NEW YORK CONFIDENTIAL

NEW YORK

Confidential

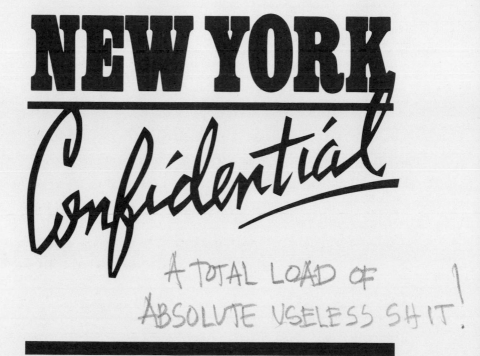

A TOTAL LOAD OF ABSOLUTE USELESS SHIT!

BY SHARON CHURCHER

I TOSSED THIS BOK. SORRY YOU FOUND IT.

Crown Publishers, Inc. New York

FOR THE FORTY THOUSAND

CONTENTS

INTRODUCTION

"ITS CREED IS CASH. DON'T TRY TO CRASH IT OTHERWISE."

Jack Lait and Lee Mortimer, NEW YORK: Confidential! *(Crown Publishers, 1948)*

Think of it as the Big Onion. Onions are murky, multilayered vegetables, and the Big Apple, with all its intimations of roseate one-bite-tells-all lusciousness, is a sobriquet that was manufactured by the city fathers as a diversionary tactic. With more than seven million natives and seventeen million wide-eyed tourists thronging it each year, the largest city in America certainly tastes good if you're among its governing classes, and with the help of a little trompe l'oeil, it's remarkably easy to keep the masses quiescent.

This book was conceived sometime after the New York Convention and Visitors Bureau touted a novel attraction for sightseers seeking a "return to the elegant and urbane world of the nineteenth century": a glossy brochure urged that they take the subway to the South Bronx. Presumably, when they arrived they would be calmed, if not fooled, by the vinyl decals of neatly shuttered windows and potted geraniums that are pasted, in a federally financed city program, over abandoned buildings in this ravaged expanse. Our work was completed shortly after it was revealed that even the parking ticket reposing on your windshield was a cover for something else. Federal prosecutors charged that an entire division of the city government, the Parking Violations Bureau, had been operated as a criminal enterprise, dealing collection contracts to firms that forked out fat bribes in return. At least, the feds called this criminal. If you want to tear yourself free from the Onion's poverty-tattered outer skin, you should discipline yourself to avoid such emotional value judgments about the city's traditional business methods. The sole value that counts in New York is the kind with enough zeroes to drop off the end of a calculator, and kickbacks are simply a tool for facilitating this.

"You can't buy everything—only almost everything," as Jack Lait and Lee Mortimer wrote of the one aspect of the city that can be guaranteed not to have changed by the time you finish reading these pages. And, since buying even *almost* everything requires dough, access, and a taste level diplomatically summarized by the axiom that in New York good is bad and bad is good, much of this book is devoted to equipping you with the techniques for successful shopping forays. As is customary, however, in travel guides, let's start by familiarizing you with some of the burg's vital statistics.

It is blessed, for instance, with one hundred museums. In chapter two, you will be renting a number of them for private soirées to which you will want to entice Ann Getty, whose husband, Gordon, is among the richest men in America; any city officials who are not on the lam; and the Texas computer billionaire H. Ross Perot, who had quite the wrong idea when he bid $70 million to move one of these halls of culture, the Museum of the American Indian, to Dallas. The Big Onion also is a city of ethnic groups (including 161 Aleuts), most of which now have their own organized crime networks, as well as their own parades along Fifth Avenue. You should learn to distinguish between the Russian godfather (according to the police, he lives in Brooklyn) and the Mafia godfather, whom you will be soliciting for loans over a steak dinner. Above all, it is a city that offers you an exhilarating better-than-one-in-twelve chance of becoming a victim of some *unorganized* felony. Should this occur, you will just pump some bullets into the perpetrator (everyone, but everyone, has a gun permit in the Wild East, including William F. Buckley, Jr.)—and boogie. To mark the release of a record about the shooting by vigilante Bernhard Goetz of four teenagers, who he said tried to rob him on a subway train, Limelight, a Manhattan discotheque, mounted a celebration called "Controversy to Dance To."

Now, you may not feel that you need this book. You may already have a system in place for bribe-taking, like the stenographers at a New York licensing office who, braving the general climate of fear—one branch of the city's official book-and-novelty store accepts only checks because cash might inspire robberies— placed dishes near their desks for permit applicants to plop "gratuities" into. But we are not concerned simply with your working life: your advancement also depends on squeezing the most out of every minute of leisure. Suppose, for example, that you are an Important Hollywood Agent. Instead of idling away your lunch hours in Frank Sinatra's favorite booth at the Russian Tea Room, you could be cultivating producers by treating them to a session at the brothel farther along West Fifty-seventh Street that specializes in corporate entertainment. Or you could be network- ing at a committee meeting of one of Gotham's charities. You'll find that in this city an eleemosynary spirit is as essential as a suitable spouse, and your role model will be such truly splendid groups as Angel Guardians for the Elderly, a New York philan- thropy that was incorporated to help oldsters obtain benefits like "pension rights." Its board at one point included at least nine union leaders with alleged links to organized crime, among them a man sentenced to twelve years for racketeering.

While none of the above should surprise even such innocents about the facts of New York life as Walter Mondale—his running mate Geraldine Ferraro's listing as an "honorary member" of the Angel Guardians was disclosed during his unsuccessful campaign for the White House—much of what you will be reading in the chapters that follow is the result of considerable excavation efforts in which the author was assisted by several fellow journalists: Peter Spielmann, a newsman with the Associated Press, who helped persuade some of God's Builders (chapter four) to open their financial records; Deborah Kirk, an associate editor for *Signature* magazine, who made reporting contributions to several chapters: *Manhattan, inc.*'s Mary Anne Ostrom, and Richard Mineards, one of the author's former sidekicks on the "Intelli- gencer" column at *New York* magazine, who surveyed places and reconnoitered parties; John Wilcock, for years the "Village Square" columnist of the *Village Voice,* who journeyed to some corners of the Night Frontier that were inaccessible to women; Phyllis Witte and Bruce Francis, who provided energetic research and insights; and Laura Broaddus, of *New York,* who located the mugshots you'll be seeing of the Cast.

And now, as you husband your energy for your debut as the

next Peter Minuit, a word about attitude. Here are three examples of the *right* attitude. For reasons that will become apparent later, all of them involve partying:

• The female guests at a Christmas shindig in the city were handed small Tiffany silver shovels and invited to dig for jewels buried around tiny, gem-decked fir trees. Obviously, the revelers did not include any of those New Yorkers, totaling nearly one quarter of the population, who live below the poverty level.
• For one of her famous "I'm Just Wild About Harry" birthday parties for the elderly real estate magnate Harry Helmsley, "Queen" Leona, the wife whom he married after divorcing from his spouse of thirty-three years, elaborated on Minuit's sale of a bill of goods to Manhattan's original owners, the Indians. The table centerpieces consisted of tomahawks, feathers, and baskets of beads, symbolizing the $24 worth of trinkets that Minuit paid for the island in 1626. Each basket was crowned by a facsimile of the Manhattan skyline. The display's authenticity was dimmed, however, by the omission of a copy of the tax abatement, valued in 1982 at $13 million, that Harry received from the city when he built the Palace, the most opulent hotel in New York. Its best suites, like the triplex where Michael Jackson stayed, go for $1,650 a night.
• Implicated in the Parking Violations Bureau scandal, Stanley Friedman, the flamboyant, cigar-chomping boss of the Bronx Democratic Party, sent out a special enclosure with the 1986 invitations to the organization's $250-a-head annual dinner dance. "This letter is from a friend to a friend," the powerful pol wrote, explaining that in these "difficult" times it would be helpful for the event to be "packed to the rafters with supporters."

All of these festivities and planned festivities were divulged to the media, and you too need never be ashamed of your activities in New York; the only thing that must be kept secret is failure. Just remember to pack your ill-gotten gains in cardboard boxes when you bank them, which is how one money launderer humped $3,409,230 in cash to a Deak-Perera currency exchange on lower Broadway. And no matter what your problems, try always to look ahead to the next move, to court the next wave of customers. As this book was going to press, Baby John, the proprietor of Caffè Palermo, a location you will be visiting in chapter ten, had just pleaded guilty in a huge narcotics case. Still, he took the time to call to give you his menu recommendation: the cannoli, a deep-fried pastry tube oozing Italian cheese and chocolate chips. Though he may be otherwise occupied, his wife, Juliana, will be around to make sure you get good service. Just remember to pay the check and tell her who sent you. All kickbacks in gratitude for listings in this book can be mailed in care of the publishers.

NEW YORK
CONFIDENTIAL

1

JOIN THE CIRCUS

"IF YOUR WIFE DOESN'T HAVE A FUR, IT DOES NOT LOOK GOOD FOR YOU AS A MAN."

From a New York Times *interview with a man whose wife was trying on a silver fox at Davellin-Balencia, a West Twenty-ninth Street fur showroom*

Come to Shangri-la. It's the only place to be in New York, your ultimate destination. One Russian émigré, a novelist, may have dubbed the city "a paradise of all the most attractive features of hell," but another, a concert pianist, rather quickly escaped the inferno. We ran into him at a flashy party that was chaired by two young Rockefellers. He was nibbling coulibiac of sole and salmon in lemon caviar sauce and engaging a millionairess in charming small talk. The other guests included a man in a gold lamé dress, the daughter of Mrs. Henry Ford II, and Robin Leach, host of the TV show "Lifestyles of the Rich and Famous."

As the world's most glittering example of human excess, New York society—a euphemism for a potpourri of rich people, well-born people, famous people, and felons—is powered by millionaires and the occasional millionairess, chronicled by Mr. Leach, and serviced by any number of amusing artistes, obliging politicians, and enterprising poseurs. It also has a niche, as in any feudal domain, for the lower classes: one new Manhattan skyscraper offers such amenities as a separate floor of housekeeping units for residents' maids and bodyguards, and a waiting room off the parking garage for their chauffeurs.

After an epidemic of recession-consciousness that peaked with the 1982 announcement of a chic restaurant called the Soup

Kitchen, it certainly is delightful that so many New Yorkers can afford to support both themselves and their scullions. Nor, despite a recent wave of scandals, should it be thought that the wealth that is flooding the city was all dishonestly won. That national reordering of priorities, Reaganomics, has given a tremendous boost to the pharaohs of Wall Street and the builders of the new Fifth Avenue pyramids; maybe even to the poverty barons of the South Bronx, one of whom has been honored with an invitation to dinner at the White House. Moreover, the Big Onion has acquired a whole new layer of gold thanks to the city's extension of the Sanctuary Principle to vast numbers of dispossessed princes, members of the Federal Witness Protection Program—one of them drives the latest-model Cadillac while minding his business interests—and tax fugitives.

What really makes this the most belle of époques, however, is the propensity of our native despots to equip themselves with young second wives with splendidly utilitarian pedigrees, such as winning the Miss Israel pageant or working in another rarefied orbit, as a stewardess for Pan Am.

So total is the sway of these new millionaire couples in a town that always has worshipped big in everything, including bucks, that when a bus stop was eliminated at Park Avenue and Fiftieth Street, it was obvious, despite all the official denials, that this was to make room for more limousines outside the Waldorf Towers. Buses have been one of the most conspicuous dangers to the lifestyles of the rich and famous, rumbling at dawn through one New York exurb where homeowners, including the King of Morocco, found their slumbers disturbed.

"Those buses are spewing out an awful odor as well," fumed a local official, announcing that if the disturbances continued, the drivers would be fined or jailed. The vehicles changed their route.

The monarchs of our burg and their courtiers need to get their rest because their days are spent in their counting rooms and on trial (only in New York do the newspapers report on an Important Indicted's choice of fashion designer) while their kept women, henceforth known as the ladies, indulge in a spirited competition to see who can run fastest through the loot. Their inspiration appears to be the turn of the last century, when Mrs. Stuyvesant Fish threw her famous banquet for a monkey, introduced as the Prince del Drago, and a gas company nabob, C.K.G. Billings, tossed a stag party at which the guests, seated on horses tethered in a ballroom, sucked champagne through tubes attached to bottles in the saddlebags. The protocol at such events can be confusing, though. The zoological diversion at a 1983 romp in a clinic turned out to be a social lioness who, propped up on the pillows in a fuchsia silk robe, was hosting a vernissage for her latest facelift.

Moreover, in the absence of a playbill, it can be hard to rate the players. Giddied by the prospect of having to choose between scores of invitations from apparent VIPs to couture shows and gallery openings (rule of etiquette: always converse with your back turned knowingly to the art), theme parties and charity dinners ("we're getting Cornelia involved with some new charities ...she's very interested in the baby seal situation," confided a public relations woman representing Cornelia Guest, New York's "Deb of the Year"), chic safaris to the Third World, and private viewings of beautiful (as in B-I-G) diamonds, you may find yourself having to seek guidance from a Social Arbiter.

"As soon as you see the name Kissinger, you know you're in the right place at the right time," counseled Diana Vreeland, the grande dame of style. We like to think she said that with an inner giggle.

THE CAST

Besides Henry the Incursor of Cambodia, his wife, Nancy, and their dog of the moment—a blond Labrador named Tyler has been glimpsed escorting Nancy to Bill Blass for her dress fittings—the nonpareils on the New York stage whom you will wish to cultivate include:

• An ex-actress who primes the social columns with such tasty details of her nuptial bliss with an elderly grandee as her bedtime apparel: "I did look divine," she scribbled to her PR man, who was instructed to pass the letter on to the *New York Post's* society scribe, Aileen "Suzy" Mehle. The former leading lady went on to document her beloved's propitious reaction: "He fell asleep early, ha, ha, ha!" The PR man censored that portion, explaining, "She gives him these really strong drinks."
• Sam LeFrak, or *Sir* Samuel J. LeFrak, as the fabulously rich tycoon (oil, real estate, and entertainment) and hobnobber with royalty ("I had tea with the queen and dinner with Charles and Diana") is described on one of his business cards. "Did you know I was knighted by the Pope, the President of Finland, and the King

of Sweden?" he asks. His family name used to be Lefrak (pronounced LEFF-rack), but only because an ancestor was anglicized at Ellis Island: "It's a French name. We've gone back to our roots."

• Adela Holzer, a cool-eyed, beautiful Broadway producer and commodities swindler who, occupying a neighboring cell to Jean Harris, the ex-headmistress convicted of murdering the Scarsdale diet doctor, became her prison champion.

• Several Episcopal ministers, but not their boss, the Bishop of New York, Paul Moore, Jr.

• Rita Lachman, a vivacious ex-maid, governess, and curtain-factory hand, who became the third wife of Charles Lachman, the co-owner of Revlon. The marriage did not endure, and at age eighty Charles took up with Jaquine de Rochambeau, a French countess forty-five years his junior who had been Barbara Hutton's social secretary. In an ensuing, unsuccessful attempt to prove that Lachman was too infirm to handle his $30 million affairs, Rita charged that Jaquine had doctored his "liquids" with "tranquilizers." Jaquine married him during all of this, and when he died, he left her $15 million. Says a lawyer for Jaquine, Rita's allegations were "totally unfounded."

• Imelda Marcos, who, even as the pundits were laying bets on the crash of her husband's fiefdom in the Philippines, was secretly piling up vast real estate holdings here, shopping our bazaars for antiques ($5 million at a throw)—and partying to the strains of David Bowie at the private disco in her East Sixty-sixth Street town house.

• Salomon Inc. chairman John Gutfreund and his bride, Susan, the Pan Am alumna, who flung a sixtieth birthday supper for Henry the Inc. that climaxed, according to a report in *Vanity Fair,* with Susan giving the doctor's favorite speech since the day Nixon screamed, "Let's blow the hell out of them." "Thank you, Henry," she bubbled, "for all the beautiful things you've done for your country, and what a privilege it was to see you here tonight!" Mrs. G's provender being the stuff of culinary legend, on another occasion it lured the pianist Van Cliburn, his mother, a clutch of Texas millionaires, and Imelda. Several members of the party, though not the Gutfreunds, adjourned later in the evening to the Sixty-sixth Street mansion, where Imelda entertained them by belting out a song on the terrace before throwing open the disco.

• Jacqueline Kennedy Onassis, whose choice of vehicle for the announcement of her daughter Caroline's betrothal to Edwin Schlossberg, the low-key social pages of the *Times,* was heralded as the most elegant moment of the decade. The princess of

Camelot's studied avoidance of the limelight is often cited as an example of what can be achieved by profile deflation. But your own fortunes in New York will be better served by reading *Financier,* Cary Reich's biography of the banker André Meyer. This claims that during her widowhood, Jackie "quite deliberately" set out to win the affections of the sixty-six-year-old Wall Street prince. Reich quotes a former World Bank president as deducing that Jackie liked money "and she felt André would be a pretty good fellow to handle the money."
• The owner of the world's most posh brothel.
• Marylou Whitney, a vivacious former Kansas City disk jockey, cooking columnist, and actress who became the fourth wife of Cornelius Vanderbilt "Sonny" Whitney, a co-founder of Pan Am, philanthropist, and descendant of the Commodore twenty-seven years her senior who had quite a reputation as a playboy. "Her job," says a Whitney friend of the longevity of his marriage to Marylou, "is making his life easy and happy."
• A well-known but, until she contracted an illustrious marriage, not super-well-heeled hostess, some of whose servants at one party we attended were recruiting for a pal of hers, a yogi. They tried to enroll us over the canapés. The guests also included a best-selling author, an Op-Ed Intellectual, an associate of Richard Nixon who told an amusing dirty story about the Screamer, and a sullen-looking physician, who was inducing faint bruises above people's Rolexes to drum up customers for his "pressure point" therapy for ailments like back pain.
• Adnan Khashoggi, or Wishbone, as the fun-loving Saudi Arabian middleman and financier was code-named by the giant Northrop Corporation when he was allegedly soliciting $450,000 in bribes for Saudi generals to fatten its fighter plane sales. The Americans urged him to make the payoffs, he maintained, and, embarrassed, "I pocketed [the money] myself." His New York pied-à-terre, occupying just two floors of the Olympic Tower, on Fifth Avenue, contains a full-size indoor swimming pool and a ten-foot-wide bed covered with sable. Supposedly the richest man in the world—there have been reports that he has suffered certain financial reverses—he has an office in the same building accented by a photograph of President Reagan, autographed "To Adnan with best wishes."
• Foreign residents and visitors. For instance, the stepbrother of Princess Diana of England, Viscount Lewisham, can sometimes be seen taking tea at the Mayfair Regent Hotel, at 610 Park Avenue. "Lewisham lent us his house in Jamaica and we gave a toga party

with a black band by the pool," another young British swell was heard whooping at Regine's, the Park Avenue night spot.

• A wealthy retired movie star whose marriage to a very pleasant gay man many years her junior is delicately alluded to from time to time in the columns. "He married her," hoots a local churchman, "for the sake of her son." The son is indeed a stunner, though his sexual predilections are uncertain.

• Claus von Bülow, who, facing a second trial on charges that he tried to kill his multimillionairess wife, Sunny, joined his mistress, a vision in polar-white fur called Andrea Reynolds, for truffled rice at Nanni Il Valletto, an East Sixty-first Street mess hall, and took the socialite's version of the AA pledge. "I will not dance," he vowed, "until this thing is over."

• Ed Koch, mayor of New York, guardian of the public cookie jar (one wouldn't want the servants sneaking in and taking what rightfully belongs to the Cast), and a supporting star of the play that follows. The mayor has kicked with the Rockettes, ridden exotic animals, hosted "Saturday Night Live," acted as ringmaster of the Ringling Bros. and Barnum & Bailey Circus, and made cameo appearances on a TV soap and in a movie called *The Muppets Take Manhattan*.

• Jerry Zipkin, owner of a storied cufflink collection (he reportedly carts as many as eighty-six pairs on out-of-town excursions), who squired Nancy Reagan to Maximilian to pick out her ranch mink for her husband's first coronation. The First Lady has described him as a "sort of modern-day Oscar Wilde. He has more depth than a lot of people in our lives." The proof of this came when he put his foot down at Mortimer's, *the* Upper East Side bistro, upon discovering that the only vegetable on the menu that day was creamed spinach.

Once you are through with this book, all of the above will be your dearest allies, patrons, friends, or servants. You also should contact the wisest guys who appear in our pages for some tips about speeding your progress. The Cosa Nostra is, after all, one of the city's largest employers, and one of its hoods, "Crazy Joe" Gallo, used to be available for social consultations, being considered quite the nicest brunch guest. He mulled over "the meaning of life" with the fashionable Mrs. John Barry "D. D." Ryan III, the *Times*'s Charlotte Curtis reported in an essay on "Mafia Chic," but unfortunately he was rubbed out some years before our story begins while celebrating his birthday in Little Italy—a territory that is fashionable with his fellow businessmen. Let's examine this historical episode in a little more detail, because in New York there is always some lesson for the future lurking in the guise of disaster, and, yes, he-e-e-re it is, folks:

Joe's wife, who was present at his demise—they'd been quaffing champagne, C.K.G. Billings's drink of choice—was attired in an *ankle-length* gown. It was evening, you understand, and if you aren't prepared to be appropriately dressed in our town, no matter how successful you are, forget it. Your success won't be self-perpetuating and you should go home to Shreveport. Whether you're a Mafia boss or not, an obsession with personal appearance is a perfectly natural corollary of your soon-to-be-burgeoning wealth, which, like the tree in the yard in George Berkeley's philosophy conundrum, will only meaningfully exist if it catches somebody's eye. Preferably that of Suzy the columnist.

The standard for men in the city was set not by Crazy Joe but by the gay hitman-turned-snitch who suggested that his testimony against the Godfather would have more credibility if the feds paid for him to have a fat-suction operation, to make him look less pudgy.

Eleanor Lambert, a fashion publicist, has set the standards for women for years with her annual Best Dressed List poll. Her father was a Ringling Bros. circus advance agent, but despite the inevitable cracks about inherited talent, she says the list is simply "a symbol of taste of a period." Determined to get on it, one parvenue flitted to Paris on the Concorde and within hours had dropped $85,000 at the couture houses. This was, incidentally, an economy, given the strength of the dollar: in New York that year, Bill Blass sweaters were commanding the same price as a no-frills Datsun, $4,550.

It also is essential that you amass collections that do not carry designer tags. If you are a man, your collection should include at least one city or state lease, negotiated at a bargain-basement rent with the aid of a politically connected lawyer. Parking lot concessions are a traditional favorite.

The income from such enterprises foots the bills for the little lady's art collection. One gal bought a Picasso for her eleven-room palace on Park Avenue.

"She wasn't there when I delivered it," says Christopher Ponsot, who owns Pack Man, a firm specializing in art shipments, "so the butler helped me hang it. I chose where to put it. There were so many pieces of fine art on the walls already that I had to take down a Calder to make room."

For their personal safety and protection, male collectors should hide that popular New York gizmo, a CCS Communication Control

Bug Alert in their pockets (see chapter twelve) at all times; in the unlucky but not infrequent event that the fellow they're dealing with is an undercover agent for the FBI, he's bound to be wired and the device will start softly vibrating.

Ladies should confine their more personal purchases to those New York stores that have portable signs—CLOSED FOR INVENTORY; BY APPOINTMENT ONLY—that staff hold up in front of the reinforced glass in the electronically controlled doors when a black person approaches.

Since so much of what they collect is for their private use and happiness, it might be thought that wealthy New Yorkers have no conscience. This is untrue. With at least 40,000 homeless in the city, over 900,000 people on public assistance, and another 560,000 estimated "at risk" of losing the roofs over their heads, some derelicts are being offered jogging lessons by well-meaning volunteers at city shelters.

Donate Your Used Adidases

"I was having lunch with Shirlee Fonda at an outside table at Le Relais," says one of the ladies, "and a black man came up and said, 'Do you know where there's a luggage repair shop?' I referred him to T. Anthony [a classy store on Park Avenue] and he said, 'If it's not there, I'm coming back with a gun to get you.' Another time, a bag lady came up and rubbed butter from the dish on our table over her face."

Take Her On As An Unpaid Servant

To review what we have learned so far:

Right: Susan Gutfreund acquired a "subway" bracelet, with sliding steel panels concealing the gemstones.

Wrong: Nancy Reagan wore a starkly contoured red silk Galanos gown to the American Embassy party in London that honored Princess Di's success in marrying up (for more on which, see chapter two). A duplicate of the garment went on sale at Bonwit Teller in New York for $2,790. No takers. The price was slashed to $1,860. Still no buyers. At $1,395, it was shifted to a back room to make space for the fall collections. When the dress finally was sold, the store declined to say for what price, but you can figure it out yourself if you remember that one matron sauntered into a reception at Sotheby's garbed from the neck down in peacock feathers, vestments significantly more *complicated* to dry clean.

Right: Fresh from jail, the city's most dapper labor racketeer, Tony Scotto, sat at the A table at a $750-a-ticket dinner for Brooklyn borough president Howard Golden's 1985 reelection kitty. "All night, the Sheraton Centre crowd lined up to greet the gangster," reported Wayne Barrett of the *Village Voice*. (You should start a clip file of Barrett's useful observations on social behavior.) Other guests included a former New York congressman who got six months for bribery, a real estate broker who mysteriously garnered over two hundred receiverships, and a builder who used to let a city official vacation at his Palm Beach home.

Wrong: Marylou Whitney sent a group of dollhouses on various tours to benefit charity. In charge were men from her husband Sonny's Kentucky horse farm, which the dollhouses duplicated down to such details as the former slave quarters where Britain's Princess Margaret stayed during a visit to the Whitneys. The tours were terminated, however. Sonny, a friend explained, "rarely issues commands, but he takes the horse business very seriously and this exhibition was disrupting the work of the farm."

Right: Marylou and her pooch Edelweiss posed for *W* magazine on their adjacent beds, which have matching lemon covers. You couldn't see the pillows on Marylou's pallet, but Edelweiss's were trimmed in what appeared to be white lace.

"MY DEAR, WHEN GIVENCHY WAS HERE, SUSAN GUTFREUND SENT BASKETS OF FLOWERS AND FRUIT TO HIS ROOM. LIKE A CUNARD STEWARD!"

An old New York dowager

Is this a tale of *three* cities?

So say some scions of old New York dynasties—dynasties founded by bandits with nickel-plated pistols strapped to their waists in an era when dangerous pigs roamed Fifth Avenue (one charged and bit one of the ladies' predecessors in 1847). They make tortuous attempts to differentiate themselves from newer arrivals like Tony Scotto, Henry the Inc., and Mrs. G.

The class system, by their account, breaks down into (1) Old Money, (2) New Money, and (3) the peasantry.

OMs are said to have Good Taste which gets passed down consanguineously, like good teeth.

"Real WASPs are never showy," says a retainer. He works for one, an elderly man who occupies his days fretting about his health and collecting small glass animals in an airless, dimly lit Park Avenue apartment where the dust-filmed furniture— inherited chinoiserie, a cheap TV set in the fireplace, and carpets etched with cigarette burns—complements the victuals. Rose Kennedy, after all, used to have her servants collect any spring-water left in the glasses after a meal and pour it back into the bottle. "Real WASPs don't serve much food," continues the retainer, himself from a family that is in the Social Register, an epistle that according to Cleveland Amory's *Who Killed Society?* was started by an entrepreneur whose other occupations included operating a one-locomotive New Jersey railroad. "We're very English. A little piece of roast beef, three little roast potatoes, and don't pass the tray more than twice."

When an organizer of one of the OM debutante cotillions tried to sell her battered umbrella to the Metropolitan Museum of Art's Costume Institute, she did not seek publicity.

OMs are said to have an innate aversion to ink, an allergy that may be contagious. Maurice Tempelsman, the diamond entrepreneur and Jackie O chaperon, had one of New York's most powerful lawyers, Edward Costikyan, demand the recall of *Endless Enemies,* a book by the *Wall Street Journal*'s Jonathan Kwitny. Among its "misstatements" and "defamatory" failings, the lawyer complained, it described Tempelsman as "the billionaire-class escort of President Kennedy's widow":

"Mr. Tempelsman is not a billionaire. . . ."

In promotional notes for the movie *The World According to Garp,* its director, George Roy Hill, graciously mentioned one of his principal locations, the Wilmerding estate on Fishers Island, the Long Island Sound atoll where families like the Rockefellers, Luces, and Roosevelts have summer homes. "The house was to be forgotten so far as ownership and location, . . ." the estate's owner, David Wilmerding, roared. "I'm probably going to turn this over to my lawyers."

Undeterred, *W* profiled Jupiter Island, a demesne north of Palm Beach that is the Fishers Island of the snow season. Its amenities are typified by a road zoned specifically for bicycles and *golf carts* and, though *W* didn't mention it, an identity-card law for the help somewhat akin to South Africa's. The story was lavishly illustrated with photos of the septuagenarian Permelia Reed wearing her profile-deflation livery—a baggy striped cotton dress from Le

Shack—and characterized this mining magnate's widow as the resort's "ruling" grande dame. The week the magazine hit the stores, she indeed did deliver an edict, visiting the island's newsstand and snapping, according to another resident, " '*W* is never to be sold here again.' ... Mrs. Reed claims she knew nothing about [the article] being done." Apparently, in view of our informant's verification of Reed's stature—"if she told me to get rid of my dog, I would"—she relented, because no such ban came into effect. So, after dark, the Doubledays, Paysons, Dukes, and Mellons presumably still slip down to the newsstand to get their weekly fix, concealing their *W*s inside the map compartment of their "woodies," old Ford station wagons with dented wood side panels.

"Preferred over a Rolls-Royce," an OM stoically muttered.

This is, of course, utter nonsense. The preference of OMs who *do* have money is to flaunt it with the best of them.

William F. Buckley, Jr., who is old oil money, wrote *Overdrive,* a Pepysian log that spoke fondly of his customized limo—"I use the car constantly, require the room, privacy, and my own temperature gauge"—as well as a Jacuzzi overlooking "the most beautiful indoor pool this side of Pompeii."

Sonny Whitney, old Commodore money, composed a diary of his meanderings with Marylou between their seven homes. It was sent to friends for Christmas. Title: *Live a Year with a Millionaire.*

The reason most WASPs aren't showy is that they've no money left to show. (See chapter two for the uses to which their fall from privilege to penury can be put.) And who wants that kind of publicity? Ironically, even as the indigent patricians secretly daydream of purloining one of Mrs. G's CARE packages for Monsieur Givenchy and eating the flowers, a number of the new-money ladies, taking the bluebloods at their word on style, have been seeking to underspend them.

One of the richest women in the city, if not America, invited an OM to fly to Newport with her. "She chartered a single-engined plane," says her guest. "I said to her, You know, Jean,* cheap is cheap."

Another fabulously wealthy virago drives less loaded acquaintances to Newport in a secondhand Rolls-Royce, has them pay the tolls, and puts them up in motels at their own expense.

Jackie O's cousin by marriage, Louis Auchincloss, who is gener-

* A pseudonym.

ally regarded as the premier standard-bearer of vieux monde virtue, was solicited for his opinion on the difference between new and old money.

"I'd be really grateful if you can help, though I realize there's nothing in it for you," your author told him.

"Well, there you are," he said politely, putting down the phone.

We wondered whether the answer might lie instead in a New York "baby benefit," the snooty "Nutcracker Scholarship" party, held every Christmas to raise money for scholarships to the School of American Ballet. One of our reporters was dispatched to investigate. As many as eight hundred mothers and youngsters, the girls attired in velvet dresses and the boys in knickers, watch a performance of the *Nutcracker* (tickets $50 to $125), the reporter was told. The holders of the higher-priced tickets also are invited to take tea (sandwiches, brownies, and cookies). Marveled Martha Rosenthal, then the school's special events coordinator, "What I can't believe is that these wealthy mothers let their kids waltz away with all the Christmas-tree and centerpiece decorations."

The Three Cities theorists weren't giving up that easily. They assured us that their progeny graduate not to Sing-Sing but to New York's debutante balls. NMs aren't invited to the "best" of these, having to be content with their own International Debutante Ball. Reeking of style that can only be called Texas, this event features flag-toting military cadets who strut alongside the girls, one of whom, representing "the United States," sinks into a curtsy to "America the Beautiful." Though the children of wealthy Republicans like Richard Nixon and Ed Meese normally steal the evening, the 1985 parade was led by Lucinda Robb, daughter of Virginia governor Chuck Robb and granddaughter of LBJ, rustling in a virginal *Gone with the Wind* concoction that vaguely resembled a meringue pie. "A hairdresser who was a *homosexual* had his boyfriend present his sister there," sniffs an OM. "She was a manicurist."

Though none of the many versions of this rumor could be substantiated, the Mayflower Society's very OM ball did seem to provide the sort of total contrast in styles that we'd been looking for. Its guest of honor was the society governor general, Dr. Dwight E. Twist, debs had to be *Mayflower* descendants, robed in maidenly white, and the menu—or rather, "ye ffeaste"—consisted of "sorrel soupe, Plimoth turkey, pumpkin bread and flaming sweete revelations." The flaming revelation shrieked by the city's tabloids in 1984 wasn't at all the sort Dr. Twist had in mind, however: Sydney Biddle Barrows, an austere-looking thirty-two-year-old blond caught operating an estimated $1-million-a-year call-girl ring, "was always very proud of being a Biddle, proud of her family history and everything" and "fond of going to the Mayflower Ball," her boyfriend, identified as a blackjack dealer, said under the year's most mellifluous headline, THE MAYFLOWER MADAM.

"YOU GO TO A PARTY IN NEW YORK AND NOBODY GETS DRUNK, NOBODY FLIRTS. EVERYBODY WANTS SOMETHING FROM SOMEBODY."

The author Michael M. Thomas, a descendant of the Bangs, one of the very *oldest families*

Leonard Schammel, formerly a mandarin at CBS television, would be flinging "the grandest beach party of the summer," trumpeted one of the society columns, at his "Ocean Estates." Not only would it be avant-garde (Bianca Jagger was to cohost), but it would launch a Cultural Event, the Brooklyn Academy of Music's Next Wave Festival (while it doesn't do for you to be from the outer boroughs, it is classy to flaunt philanthropic feelings toward them). The guests—"all of whom are required to wear white"—were expected to include Dick Cavett, Calvin Klein, Richard Gere, and Yoko Ono.

Celebrities are accorded a status in the circus similar to the mayor. And the dress code sounded so right, so suitable to Amagansett, where Schammel's Xanadu was located. This resort is in the stretch of Long Island called the Hamptons, and parties with color themes are as ubiquitous there as summer residents with names like Woody Allen, Billy Joel, Candice Bergen, Lauren Bacall, Cheryl Tiegs, Cliff Robertson, Gloria Vanderbilt, Willie Morris, and Howard Cosell. One wingding was done completely in black and white with, as its centerpiece, a rented Holstein calf.

Schammel, as it happened, had something less rural in mind.

Wandering over the sand dunes, we encountered strategically posted maps, informing us that he had subdivided his thirty shorefront acres into twenty-one building lots. "As guests stream onto his property...Mr. Schammel will get to see his marketing plan move into gear," said a release helpfully distributed on the bus speeding musicians and reporters to the fête. "He hopes that [the guests]... will be inspired by the natural beauty of the land and purchase an acre, at the starting price of $125,000 up to half a million dollars."

We expected to read about this in *Women's Wear Daily*'s report on the party, since the paper prides itself on its social acuity. "Edward Albee and Henry Geldzahler having fun...," said a photo caption, but we searched in vain for some allusion to Schammel's accession to the real estate peerage. Kurt Vonnegut, however, was quoted grumbling, "What I don't understand is why women don't wear hats anymore."

As milliners rush to take out full-page ads in the paper in gratitude for its discretion—"Yoko Ono, in a pea-green Adolfo, having fun waiting for Leonard Schammel's bulldozers" just wouldn't have had the right tone of romance to it—it occurs to us that even the media want something out of New York society. But let's consider the upside to Michael Thomas's dictum.

Like libido and drunkenness, emotion is an uncommon syndrome among people on the rise in New York, because it gets in the way of making money and displaying it suitably, and that's immensely hard work. So, while you may not have fun, neither will you ever be unhappy. Shortly after one of the city's wealthiest businesswomen was widowed, she was invited to dinner by a property czar and his wife. "She said she could only stop for a few minutes, to say hello to Charlotte Curtis [the *Times* columnist]," recalls the wife. The widow swept into the room, awash in perfume and enough jewels to buy the Empire State Building.

One of the guests threw her arms around her and commiserated: "I'm just so sorry about ———."

The widow started to cry softly.

"This goes on for about two minutes and is very touching," says the property czar's wife. "Then all of a sudden the crying stops. She looks at her watch and says, 'You know, I have to go now to the ———'s party.'"

2

APING MRS. FISH

"THINGS HAVEN'T CHANGED MUCH, EXCEPT THAT TODAY'S MONKEYS DON'T GO BACK TO A CAGE, BUT MORE LIKELY TO THE EXECUTIVE SUITE OF A MAJOR CORPORATION OR TO ONE OF THE GREAT WASHINGTON CHANCERIES."

Michael M. Thomas, in Vanity Fair

Some people find it easy making the first $10 million. Unless you're a big public official, $10 million is the rock-bottom financial requirement for crashing the ruling class in New York.

Should you, for instance, be the front personage for a foreign despot, you'll do just fine as long as you don't get carried away and blow your lucre on losers. Before the demise of Imelda's regime, the two brothers who were her New York property managers ran through a small fortune restoring a gaudy gold medal of Napoleon III atop their New York offices. To this day, the twenty-three-karat visage of the ruler who was France's Gerald Ford broods like the head on a devalued coin on Ralph and Joseph Bernstein's 29 West Fifty-seventh Street building.

A job as a high-powered broker for an old-line firm on Wall Street is another excellent entry point. "We churned the shit out of clients," confided a former employee of Lehman Brothers, now Shearson Lehman. Churning involves buying and selling stocks just to pile up commissions and is heartily recommended if you go in for any of the modish vices to which we'll be introducing you. "I . . . was continually catching up with my gambling," the former employee elaborated. These observations were recorded by one of those FBI devices that are a constant refrain in the life of the Cast of This Book. However, he now says he invented his account out of pique at Shearson, which is denying that he did any mischief.

Should you too be in a situation where you are denying everything, but especially if you are an *ex*-public official, the prospects have never been better, if only because Pepsi-Cola undoubtedly will be in the market soon for a new $500,000 shill. Though that former New York congresswoman and vice-presidential hopeful Geraldine Ferraro was a model of good taste when she appeared in a thirty-second spot telling her daughters, "There's one choice I'll never regret . . . being a mother," the company seems unlikely to hire her again. "My mom may drink Pepsi, but I like COKE," guffawed the spoof advertisement in a magazine put out by college mates of her son, John "the Pharmacist" Zaccaro, Jr.

The following plans for becoming a featured segment on "Lifestyles of the You-Know-What" are for those of you who drink New York State sparkling wine but would prefer to be imbibing Dom Pérignon.

PLAN A

This strategy is recommended if you are a face that Mrs. G remembers from Pan Am Business Class, and it should be commenced the moment that the first invitation flutters into your mailbox. The trick is to think of the entire city as a souk, and of the drawing rooms of its swells as its busiest quarter. Keep your palm up and your pitch oiled and in no time at all you'll beat out the yogi and the collagen clinicians, the divorce lawyers and gynecologists, and be in the home stretch with the florists, hairdressers, and gigolos.

"Doesn't she look wonderful!" exclaims that up-and-coming participant in this plan, the couturier Count von Zoot,* gently taking a bejeweled crone by the arm. He waves animatedly at the nineteen-year-old nymphet who is nuzzling against the crone's husband to the accompaniment of a Lester Lanin fox-trot at the ball we are attending at the Plaza. The phone is ringing as Zoot arrives at his office the next morning. "Uh, who was her dress by?" pleads his victim. A beam spreads like the sunrise across Zoot's expensively tanned jowls. "Darling, by me," he purrs. "And it just so happens that Barbra had to postpone her fitting for her new picture, so if you wanted to come in at eleven . . ."

Bill Blass, who was among those to get the call when Brooke

---

* A pseudonym

Astor assembled Gotham's "elite" for inspection by President Reagan, once excused his strenuous social perambulations as follows: "I've found that ladies who spend a lot for clothes like to relate to the designer."

Since the same festive principle holds for their châteaux, some real estate brokers have been lofting into the multimillion bracket as effortlessly as the balloon, loaded with joyriding captive prospects, that swooped over Leonard Schammel's Hamptons subdivision celebration.

The doyenne of the real party estate is Alice Mason, the property dealer who found a cozy $4 million Fifth Avenue suite for Al Taubman, an affable shopping-mall potentate known for his purchase of Sotheby's, the venerable auction house, and his marriage to the former Miss Israel.

A seating chart for one of Mason's frequent repasts is a virtual atlas of the nodes of million-dollar power.

The horizon over her paupiette de sole florentine may include Mike Wallace (she installed him in his East Side pad), Alexander Haig, William Randolph Hearst, Jr., Barbara Walters, the Shah's last ambassador to the UN, Claus von Bülow, and Jimmy Carter. The realtor, who practices numerology and astrology, became one of the Georgian's largest fundraisers after casting his horoscope and discovering that he had "energy" in his stars.

She invited Michael Thomas to her groaning board after the writer sent her a note requesting an interview. He was out when she phoned.

"I just had the strangest call from Mrs. Mason," said his wife when he returned. "She is giving a party tonight, and she said we could go and mingle with the guests as long as we dressed 'appropriately,' but, she said, 'If you're willing to put on black tie, you can stay an extra half hour and watch the seating.'" This episode, it can now be revealed, was the genesis of "Mrs. Fish's Ape," Thomas's seminal *Vanity Fair* essay on the New York hospitality boom.

For those of you with nothing to sell but yourselves, we have drafted instructions for the social equivalent of cold-starting your Honda Civic on a January midnight.

PLAN B

The basic skill that you will be learning is "social engineering," and you can be quite upfront about it. The ladies use the phrase themselves in burbling about their aerobatics. "SE" bears no more resemblance to the vulgar sport of social climbing than do slimy little fish eggs to the caviar that, heaped in Indian burial mounds at the ladies' buffet parties, will stick in their snobbish throats as they watch you taking:

Step One, which is to get through the right door. Preferably the portal of the other Mrs. G, Ann Getty, the oil billionaire's consort, who, dividing her time between New York and San Francisco, is said to be Saks Fifth Avenue's biggest customer. If you're bashful about accosting her in the lingerie department, various alternative entry methods, most of them not explicitly prohibited by law, can be found in chapters three and eleven.

On to **Step Two,** making the crucial moolah without lifting a finger. The most common way, very frankly, is to marry up, naturally for love. You will meet plenty of eligibles chez Mrs. Getty.

• Rita Lachman, who arrived in this country in 1939 as a refugee from Germany, was working as a department-store salesgirl when, she says, a Long Island bank president set her up in a sumptuous Upper East Side apartment and endowed her with her first mink. He died. Another well-to-do boyfriend asked her what she would like for Christmas. A plane ticket to Paris, she chirruped. Three other male chums each popped the same question and she gave the same answer. "So I cashed three of the tickets in," says Rita. From Paris, she decamped to Monte Carlo, which is where she met Charles Lachman, the cosmetics potentate. "He just fell in love with me, this tall, long-legged brunette," she says. The complexion smoother, who was married to someone else at the time, had no natural children. "I got pregnant," says Rita. "I was going to have an abortion. He said, 'You must make me that person. I will marry you for that.'" Since the marriage didn't take place until some years later, the baby was born out of wedlock. Hobnobbing with the Begum Aga Khan, Tennessee Williams, and the Duke and Duchess of Windsor, Rita became a renowned hostess, her Pisces entertainment perhaps being the standout among her many theme parties, with its live goldfish and cakes shaped like fish. Upon her divorce, she is said to have obtained $3 million outright and a tax-free annuity for life.

• Pia Zadora, the singer-actress daughter of an Italian orchestra violinist, knotted the golden cord with her Daddy Warbucks, Rapid-American Corporation's Meshulam Riklis, when she was seventeen to his forty-nine. She has divulged that she was wearing "short" hot pants when the tycoon, whose industrial harem includes Schenley liquors and Fabergé, first said hello to her. More recently, her full-disclosure policy has seen her treating our local tabloids to a perfectly darling account of the pangs she suffered giving birth to a Riklis heiress. Though her provider's baroque efforts to mold her into the Jayne Mansfield of the Jacuzzi generation have evoked howls of media scorn, she can be comforted that he at least has the savoir-faire to hoist her to the only high-wire that counts: "When he bought his estate in Locust Valley, he invited me and the other neighbors over," giggles a très oldveau lady. "I'll never forget the sight. He had a carnival with a Ferris wheel and cotton candy."

Better things are surely to come, since the Queen of England was among those attracted to a birthday bash for the fifty-seven-varieties panjandrum, Jack Heinz II, that featured vegetable decorations, a fairground, and servants togged out as clowns. Actually, the Heinzes seemed to have reached the pinnacles some moons before this when, acquiring a London apartment from the Henry Luces, they were reported to have celebrated with a house-wrecking party. However, the monkeys perched on the ladders in painters' coveralls are believed to have turned out to be toys.

• The author William Wright found himself sitting in the Ritz bar in Paris with Loyce Stinson, a thrice-divorced southern belle who seems to have that honey-and-the-bee effect on rich men. "Champagne was brought," Wright wrote in *Ball,* his book about New York's April in Paris cotillion, and one of the ladies, Brownie McLean, "proposed a toast to Loyce's divorce settlement." Brownie estimated that Loyce had collected $1.5 million in the latest crackup. Some time after this, clasping a white Bible and matching baby orchids, Loyce took another plunge into marital bliss, exchanging vows with Thomas Milbank, whose great-grandfather had founded Borden milk. The columns announced that he would be giving her debutante daughter by her first marriage a buttercup-yellow sports car.

A year later, poor Loyce was back on the shelf.

Milbank filed for divorce, charging that Loyce had marred their honeymoon by caviling, "I can't sleep in the same bed with you, my legs are too long." If any such problem existed—Loyce denied it emphatically—it was soon resolved, because Milbank passed away before the suit came to trial. Noting that his death certificate mentioned alcoholic cirrhosis, his sorrowing bride laid siege to half his $8.4 million estate. She settled, after a brawl with his executor, Roy Cohn—a subsequently disbarred lawyer renowned for his scorched-earth policy in matrimonial as well as political cases—for $1.2 million, a Rolls-Royce, and two houses.

• Soon after forty-four-year-old Evangeline Gouletas married sixty-two-year-old New York Governor Hugh Carey, who had tinted his hair carrot in testimony to his ardor, it emerged that his buxom bride, a self-styled "widow," had three living ex-husbands. Still, in this instance it was the man who had married up. Engie was a real-estate millionairess—and she wasn't permitting her latest mate any status slippage. Several months after Carey had left office, she was still mailing out greetings from "Governor and Mrs. Hugh L. Carey," with the Executive Mansion as the return address. "A clerical error," she told us. But only a partial one. Governor would remain anchored to his name, if not the pigment to his locks, "because that's what I call him," she flounced. Though the usual protocol is only to use one's old title in speech—*never* in writing, steamed another ex-incumbent of the office—Carey knew when he was on to a good thing. No, he wouldn't be overruling Engie, he said: "She is a woman of taste."

• Brooke Astor has said that she was sixteen when she was shanghaied into marriage with a lecher because her mother was "dazzled" by her swain's wealth. Her second marriage was happy, ending when her husband, a stockbroker, died in her arms. Vincent Astor, a fabled melancholic, started courting her. She married him a few months later, and if their time together was trying (he requested that she not use the phone while he was in the house), she has been endeavoring to make up for it: on his death, he willed her $2 million, the income on another $60 million, and the charge of the Vincent Astor Foundation, which, under her tutelage, has given away well over $130 million. Unfortunately, while philanthropy, as we will see, is as essential to one's social certification as orchid bowers and initialed toilet paper, anything over $100 million is rather overdoing it, because your relatives will resent being treated like poor cousins. Sure enough, an article in the *Times* about Brooke's largesse detonated one of those delicious little feuds that are much advocated by society shrinks as a tension-relieving therapy for patients whose upbringing precludes them from attending pitdog fights. The *Times* had claimed in passing that another Astor by marriage, Candace Van Alen, screeched "You're a disgrace" at Brooke, who had been delivering a talk about the family at the terribly sedate Knickerbocker Club. "It wasn't Mrs. Van Alen who yelled. It was Brooke," shot back a Van Alen partisan. "She believes she is the biggest money-giver in New York. You know, Mr. Forbes does his four hundred, and she's

not in it." Another Van Alen friend called a journalist and intimated that Brooke was receiving counsel from "that PR man
George Trescher." An *Astor* with a PR man? "George has a *special
events* firm," hissed a Trescher sidekick. "It's simply that he and
Brooke are bosom pals. She is his mentor and vice versa."

And what advice might a society mentor offer? Certainly, after
marrying well, you'll need to learn to sustain some high-powered
conversations. To enhance her ability to banter with her
investment-banker husband about the Federal Reserve system,
mergers, acquisitions, and so forth, Susan Gutfreund has joined
the Forum of Women Directors, a brainy financial discussion
group. One of her proudest possessions is the prize she won from
it, an engraved Tiffany sculpture, for correctly guessing the trea-
sury bill rate.

Step Three: Hire a social secretary who is better born than
yourself to corral the Cast for your first party. At this stage you
probably will be working out of a suite at the Helmsley Palace
Hotel, because your husband lived a quiet life with his first wife of
thirty years in Scarsdale before marrying you and you don't have a
permanent home yet in the city. But that doesn't mean you have to
act like some common tourist and place your own phone calls.
Besides, you'll need the guhl (by now you should be taking
elocution tuition from a Long Island Lockjaw specialist) down the
line, when you do find an apartment, to usher your guests on
instructional house tours—"these are Fabergé . . . and this is from
the Winter Palace," a blueblooded employee of Mrs. G's has been
known to tell visitors. The word is that there has been nothing like
it since the halcyon era when Jayne Wrightsman, wife of the late
oil industrialist, displayed Marie Antoinette's velvet-lined dog-
house, the new domain of Choux-Choux, the Wrightsman pooch.

Though vieux New York generally charges for its stenographic
services, it should be only too ready to swill unpaid at your
trough—to allay the starvation symptoms that we discussed in
chapter one. Outright bribery is reserved for more serious projects in this book. Lee Israel, the unauthorized biographer of Estée
Lauder, did report in *Beyond the Magic* that there was gossip that
the ambitious cosmetics manufacturer had bagged the Duke and
Duchess of Windsor for her table with an outright cash payment
of $25,000. "That is unlikely," Israel wrote. And George Plimp-
ton, of the Plimpton Plimptons, was enraged by a *Women's Wear*
report that said he had charged $2,000 to grace the opening of a
new office building. "Hiring oneself out as a party guest," sniped
the gospel according to the needle trades. That was no party,

retorts the *Paris Review* editor. It's what you charge when you have to clip a ribbon and deliver a little oration.

Let's see if you now have it straight.

Right: Estée hired a Salvation Army band to serenade Princess Grace of Monaco.

Wrong: Estée bombarded Wallis with so much free lipstick, according to the Israel biography, that finally the duchess, who credited her wrinkle-free autumn to *Erno Lazlo,* graciously informed her benefactress that her supply had reached the point of glut.

Right: While the Social Registerite help works the phones, telling your old friends they've got the wrong number and selling *her* aristocratic pals on the authenticity of your fifty identical pairs of Susan Bennis Warren Edwards shoes and your dog's onyx parure and Patricia Henderson mink coat, ask any social heavies you already know to mail out testimonials about you. Le tout New York took Arianna Stassinopoulos to its bosom after being deluged with introductory letters about the unconventional Greek-born biographer. She was moving here from London, where she had been through a bit of a media drubbing because of her advocacy at a seminar in a well-appointed Chelsea drawing room of a training scheme that's marketed by a California cult. The cult is run by John-Roger, who calls himself a "way-shower."

"I got a quick note about [Arianna] from her pal Fleur Cowles," says William M. Fine, a debonair New York business executive and writer who is an excellent jumping-off point because of his longtime friendship with the Reagans. It was to him that the First Lady confided that she planned to put the White House "up on a hill, in people's minds, in a philosophical sense." Hilton Kramer, who edits one of the city's prestigious intellectual magazines, *New Criterion,* was introduced to Arianna at nine-thirty in the evening at a party he left a few minutes later "without giving her my card." At nine-thirty the next morning, a daintily wrapped, inscribed copy of her best-selling work on Maria Callas arrived at his office. Around that hour, Arianna could be found at an exercise class whose only other member was Barbara Walters.

Alternative Step Three: If your style is more the Palladium than the Plaza, get Andy Warhol to sponsor you. The ink on his fortune (estimated at $20 million) is so green that it may rub off on your Valentino (one young countess discoed in hers with her dismembered tiara pinned to her décolletage). But think what he did for First Daughter-in-Law Doria when she worked for his magazine *Interview.* Think of his rank as staff portraitist to the rich cow who thought she was going to stop her son's setting up housekeeping with you. Above all, think of the vedettes he created. Baby Jane Holzer, a coltish young Park Avenue matron, performed in about half a dozen of his underground movies. She sweated it out without salary, according to *The Beautiful People,* Marylin Bender's classic sixties account of the fashion industry's courtship of society, but then New York always was a quid pro quo town. Holzer now runs Sweet Baby Jane's, a Palm Beach dessert parlor where the most popular ice cream flavor for a while was Absolutely Nuts.

"Andy's one of the most misunderstood figures of our time," said Maura Moynihan, a more current Warhol protégée, when one of our reporters asked the singer-writer daughter of New York's senior senator about Edie Sedgwick, the Warhol star whose drug-dazed work has become a sort of memento mori to an entire generation of beepees. "He's very antidrugs. . . . None of the people around him today do any drugs. In the sixties, [they did], and he's told me, he thought that they were straight . . . and then he found out they were all on drugs. He was really surprised."

Step Four: A restaurant will have stood for your first party, (see chapter three), but by now the invitations are going to be rolling in, and you'll want to return them graciously. It's time, therefore, to check out of Queen Leona's palace and get your own good Manhattan address. This isn't necessarily the same as a good *building*—one of the most publicized high-rises on Fifth Avenue "is really cheaply built," says the socially connected realtor Bob Watt. "I've heard of people bursting into tears when they moved in there, but very rich people don't complain because they don't like to admit they made a mistake." Or because they're smart enough to realize when they're in a social climber's heaven. As the late Henry Post, a reputed descendant of Emily, urged in *New York* magazine, such mutual adversities as "overflowing toilets . . . garbage problems, doorman strikes" will ensure that you get to meet the triple-A neighbors. "You wind up discussing leaky plumbing with Leonard Bernstein or a Whitney, operating the elevator with Lyn Revson or Nancy Kissinger. All in all, a good beginning."

A word of warning, though. The choicest residential sanctums on Manhattan's so-called Gold Coast will accept you only if you make the grade in the Bishop's report. One of the city's more closely guarded secrets, the report has no more to do with spirituality than anything else in the haut monde. Bishop's Service, a firm that conducts confidential background checks for clients like the New York Stock Exchange, has a subsidiary man-

aged by former FBI agents that pries open the pasts of prospective
co-op purchasers. As a brochure for the firm points out, "All too
often, impressive credentials turn out to be exaggerated and
misleading, if not completely false—and personal chemistry that
seemed so right turns out to be all wrong." For instance, maybe
your husband, a former Louisiana wildcatter, surreptitiously
schlepps his lunch to work in a bag, his Thom Mc An patent
leather flashing like the Christmas sleigh scene on the roof of your
Scarsdale split-level. Worse, maybe the tableau was mounted to
amuse your six-month-old. While it certainly was smart to get
pregnant on your wedding night, as a way around that mean-
spirited prenuptial agreement your beloved's lawyer forced you to
sign, the only time you hear about children in your new milieu
before they burst into kleptomaniacal bloom at the Baby Benefit is
when Nanny or Mamzelle the French Governess wheels them out
to the park for an airing. Ideally, the *Gardenia jasminoides* in your
conservatory will be aired in the same sentence. "We check with
the previous landlord," says a Bishop's executive, "and neighbors."

Since the investigators will also grill you, it is time for some
warm-up exercises, in which we will study what the Madison
Avenue public relations maven Count Lanfranco Rasponi, a social
Svengali who has now departed for the big party in the sky,
labeled "the tribal customs" (for more on his career, turn to
chapter twelve, where we deal with charity fraud).

Okay, so the ex-G-man asks you, "What is the socially correct
drug with which to finish up lunch at Le Cirque?" The answer, of
course, is papaya-and-garlic pills, the ones from Peru at $60 a
bottle. "They break up the food in your system," a social user
advises.

If the gumshoe invites you to the theater, ostentatiously join
him in the front row twenty minutes after the curtain goes up.
Rasponi liked to recite the cautionary tale of the tyro who asked
permission to leave a dinner party before coffee was served in
order to be punctual for the glorious title aria of *Aida* at the Met.
"Now, Marie," a sophisticate at the table reprimanded her, as
recounted by Rasponi in his book *The International Nomads,*
"surely Verdi did not have a great opinion of this aria if he placed it
at the beginning of the first act."

But how to respond when the sleuth demands during intermission, "Are those *real* diamonds?" Aha. You got it. "Harry Winston's," you retort frostily, "doesn't make fake ones." At least
that's what one of the newly minted ladies said when someone

asked her. She tactfully lets her guests know what she paid for some of her fine Victorian etchings and burled walnut whatnots by leaving the price tags on them.

You don't have any diamonds? After burglars relieved Rita Lachman of her $5 million gem trove, the cosmetics tycoon's ex calmly proceeded to compile a scrapbook about her collection-that-was and the subsequent police probe. "My robbery album," she smiles. "What other person do you know who has owned a Mazarin diamond?" Incidentally, should you too become a crime victim, keep your priorities straight. Your paradigm should be the socialite who, jumped by muggers, balked at yielding up her glittering necklace even though the men were poking a gun at her boyfriend's head. And no matter how safe you feel, act paranoid. It enhances your importance. Imagine that you're Baby Doc's wife when she was here on one of her shopping expeditions. This is not totally dishonest, since you never know when the class war is going to start. We are particularly taken by the lady who orders her chauffeur to cut red lights whenever she spies a bag person; given the statistics, she found no shortage of opportunities to demonstrate her tactics during a test drive one evening, squealing as her limo narrowly missed hitting one bundle of rags: "She'll smash the windows with a hammer." The Countess Aline de Romanones arrived at a lustrous reception bundled up in a baseball jacket. To "disguise" her emeralds.

Step Five: Hire a posh decorating firm. You'll be rewarded with a lot more than its impeccable taste. For instance, MAC II (212-249-4466) is run by Mica Ertegun and Chessy Rayner. Mica's husband, Ahmet, is the Atlantic Records supremo, meaning there's the possibility she'll deliver his chums the Rolling Stones along with the curtains (never, on any account, call them drapes). Chessy is from such a well-to-do old family that her mother, Mrs. Iva Patcevitch, is reputed to have quashed an impudent clerk at a perfume counter by snapping, "Charge it!" as she swept all the bottles to the floor with her parasol. Though Patcevitch has no recollection of any such incident, J. Allen Murphy, an old-money decorator (516-922-4007), offered us conclusive proof that there is nothing like an interior designer whose lineage rivals his linens in quality. For instance, he explained, the designer might take a promenade with a new client along the upper reaches of Madison Avenue:

"With the right decorator you can bump into at least three of the best people in New York in ten minutes and then you lunch with them at Le Cirque." More than that, "If he's giving a dinner party, he'll invite you, and if he's doing a house for one of his other families, he'll tell them how nice you are."

Since personal introductions like this can only go so far, you also need certain objets retrouvés. So we are proud to present Murphy's Law—of marketing.

Patronizing the "right" stores and service establishments, as the interior designer points out, while not always the same as shopping for value, will nicely propagate your name in the social hothouse. "If you see a face enough in a right place, it becomes a right face," as Murphy puts it. The following list incorporates his recommendations with some from other social cognoscenti; all numbers are 212 area code.

Butcher shops

Albert's Prime Meats
836 Lexington Avenue
751-3169

Akron Prime Meats
1605 Lemoine Avenue, Fort Lee,
  New Jersey
744-1551

Ottomanelli Brothers
1549 York Avenue
772-7900

The way this one works is that the butcher wraps the twenty-one filets and puts them on the counter for your chauffeur (send your son in a uniform) to pick up. Mrs. T's driver, arriving for her twenty filets, notices your name on the wrapping and dashes back to rat to her.

Greengrocers

Grace Balducci's
1237 Third Avenue
737-0600

Rodney Dangerfield gets no respect here. He has to take his turn with folks like Neil Simon, David Rockefeller, Lucille Ball, Mick Jagger, and Liza Minnelli.

Paradise Market
1100 Madison Avenue
737-0049

Paradise customers include Ben Gazzara, Tony Roberts, and Peter Kalikow, the developer who proposed evicting some twelve hundred tenants from a working-class Manhattan apartment complex in order to build a paradise for upscale bananas on the site.

Pastries

William Greenberg, Jr., Desserts
1377 Third Avenue
861-1340

The brownies are popular with Jackie O. Claudette Colbert favors the schnecken.

Bonté Patisserie
1316 Third Avenue
535-2360

The Bakery at Bloomingdale's

Fancy foods

Fraser Morris Fine Foods
931 Madison Avenue
988-6700

This is where Jackie O's aristocratic sister, Lee Radziwell, shops for caviar and Woody Allen buys his assorted nuts. Gene Wilder, Pearl Bailey, and Gilda Radner have been seen browsing the salads.

William Poll
1051 Lexington Avenue
288-0501

Hair (women's)

Kenneth
19 East Fifty-fourth Street
752-1800

Jackie O packs manuscripts here in a Hermès book bag from the publishing house where she is an editor. She pores over her paperwork as her hair is blow-dried in a private room.

Elizabeth Arden Salon
691 Fifth Avenue
407-7910

Nancy Reagan invites you to join her for a brushout at Monsieur Marc, at 22 East Sixty-fifth Street, which is where Rita Lachman says she had her successor in the cosmetics tycoon's affections, Jaquine, slapped with the "tranquilizers" lawsuit (chapter one); phone 861-0700.

Hair (men's)

Bonaparte Hair Designers
521 Madison Avenue
753-8545

Manicurists

Josephine's
200 East Sixtieth Street
758-3090

Dinmar Beauty Salon
35 East Sixty-fifth Street
249-9268

Dresses

Martha
475 Park Avenue
753-1511

St. Laurent Rive Gauche
855 Madison Avenue
988-3821

Givenchy Boutique
954 Madison Avenue
772-1040

Other women's wear
Bloomingdale's
Henri Bendel

Ensure that you are au fait with the correct pronunciation for Bendel's. It rhymes with Wendel's.

Resale
Encore
1132 Madison Avenue
879-2850

Jackie O is said to bring her duds here after wearing them once or twice or not at all.

Pet wear
Canine Styles
830 Lexington Avenue
751-4549

Tyler can have his toenails enameled grape here as well as choose a complete wardrobe, including booties, suspenders for his socks, and pajamas. For a leash, we recommend the twenty-four-karat gold-plated "Princess" model. It's named for a human who used to patronize this salon, the late Princess Grace of Monaco.

Menswear
Dunhill Tailors
65 East Fifty-seventh Street
355-0050

Paul Stuart
Madison Avenue at Forty-fifth
　Street
682-0320

Sills of Cambridge
18 East Fifty-third Street
355-2360

Bijan
699 Fifth Avenue
758-7500

Lured by the $24,000 chinchilla-lined trenchcoat and the $2,200 suits, Bijan's customers include Ronald Reagan, King Juan Carlos of Spain, Adnan Khashoggi, and the Rev. Jesse Jackson.

Jewels
Harry Winston
718 Fifth Avenue
245-2000

Marina B
809 Madison Avenue
288-9708

Alexander Guest works at Marina B. His mother is C. Z. Guest, the noted horsewoman, social Brahmin, and gardening columnist. His father, the late Winston Guest, was a Phipps steel heir whose family tree included a British duke. His sister Cornelia sang "It's My Party and I'll Cry If I Want To" on the David Letterman Show and a rock version of "Frosty the Snowman" ("Thumpety thump-thump, thumpety thump-thump, there goes Frosty!") at a disco. She also posed topless on a Cap Ferrat diving board for *Life* magazine, which photographed her with her hands folded modestly over her breasts. Then she wrote a book about it all, *The Debutante's Guide to Life*.

Furs
Maximilian
20 West Fifty-seventh Street
563-4490

Revillon at Saks Fifth Avenue

Flowers
Renny
27 East Sixty-second Street and
    1018 Lexington Avenue
371-5354

The final recommendation is from our friend J. Allen Murphy. C.Z. runs C. Z. Guest Garden Enterprises from Templeton, her Long Island family estate. It is known for its great orchid houses, and for assistance in setting up your own collection, you can write her at the *New York Post, Ladies' Home Journal,* or any of the other publications that carry her columns. She also designs gardens and patio and porch furniture.

Step Six: Have your decorator fill you in on the Lexington Avenue antiques store that supplies sets of Compleat Heirlooms. Maybe an oil of your grandmom's palazzo in Leningrad, a family Bible with flyleaf genealogical tree, and hides of tigers your paternal forebears slaughtered on hunts in the British Raj. Male readers should embark immediately on polo lessons and practice barking gruff asides about how they resigned from the Brook— "the family club, y'know"—"because one day I walked in and there was this fellow lounging in a chair who looked like somebody's guest and he was a *member!*"

Depending on your previous career and origins, you should also study the following case histories, which are presented here without comment:

• Merle Oberon used to have her half-Indian mother dress up in a maid's cap and apron. Thus disguised, she would be permitted to serve the late actress's guests tea.
• The boss of the Democratic Party in Manhattan, Denny Farrell, applied to join the Friendly Sons of St. Patrick. Since he had scaled the political heights by identifying himself as black, this seemed almost as confusing as his light skin, but Denny explained that while "both grandmothers were black," he had "a grandfather whose parents were from Ireland, and a grandfather who was Scottish. The bottom line is that black is a state of mind, and black is what I am."
• The fashion designer Oscar de la Renta was called Oscar *Renta* when the New York TV personality and writer James Brady first knew him as a gangling youth from the Dominican Republic. Oscar responded that his "original family name" was "Ortiz de la Renta." His late wife Françoise, an eminent New York hostess, also

seemed something of an enigma. She consistently claimed Paris as her birthplace, even though, *Women's Wear* informed its readers, there was talk that "she was born in the French West Indies." The memorial service for her was delayed until three months after her death and was widely described as the kick-off to the 1983 social season. She was eulogized by Henry the Inc., Baron Guy de Rothschild, and Bill Blass. Music was by thirty-five members of the New York Philharmonic and Placido Domingo.

• The late Alfred Bloomingdale, a socialite and Reagan confidant whose family established the eponymous New York department store, was described in his résumé, and is still described in press reports recalling his predilection for spanking his young mistress, as having founded Diners Club. Not so, according to the credit card company. Evelyn Capone, widow of a Long Island business-man, Frank McNamara, takes up the tale: "My husband founded the club with one hundred percent of the stock in 1950, and Alfred Bloomingdale came into the company about two years later."

• One of the NM ladies regularly writes Buckingham Palace, volunteering her help to the royal charities and enclosing garish little presents. When, as invariably happens, a flunky or even one of Their Highnesses replies with a bread-and-butter note, she adds it to a leather-bound collection that she intends donating in her name to an Ivy League university.

• Estée Lauder (maxim: "If you don't smell it, you can't sell it") is from a "beauty-conscious Viennese family," counseled the résumé her company sent us some time before the publication of the Lee Israel book. However, reporters who have interviewed the moth-erly self-made tycoon over the years have tended to come away confused. One wrote, for instance, that she was partly French. Another, Virginia Lee Warren of the *Times,* was briefed shortly after Mrs. Lauder moved into an East Seventies mansion with silver doorknobs and gold-plated bathroom fixtures. "In Milwau-kee," declared Estée, "a woman used to come to our house every day just to brush my mother's hair." These heartland reminis-cences "interchanged with anecdotes about Scranton, giving rise to reports that she was a coal miner's daughter which she denied," according to *At the Top,* a book by Marylin Bender.

There were even intimations of royal connections: Estée adorned the mansion with looming portraits of Spanish nobles and sailed into the opening of the new Metropolitan Opera House in a gold-and-diamond crown.

Women's Wear related that she was raised in a large house on

Long Island with a "stable, a chauffeured car and an Italian nurse."

At least her religious affiliation seemed unequivocal: "You know," an acquaintance of hers recalls her saying, "Christmas means so much to me."

"I got the impression," he says, "that she was brought up by nuns in a convent."

Her late husband and Lauder company cofounder, Joseph, was brought up Lauter, the *d* being substituted after he met Estée. Lauder was the original family name, she has explained. *His* religious affiliation was devoutly unequivocal. He was Jewish, and so, according to Israel, is Estée, who was born Josephine Esther, and grew up above a hardware store in Corona, Queens—"the valley of ashes" in F. Scott Fitzgerald's *The Great Gatsby.*

Milwaukee? "See, a lot of my family are in Milwaukee and I spent a lot of time there," Estée told us. "My mother's mother was French Catholic, and her father wasn't. She died and my grandfather remarried a Jewish person, so my mother was brought up by a stepmother in Hungary." We thought it was Vienna? "*Austrian* Hungary." As it happened, her autobiography plopped into the bookstores at the same time as the Israel work. In *Estée: A Success Story,* the businesswoman says she belongs to both the Catholic Sisters and Temple Emanu-El—and that her pa was Czechoslovakian. "When my father was a young man, Emperor Francis Joseph wanted his niece, who weighed about 300 pounds, to marry him ..." Size apart, this would have been the perfect ad for Estée's Youth Dew line, since her father, according to his death certificate, was only thirteen when he arrived in New York; or sixteen if you go by his naturalization papers, which Israel concluded probably were less accurate.

Still, if Estée was doing a dervish dance around her roots, it may have been for more complex reasons than her position in an industry that sells the impossible dream by packaging it in images of glamour.

"Look at the dirty Jew...!" an employee of the Maidstone Club, a Hamptons WASP sanctuary, reportedly sneered as the daughter of a member of a more ecumenical club walked by during a children's swim meet. Moreover, Denny Farrell, the political boss, was wise to get his Irish up: the circus is eclectic in its prejudices. One famous instance of this, or so Gloria Vanderbilt charged, was when the board of River House, a fortresslike East Fifty-second Street co-op where Henry romps with Nancy and Tyler, rejected her bid to buy a duplex that had once belonged to Marshall Field because she was rumored to be enamored of the black entertainer

Bobby Short. The board responded that it wasn't that at all: it didn't want a "public person."

A Korean immigrant, Kyu-Sung Choi, tried to open a twenty-four-hour delicatessen on Park Avenue. Remonstrated a neighborhood leader, "Do the residents of Park Avenue want to look out the window at vegetables?" Choi settled for working seventeen hours a day and decorating his windows with fruit, not vegetables. Fifth Avenue is the new front line. Wails a Social Registerite, "Just the other day, I was in the Tiffany area, and I saw nothing but Japs and chocolate drops."

Still, there is chocolate and Godiva chocolate. **Step Seven** will win you the undying friendship of huge retinues of hangers-on, even if you're Michael Jackson and plan stuffing your croustades with tracts for the Jehovah's Witnesses instead of scallops Saint-Tropez. We're talking about your purchase of a private plane and a yacht. Seagoing palaces, wadded with little decorator touches like fireplaces, silver faucets, and English antiques, are so dime-a-dozen off New York these days that the FBI bugged one to snare a clutch of mobsters, who were hosted aboard by two agents posing as lovers. Our only cautionary note is that much as the feds' choice of moorings may have sent one of their guests, Carmine Persico, the boss of the Colombo crime family, panting for his custom-made yacht cap, there are more socially effective places to drop anchor than Staten Island.

For instance, trucking sachem Arthur Imperatore became the gleam in *Women's Wear*'s "Eye" column when he loaned his 142-foot *Imperator* (drop that cumbersome final *e,* and in the eyes of the ladies, all of whom have excellent Latin, you're an instant Emperor) to the New York City Ballet for a fundraising cruise on the Hudson River. His boat is stocked with artworks by Monet, Toulouse-Lautrec, Renoir, Pissarro, and Matisse, which is as good as pasting up a net asset statement, since even Stavros Niarchos stripped the Impressionists from one his of tubs, the *Creole,* for fear they would be damaged by the sea damp.

Publisher Malcolm Forbes lent one of his floating Winnebagos—he's had a series of them, all called the *Highlander*—to Imelda while she was still Queen Bee, for a party. The guests included a Vanderbilt and Andy Warhol, and uniformed soldiers stood in the background, reported *New York Post* columnist Cindy Adams.

The latest *Highlander* has fourteen bathrooms. The reason for this can be deduced from the usage record of one of her predecessors, which, says a glossy brochure Forbes has issued on his ultimate Capitalist Tool, hosted thousands of "corporate Consequentials . . . In several instances, major American corporate mergers resulted from friendships formed."

Adnan Khashoggi, who uses the same yacht designer as Forbes, named a 282-foot colossus after his daughter Nabila, and two other boats, the *Mahomedia* and the *Khalidia,* for his sons. The *Nabila,* which served as a setting for the James Bond film *Never Say Never Again,* is equipped with a U.S. Navy–quality satellite guidance system, a hospital (with an operating room, two nurses, and a doctor), safes in each guest room, three chefs, a crew of forty, and a heliport. "Strictly for fun," *Town and Country* instructed its readers, "there's a discotheque and a cinema." Truth to tell, it was just so cramped on board that shortly after the story hit the newsstands, blueprints were drafted for the *Nabila II.* Denying talk that Khashoggi is running low on cash, an aide said it will have his and her helicopter pads and *two* satellite guidance systems. Also, it has been bruited, antiaircraft missiles, but we think that is a confusion with the four state-of-the-art warheads the Pentagon leased out to the *Abdul-Aziz,* Saudi King Fahd's new yacht. "We've never rented missiles before," remarked a Pentagon official. "We'll charge the Saudis for refurbishing them when they are returned."

Khashoggi's arsenal does include:
- a helicopter
- a stretched Boeing 727
- a DC-9
- a DC-8

The DC-8 is done out like a midscale Holiday Inn, with staff quarters, a semicircular dining room, two lounges, a conference room, and, in the private quarters, a king-sized bed. The belly of the plane hides a camera, which projects close-ups of the salaaming peasants in the fields thirty-thousand feet beneath onto a horizontal screen. This apparatus doubles as a coffee table.

Such comfort should be shared. Indeed Cheryl Rixon, a *Penthouse* Pet of the Year, told us that a Khashoggi representative offered to dispatch one of the airships to New York to transport her and some girlfriends to the billionaire's forty-seventh birthday bash in the Mediterranean—"they said Khashoggi was an admirer of mine and they'd provide designer clothes." Khashoggi's chief of staff, Robert Shaheen, demurred, insisting that a typical soirée chez Adnan would be the New York dinner attended by: American University president Richard Berendzen, whose school has been endowed by Khashoggi with a sports and convocation center; President Reagan's agriculture secretary, John Block; the wife of

White House deputy chief of staff Michael Deaver; and twelve other Washington notables. One of the arms magnate's smaller silver birds, the Boeing 727, had sped them north from the capital. After the dishes were cleared, at one-thirty in the morning, Khashoggi called on Berendzen to perk up the bleary-eyed guests with an astronomy lecture. Berendzen ran into the Queen of England's favorite porno star at another of these Olympic Tower salons: "There was this young woman who looked like one of my students, standing all by herself and almost matronly in her dress. I walked up and said, 'Hi, I'm Richard Berendzen,' and she said, 'I'm Koo Stark.'"

The image problems of Koo, Prince Andrew's ex, were trivial compared to the calumnies that hounded Judy Taubman, the Israeli beauty pageant winner, after she wed Alfred Taubman, the Sotheby's owner and property sultan. Since she had been a receptionist at Christie's, a principal rival to her husband's New York auction rooms, it wasn't hard to guess the motives behind some of the scuttlebutt. "She had these *fabulous* tits," snickers a fashion plate who worked with her there. "One day an old man was coming upstairs with a Ming vase he wanted to sell. He took one look at her and fell backwards, smashing the vase." A specialist in Christie's Oriental department concedes that the story seems apocryphal, since no breakage claim was submitted to the auction house's insurance company. A magazine retracted a report that had the former beauty queen turning up in a "white leather miniskirt" at a gathering of debutantes' mothers. Judy, complaining that she wasn't at the event and that the story implied she was "ignorant of appropriate apparel and of proper social behavior," had filed a $20 million libel suit. Her husband had more serious baggage. No sooner had he taken over Sotheby's than rumors began to circulate that he planned topping its New York showrooms with a Godzilla of a condominium tower. Correct, as it turned out, but the design of the proposed monolith was neoclassical, and, after perusing other evidence, we prefer to think of this magnificent couple as the New Kennedys.

Shortly after Jackie Kennedy Onassis left for a visit to New Delhi, the Taubman Learjet streaked off in the same direction. "I've got to see the Taj Mahal!" vowed one of the pilgrims they had invited to accompany them, Jerry Zipkin.

What you are aiming for, you see, is to start a trend.

Later in the year, oil heiress Camilla Blaffer Royall scampered to Jaipur to marry a Boston financier in a Hindu ceremony in a government-owned palace. The plump, pretty bride was girt in pink Rajasthani wedding robes and a nose ornament, and the groom, also in traditional garb, lurched in clinging to an elephant. "India is so in now," said Asha Puthli, an Indian-born New York socialite and recording artist who was among the glitter people who jetted there for the occasion.

So many of them were jetting there that all flights were fully booked.

Town & Country weighed in with one of its periodic geopolitical screeds. Gazing dreamily up into a Bombay sky that was "diaphanous as a silk chiffon sari," the magazine's commentator was seized with the excitement of the election of the "handsome, forty-year-old Rajiv Gandhi." Presumably society's Anthony Lewis was seeing all this through a bit of a haze—the haze of dust devils thrown up by the wheels of the "snappy red" coupe driven by the wife of a film mogul. "Smart cars are not the only shape of things to come," the piece continued, caroming to another rajah who was expecting "a new industrial revolution. It may be late in coming, but I think we are ready for it."

Maybe we could do a swap. All New Yorkers earning less than the median income needed for a middle-class lifestyle here, $80,000 a year, would move to Bombay (Zipkin, the sweet thing, says he'll ask Ronnie to lend some life preservers for the journey), and all rich Bombayites would move to Manhattan. The other boroughs would be razed and enclosed in a giant Bohemian crystal bubble for a limo garage.

Alternative Step Seven: If you can't afford to buy a plane or a ship, *borrow one from your employer.* The chances of being caught by irked stockholders are remote. Corporate jets used to carry identifying markings, but most of these were obliterated after elderly investors began staking out airports in vacation spots like Palm Springs and ratting to the IRS. One CEO was caught red-handed as he and a young floozy boarded their crate accompanied by a vassal carrying Vuitton luggage and a lemon tree in a ceramic pot.

Right after President Reagan was first elected, America's power-sick Metternich whirled through the Middle East on what was billed as a "fact-finding" tour. Henry Kissinger's companions on the mission were his wife, Brooke Astor, and William Paley. Paley was then the chairman of CBS and they were riding in a CBS Gulfstream jet. "I think the whole thing started as a lark, to go look at the ruins in Egypt," said a Paley aide, Franklin Mewshaw. Paley reimbursed the company ("Normally, we charge first-class airfares," explained an aircraft department staffer), and no one made a big deal about it because the key to this sort of subsidized living is to comport oneself with sangfroid. Like the New York captain of industry who, playing golf one afternoon in the Hamptons, phoned in a reservation on his company credit card for a charter chopper to ferry him home to Manhattan. As he reached the eighteenth hole, the machine came in to land. Three minutes later, in thrummed another of the $395-an-hour flying machines. "Shit!" the industrialist exclaimed. "I forgot I ordered one already."

Laura Utley, a not especially well-known New York businesswoman, and her husband, Bentley Blum, enticed 450 guests, including a prince (the designer Egon von Furstenberg), Anne Eisenhower, and a granddaughter of Sir Winston Churchill, to a "one night cruise around the world" on their imposing country estate. The calligraphic invitations popped like Easter chicks out of small packing crates, which also contained a split of Moët et Chandon and the evening's itinerary:

7:30–9:30 P.M.

Point of embarkation, Japan
With cocktails and champagne enjoy fresh sushi and hibachi-grilled hors d'oeuvre and an array of international appetizers.

9:30 P.M.

Havana, Monte Carlo and New York
You will dine on delicacies from around the world, dance the rhumba in old Havana & enjoy the strolling violins as you try your luck for Gift Prizes at roulette, black jack and dice tables on the terraces of Monte Carlo and reminisce to the old standards played by a big band in the ambiance of an authentic New York supper club as you enjoy the splendor of a transatlantic voyage, circa 1935.

1 A.M.

Breakfast Buffet will be served on the main deck. A selection of crepes, omelettes and smoked fish.

BON VOYAGE!

Laura and Bentley

As an inexpensive beginning to **Step Eight,** the photo opportunities that will be a recurring concern during your voyage to the top, we suggest inviting your chosen columnist on a yacht cruise and impressing her as soon as she walks up your gangplank with a *gimmick*. Nothing too outré, please. One big real estate owner declines to wear anything on his feet except sneakers, including a pair that are dyed black to go with his tuxedo. Khashoggi's unassuming trademark is a pet puma, declawed, and with filed teeth. Marylou Whitney clops through the streets of Saratoga, the racing resort, to her annual summer party in quaint vehicles—on one occasion, a sleigh; on another, a pumpkin coach—waving gracefully to her friends, the tourists, and photographers. Her husband, Sonny, acquired an "amphi-car," an automobile that, upon pressing a button, transformed into a boat. Another social tiger bought a similar machine and went to demonstrate it to friends. It promptly sank, so maybe publishing is a better field to investigate. A group of the ladies got together to issue a recipe collection. Only after it won them the coveted Tastemaker cookbook award did a professional food writer, Paula Wolfert, come forward to point out the remarkable similarity, down to "the decorative parsley bits" in an illustration, between seven recipes in the work and ones she has had published in national magazines.

James Van Alen, the founder of the International Tennis Hall of Fame, father of the game's tie-break principle, and husband of Brooke Astor's antagonist, has frequently gotten attention as a talented amateur lyricist. Lunching at Le Cirque, shortly before the 1984 presidential election, he launched into his latest number:

> *Believe me Mister President*
> *We're proud to shake your hand*
> *You got here just in time to save*
> *Our dear beloved land*
> *From four more dumb defenseless years*
> *Of Carter and Mondale*
> *Intent on our disarmament*
> *On a suicidal scale*
>
> *You stand for freedom*
> *Above all else on earth*
> *The heritage we've treasured*
> *Since our country's day of birth*
> *You've turned the White House bright again*
> *From Commie-Cratic gray*
> *And we're giving you a landslide vote*
> *To keep it just that way*

The ode was a smash when its composer, accompanying himself on a tenor guitar, performed it at campaign events.

You're not musical? Consider this: Even the misfortunes in your life may make you worthy of ink. After the très soignée Carolyn Amory and her husband patched up a temporary lacuna in their marriage, the *Post*'s society column carried this Valentine's Day bulletin:

"All is well with Carolyn and Thomas. . . . She entered in a new Russian sable coat which her husband had ordered for Christmas but had just been delivered by the furrier.

"Under the sable she was wearing a white satin dress and a diamond necklace with a 44-carat sapphire pendant outlined by diamonds that was Tom's Valentine's present.

"'I'm so happy,' Carolyn says. 'We're starting a second honeymoon next week.'"

And after a freak tropical storm dumped a Venezuelan freighter next to the swimming pool of Mollie Wilmot's Palm Beach mansion, do you think the department-store heiress went whining about it to her neighbor, Rose Kennedy? The uninvited guest might be a rustbucket in need of a good spritz of Lauder for Men, but there it was splashed across the bow—MERCEDES. A veritable talisman. Wilmot posed for the *Times,* sitting demurely on a damask couch. She was clutching her white Pekinese Fluff and the ship loomed over her shoulder. A friend of hers urged your author to write a major magazine article about how the episode had made the hostess into a media hero. Perhaps there was even a film in it? A thick dossier of supportive material quickly followed in the mail, including photocopies of letters from a number of men who, somehow confusing the snap of Mollie and Fluff with a lonely-hearts ad, proposed relationships with her: "I have been unemployed for 5 yrs," one of the enclosures implored, " . . . and I haven't had sex with a woman for 5 yrs."

Susan Gutfreund, these days a neighbor of the Taubmans in the best building on Fifth Avenue, peers down through the foliage at all of this. Like *Macbeth,* she has trees as her colophon.

As her guests arrived at Britain's Blenheim Palace, which she had rented for one of her intimate little entertainments, the queen's trumpeters blasted a salvo of welcoming fanfares. After dinner there was dancing to a society orchestra from New York in an anteroom decorated with potted palms.

For one of her first Christmases with her Wall Street king, the banker's wife selected a twenty-two-foot Douglas fir from a tree grower who had previously donated a fifteen-foot shrimp to the president's quarters at the White House. Since the Gutfreunds' quarter-ton monster wouldn't fit into the elevators at River House, where the couple at the time were the Kissingers' neighbors, it had to be winched up the outside of the building into their galactic Dunsinane.

"It's not coarse, it has a nice soft needle, very good branching habit and excellent needle retention," its proud breeder told *Manhattan, inc.* magazine.

As her old employer would say, you really can't beat the experience of an evening with Mrs. G.

The chef for some of her early dinner-party triumphs was one of the world's foremost food showmen, Michel Fitoussi, a part-owner of the now-defunct Palace. Probably the most expensive restaurant in the world, its trademark was towering lamb-fat-and-pasta effigies—which, luckily, weren't labeled "on loan" when Fitoussi hauled them to the Gutfreund residence for one party. There was a fisherman, an octopus, an Oriental birdcage . . . not a monkey in sight, though. Michael Thomas must have confused the admirably restrained Gutfreund at-homes with the blowout at Jack Heinz's New York digs at which guests were greeted by a robot shaped like a ketchup bottle and supped alfresco on the lawns where two sheep (live) and several pheasants, owls, partridges, and quail (stuffed) had been moored to the trees. Or maybe Thomas was thinking of the New York Explorers Club soirée that featured a leopard (live) as its centerpiece. The black-tie crowd nibbled on lionburgers, mountain-buffalo roast, and hippo pâté, prompting the Queen of England's husband, Prince Philip, to resign his club affiliation, snarling that he had been "appalled by this exhibition of bad taste."

Alternative Step Eight is to hire a PR person. Even if, like Marylou Whitney, you do this just to help you with various *projects* (she uses Budd Calisch, the former representative for the Queen of England's dress designer), don't ever admit to it in public. It would make you sound pushy. And, depending on who you are, professional assistance may be unnecessary.

No Need: Donald Trump is the developer whose Trump Tower, built with the help of a tax abatement valued at as much as $50 million, is the Fifth Avenue home to a slew of celebs and, until he was arrested in his condo there on a murder charge, one reputed Mafia gambling czar. To trump this, Donald proposed raising a sixty-story castle—*Trump Castle*—on one of the plushier sections of Madison Avenue. It would have six spires, with gold-leafed crenellations, and would answer the crime problem by being equipped with a moat and a drawbridge. Though the reaction of the populace to his plan is not recorded, Trump's connections in high places are such that he could crenellate the Statue of Liberty and the federal government would put up the financing, Mrs. G would give one of her little speeches, and local politicians would fight for the privilege of snipping the ribbon.

Crying Need: Barry Trupin, a computer-leasing millionaire, and his wife, Renée, had no known links to the power establishment when they began transforming a mansion in the Hamptons into a turreted pile with Gothic architectural details of an ilk that one is not often privileged to see outside of Epcot Center. The highlight of their home improvements was a replica of the Great Barrier Reef with a gushing twenty-foot waterfall and an "underground grotto for deep-sea picnics." The ladies nudged each other and whispered that Trupin was digging a shark pool.

"Barry Trupin wants to be the most famous man in the world," said an acquaintance of the millionaire after he prepared to deal a blow to the gossips by retaining Howard J. Rubenstein Associates. This heavy-hitting PR agency, which normally represents clients like labor unions and property moguls, achieved a textbook image rescue.

"Renée looked pretty, all in white, wearing what she described as Victorian underwear..." drooled a society columnist. "She proudly pointed out one of her favorite rooms, which featured wall-to-wall dog paintings." The couple started returning phone calls to publications like *New York* and the *Washington Post,* and a public-television crew pleaded to fly over the pile for a special on people who own castles.

Such damage control might not even have been necessary had the Trupins consulted a publicist *before* their debut. Maybe Gus Ober, a stout, humorous southerner who helps shape up corporate heads who are new to town and want to make the scene. He refers to himself as a "helper"—as in, he chuckles, "we tell people that they can do it by themselves if they want to, but, with the proper help, you can do in six months what would take six years. Maybe we'll get somebody to give a dinner party for you, and you'll pick up the tab."

Your publicist can also give you a leg up on **Step Nine,** which is to "get yourself a charity," as the journalist-businessman and Reagan friend William Fine, whose writings have included an article on such social nuances, puts it with a knowing smile.

This step will swallow up what's left of your $10 million start-up trove because you'll want to buy *two* tables at *every* benefit—one for you and your guests, one to donate to a second-tier charity, an impoverished member of an old family. She'll pretend she paid for it herself. "If Estée has bought two tables," gushes one of the have-nots, "she'll call you and say, 'Here's ten places. Bring anyone you want.'"

You'll also need to get on the committee of at least one first-tier disease. "Everyone wants cancer," a Park Avenue belle dame says dreamily. "Memorial Sloan-Kettering [cancer center] is just so exclusive. It has Benno Schmidt and Laurance Rockefeller. It's much nicer than Hospital for Special Surgery." Consequently, to be on the committees of the group that raises money for Memorial Sloan-Kettering is no sinecure. "There's so much competition," says a public relations maven. "I know a lady who was warned about being late for meetings, so now she always arrives twenty minutes early."

Disabled people are big too. The Feather Ball, which raises money for them, "is very nice," says the Park Avenue lady. Maniacs, on the other hand, have yet to catch on, despite the premiering of *Star 80,* the movie about a psychotic who butchers his Playmate wife, as a benefit for the Postgraduate Center of Mental Health. Nor would you want heart disease. "It's the number-one killer, I guess," Jane Pickens Hoving, who used to run the Heart Ball, opined to the *Daily News,* "... but you can't demonstrate it. People don't really get close to the disease. You can't get someone with a heart attack standing up in the middle of the room. They don't look different."

Some of the guests at New York's annual April in Paris fund-raising ball do look different. The event, which has *sixteen* committees, cunningly mixes refined patricians with Texan ladies grease-painted and ruffled like the transvestites in *La Cage aux Folles.* "Hello, sexpot!" they foghorn to each other before tearing into a hearty steak-and-fish dinner. The ball's gift boxes are slightly larger and the same weight as a small room air conditioner, and the contents explain why only poor people have to buy perfume in New York.

Some of the arrivistes have asked us whether they were right to buy $1,000 "archangel" tickets ($500 for an "angel" pew, $300 for a "seraphim," and $150 for a "cherub") for the Cathedral of St. John the Divine's 1986 centennial supper. Absolutely not. Turn immediately to chapter four, then demand they send your money back.

"LEARN HOW YOU CAN PROVIDE CREATIVE AND COST-
EFFECTIVE ANSWERS TO YOUR MARKETING OBJECTIVES BY
IDENTIFYING YOUR CORPORATE NAME WITH VINCENT VAN
GOGH . . . CANALETTO."

Mailing from New York's Metropolitan Museum of Art

The arts are probably the classiest alternative to the best diseases. Especially the Whitney Museum, says one aesthete: "It's
much more important than the Met because it's smaller and a
newer form of art, so you become proportionately more of a
benefactor and they have these *living* artists to come to your
parties." The Met, on the other hand, is very popular with
corporations. (Just be aware that if you want the press to record
the launch there of your new spray paint, a $35,000 contribution
instead of the usual $25,000 is required. Try to cheat and a
security guard may confiscate the photographers' cameras.) Nor
did the fuddy-duddy dead masters bother San Francisco's Ann
Getty when she fed smoked salmon and fresh caviar to la crème
de la crème at the Met after becoming one of the museum's
trustees. Investing in any of New York's great cultural causes is a
sure way for an out-of-towner to make a mark in the circus
because the newspapers will write grateful stories about you. Like
Mrs. Getty, you'll need a little mansion away from mansion here,
of course. Maybe the IRS will let you treat it as a charitable
deduction.

Anne Bass, the wife of one of Texas's billionaire Bass brothers,
had all the girls flitting in from the oil fields for two galas she cochaired for the New York City Ballet's School of American Ballet.
These raised nearly $1.3 million, some of which was invested in
the future—through the purchase of seventy dozen white cotton
damask napkins. The ballet school's director of development,
Mary Porter, explained that these would be used at a ball, then
washed and stored with Mark Hampton, a society decorator: "It
would cost three-fifty to rent the same napkins, so by the time
we've used them four times, we'll have saved money. You know,
synthetic napkins are awful. The food rolls off them." Porter
subsequently was dismissed from her job, amid allegations that
Mrs. Bass was attempting a "Texas take-over" of the school.

If such scrimmages do not have you leaping to your pointes,
there is no shortage of other options. It's true that, with the

demand to give money away showing temporary signs of exceeding the supply of socially worthwhile charities, some of the ladies in the Lone Star state and other remote territories were panicked. But then the Creo Society, a not-for-profit organization, was founded by a New York classical music buff and a former soap-opera writer to think up awards and projects celebrating "creativity," oversee the selection of the prize recipients, and organize benefits and ceremonies, which, of course, are crying out for wealthy chairpeople. Martha Hyder, the heiress to a Fort Worth oil-well-equipment fortune and owner of two of Nicholas's and Alexandra's crowns, endowed the society with what it describes as a "crucial" start-up gift. Its events have included:

• The presentation of the "Albert Schweitzer Music Award" to Van Cliburn at a spectacular benefiting a Michigan business school that, said a program note, is dedicated to the philosophy of free enterprise. The evening was cochaired by Martha Hyder and W. Clement Stone.
• A Rockefeller University Founders Ball, cochaired by Ann Getty and Anne Bass.
• Twenty-six black-tie musicales commemorating Johann Sebastian Bach's three hundredth birthday, cochaired by Mrs. Hyder, and hosted by, among others, Getty, Bass, Oscar de la Renta, Bill and Pat Buckley, and Mayor Koch. We do not know whether party favors at the concert at the executive seat included those police shields, entitling holders to park illegally and get free passage through toll plazas, that the mayor has bestowed on such top aides as his chef. But Judith Norell, banging away at the harpsichord, was a picture in her $1 million worth of diamonds and sapphires. On loan from Winston's.

Unfortunately, by the time Mrs. Getty got to host concert number twenty-four, there was some wriggling of immortal posteriors on the little gold chairs during Partita No. 4 in D Major, BWV 828. With the Creo Society now planning an art auction to benefit an *unfashionable* cause, the homeless, it's time, therefore, to weigh the pros and, yes, cons of another charity that, for obvious reasons, strikes a chord in some New Yorkers' hearts. Criminals. And accused criminals.

Your efforts in this sphere may come about totally unwittingly. "It turned out that the man I presented my award to was alleged by the press to be somehow connected to organized crime," wrote Geraldine in her memoirs, *Ferraro: My Story,* referring to a good deed that she did for Angel Guardians for the Elderly, the shady labor leaders' sometime charity of choice, at its 1981 annual dinner. "For crying out loud, do you know how many times a member of Congress is asked to present awards? . . . How could we run in-depth checks on every one? Most of the time we don't even know who we're giving the awards to until we get to the event," she recalled complaining when the *New York Post* reported her association with AGE.

Or it may be that you firmly believe the person you are benefiting is innocent. The Countess Christina Paolozzi, a New York model, appeared eager to help fundraise for Dr. Jeffrey MacDonald after this handsome physician was charged with slaughtering his pregnant wife and two small children. "We've got a lot of guest rooms in this eighteen-room apartment on Park Avenue," she wrote him, according to a letter quoted in Joe McGinniss's book about the case, *Fatal Vision*. "You've got a room here when you get free, and we will show you how the rest of the world is living during this year of monetary crisis. . . ." The countess now claims that the letter was composed by her husband at the time, Park Avenue plastic surgeon Dr. Howard Bellin; by Christina, he retorts, though he did issue an appeal for contributions to a Jeff MacDonald Defense Fund. In any event, MacDonald was convicted, which does seem to be the snag with this type of compassion. No sooner were the ladies planning dainty menus to tempt the prison-jaded palate of Jack Abbott, the paroled holdup man whose jail letters had been collected into a book with the help of Norman Mailer, than Abbott stabbed a twenty-two-year-old actor to death in the East Village. He later had this to say about his champion: "Norman and I are enemies, we're class enemies." Mailer next went to bat for Richard Stratton, who was on trial for a drug conspiracy that, the accused man explained very reasonably, was all to do with a book he was planning on dope smuggling. *He* got fifteen years.

Claus von Bülow, or, as he was born in Denmark, Claus Borberg (he took the name of his maternal grandfather, Frits Bülow, after his father was accused, though later acquitted, of being a Nazi collaborator), would have been a much better bet. Not only was he eventually found not guilty of attempting to murder his wife, but he meticulously kept up appearances during his two trials, gracing only the best tables in town. Suzy did report that a debate was raging about whether he could legitimately carry the aristocratic "von" in his name, but we obtained a copy of a letter from him to one of his witnesses that will set your mind at rest:

"Clearly, [this] ought not to have a bearing on the major

question of my guilt or innocence, but I feel it may be politic to put the record straight," the dapper socialite wrote, reeling off scholarly citations attesting to his membership in "the Plüskow-Aggerupgaard-Björnemose branch" of the nobility. He concluded, "Finally one more misconception: Some people believe that I claim to come from a 'family of musicians' and named my daughter Cosima in order to ally myself to that branch. This is nonsense. Of the various members of my family listed in the *Encyclopedia Britannica,* only one was a musician, and he came from a different branch. Cosima was named at the request of her godmother, the Marchioness of Londonderry, whose own daughter is called Lady Cosima Stewart."

"WHAT DO NEGROES FEEL? WHAT DO NEGROES FEEL?"

What Leonard Bernstein reportedly implored the Black Panthers at his 1970 at-home for them in his Park Avenue duplex

---

Though Bernstein quibbled at Charlotte Curtis's famous account of his remarks on that quintessentially elegant occasion, there is no denying that our social leaders' continuing flirtation with radical chic has tended to take some embarrasing twists. Kitty Carlisle Hart, the actress and philanthropist, opened her home for a benefit for the American Indian Development Association, at which the attractions included Marlon Brando, real Lummi smoked salmon in doggy bags—and a real Lummi Indian chief. Curtis's newspaper, the *Times,* persisting in its study of the divided city, asked the tribal leader how he felt about being in a room with some of the richest people in New York. "My innermost feelings," he replied, "are not printable."

Denise LeFrak, daughter of New York's very own real-estate knight, Sir Samuel J. LeFrak (see chapter one), opened *her* Park Avenue duplex to the First Ladies of El Salvador and Costa Rica, who were in town to combat communism by helping "the children of Central America." After the pair's gun-toting bodyguards had scrutinized the yawning platters of roast beef and shrimp in the kitchen for possible booby traps, an artist presented Costa Rica's De Monge with a portrait inscribed: "Your constant Mona Lisa smile and magic energy inspires one and all." Including, unfortunately, the pianist, who slammed into a rousing rendition of "On This Night of a Thousand Stars." In tribute, you might say, to De Monge's look-alike, Evita Perón.

Shortly after this, Yippie cofounder Abbie Hoffman solicited the city's liberals to accompany him to Nicaragua for New Year's. The pilgrims were promised a hotel with a "fine pool, tennis courts and horse riding," a church service "utilizing the theology of liberation," the beach, a brewery tour, a "gala party at one of Managua's popular nightclubs," and, not to forget what you were going there for, a chance to schmooze "formally and informally with the highest government officials." Not even any need to pack your flak jackets for this countercultural correlative to New Year's in Palm Springs with the Annenbergs, because, as Hoffman's mailing said, "Those having misconceptions about danger, should know that I'm bringing my daughter along."

Mrs. G herself began to do unpublicized good works—with an illiteracy project and, disguised in blue jeans and accompanied by other socially prominent women, in neighborhoods like the South Bronx. "We've got to make some efforts," the banker's wife said.

Around this time, the PR man Budd Calisch marshaled a fiftieth anniversary fiesta that raised over $250,000 for Casita Maria, the city's oldest Hispanic service organization. The committee bulged with names like Biddle, Carhart—and Somoza. "In the past, they had a committee of local people who didn't understand what to do at all," explained an organizer. "They would have very nice Hispanic evenings—a very good B list. We're slowly changing the board."

The $250,000 evening started with a concert at Radio City Music Hall by Julio Iglesias. The ghetto youngsters and their parents to whom Calisch had given seats were delighted by the opening routine, a juggler manipulating egg yolks and spitballs. But the ladies gossiped or looked bored, occasionally prodding a dozing husband. Luckily, Iglesias knows how to work an audience. "I want to feel your body close to mine," he crooned. Then he coaxed a seven-year-old girl up from the audience and asked her, "How old were you when you learned 'shit' was a bad word?"

Ah yes. **Step Eleven.** Keeping going. Biting the gold bullet when things get bad. Which they will. Do you think that Donald Trump's helper, his glamour-girl wife Ivana, enjoys picking through the puddles on his construction projects in her Thierry Mugler jumpsuit and Christian Dior pumps, yelling at recalcitrant Teamsters? Do you think Donald was pleased when his partner in the castle project, Prudential Insurance, announced that it made "more sense" to sell the site for its appreciated value? Darn right he was. Maintaining that the sale had been his idea, the young developer brokered it, for $105 million, collected his multimillions in commission, and proceeded to announce his plan to adorn the New York waterfront with the world's highest building. One hundred and fifty gorgeous floors of it. Here, in concluding this chapter, are some little pointers to stop you falling off your 150-story pedestal.

Right: Biting into one of Michel Fitoussi's specialties, a mousse-filled spun-sugar apple, a Gutfreund guest was spurred to spring to his feet and exult that it was the best meal he had ever eaten, recalls the chef, who now presides at the restaurant 24 Fifth Avenue. Another invitee took this as an insult to *his* hospitality and retaliated by retaining a maestro from one of the city's top French eateries to prepare a repast to which Mrs. G was bidden.

Whether or not she was aware of such jealousies, the banker's wife did not allow herself to become embroiled in an unseemly competition. Her next Christmas banquet featured . . . miniature hamburgers. "I feel we're in a period now where people want to go back to nursery and gut food," she explained. "I called James Beard for advice and cooked half of it myself."

Wrong: A Gutfreund pal, Edmond Safra, who is probably the world's richest banker, sold his hundred-foot yacht, reported *Institutional Investor* magazine, after receiving an $800 bill for soap in the cabins.

Right: A New York property heiress wrote an article for the society magazine *Palm Beach Life* under the pseudonym T. L. Jones and the title "Memoirs of a Burned-Out Social Climber." Burned out? But whenever we phone our mutual acquaintance — ——, her housekeeper says she is out riding her bicycle or playing bridge or serving The Committee croissants. "Actually, the woman is sleeping," responds the heiress, "but to rest is considered terribly gauche. You must never show that it's all too much."

3

IF ONLY YOU WERE CALLED VANDERBILT

"WHAT'S IN A NAME? THAT WHICH WE CALL A ROSE BY ANY OTHER NAME WOULD SMELL AS SWEET."

The Bard, writing some years before Andy Warhol autographed a string of Campbell soup cans for two well-known members of the DuPont family

When Pilar Crespi, a social meteoroid whose elegant purchases had made her one of the jet set's most incandescent clotheshorses, made her debut as a fashion designer at Saks Fifth Avenue, the store intimated that this was no rich dilettante, no superannuated debutante like Charlotte Ford dangling her hang-tag on oeuvres by professional technicians.

The collection of sensuous evening blouses reflected the "distinct fashion sense," declared a Saks press release, of an Italian count's daughter who had actually toiled in the industry—as a model, Valentino's fashion coordinator, and the owner of a South American boutique where the collection was conceived after customers "admired the blouses she designed for herself."

And quelle collection! Veterans in the industry sang its praises. *Women's Wear Daily* showcased it. To be sure, as is usual when New York sets out to sell the rest of America on a new product, the publicity did gloss over one or two cumbersome technical details: though Crespi says she had expected the blouses really would be all her own work, we discovered that they actually were made from sketches by Adam Yankauskas, a highly talented professional designer on the staff of the collection's manufacturer. Still, he consulted closely with the young aristocrat, who says she "wouldn't have known how to sew," nor how to make a pattern. "I'd sit down with her and say, 'You mean something like *this*?'" he explained. This quiet arrangement ("I didn't know about it," says a Saks spokeswoman) clearly was to everyone's benefit. Crespi's customers hardly would have felt so deliciously *aristocratic* if the garment they were slithering into had been labeled "Adam Yankauskas." Moreover, though Crespi says she was chagrined by her lack of hands-on involvement in the venture, such misgivings are not only naïve but can be an impediment to one's progress. If you have a bankable name like she does, or certain bankable skills that we will be exploring later in this chapter, the ringmasters of the New York circus expect that you will exploit them shamelessly and with minimum effort, in order to expand your net worth. Effort is vulgar. Does Crespi think the Queen of England personally does the sketches for those little By Appointment labels?

For that matter, does the queen realize what a killing she could make if she relocated to the Big Onion? One of her subjects, Simon Allen, the twenty-four-year-old son of a British theatrical set designer, financed his acting studies when he moved here by selling, under the impressively hyphenated label "Dingwell-Fordyce," what he described as Turnbull and Asser-*type* shirts (as distinct from the prestigious real product). Much as we admired his honesty, such timid disclaimers are quite unnecessary. "Who is Dingwall-Fordyce?" we asked Simon. Another demerit point: "My great-great-grandmother was Lady Dingwall-Fordyce," he replied. The correct answer, of course, would have been to glare, "I'm Lord Dingwall-Fordyce."

By contrast, Charlotte Ford, the automobile magnate's daughter, perfectly understands the city. Going into business with Herbert Rounick, a Seventh Avenue executive, she made it clear that, while she was all *for* the working women who would be the market for her clothes, she was not *of* their class. Explaining her previous experience with the dignity of labor to *New York*'s Anthony Haden-Guest, she said, "The girl I lived with had a job, and I thought it would be kind of fun. I worked for two years for McMillen, the decorating firm." This time round she would be "editing" the clothes bearing her name. These were by no means the whole output of Don Sophisticates, the company in which she was involved with Rounick, first as a partner and later as a consultant. For instance, the $400 Chinese wedding jackets that the company sold under its "Dynasty" label in the United States and in London (where Gloria Vanderbilt personally snapped up two of the garments, according to a Ford PR woman) did not need editing, says a former Don Sophisticates employee. "We bought the jackets at little shops around our factory in Hong Kong," he recalls. "Still, you couldn't reproduce them now for four hundred dollars. You know, Ralph Lauren made skirts out of antique quilts."

Ford knew nothing about the episode, says her PR woman.

"IT'S THE NORM THAT YOU HAVE TO GIVE TO GET."

A PR man for haut monde retailers, explaining why the Cast of This Book get so much

---

The Vanderbargain

Never mind what the Bard said. If you are called Vanderbilt—or *once* you are called Vanderbilt—your financial situation will get an immediate lift if you set aside a half hour a day to comb the society columns to see who is trying to make a fast buck off you sans permission. Jackie O's little sister, Lee Radziwill, apparently had an eagle eye for such opportunities in the days when she was a patron of Jean-Jacques Bloos, a Lexington Avenue florist whose store provided a discreet flow of pin money to a silent partner, according to Tom Foster, Bloos's PR man. Since that partner, Babe Paley, the late wife of the CBS grandee, hardly would have wanted it bandied about that she was selling the spousal patrimony (spare blooms from the greenhouses on the Paley estate were shipped to the store), we assume she was sympathetic to Radziwill's feelings when *her* name began appearing in the columns as a customer of Bloos's boutique. Lee quietly contacted the florist, says Foster. "She said, 'If you're going to go on using my name, I should have a discount.'"

First Freebies

Another Foster client was Monsieur Marc, Nancy Reagan's long-time New York coiffeur. Women would be fired by the First Lady's example to dust off their rollers and "look like ladies" again, Monsieur had opined shortly before the 1981 inaugural. And to wear rhinestoned T-shirts with their slacks? Although setting an example to the masses is indeed a First Marketing principle, Foster can't remember whether Nancy was among the prestigious Marc clients who were showered with the glittery garments, when they became a sideline of the hairdressing salon. The shirts' recipients did include the ladies. Also the late society columnist Eugenia Sheppard, who, in a courtesy frequently extended by the beauty industry to influential scribes, already enjoyed a "generous" discount at the salon on hairdos: "The shirts averaged seventy-five dollars and I knew at that price we'd never get a volume business unless we created a little bit of a status following for them," says Foster.

Though it was French fashion merchants who pioneered the custom of drastically reducing their rates to photogenic social types, as a schmear (politely called an *exclusivité*) for publicity purposes, it was ladies like Nancy who gave the habit that all-American touch—by *Going on the offensive.* T-shirts and the occasional discounted tea rose are all very well, but a girl has to own more than that to keep up with Betsy Bloomingdale, Alfred's widow (chapter two). And how about the genial, self-effacing Dutch? No way could Neiman-Marcus have known that the White House table would be quite bare at El Presidente's seventieth birthday party unless the store pitched in and donated twenty-five tablecloths. No way, that is, unless his wife hustled . . . which, according to a store spokesman, she did, though a Reagan aide insisted that "the Reagans do not accept gifts" and told us in shocked tones that the First Lady "would *never*" have solicited so much as a coaster.

What with First Manicurist Jessica scooting in from Los Angeles at her own expense to groom Nancy's nails (a *necessity,* not a gift), it looked briefly as if the go-getter merchants of Dallas and Beverly Hills were going to leave New York tradesmen in the promotional cold. Luckily, the entire fashion industry had been silently boarding the First Publicity wagon. With "loans." Long-term ones, to be sure. For instance, the $250,000 worth of diamonds twinkling on Nancy's slender neck and ears at the 1981 inaugural were Harry Winston's founding contribution to a new White House Jewelry Collection. After the ease with which the First Lady had been quietly accumulating designer togs threatened to cause a peasants' revolt (shopping being for the hoi polloi, one couturier, Bill Blass, had been tantalizing her with his wares by sending videos to 1600 Pennsylvania), it was announced that twelve "borrowed" outfits would be removed from Nancy's closets and donated to museums. The jewels went back to Winston's.

Someone once asked Rose Kennedy how long she'd had the magnificent tiara adorning her at a ball.

"About two hours," Rose snapped. "It's borrowed from Van Cleef & Arpels."

The Rockefeller wife co-hosting the party where we met the Russian defector in chapter one had an emerald the size of a cherry tomato strapped around her neck on a diamond collar—another loan from Winston's.

The ladies are functioning in this regard like show people, who commonly are solicited to wear loaned finery. The young New York designer Marc Bouwer, whose clients include Barbra Streisand, Morgan Fairchild, and Lesley Anne Warren, says his career "just skyrocketed" after he gave Liliane Montevecchi, star of the hit musical *Nine,* a fecund wing-shaped creation for the Tony awards. Huge folds narrowed from her shoulders to a front-slit, thigh-skimming tip. Saks phoned the designer the day after the nationally televised ceremony. *Nine, the Clothing Advertisement?* Why not? The store took out a large space in the *Times*. Montevecchi, flapping her arms like a hawk swooping in for the kill in a sequined version of the Bouwer outfit, appeared over the caption: "Show-stopper!" We tried not to imagine how the ladies were going to look as they tried to wriggle into the concoction. "One size for all," said the caption, "$2,000."

While most designers, angling for such publicity windfalls, will be happy to dress you for free, there is always the occasional stubborn hold-out. The Seventh Avenue impresario Frank Composto hollered that he had been stiffed by the Superbitch: by the designer's account of it, Joan Collins owed him $2,600 (a 50 percent discount from retail) on a little bevel-beaded number that she'd slipped into for the "Tonight" show seven months earlier. "Generally," a Collins lawyer replied, his client doesn't have to pay for things because the studios pick up the tab. However, a few days after Composto took his grievance public, the star created an unfortunate precedent by sending the designer a check. "I do freebies if the person buys a lot of clothes from me, like Linda Evans. She'll buy four dresses," Composto said, "and I'll give her one free."

Return Policies

The city's best-known mendicant is not a politician's relative, not a socialite, not an actress. He is a host at WNBC Radio, a network-owned station. Don Imus for years has appealed on his satirical morning show for alms. "It's a joke. As an on-air personality, he's not supposed to do this, so of course he's always done it," explained a station executive. "Our policy is that anything worth over twenty-five dollars must be sent back."

In line with this, Imus has returned a room air conditioner to the donor, declined to cook the slab of liver that arrived packed in a bag with a cucumber and a bottle of Crisco oil, and changed his mind about equipping a 1957 Chevy (which he actually had *bought*) with something essential, even if it hadn't been free. A motor.

"All these people offered him engines, but since he doesn't know anything about cars, he didn't know what they were talking about," an Imus aide said disconsolately. Although any engine worth its pistons would have violated the $25 rule, Imus might have considered *borrowing* one. A German prince, Juergen von Anhalt, became known for erecting huge canvases near the engines of beau monde jets, such as the aircraft volunteered by a Texas oil heir, Baron Ricky di Portanova. As the pilot gunned the big bird to full throttle, the prince tossed paint into the exhaust stream, and the wind spattered it back for an effect that, cooed a New York society columnist, "is slick, colorful and good for many contemporary rooms." According to one valuation, it will cost you around $100,000 to hang a von Anhalt next to your Tintoretto.

Escape From New York

As a Vanderbilt you not only get the Vanderbargains—the free clothes, free jewels, free apartment (in one of those Good Buildings that made people weep in chapter two), free eyelift—you also get free vacations. "The trouble is, they wake you up by ringing a little bell when the animals come to the waterhole," whined a social leader upon her return from a safari to the Best Hotels in the Kenyan Bush. These goodies also are available to journalists (a short course in journalism is available in chapter twelve) and, unlike Dom Imus, some journalists aren't shy about accepting them. Thanks, for instance, to the eleemosynary spirit of Pan Am, "The Nikki Haskell Show," a little cable-TV program named for its host, New York's unofficial Queen of Comp, traveled to Rio (for Carnaval), Monte Carlo (the Grand Prix), and Manila and Cannes (film festivals). After an opening shot of Nikki, reposing in a bubble bath, the airline would be promoed. The symbiotic relationship between girl and airline continued until Nikki filed for bankruptcy, declaring debts of $349,000.

Pan Am vice-president Jeff Kriendler said that his corporation's relationship with her had terminated: "The show was not reaching out to a Pan Am market." We expressed our condolences to her.

"I'm out of bankruptcy," Nikki said brightly.

We assumed she was paying the usual Chapter 11 arrangement, so many cents on every owed dollar.

"Nah," said Nikki. "I don't have to pay anybody anything. I took personal bankruptcy. Chapter 6. I'm working on a new celebrity show. Lots of travel. Wherever Pan Am goes, I go." Kriendler expressed astonishment when we told him this. He said he'd have to look into it. Maybe another department at the company. . . .

Very Confidential!

Eve Hatch Holmes, of the Murray Hill Hatches (her ancestors are hung in the Met), throws her mink over her bouclé designer dress (bought at wholesale, which is one-third to one-half off retail) and hops on a bus to escort her Social Registerite friends on Seventh Avenue showroom sprees. They select an outfit and buy it for wholesale plus 20 percent as Eve's fee.

We wondered what was in it for designers and their representatives, selling through "personal shoppers" like Eve rather than through stores. "We don't mention it," said a socialite who does her purchasing via another shopper, "but I pay [the designer] in cash and no sales tax and what he does about tax is up to him."

"I AM SURPRISED BY HOW BUSINESSLIKE SOTHEBY'S IS. THIS IS REALLY MUCH MORE OF A BUSINESS ATTITUDE THAN I EXPECTED FROM AN AUCTION HOUSE."

A new executive at Sotheby's, interviewed by the Washington Post *at a $250-a-head benefit for the Metropolitan Museum of Art thrown by the auction house. The 1984 affair also benefited Sotheby's, since guests sipped their cocktails among objets that would be auctioned that fall.*

The fun part about fashion discounts and jewelry handouts is that you can flaunt them at philanthropic events and hence get a tax deduction for eating with your dressmaker. Charitable bashes honoring designers and other darlings of the circus have become quite the rage in New York.

Macy's, for instance, fêted Oscar de la Renta's new Ruffles fragrance with a benefit for the New York City Ballet. Heather Watts and Bart Cook whooshed into a specially choreographed pas de deux (title: *Ruffles*) and a tasteful ice sculpture (depicting a Ruffles bottle) loomed over guests like Nancy Kissinger. Yves Saint Laurent was honored at a $500-a-ticket dinner dance at the Metropolitan Museum, benefiting Diana Vreeland's Costume Institute. Many of the guests arrived before the official seven-thirty start of the event so they could peacock around and allow the press to snap their YSLs. The tables and columns were swathed in pink, orange, and red silk from a YSL fabric supplier—just so nobody could confuse the Met with Lamston's.

"It's all for Yves. He's such a charming boy," Vreeland smiled.

The unofficial opener for the fall social season in years when there isn't a good funeral is the "SFA/USA" fashion gala. It is held, as the initials suggest, at Saks and each of the six philanthropies it helps is represented by a designer—Oscar de la Renta for the Hospital for Special Surgery, Bill Blass for J.O.B. . . . *Women's Wear* didn't explain what the initials stood for (Just One Break, funding jobs for the handicapped) in its cover story on the event one year. Still you musn't get cynical: "The real show was Oscar de la Renta . . . and his Ladies mugging mercilessly in the front row," the newspaper, which enjoys a little wickedness, reported. "He coaxed and cajoled them, tormenting them with naughty remarks and pranks and titillating them into paroxysms of giggles." J.O.B., for its part, threw a slap-up Tribute to Bill Blass, to thank him for his support. Bergdorf's picked up the tab and the ladies modeled their old Blasses. Up the steps, skitter along the runway, swivel, down the steps, and a hug from the Beaming Storekeeper.

"Marvelous," Blass burbled, as each customer fell into his arms. "Divine . . . you're a real pro!"

The Russian defector in chapter one was noshing courtesy of another real pro, the designer Karl Lagerfeld. You see, the party in question, while co-hosted by the Rockefeller wife in her borrowed jewels, was *benefiting* a music project planned by a friend from chapter two, the Creo Society, and *debuting* a new Lagerfeld scent for men, K L Homme.

"I'M CONSTANTLY SEARCHING FOR A NEW CUTIE, A NEW ROCKEFELLER."

Alan Rish, one of New York's professional partygivers

If You Don't Ever Intend Becoming a Vanderbilt...

Just as some people choose to become executive headhunters rather than executives, some confirmed plebs do very nicely by headhunting aristocrats. The market for this can be explained as follows: like designers, restaurants and clubs need beautiful customers in order to get publicity in the columns. Your indispensable function is to organize the parties that bring the beautiful customers that bring the publicity. . . .

Your remuneration will depend on your guest list. As both the very dear friend of beepees like Liza Minnelli and Margaux Hemingway and the founder of Celebrity Service, a New York firm that tracks the very dear friends' whereabouts for journalists in return for an annual bounty, Earl Blackwell could command $50,000 an event in his heyday. He shipped Marilyn Monroe to Madison Square Garden to serenade President John Kennedy and enlisted Princess Grace for a bal masque in Venice that was hailed as the "party of the century." This was without even having to resort, in the style of the doyenne of the party-promotion business, Elsa Maxwell, to a gimmicky fish course (live seals).

For a younger party promoter like Alan Rish or Dallas Boesandahl, $2,500 an evening would be more like it.

"When you're growing up, you want to be a king or a movie star, right? You don't think you'll be a *party*-thrower," Alan mused to the *New York Times*. "I wanted to be an actor but my parents thought it would make me crazy. When my allowance stopped, I realized I had to become an adult and work."

Work?

"You have to get to know the daughters, so their mothers come to your parties," says a PR man who has worked with Dallas. Maria Burton begets Elizabeth Taylor. That sort of getting-to-know. Dallas's impressive Dear Friend division also includes: Christopher Atkins, Rita Jenrette, Phyllis George, Maureen Stapleton, Tommy Tune, and a Philadelphia big spender whose bar tab handily compensates the host establishment for its costs.

While most party promoters collect only one fee per event, a Parisian immigrant, Ludovic Autet, runs the Junior International Club, a New York company that effectively gets two. The organization cocktail-shakes wealthy young Americans with the HRH emigré set (Prince Jean of Luxembourg, Prince Albert of Monaco, Anne Eisenhower, a Carnegie, a Woolworth . . .) at dinners and dances at restaurants and discos. The establishments pay the club a fee. So do the five hundred club members, one of whom once explained that it would be frightfully common to frequent such dives unless it was a JIC event. The club's 1986 dues scale was set at $350 for the first year, $150 thereafter, entitling its flock to such privileges as a "special price" for their chow and a free glass of Moët et Chandon. Autet, who wears Yves Saint Laurent suits, occupies a tiny office where the reference manuals include *The Emerging Business* (a JIC branch is opening in Los Angeles) and *The Amy Vanderbilt Book of Etiquette*.

Baird Jones, a pink-faced man in his late twenties who lives with his parents and distributes passes by the million (seven million at this writing) to shindigs at those just-so-exclusive nightclubs, has another tip for coining it: "The clubs give you a bonus according to the press you get," he says. For instance, $200 for a mention in "Page Six" in the *New York Post*. Naturally, the story should not let the shill out of the bag with any déclassé reference to money exchanging hands. Jones showed us a typical clipping: "**Baird Jones,** son of *People* magazine's senior editor, is birthdaying. Invitees are **Walter Cronkite's** kid, **Chip, Otto Preminger's** daughter **Vicki, Walter Hoving**'s grandson **John;** plus **Caroline Kennedy, Sydney Lawford, Tina Radziwell**...."

"If you promise ten nice names and you get four, that is a nice record," says partygiver George-Paul Rosell, gazing pensively into his champagne glass. He is lunching at a marble table at Serendipity, on East Sixtieth Street, with Patty Hearst's sister, Anne, and a young designer, Contessina Francesca Braschi. The restaurant is paying, because the meal is a rehearsal for the feast for forty that Rosell has enlisted the women to *host* there to *honor* a beautician. The distinction between these two functions is pertinent. Just as an honoree is not a host, a host is not a promoter. Though a few socialites, having roared through the family fortunes, are notorious for demanding payments off the books from businesses that use them as hosts, and for refusing to tip, this is considered *bad form.* In return for their names being fed to the columns, the contessina and the publishing heiress will be rewarded simply by the chance to invite some of their friends to a free dinner. It is polite, by the way, but not essential, to show up if you are selected to be *honored* at one of these endeavors.

Many of the most publicized "private" parties you've heard about have been organized along these lines, benefiting both party-giver and party-goer. For instance, former Studio 54 owner Mark Fleischman says the disco footed the bill for the spectacular dinners that Roy Cohn, the powerful lawyer who was Senator Joseph McCarthy's right-hand man, hosted at the club: "He brought a lot of people you wouldn't ordinarily get, like Barbara Walters." And like judges, members of the Reagan administration, United States senators . . .

Another Fleischman investment was the $10,000 he estimates it cost to celebrate Cornelia Guest's twentieth birthday at Studio. "Cornelia's a sweet girl. She really wanted this and you've got to be happy," her mother, the blue-blooded gardening expert C. Z. Guest, told the *Times,* which devoted almost an entire column to the frolic. If you detected a note of resignation in the social lioness's comment, that may be because the evening's "Swiss" theme—slides of the Alps and fake snow—was Fleischman's idea, he admits with a bashful grin, not C.Z.'s. "At first C.Z. wanted a formal dinner," confides the then club owner, who clambered up on a catwalk after the tortellini, potato salad, wursts, and sauerkraut were cleared away and belted out "Hit the Road, Jack."

Apart from the risk of such impromptu gigs, there is another danger in accepting the courtesy of a disco. At some predetermined witching hour, which can be as early as ten-thirty, your invitees will have to waltz a little closer, and risk deafness as several hundred youngsters fork over their door charges, smirk a second or two at any VIP who hasn't had the sense to split, then charge onto the dance floor to a blast of music that sounds like the liftoff of your private DC-8. We do not advocate such mergers of the two cities.

"I SUPPOSE PEOPLE COME TO ME BECAUSE I GREW UP IN THE PALACE OF VERSAILLES AND IT'S THE HALLMARK OF QUALITY."

Barbara de Portago, a New York socialite who reportedly earns $6,000 a crack for the lectures she gives around the country on her childhood as stepdaughter of the palace curator

---

The name of Barbara de Portago, society's grand organizer, at the top of an engraved invitation virtually guarantees a rhapsodic review by Suzy. Barbara accepts only the hospitality of the classiest restaurants for her parties. She acquired her taste for fine things when she played with Marie Antoinette's diamond necklace as a youngster and discovered Madame de Pompadour's skin-care formula in a secret drawer in a Louis Quinze palace desk. All she asks, in return for hosting an event, is that you feed her and her guests for free. With cake, not bread, admittedly, but she provides the wine, the flowers, the table decorations, the calligraphy. She will even order around the staff. Politely, of course. Here are excerpts from her instructions to Les Tuileries, the Central Park South restaurant where she presented a mega-rich royal, His Serene Highness Prince von Thurn und Taxis, of Germany, and his pretty wife with an elegant macédoine of lobster. [Brackets are ours.]

1. By 12 noon, *I want all tables laid out according to attached plan.*

2. *1* P.M.: *I arrive to put castles up [sand replicas of Regensburg, the serene family pile], flags, plants.*

3. *7:30* P.M.: *Musicians [an oompah and jazz band] arrive. Offer nonalcoholic beverages while they wait.*

4. *8:00* P.M.: *Guests arrive.*
      (a) Doorman to help open car doors.
      (b) Coatroom girl to be at door to take coats. She is not to accept tips. [The prince is one of the wealthiest men in Germany but, as the columnist Taki once pointed out, the truly rich never pay for anything.]

5. *8:00* P.M.: Back Room:
      Waiters ask guests what they wish to drink: "Please and Thank you" and bring the drink on a tray.
      Waiters pass canapés with little white paper napkins.
      Musicians play seated in the inside of tables, see plan [There were three tables, "Thurn," "Und," and "Taxis"].

6. *8:30* P.M.: *Waiters fill water glasses with ice water.*

7. . . . I GET UP TO MAKE SPEECH. NO WAITER ACTIVITY PLEASE.

> *I do not want to hear your cabaret chanteuse till 11:45! PROMPT SERVICE BETWEEN COURSES, MAITRE D' HOTEL IS TO COME SEE ME AT LEAST ONCE EVERY ½ HOUR. . . .*

Another restaurant received a list from de Portago for a luncheon she was hosting on its premises in honor of the late Princess Grace: "I went over [it] with them and all of a sudden I discovered it was not being done," de Portago says, wagging her finger. "They were going to serve a very bad white wine and their regular patrons were going to be allowed to come and eat. They were supposed to be closed. It was so foolish and so wrong. So I took the party over to Le Cirque." Where, she says, she paid for the whole thing.

The crush celebrating Barbara's marriage to Jason Grant—a member of a wealthy Philadelphia family and former actor on "The Edge of Night"—culminated in what appeared to be an exception to her rule of accepting at most the bare minimum in freebies. "Page Six" reported that the happy couple's bijou Greenwich Village apartment had been submerged in an "avalanche" of "bills, bounced checks," and "threatening letters from lawyers." A florist, for instance, Richard Salome, was said to be out $1,500 on the event.

De Portago assured us that the story was inaccurate.

"Mr. Richard Salome . . . the poor man could not have done my wedding because he didn't have the people and all he did was the bouquets," she said. She recited from a card from the florist: "This bouquet is my wedding gift to you," it read.

We put this to Salome. "I gave her *her* bouquet, not the bridesmaids' and all the other flowers," he said curtly. About four months after the wedding, however, he did receive the $1,500.

"Page Six" wrote that Pauline Trigère did get paid for the delicate gold lace wedding dress she designed for the bride.

"She *gave* me my wedding dress as a gift," de Portago said triumphantly.

Jean-Pierre Radley, the Trigère company's president, confirmed this. As for some bills de Portago did owe at the time, she subsequently paid them, he said, "at least half a year late. My bank charges *me* interest [on debts]," he added wearily. But, as we attempted to explain to him, he has to pay on time or pay extra because he is not a Manhattan hostess.

In Service Caterers claims to have provided the Grant–de Portago nuptials with custom-made red carpets, handblown glasses, and waiters. Ann Getty, Sao Schlumberger, and Princess Chantal of France were on the guest list, so obviously everything had to be just so. In Service owner Bob Goldberg said that de Portago had called him at the hospital where he was recuperating from an illness and implored him to help with the reception: "It had to be the tallest, most handsome waiters I could find, and special collars on their uniforms." The evening of the event, Goldberg implored the bride and groom for something, a check. He got one—the kind that has that tennis-ball tendency when you present it at the bank. Things became clearer, however, when he received a letter, two months later, blaming the problem on a "gargantuan snafu" entangling not only Jason Grant's "trustees" and banks but Merrill Lynch. The bill, for just over $9,600, was still outstanding when we interviewed de Portago about ten months afterward.

"We disputed In Service's bill. It is still in dispute," said the elegante. Her husband was also saying something. "Jason, may I please continue," snapped his wife. "I gave them nine cases of magnums of champagne to hold until the bill is settled."

Shortly after that, it was reported that the marriage had broken up. The catering firm agreed to a $7,500 settlement.

"IN THE UNITED STATES, ALMOST EVERY PROSPEROUS SUBURB HAS HAD A DRESS SHOP WHOSE OWNER WAS FINANCED BY HER AFFLUENT FRIENDS WHEN HER OWN FORTUNE DECLINED."

Marylin Bender in The Beautiful People

If you are a blue-blooded indigent, dress shops are the last resort to keep body and wallet together. Some clues to alternative survival tactics are scattered through chapter two, but to summarize here:

1. Take a job as a receptionist at Christie's, then marry up.
2.* Lend out the family name to the Arabs. The wife of a man whose ancestors came over with the Mayflower Madam's lent his name to property that was being accumulated in the New York area by a minister in a Middle Eastern government. Her frontwomanship apparently did not go unrewarded, because though her husband had no more money than any other vieux WASP, she was able to throw parties with the ritual heapings of caviar. For entertainment, there were belly dancers. She was chauffeured by an elderly man whose duties also included collecting satin purses, which did not have to clear customs at Kennedy Airport because of the minister's diplomatic status.

Often the Mayflower Matron would meet friends for cocktails at the Plaza carrying a jewelry presentation box, the latest token of the minister's gratitude. One velvet chest held a string of perfectly matched Oriental pearls. The relationship ended abruptly, however, when, in a snit about her spending (she was investing some

*Some details have been changed to protect this lady's identity.

of his money in the stock market), the minister removed the properties from her control and placed them in the trust of a lawyer who had once compared him to Abraham Lincoln.

"The Arabs are getting to be real tightwads now they're better-educated," an aide to the frontwoman sighed. "They've started asking for open bids for this kind of thing."

3. Lend out your name to the masthead of a glossy magazine. Caterine Milinaire, a highly acclaimed journalist who is the step-daughter of the Duke of Bedford, was "discovered" by *Vogue.* "The press learned how to spell her name," Bender wrote in *The Beautiful People,* when Caterine upstaged ladies like Audrey Hepburn at a movie premiere "by arriving in a black, chiffony dress that [made] the photographers suspect there [was] nothing between it and [her] bare bosom." Many years later, there was another chic addition to the staff at *Vogue*—Issie Taylor, a pert British society girl whose maiden name, Delves Broughton, had that ring of delicious decadence about it, something, like her predecessor's breasts, for the ladies to cluck about. Her grand-father, Sir Jock Delves Broughton, had been charged with dis-patching a belted earl with a bullet through the head in Kenya, where a chap normally shoots only game. Sir Jock was acquitted in the World War II case, but *White Mischief,* a well-reviewed book claiming to bare his Secret Confessions, hit the American stores in 1982. It was the mid-eighties when Issie, who casually let it be known the first time we met her that Taylor was only her married name, landed her fashionable job. She'd previously been in Texas with her husband, accumulating interests in oil proper-ties the way *Vogue* readers buy furs. "We intended," she said with a demure giggle one evening at Regine's, "to become the first English wildcatters—we though we'd be like the Ewings in 'Dal-las.'"

Both breasts and murders-in-the-baronial-closet should be kept hidden when you apply to fly your family crest from *Town & Country*'s mast. The ladylike style of its ménage was long epito-mized by a staffer called Nancy Holmes. Gathered at a party to celebrate her first novel, *The Big Girls,* one of the ladies trilled to another, "I heard it's a little dirty, so we'll like it." Holmes rapidly quashed this buzz, according to a story in *Women's Wear:* "I'm sick of all the pornography in books," the author said stiffly. "People with real style and manners don't use four-letter words." Until then we'd thought they simply used their husbands. . . . "Big girls understand men, money, power and sex," said Holmes. "But they also understand sacrifice, patience, and giving more than they take."

"PART OF [HER] SUCCESS IS DIANE'S ABILITY TO INFUSE HER CREATIONS WITH A PORTION OF HER OWN MYSTIQUE AS A GLAMOROUS, MULTI-LINGUAL BEAUTY. BORN IN BELGIUM AND EDUCATED THROUGHOUT EUROPE, SHE WAS ONCE THE WIFE OF PRINCE EGON VON FURSTENBERG. AS SUCH, SHE BECAME A MUCH-PHOTOGRAPHED PART OF THE GLITTER-ING WORLD OF EUROPEAN ARISTOCRACY."

From a press kit issued by Diane Von Furstenberg

The trend that reached its climax with Princess Chantal of France announcing a line of dishes and Pilar Crespi a line of sunglasses (après the blouses and all her own work) started when Jackie Kennedy wore to the 1961 inaugural a beige coat designed by Oleg Cassini, or, as he was born, Oleg Loiewski. Oleg's father was a White Russian exile who, according to *Esquire* magazine, had failed in a diplomatic career, "failed with a Russian tearoom in Florence," and finally sailed for America lugging a life-size portrait of Czar Nicholas II and an electric hot plate. Understandably, when Oleg's brother, the late Igor, caught the boat for New York, the boys' mother, the late Countess Marguerite Cassini, cupped her hands and shouted, "In America, remember who you are! Remember, Cassini, Cassini." Her father, Count de Cassini, had been the czar's ambassador to Washington. Igor became the gossip columnist Cholly Knickerbocker, and his contribution to posterity was the invention of the phrase "jet set."

"I think my brother and I survived because we're adaptable. We're democratic," Oleg told *Esquire.* This was during an inter-view at the House of Cassini, which was established in 1964 in a Renaissance-style mansion in Manhattan. The Cassini coat of arms (motto: "Spes Mea in Deo Est") emblazoned a wall, the brocade dining-room curtains, and the designer's ring finger.

Adaptable to the mass marketplace is, of course, what he meant. As the U.S. economy moved into the post-tertiary, Bill Blass chocolate phase, the Cassini family tree branched out to include cars (an Indian motif for the American Motors Matador and Chero-kee) and carpets. Cassini was hired by Galaxy Carpet Mills, he explained in a newspaper interview, "to elevate the standards of taste. . . . It was all too aggressive." We agreed. We ripped up our Oriental area rugs, burned the antique Axminster, and installed the $20-a-yard wool-look-alike Cassini nylon pile. For some rea-son, Cassini's PR woman was reluctant to discuss that phase in the designer's artistic development. She said it was in the past and we should concentrate on telling you about his evening wear.

Diane Von Furstenberg has never been shy about discussing her efforts to raise aesthetic standards in American households, any more than she was bashful about using her *ex*-status as a princess in that press kit. Let's consider for a moment the DVF Tissue Box. The box was an example, said the press kit, of the designer's diversification "into territories yet unexplored" and was "a new art form!" As for the little wrap dress, which was the cornerstone of the Von Furstenberg fortune, Mrs. Middle America was assured that she was donning a garment that was a "direct extension" of Diana's own "lifestyle . . . sensibility & sensuality."

Perhaps it was the sight of the designer's ample breasts straining against the dress's simple jersey knit that prompted her prince, Egon, in the days when they were still married, to leap out of his clothes and into a *New York* cover story about their relationship. The young aristo, whose ancestral home is an Austrian schloss with fifty-two bedrooms, was photographed with a towel clasped around his loins, hair curling down his pectorals, alongside the caption "Anything Goes."

"Once in Paris we tried it with a different woman," he yawned. "There were three of us. But you know what?" He shrugged. "It was just twice as much work for me." Were he to meet an attractive man, he would not be loath to experiment, he confided. Diane was not so sure. Homosexuality, *she* yawned, was "a big bore."

Diane reappeared in the magazine some years later, after her split from Egon, with a new terra incognita, a $130-an-ounce perfume, Volcan d'Amour. The designer explained that she was selling it for symbolic reasons:

"I think," she informed *New York*'s Julie Baumgold, "I found my mate." The scent, a powerful brew of violets, was marketed with a brochure describing how Paulo—a Brazilian beach boy who pad-dled into America's consciousness wearing a small green stone in his earlobe—had inspired this "volcano of love." Diane had met him in Bali. A poem in the brochure elaborated:

Into my life you came
Bringing peace to my heart
Fire to my body
Love to my soul
In your eyes I see myself
Feeling, reaching, looking
For perfect harmony.

You're panting to hear about the perfume bottle? It was the same shape as Manhattan's Citicorp Center and took "over a year and a half" to craft, said the brochure, in France. And the box that houses the bottle that houses the perfume?

"Only something heavenly could house the brilliance, the magic that was Volcan d'Amour. Diane knew it. And so did Paulo," said the brochure. Antonio, a painter Von Furstenberg had met in Bali, was commissioned to do the packaging. Pressures were building. "Paulo was rapidly becoming a raving Brazilian," confided the brochure. "The box didn't sing. He deluged Antonio with data. He appealed to his cunning with strategy. . . . And the perfect shelter was at last invoked."

Some time later, we asked an advertising executive at Diane's firm what had become of the fashion industry's most extraordinary launch. Not much, it seemed. "It didn't do well. It was too heavy for people," the executive said. She was referring to the fragrance, of course. Though Volcan d'Amour is no longer manufactured and, according to a Von Furstenberg staffer, Paulo and Diane are no longer à deux, some bottles of the scent are still in stock at the DVF boutique on Fifth Avenue. These days it costs $140 an ounce.

That's what came Out of Bali. The designer Mary McFadden came Out of Africa. Via New York society. She rebelled at the early age of fifteen, when she cashed in the emeralds her grandmother had given her in favor of a Dalí that eventually would hang in her bathroom. Marrying an executive for De Beers, the gold and diamond company (some of the women guests at the wedding sported Goldwater buttons with their feathers), Mary departed for Johannesburg, where visitors reported that she was creating a formal Italian garden and dressing her Zulu male domestics in enchanting beaded hats above their gray-and-white Italian uniforms.

"They were the hats of Jomo Kenyatta's Kikuyu tribe," says Mary. Kenyatta, of course, was the grand old man of politics in nationalist Kenya.

Back in New York, after that marriage, and a second, broke up, Mary's first fashion collection consisted of quilted jackets and floating togas over flimsy chiffon pants. "African" togas, as they're called in McFadden's listing in *Current Biography,* which records how "chic women followed suit" when Babe Paley started wearing the robes. But Mary, who once told a society writer that she had spent eight years "studying all the primitive cultures," now says the inspiration was "Eastern."

Carolina Herrera, a fabulously rich Venezuelan-born luminary of Seventh Avenue, was selected by De Beers as one of twenty Women of Quality. Ms. Herrera included this information in her corporate biography when she started designing clothes—along with the precept "Motivation is nothing without discipline." Indeed, though she is married to a landowner who, queried about what he does, has been known to answer, "Have a good time," Carolina is taken seriously by veteran couturiers. Her gorgeous, hand-loomed silk gowns invariably have sleeves bigger than the maid's room, and sleeves are what matter because they are all you see above the dinner table. The protuberances are a little difficult to stuff under a coat, but as the late writer Henry Post pointed out, Herrera customers "don't wear coats, they wear limos."

"CONTESSINA BRASCHI, DAUGHTER OF COUNT AND COUNTESS PIER ARRIGO BRASCHI, IS DESCENDED FROM A 12TH-CENTURY FAMILY OF ITALIAN NOBILITY. . . .

CONTESSINA BRASCHI WILL BE BRINGING COUNT PIER BRASCHI CHAMPAGNE FROM HER FATHER'S VINEYARDS IN ITALY TO INTRODUCE HER COLLECTION AT SAKS. AMONG THE FRIENDS EXPECTED TO ATTEND HER RECEPTION ARE MARISA BERENSON, CORNELIA BIDDLE, PANDORA DUKE BIDDLE, WENDY CARHART, CORNELIA GUEST, ANNE HEARST AND ALISON MAZZOLA. CONTESSINA BRASCHI WILL ALSO BE AT SAKS TO GREET FRIENDS AND CUSTOMERS ON FRIDAY, MARCH 22. . . ."

From a Saks Fifth Avenue press release

The designer Contessina Francesca Braschi, who lives in New York and looks like the Mona Lisa, derives her title from San Marino, reputedly the oldest and smallest republic in the world. It measures twenty four square miles, matching the contessina's age when we interviewed her.

"I'm part owner of a factory in Tennessee with a Chinaman. He's very sweet," she said. "All the society girls in New York are my dear friends and they buy my clothes. They're very sweet. You see, always being around these people, you learn what the needs of the ladies are. My clothes are for the working lady, but I like to be feminine." Her West Coast representatives, she added, were Ricky Hilton, heir to the hotel fortune, and his wife, Kathy.

C. Z. Guest, whose late husband, the Phipps heir Winston Guest, received around $600,000 a year from trust funds, made the cover of *Time* in 1962 as an archetype of the Leisure-Class Ladies. Some years later, the family's leisure options were depleted by a half-million judgment against Winston that was followed by what some social rivals interpreted as a fire sale of certain Guest Chinese porcelains and French furnishings. These days, C.Z. is a Leisure-Class Worker, one who is energetically staking her claim to the *practical* end of the design business. Her first productions included a $48 gardening jumpsuit. To ward off pesky insects, she now markets "C.Z.'s Fragrant Repellant Spray" ($5.50). Then there is the $12.95 *C. Z. Guest's Garden Planner and Datebook*. Should you get mud on one of your "C. Z. Guest" cashmere sweaters while lounging in one of her "C.Z."-initialed garden chairs, just wash it in Woolite, C.Z. counseled the society magazine *W.*

"I spent my whole life spending money and now I'm going to spend the rest of it making money," vowed the mom of the nation's most precocious debutante.

Truly, even if you don't have a mosquito swamp in your Manhattan high-rise, the choice can be grueling. How *do* you decide between a Lyn Revson (a sweater knitted by the ex-wife of Charles Revson, the late cosmetics tycoon, *with her own fingers,* will set you back maybe $1,500) and a Donina, when a gown with "Donina, Countess Cicogna" on the label could grace your closet for under $1,800?

Well, here it is. Our recommendation for the Buy of the Decade: a ruby-red crêpe georgette evening gown by Princess Katalin zu Windisch-Graetz for as little as $600. Pour yourself into one of her creations, says her publicity kit, and you will have "an aura of royalty." You also will have Katalin's full title on the label, though not the Windisch-Graetz coat of arms, a crown above a wolf's head. This crest is reserved for embossing the princess's publicity materials; she scribbles notes to her friends on snowy white parchment with just a modest "K" floating beneath the same diadem.

"The social designers, it's so ridiculous," sniffs Her Serene Highness, who began designing in Hungary, where, she says, she was a baroness before the revolution. Her current title is from her marriage to an Austrian prince, with whom she lived in Germany in "a beautiful Renaissance castle." She now lives in a small Manhattan apartment, and the prince lives in Europe. "For him, New York is too complicated," she explains. "But he comes to my shows. This is my family's coronet." She shows us an elaborate turquoise-and-gold crest. "But I can't use it because if you are married, you have to use your husband's."

"We are separated," her husband, an engineer who did not use his title during his twenty-seven-year stay in New York, said when we contacted him. The castle? "That now is owned by the government. It's not a very livable castle," he said. He seemed amused by our questioning. "Huge, huge rooms that are impossible to heat." We were curious to know how he felt about seeing the family title hanging on little cards on clothes in Lord & Taylor in New York, Garfinkel's in Washington, Neiman-Marcus in Dallas. "She has great talent, that I must say," responded the prince with another chuckle. By the way, how long did he live with his princess? "We've been married since 1979," he said, "and we've been together off and on."

Rumor has it that Antonia de Portago, the second wife of the dashing Marqués de Portago, was a marquesa for not much longer than it takes the marqués's *first* wife, Barbara de Portago, to inscribe a place card. Could it be that Antonia, the former Mademoiselle Lynch, of Paris, ("my father was not working," she says, "he was rich"), kept her distinguished married name to burnish her budding career as a singer?

Antonia bats her eyelids and hikes her right shoulder toward the streaky orange earrings that hang below her spiky haircut. She is all Gallic amazement.

Then how long *was* she married?

"It took at least a year to get divorced," she says shortly. "I spoke to my lawyer immediately and asked to get back my maiden name and he told me it was very difficult. Everyone keeps the name of her husband."

And who wouldn't make use of her childhood experience? As a school chum of Barbara de Portago, Antonia too has romped at Versailles. So, around the time that Barbara was out working the lecture circuit, Antonia was composing a song, "Versailles," about the palace ghosts. She has performed it on an album and at New York clubs, where she appeared dressed as Marie Antoinette.

"EVERY DAY IS THANKSGIVING."

From the lyrics of Subways Are for Sleeping, *the hit musical about a special breed of New York bum, the well-dressed drifter.*

...Change Your Name to Vanderbilt

Michael Manos, aka Dain Vanderbilt, a twenty-one-year-old who is said to have described himself as a black sheep of Little Gloria's family, swanned around the city in a rented limo and was showered with loans. Against his inheritance.

One woman gave him a $1,200 necklace.

"He dressed like Boy George. He was so outrageous that it was believable that he was a Vanderbilt," says a detective. When a limo service, unpaid, got on his trail, one of this "Vanderbilt's" last addresses was determined, said the police, to have been a hospital psycho ward where, according to a press report, he'd been in a drug detox program.

Other self-styled blue bloods have lasted longer than "Dain." An Austrian prince, a Getty, a Mellon, and Andy Warhol hied to a Manhattan bistro to hoist a welcoming toast to a matching set of blond nineteen-year-olds, the "DuPont" twins, when they took up residence in the Big Onion.

"Andy Warhol's discoveries," announced the *Hollywood Reporter,* the movie industry's trade magazine, printing the pair's picture.

"**Richard** and **Robert** . . . were adopted when they were three months old by **Henry George DuPont,** who died when they were eight," effused the grande dame of society columnists, Eugenia Sheppard, bestowing the ultimate seal of approval on the youths' account of their lineage—which supposedly connected them to the Delaware chemical dynasty. Indeed, though there is no Henry George in that family (which spells its name with a lowercase d), we discovered that the twins' dad *was* in a chemical business of sorts—running a Connecticut gas station. "I did adopt them, but I didn't die," snorted Jack Lasko. "No way they are du Ponts."

Though Warhol insists he was never fooled, the twins were afforded the same House Privileges as the pop artist's truly upper-crust satellites. The pair's memorabilia from this period—soup

cans, cloth, and other art daubed with Warhol's autographs—
would do justice to any gallery. By the same token, *you* may own
the twins' John Hancocks: when fans asked Warhol to sign shoes
for them (the artist got his start with shoes, sketching them for I.
Miller & Co.), he would gesture at the twins, they recall, and say,
"This is Robert and Richard DuPont. They're famous. They'll sign
too." Another high point for the duo was the dinner party they
attended with Warhol at Regine's. It was one of the openers for the
1982 fall social season. "*Everyone* came," says Richard, "Mick
Jagger, Diana Ross, Neil Sedaka . . . "

Mick should wish he made the same society sheets, from New
York to Houston and Beverly Hills, as the twins DuPont.

Pearls of gossip, daggers of sardonic wit, the latest information
on who is in and who is out spill from their lips. Tall and
mannerly, with eyes as blue as a maharanee's sapphire and the
weak, sloped chins of aristocrats whose ancient bloodlines have
worn frail as Limoges porcelain, they have enjoyed leisurely tête-à-
têtes with many *real* aristos, like the King of Sweden, and squired
actresses like Kristy McNichol and Brooke Shields. Salvador Dalí
would arrange the pair like bookends on either side of his bejeweled, brocaded wife, Gala, at the Sunday-night dinner parties
he threw at his favorite New York restaurants, Trader Vic's and
Laurent. Through Dalí, the lads met the Duchess of Windsor and
Happy Rockefeller.

Neither of those ladies offered them bed and board, but just
about everyone else has obliged, including a rock star who
accommodated the youths at his home in Benedict Canyon and an
heiress who rented a house in Round Hill, Jamaica—"*Ringo
Starr's* house," says Richard—and invited them to visit there. She
also invited them to Thanksgiving dinner at her apartment on
New York's swanky Sutton Place: "We asked if we could stay the
night and we stayed a year," says Richard, "with the maid, the
cook, and the chauffeur."

Now in their early twenties, the twins are no longer believed to
be du Ponts by most in their circle, but their entrée, free, to the
best oases of the haut monde is undiminished. Sit them at your
table and are they going to ruin the poularde Derby by reminisc-
ing about the golden era of leaded gas at their pop's business in
Connecticut?

Another putative member of the du Pont tribe, *John McLana-
han* du Pont, popped up on Wall Street as a "consultant" to John
Muir & Co., a brokerage house that launched high-flying new
issues of a parentage only somewhat more definite than his own.

The climate of optimism at the firm doubtless also owed something to its director of business development, ex-Yippie Jerry Rubin, and its general partner, Ray Dirks. Dirks, a colorful securities analyst, had been waging a running battle with the Securities and Exchange Commission ever since it brought an insider-trading action against him in connection with the Equity Funding swindle, a massive insurance brokerage scandal that he'd exposed in 1973.

Du Pont, who was an aide to Dirks, sported a chic ponytail. It often could be seen bobbing over the table at hangouts like the Russian Tea Room, where he was said to be bringing in *deals*. Was the du Pont name the catalyst? "I never claim I'm with the chemical family," he said. Dirks recollects it differently. "He wanted people to think he was. I would suppose initially it impressed [clients]."

Certainly, something about the rotund bon vivant drew the glitterati. Like the DuPont twins, this du Pont hobnobbed with sports, show business, and media personalities. With people like Peter, Paul, and Mary's Peter Yarrow, John Denver, Dick Clark. The Wall Streeter was godfather to Yarrow's daughter and, some time before Muir went bankrupt—the brokerage firm's reserves having paralleled the earthward plunge of many of its stock issues—the singer implored a reporter who was asking awkward questions not to sully du Pont's reputation:

"Bad publicity can be very harmful," Yarrow urged. He proceeded to cite an example. "People think 'Puff the Magic Dragon' is about marijuana, and I know it's not because I co-wrote it."

ALTERNATIVES

"I DON'T THINK I COULD LIVE THE LIFESTYLE I DO IF THE REST OF THE PEOPLE IN NEW YORK WEREN'T CRAZY."

Lew (not his real name), a free-lance illustrator and master forger who lives like a king, or at least a king's courtier, on $5,000 a year

"EVERYONE WAS THERE EXCEPT SYLVIA MILES AND I DON'T UNDERSTAND WHY BECAUSE SHE'D GO TO THE OPENING OF AN ENVELOPE."

Madame, the puppet of ventriloquist Wayland Flowers

If you aren't a Vanderbilt, don't want to masquerade as a Vanderbilt, or refuse to woo Vanderbilts as a party promoter, there is still hope.

1. The Eighteen-Karat Garbage Trick

Like the collages that are his métier, Lew, a New York free-lance illustrator, has a lifestyle made up of multitudinous pieces—most of them picked up on the sidewalk and hauled back to his downtown loft, which was bought with the income from the four years out of his twenty as an adult that he has worked as a salaried employee. His finds include:

• The ladies' discarded antiques (what else to do when your decorator sulks that Hepplewhite is out and the Delacroix is too tedious?)
• A seaman's chest that was featured in *New York*'s "Best Bets" column. Lew has a clipping pasted to the inside lid, to remind himself that someone could afford to throw out $125 in 1982.
• Towering tropical trees that would not be out of place at Mrs. G's. "This plant looks unhealthy," Lew says, casting a knowing eye over the *Ficus benjamina* in a Chinese restaurant where we're eating lunch. "They'll soon be throwing it out."
• An entire wardrobe. The garments have been dumped in dry-cleaning bags, the shoes in their original boxes. "Clothes I don't want, I give them to St. Vincent's Hospital for a tax break," Lew says. He deducted around $1,000 that way last year. Any furniture and books he doesn't want, he sells, to supplement his $5,000 earnings from occasional work doing illustrations for publishing houses.

"Now, I don't want you telling amateurs how to imitate this, because this means literally hundreds of dollars to me a year," he says, dropping his voice to a conspiratorial whisper. "This" is a CBS News correspondent's ID card signed with one of Lew's pseudonyms. His sheath of forgeries also includes a membership pass for the Museum of Modern Art and credentials for the Japan Society.

Though Lew is a culture buff, in his books money speaks louder than great works. Thus the higher-*priced* an event, the more likely a press agent is to get a ticket request from this "newsman." Lew was ecstatic at the announcement that it would cost $100 to see the eight-and-a-half-hour marathon play *Life and Adventures of Nicholas Nickleby:* "If I don't want the tickets, I sell them," he explains. But never at a scalper's premium. *That* would be dishonest.

(The Circus was also ecstatic at the record *Nicholas Nickleby* price. In his book *Ball,* William Wright reported that Claude Philippe, the late ringmaster of the April in Paris Ball, instituted a two-tier pricing system for a pre-ball party: $100 for Americans; $50 for the French. "[Philippe] knew that the French would not pay more than $50 for an evening's entertainment, and on the other hand, he knew that Americans would think there was something wrong with a charity party that cost *less* than $100," Wright wrote.)

2. You Could Become the First Mrs. Beatty

Arthur Schlesinger, Jr., was enjoying a quiet evening at home, a member of his family recalls, when he began to receive a frantic series of phone calls from Jan Cushing, a New York socialite.

"Warren's in town," she said. "He wants to talk to Arthur about a film."

Norman Mailer is said to have received a similar message: Beatty wanted to talk with him about a project. The powwow was set for some minutes hence at Elaine's, the literati's Mortimer's. The party assembled. Schlesinger and Mailer looked blankly at Warren when the actor asked just what was this idea for a screenplay that *Arthur* had had that *Norman* wanted to write that would be ideal for Warren. . . .

"I think Arthur did have an idea for a screenplay," Cushing says obdurately, "and all I did was introduce Beatty to Norman and Arthur."

Whether you go in for alternatives #1 or #2, the one choice that—to paraphrase Geraldine Ferraro's Pepsi spiel—you will never regret is:

3. Learning to be the Perfect Guest

Sylvia Miles perfected this art. A friend of the flamboyant actress first encountered her at a preview party for John Schlesinger's movie *Midnight Cowboy* at a Fifth Avenue hotel. "On her left hand," says the friend, "Sylvia had this line of hors d'oeuvres running up from the tips of her fingers to the wrist. With her right hand, she was holding a glass of champagne and my shirt collar."

The many subsequent evenings that the friend chaperoned Miles from party to party around town included one that began with cocktails and canapés at a new Chinese bank. The star was in one of her trademark turbans and a leopard-skin outfit. "We were the only Caucasians in the room," her friend says.

"It got so that if Sylvia was at an event, it wasn't chic," he adds.

We asked Miles about Madame's famous line connecting the actress with an envelope.

"The line came from me," she screamed. "Someone asked *me* if I'd gone to an opening and I said, if I'd have gone there, I'd have gone to the opening of an envelope. I do not like to be thought of as the queen of the night. I've had two Academy Award nominations and one of the reasons I've had difficulty here is people have trivialized my career.... I am one of the leading actresses in America. I happen to live here. I go out. I don't go to *everything*. I make my living in the theater. I have made thirty-two films."

"I'M LIKE A COURT JESTER. ALL I HAVE TO DO IS SMILE AND BE WITTY, AND IT DOES HELP TO BE DEVASTATINGLY HANDSOME. I WOULDN'T ADVISE ANYONE TO TRY TO LIVE FOR NOTHING IN NEW YORK IF THEY'RE NOT."

Peter (not his real name)

While you meet him at all the best parties, Peter is no Sylvia Miles, because he does not have a job; no Barbara de Portago, because he does not have a patrician name; no Nikki Haskell, because he would consider it most ungentlemanly to hustle—and on no account should you compare him to our illustrator-friend Lew. Peter's Gucci loafers seldom touch Lew's hunting ground, the sidewalks of New York. Generally, he whooshes past you in a limo. Someone else's limo, of course.

Peter does have two expenses—rent (earned by lending his assumed Old Etonian accent to PR firms for special events), and $3 for coat checks when, after he has walked the ladies to the shops, he lends them emotional support as they make the excruciating choice between Le Cirque, La Côte Basque, and La Grenouille. Of course, Peter will be at their side as they pick at a spinach salad. "Lunch is their big thing," he says. His voice rings with professional sincerity. In his line of leisure, you must never let down your guard. "They're always running out of venues." The same way that they're always running out of ideas for little presents for their walker. Since you can't eat a watch collection

(Peter's, all gifts from his "dates," includes a Bulgari, a Cartier, a Piaget, and a Patek Philippe), on mornings when the phone doesn't ring, he'll arrange a spiffy handkerchief in the breast pocket of his pinstripes, check the folds in his silk cravat, and stroll over to a mess hall where it's chic to hang out—generally those Upper East Side staples Le Relais or Mortimer's. "Someone will say, 'Oh, do come and join us. I want you to meet so-and-so,'" Peter explains haughtily, "and then that person will buy you lunch."

Evenings, he crashes gallery openings for a bite of smoked salmon and his regular glass of Moët. Among the galleries he recommends are Leila Taghinia-Milani, Wally Findlay, the Fox-worth, Marlborough, Dynasen . . . "the Dynasen uptown," he qualifies. "They have one in Soho but anything below Tiffany's is a drag. I mean, *cheese* lumps on toothpicks." After the hors d'oeuvres, Peter ambles on to some large private dinner party. It has to be large enough to have a retainer at the door with a list. Peter is a specialist at reading lists upside down: "You just look for a name that isn't crossed off that's plausible and say you're him."

Infiltrating parties at suburban mansions, mansions with *driveways,* is a snap: "The peak time to hit them is when there is a line of cars waiting to go through the gate," explains Peter. "You go up to about the third car behind your taxi and say, 'We're checking names, sir.' Then you get back into the taxi and use his name."

Since there is no such thing as a fashionable *private* party in New York—virtually every party is an advertisement for some product or person—the savvy hostess doesn't even consider having crashers arrested for trespass. By counting the number of them at her tables, she can gauge whether the column her press agent fed the predinner story to has pull, whether *she* has pull. We recall the time when the Onion's then Numero Uno Crasher, Arthur Weiner, commonly known as Bullet Head for his mirror-polished cranium, came face to face with the press agent for an event that had not invited him through its doors. The press agent, a sallow, twitchy man, who lives in fear that a client will fire him for missing two Suzy's or slurping the butter on his asparagus, was transformed by an unaccustomed feeling. Pride. "Bullet Head doesn't crash every party," the press agent exulted. "Only the best ones."

A Crash Course

1. Do not drink to excess when you crash. You will be taken for a visiting producer from Hollywood. An unsuccessful New York

lawyer does tiptoe around the bar table, filling small Tupperware containers to take home. That is different.

2. Do not grope celebrities. The crasher who was photographed by the *Post* dancing with Olivia Newton-John was not groping her.

3. Do not steal anything more serious than the silverware.

Learned studies have been made of crashers in New York: William Van Precht, a Manhattan psychoanalyst, determined that they had been emotionally starved in infancy. "They resented [this] but could not express it for fear of ridicule," he said. "Obviously, they risk exposure and embarrassment, but they think since nobody cares about them, nothing that happens really matters." The other study did not reference Freud since it was by Richard Falk, a public relations man. He drew up a list of the Ten Most Wanted Party Crashers, which he planned to circulate, with pictures, to partygivers. Fortunately, word of this nefarious plot leaked to "Page Six," the *Post* column that is the crasher's version of stock price tables.

"The Colonel [a noted crasher who's a supposed friend of the late Gen. Douglas MacArthur] called and threatened a lawsuit, Bullet Head said he was growing an Afro, and another crasher threatened to bomb me," Falk says. The Secret Service requested a copy of the list for its files.

"I am preparing a profile of the average crasher," Falk adds. "He has a furtive look, always carries something—a cane, briefcase, camera—is hatless, five feet nine, clip-on bow tie, pants usually too short, ring around the collar, highly polished shoes with worn heels, rapidly heads for the food table . . . "

The story is told of the manufacturer of a fire-prevention device who was touched by the spectacle of a swarm of safety-minded "journalists" devouring the turkey, the ham, the barbecued ribs, the fried chicken, at a demonstration of the gizmo. His PR woman took a deep breath—and did not exhale it. Though there were only two scribes among the uninvited gluttons, mindful of her monthly retainer, she wisely decided not to disillusion her client with a head count of who was invited and who just came.

The story also is told of the pseudonymous Sammy Green. For some reason this crasher did not receive a Mailgram summoning him to the "21" Club for the launch of Finlandia vodka. Still, posing as a reporter, he, like Ann-Margret and the other guests in the crush, was given a free raffle ticket. And the winner of a vacation for two to Finland was . . . Little blobs of sweat dribbling down his face, Sammy rushed to the microphone to claim his loot.

"We would have hoped Ann-Margret could have been the winner," huffed an organizer. The *real* reporters joined the keen. The sound of mass mourning was too much for the Finns. They conferred with the event's publicists and Sammy stayed in New York.

David Susskind had three New York "crashers" on his TV show. *Life* also interviewed the trio. Terry Weldon, a fireman, and management-recruitment executives Frank Fusaro and Steve Goldstein had come in for this media attention because they had succeeded in slipping past 120 policemen and 77 security guards to pose in a group portrait with 126 stars on the stage of Radio City Music Hall at an Actors Fund gala.

For the price of their $89 polyester tuxedos, the men bragged that they had finessed their way into being photographed with every living President, into sharing the reviewing stand with Mayor Koch upon the return of the Iranian hostages, even into drinks with George Steinbrenner during the World Series.

"*Real* crashers," grunts the compiler of the Most Wanted List, PR man Richard Falk, "publicity is the last thing they want."

"I LOVE TO SPEND MONEY. IT'S AN OBSESSION WITH ME."

Arthur Ringwalt "Burke" Rupley IV

The living proof of the adage that if you can make it here, you can make it anywhere is Burke Rupley, a handsome eleventh-grade dropout from Florida's South Plantation High School who when he arrived in New York was a social unknown—though not for long. He lodged at the Helmsley Palace Hotel, dropped $100 tips at discotheques, and drenched a retinue of hangers-on with Dom Pérignon. World-weary at twenty, his pampered skin pale as white bread, manicured hands flashing a double-band diamond ring, the youth clambered into a limousine for the one-block ride from his hotel to the Waldorf, where, over a cocktail, he told a *New York* reporter that he had inherited a real estate empire—worth $125 million, according to a lawyer in his entourage. Because his money was tied up in trust funds, "Young Rupley must restrain himself with an allowance of $80,000 to $120,000 a month," wrote another reporter, who interviewed him for his hometown newspaper, the *Miami Herald*.

$120,000 a *month*?

Burke had been raised by a Florida woman, Mary Westerberg,

who was not known to have any great wealth. He subsequently would say that he was left the money when his grandfather died, but that relative was also an unknown quantity. What *was* known was that his grandmother, Mildred Rupley, once owned a chunk of a huge Virginia apartment complex. The property was sold, reportedly for $23 million, around the time Burke took a shine to New York and *she* certainly seemed loaded since she drove around in a Cadillac limo with a chauffeur. The *Miami Herald* attempted to interview Mildred about her grandson. "I really don't like to talk about this," she said, "Let him speak for himself."

Burke's lifestyle when he moved to an apartment from his luxurious hotel spoke for him quite effectively. His cook served the *Herald* reporter Veal Orloff, baked endive, watercress in a tart dressing, and coeur à la crème—"a heart-shaped sweet cheese mold dressed with strawberries," elaborated the newspaper. The youth's girlfriend, Britt Ekland, didn't hurt his image either. Her previous squeezes, noted one news report about Burke, had included Rod Stewart, Ryan O'Neal, and Peter Sellers. Britt was thirty-ninish, maybe too young for Burke, because he passed her over and married Soraya Khashoggi, the raven-haired fortyish ex-wife of Adnan Khashoggi, the *Nabila*'s owner.

Your Next Clue: Obviously, neither party to the match needed to be a gold digger. The British-born Soraya had made international headlines with a record $2.5 *billion* divorce suit against Khashoggi. To be sure, despite press reports estimating that she eventually settled for $100 million, a Khashoggi aide values it at more like $2 million, plus $10,000 a month for life. A bit of a whimper. Still, if you believed what a London tabloid, the *Daily Star,* touted as Soraya's confessions—she griped that she did not get to approve the series, a dispute resolved when the *Star* upped her fee—there was one driving force in the life of Burke's adored. Passion:

"His rich, cultured voice echoed across the grand but gloomy marbled lobby. 'Soraya . . .' It was Winston. Then and there, right in the bustling heart of Parliament, I fell in love with Winston Spencer Churchill, MP [the grandson of the wartime prime minister]."

Despite this romp with the married British parliamentarian, which took place after her divorce from Adnan, Soraya clearly was no vamp. The series revealed that she had passed up a chance to meet Neil Diamond that "probably" would have culminated in "a night of love." She did go on a blind date with Frank Sinatra—"I knew instinctively that I would finish the night with him"—but after one of those poetic evenings of which romances are made (heaving the furniture at a Monaco restaurant "into the fire"), she "thought of my ex-husband [she and Khashoggi were divorced by then] at home and suddenly got cold feet." As for the randy Ted Kennedy, he would have to warm his tootsies on the cat: "One of his emissaries knocked at the door.... I was outraged. The man was just pimping. If Kennedy had arrived himself with a bunch of red roses I might have accepted."

After only eight months, Burke Rupley joined the ranks of dejected ex-suitors. With his marriage on the rocks, what was the lad to do? Maybe tell all. A series began to run in another London paper, the *News of the World,* under such titles as "Confessions of Rich Boy Robert Rupley" (he apparently was using "Robert" as his name in this unhappy period) and "Sexy Life of Robert Rupley."

"Confessions of a Toy Boy," some cynics in the media might gibe, but this was a *man* smitten. Ekland occupied some of his post-marital reveries—"I didn't speak, but carefully slid down the straps of her silky white dress until it made a gleaming patch on the sand ..."—but mostly it was *Soraya, Soraya:* "She told me I was the best lover she ever had." She walked out on him, the series quoted him as saying, soon after he bought her a white mink: "I'm still wondering exactly what went wrong."

Some answers may be contained in lawsuits against Burke and other documents that we found on file in courthouses from New York to Florida. Researching these, and interviewing some of the plaintiffs, we learned about allegations of:

Lonely Nights: Soraya wailed in a divorce suit against Burke that the Romeo of the western world didn't even spend the marriage night with her. "I was married in July, and he didn't bother to come over to England until September. And then he didn't come to visit me at all." Burke denied this. She claimed he'd forged checks and American Express charges in her name. The charges were at her request, Burke responded. "He conned me," stormed Soraya.

Jetting Away: Robert Stecher, an owner of East Wind Limousine, said this New York company had provided Burke with a stretch Cadillac, a Mercedes, a Rolls-Royce, and a Ferrari. At first, the newcomer to town was a prompt payer. But, "One day at Le Relais, he took my wallet and said, 'I'll be right back,' and the next thing I knew he'd chartered a Learjet with my American Express card and gone to Florida," claimed Stecher. Burke demurred: "Soraya and I used to take a Learjet all the time, but never on [Stecher's card]." Stecher and a business partner, Arthur Davis, obtained a judgment for $195,000 against Soraya's ex, in an effort to recoup various alleged debts. For instance, Davis claimed that Burke had wheedled a $29,500 loan out of him: "He told me," Davis said in a deposition, "that he owed money to certain people and that they threatened to kill him if it was not repaid."

Moneybags: Henry San, credit director of Mayor's, a swank Miami jeweler's, claimed that his company was out some $250,000. Burke, the executive said, used one of the articles about his "inheritance" to get an increase in a credit line he had at the store. "We went to see him to collect our money when he was into us for about two hundred thousand," San recalled. "He opened the trunk of a Rolls-Royce and in it were two satchels filled with money wrapped in plastic. He said that he was holding a reception on a boat he had rented and he counted out ten thousand dollars he said was to pay the caterer." So why didn't San leave with his money? "The excuse we got was he had a cash-flow problem, so he'd pay us within two weeks," said the credit director. "We got a call a week after that saying the caterer was looking for him."

The Party at the Pawnshop: It's unclear whether it was worth it for the caterer to look for Burke. Probate records indicate that his grandfather, the putative source of his wealth, left an estate valued at just over $700,000, one quarter of this in trust to his grandson. Burke's income from this is $3,000 a month, according to his grandmother's testimony in a deposition when Mayor's sued for its alleged debt.

"Does Arthur own any real property, any land?" asked the high-powered lawyer representing the jewelry store.

"That I don't know..." his grandmother said. "He is very secretive..."

Maybe Mayor's could at least find what it said was its jewelry. Burke testified that he had rained "tons" of trinkets on Mary Westerberg, the Florida woman who brought him up, and her family. In that case, the Mayor's lawyer wondered, what had become of one of those pieces, an opal-and-diamond Piaget watch? Westerberg's daughter, Dorothy Van Kleet, said Burke had lent it to her for a party.

"But you went to a party at a pawn shop?" asked the lawyer. A claim ticket suggested that that indeed was where the watch ended up. Van Kleet explained that she had pawned the Piaget because she needed money. What about the Rolex Cellini, another time piece? "He lent it to me with the Piaget," said Van Kleet.

"To go to the same party?" asked the lawyer.

"He's very flamboyant," said Van Kleet. After redeeming both watches from the pawnbroker, she returned them to Burke, she claimed.

Westerberg testified that she had "begged" Mayor's to stop giving Burke credit, that she was "in the midst of having a nervous breakdown" and that she was selling her "plate collection."

Like the partners in the New York limo company, the jeweler's obtained a judgment against Burke, for $312,000. But, at the time of writing, again like the limo firm owners, the store claimed it had been unable to collect its money. "In all the years I've been in retail," San, the Mayor's credit director, brooded, "I've never, never seen a situation like this."

We asked Burke to elucidate it for us. His version of events certainly sounded plausible. He didn't owe the East Wind Limousine owners anything, he said, because he had invested $595,000 through Term Leasing, a vehicle leasing and finance firm, to provide a fleet of Mercedeses for the New York limo concern. Replied Term Leasing vice-president Clare Sawchuk, Burke indeed paid her firm $595,000—in repayment of "money given to him for personal use and personal debts." The Mayor's debt? Burke's story on that sounded plausible too. Though the store seemed unaware of it, he had "settled" with it.

As for the $125 million, "one day I will inherit a considerable amount of that." For the moment, however, Burke Rupley had turned, like so many of our social titans, to earning his living.

"I'm doing a real estate thing in Harrisburg, Pennsylvania, converting ten buildings owned by my grandmother into co-ops, and I'm starting a computer company, marketing computers." Oh yes, and he had started a company with a partner to design bathing suits. Pilar Crespi, who has been taking design courses at New York's prestigious Parsons School and hopes to do a swimwear line herself, can relax, however. Burke said he would be selling under the label "Oooh Can't Wait." Not his name.

4

GOD'S BUILDERS

"PRESUMPTIONS THAT THE CHURCH SHOULD BE TRYING TO IMPROVE HOUSING FOR THE POOR...THE PRESUMPTION THAT THE CHURCH SHOULD BE SMALL AND IMPOVERISHED. THESE ARE HIDDEN PRESUMPTIONS THAT I SEE ALL THE TIME."

The Rev. Dr. Bryant Kirkland, of the Fifth Avenue Presbyterian Church

In the spring of 1984, Dr. Kirkland's church, an imposing brownstone edifice that sits kitty-corner from Trump Tower, did what more and more tax-exempt New York institutions are doing these days—it cut a lucrative property deal. In return for transferring one of its buildings and certain development rights to a consortium planning a controversial horizonscraper next door, the parish would be paid about $17 million. The happy event is said to have been sealed with a 10 percent deposit by the time that a deputation of social activists met with an aide to the Fifth Avenue Presbyterian pastor almost a year later to lobby for help for the homeless, five or six of whom had taken to huddling outside the church's locked doors at night to shelter from the cold. The deputation leader, Joe Gilmore, a Presbyterian minister from a suburb north of New York, wondered whether something couldn't be done to make conditions for the uninvited guests "more human?"

For instance, the church was known to have a kitchen—"Dr. Kirkland is a real elegant man," drawled a socialite who has attended dinners there—so maybe it could feed the destitutes. Or allow them to use its toilets. Of course, it could always open its sanctuary for twenty-four-hour prayer, Gilmore murmured. That way, should anyone snatch a few minutes' sleep, it would be between him and his Maker.

What the out of town minister couldn't have known, of course, was that he was asking for help from a flock that had its own financial problems. Until the balance of the $17 million was paid, Fifth Avenue Presbyterian was having to scrimp along, like many an OM dowager, on passing the plate and the income from what Dr. Kirkland describes as a "very modest" $8.5 million endowment. Besides, would the Lord really want these people in his house? Three or four months passed, then the church made its response to the deputation. With *action,* not *words.* A security guard loomed over the indigents and ordered them to get lost. "We let people stay on those steps for fifteen years, but increasingly there have been security problems and damage to the property," said Carl Nelson, a Kirkland staffer. "They were using the place as bathrooms, causing corrosion to the wood and stone, and there were potential fire problems because people were building little homes of cardboard and using little candles."

Some months after this, church officials apparently had second thoughts, because it was announced that the kirk would be providing the homeless with cots—six cots, five nights a week— and Dr. Kirkland assured us that the homeless were welcome on the church steps again. The church was planning to use about one third of its income from the property deal to add to its already considerable annual program (over $200,000) of philanthropic works, which include grants toward housing projects for the poor (the other two thirds of the development proceeds would help to support building upkeep and "program services").

The generosity of this plan does not surprise you? It should.

The Fifth Avenue church doesn't *have* to do any good works. As Dr. Kirkland points out, the presumption that New York's religious institutions—among the wealthiest in the world—have some kind of duty to take a vow of poverty and give every cent away is, well, presumptuous.

"Are *you* housing the homeless in your home?" the pastor asks.

Well, are you?

"What's the Empire State Building doing to help the homeless, what's Rockefeller Center doing?"

Good question.

"Why should people just pick on the churches? There's a fairness element here," snaps the pastor.

It is important to be fair. What follows should reassure the forty thousand homeless to whom this book is dedicated that their situation is absolutely fair. Moreover, once you realize that our great religious institutions are nothing more than slightly richer versions of Rockefeller Center, it ceases to be a puzzlement that their techniques, and sometimes those of their leaders and followers, for achieving the spiritual include making use of that by now familiar temporal trinity:

Photo Opportunities

New York's Roman Catholic primate, John Cardinal O'Connor, is rivaled only by Ronald Reagan as a communicator of traditional values. The bon mots that have made him a household name with women across America include his observation that, "I always compare the killing of four thousand babies a day in the United States, unborn babies, with the Holocaust." Contrary to what you might believe, the prelate does not employ any of the PR firms from chapter two to leak those intime little details about his personal life that keep popping up in the gossip columns. The archdiocese has a very adequate press office of its own, besides which, O'Connor is a master of the kind of off-the-cuff announcement that grabs reporters. It was his revelation, for instance, that despite his God-given knowledge that practicing homosexuals are sinful, he was "seriously considering" setting up a shelter for AIDS victims, that brought him some of his most admiring press. The chancery was inundated with calls from astonished journalists. At least one of O'Connor's own staffers was astonished too. "We had no new shelter, no new programs planned, that I know of," says this aide. "A local reporter had asked him a question. He does tend to shoot a little from the hip, but he doesn't do it to get headlines. He sees his strength in talking directly to people, and why not use the media?"

After some quick looking around, the archdiocese corralled the nuns of Mother Teresa of India's order to run the Gift of Love, as the shelter is called. This was a *perfect appointment,* even if it did pass over several New York nuns who had been doing dedicated work with AIDS patients at three Catholic hospitals. For one thing, the ladies of the circus now knew there was a serious purpose to sari chic. For another, members of Dignity, a religious organization of gay Catholics, were rebuffed in an attempt to enter the new residence and minister to the dying men. This did not become a photo opportunity for the cardinal, but should have if you believe that the buck stops with him. The saving of these sinners' immortal souls from further pollution is due not only to Mother Teresa's upholding of his ban on the renegades (Dignity isn't recognized by the archdiocese), but to her introduction of a ban on television (residents are allowed radios, a stereo, and board games). The men are confined to the building most of the day, are permitted visitors for just two hours in the afternoon, and must be in bed by eight-thirty at night. Says John Wright, social services director at St. Clare's Hospital, a Catholic center that pioneered the city's first specialized ward for AIDS victims, "We tell people [the shelter] is an alternative if they really have nowhere else to go. One of our sisters says the place reminds her of your basic training as a nun."

To monitor his progress at training New Yorkers in his take on the divine laws, the cardinal likes to watch videotapes of himself. Accordingly, an interview room in the Chancery press office has been converted into a video recording center, equipped with three new professional-quality cassette machines, in addition to the one that was felt necessary during the regnum of his predecessor, Terence Cardinal Cooke. Nicknamed Cookie, this quiet, unassuming man disliked pomp and publicity and would spend eighteen hours a day squinting over diocesan paperwork, absentmindedly spooning soup into his mouth during dinner. "Periodically, the press office would get a call requesting an interview with him and they would say, 'No. Do you want somebody else?'" says an archdiocesan staffer.

Would the Pope's new man on the job want to miss the chance for comparison if he was on four major local stations at once?

"They record everything they can, then edit it down so [O'Connor] can just watch a tape of his section," says the staffer.

Financial Opportunities

Preservationists have raised a hue and cry about the proclivity of religious institutions for real estate development. They complained for instance, that the skyscraper planned for the site next to Fifth Avenue Presbyterian, would destroy two other edifices—the Coty and Rizzoli buildings—which they claimed were architectural treasures. That was the WRONG way to look at it. The RIGHT way, along the model of old-fashioned ward politics, was that there tends to be something in God's Building Plans for everyone. The prime example of this involves the drama that began when the headline $100 MILLION OFFERED FOR PARK AVE. CHURCH glowered from the front page of the *New York Times*—Saint Bartholomew's

Church, selling out for a skyscraper. Its ornate neo-Byzantine basilica is one of the last pools of human-scale serenity on congested midtown Park Avenue. But who wants human if they can rig a tower tall enough to touch the pearly gates? And use the money to avoid bankruptcy (the church has a paltry $13 million endowment) and serve the poor? As with Fifth Avenue Presbyterian's property plan, a chunk of the profits would be given away and a chunk retained for such projects as a rector's TV ministry. The *Times* story quoted Marc Haas, a multimillionaire financier and world-class stamp collector who was the church's senior warden, as saying that an unidentified "very prestigious American corporation" was behind the bid to buy the place lock, stock, and Bibles. The word according to Haas was as remarkable as his taste in conveyances for arriving at Sunday services (a navy Rolls-Royce): the bid valued the property at $2,000 a square foot, almost three times the going rate in the neighborhood.

Still, his account of the supposed offer was taken seriously. The entire preservation community rose up in wrath and another millionaire, Andrew Stein, felt called to help these potential voters carry the protest flag and picket the church. Stein at the time was the Manhattan borough president and in following our parable you should bear in mind that he had not lightly earned his sobriquet, the Kellogg of Flakes. He had been propelled into politics by a third millionaire, his dad, who doubtless was impressed by his ambition to become the first Jewish President of the United States—and, in his incubatory years as a state assemblyman, he was once observed scurrying around the legislative chamber, buttonholing colleagues and imploring them to tell him which would be the most politically advantageous way to vote on a move to reinstate capital punishment.

A meeting was convened: plastic Andy meets the Rector of St. Bart's, the Rev. Thomas Bowers, and Haas the Collector.

Who said *Andy* had a monopoly on plastic?

"Haas looks at Andrew, this big grin on his face, and says, 'The price has doubled since the [*Times*] story appeared,'" a Stein acquaintance recalls. "It was very clear that they'd leaked it to jack up the bidding." And that the idea had been to scare the city into accepting a compromise—preserving the church, and shoe-horning the skyscraper into the space currently occupied by its community house, a designated landmark.

Stein, who is now New York's city council president, rechained himself to the railings. Publicly, at least. The *Times* quoted Father Bowers as saying that the politician privately had been lobbying him to do a little favor for the Fisher Brothers real estate company, a developer that has contributed rather generously to Stein's ascent to the Oval Office. Bowers said that the suggested favor consisted of letting the tower be built after all, by Fisher Brothers.

The borough president denied this, and since it indeed would have been unusual for him to have made such a pitch—he has a short attention span and, like the man who may be seen as his role model, Ted Kennedy, generally delegates such complicated matters to aides—we made further inquiries.

Ah yes. The truth before God. Says a well-placed source, it was Theodore Kheel, a powerhouse lawyer and friend of one of the Fishers, who barreled into a homily, as Stein nervously stretched his mouth into its famous smile, about how, with young Andrew's help, all things on earth could come to pass. Even swinging a wrecker's ball at a building that had been designated a historic landmark.

Kheel is said to have brought his case to a conclusion so incontrovertible that you could almost hear the jackhammers start. Go it alone without Stein, the source recalls him admonishing, and it could take *years* to thwart the opposition.

Haas the Collector treated the lawyer—who has only a "faint recollection" of these events and "doubts" he would have held out Stein as a savior—to a long, contemptuous stare.

"Mr. Kheel," he said, getting up to leave, "the church is eternal."

Advancement Opportunities

In New York, it's not only what you believe, it's where you believe it. So for those of you who have been struggling to weigh the social cachet of Christmas Eve at St. Thomas against a performance by the Harvard Glee Club (during morning worship at Brick Presbyterian) and Lenten Lectures at All Souls, here is a quick rank ordering which we prepared with the assistance of Marianne Strong, a bellwether of Old New York's haut monde:

Catholic
1. St. Thomas More's, 65 East Eighty-ninth Street. (Marianne's church. Also that of Letitia Baldrige, the Jackie O pal and etiquette arbiter.) In a dead heat, St. Vincent Ferrer, Sixty-sixth Street and Lexington Avenue.
2. St. Ignatius Loyola, 980 Park Avenue.
3. St. Patrick's Cathedral, Fiftieth Street and Fifth Avenue. (Voguish for politicians and other bigwigs, but really only recommended for funerals.)

Protestant

1. St. James Episcopal, 865 Madison Avenue. (*The* Social Register church. Big on noblesse oblige, so pretend you already put your worldly goods into trust for the Second Coming.)
2. St. Thomas, 1 West Fifty-third Street. (Old families still use it for those special occasions, like weddings and burials, but social-climbing conditions can be slippery as doctors, lawyers, diplomats, and other members of the underclass mingle with the largest supply of rich widows in New York. Christmas Eve here, boys and girls, is strictly for the tourists.)
3. Brick Church, Ninety-first Street and Park Avenue. (Although this was John Foster Dulles's church and is now Laurance Rockefeller's, it is also popular with wealthy young families, and has a nursery school so fashionable that little Johnny would murder his designer teddy bear to get admitted; fees $2,700 a year for mornings only, or $3,600 for an "extended" day.)
4. Heavenly Rest, 2 East Ninetieth Street. (The rector, the Rev. Hugh Hildesley, is a presumptionist liberal who has set up cots for the homeless without any pressure from activists. He also hosted a press conference at which an interfaith coalition attacked the city for its success in resembling Calcutta on Mother Teresa's morning off. Mayor Koch's response to this rubbish was to mail the protesters a copy of a speech he had given on the subject.)
5. St. Bartholomew's, 109 East Fiftieth Street. (While taking periodic emergency measures to keep his flock out of Chapter 11 bankruptcy proceedings, such as closing the church for weekday worship, Father Bowers has maintained a tight grip on spiritual priorities. "This season," said a mailing we received at the height of the place's fiscal emergency, "St. Bartholomew's . . . has kindly and graciously made available to Mr. Tannen's Free Theatre Productions the use of its 1,200-seat church." For a program of readings by the Tony-award-winning actor Jeremy Irons.)
6. All Souls Unitarian, Eightieth Street and Lexington Avenue. (The minister, Frank Forrester Church IV, is the son of the late United States senator, and climbing conditions here are ecumenical. Roughly a third of the worshipers are of Jewish origin, another third originally Catholic. The cross has been replaced by an impressionistic sculpture made of nylon string, and the services include a "celebration" of Chanukah and a Passover seder.)

Falling somewhere off the bottom of this list is the world's largest, and largest unfinished, Gothic cathedral, St. John the Divine at 1047 Amsterdam Avenue. The address, just to clarify matters, means that it has a splendid view of West Harlem, legions of whose youths are to be trained as stonemasons in an $80 million push to complete a structure on which work has occurred sporadically since 1892. Its dean, the Very Rev. James Parks Morton, classifies himself as an apostle of Bauhaus before this movement was "co-opted by the rich" and is backing a plan to eventually encase the south transept in glass to form a giant "bioshelter" that will act as a solar collector and contain an experimental fish, flower, and vegetable farm. The diocesan bishop, Paul Moore, Jr., comes from a family with substantial interests in companies like Bankers Trust—and caused several of the ladies to choke on their cream sherry when he ordained a lesbian. You will not see a line of limousines triple-parked outside such functions as the interfaith AIDS service and exposition by the Dalai Lama.

Jewish
Ronald Sobel, the senior rabbi at Temple Emanu-El, the synagogue that Our Crowd built at Sixty-fifth Street and Fifth Avenue, fulminates that Stephen Birmingham was mistaken when he wrote that trustee meetings here used to be black-tie. "Birmingham is enchanted with social mystique," Sobel says, gritting his teeth. "It has nothing to do with the reality of American-Jewish life today." It's best, therefore, not to let the rabbi know what you're up to. A careful placement in the main sanctuary can afford contacts in government (Maxwell Rabb, President Reagan's envoy to Rome, is not Catholic), law (Robert Morgenthau, the Manhattan district attorney, will be glad to guide you), publishing (try for an Annenberg or a Sulzberger), or real estate development (Andrew Stein always needs new contributors).

Yuppy
Religion, straightforward Judeo-Christianity, hat on your head, money in the plate, is hot with the upwardly mobile. And one branch of it is near meltdown point, Grace Church, at Broadway and Tenth Street. The parish has experienced at least a 500 percent surge in its membership in the past decade, most of the growth coming from singles in their twenties and thirties, and at least some of it spiritually induced. The religious awakening and baptism at Grace of a twenty-five-year-old writer and close friend of Caroline Kennedy, David Michaelis, was the subject of a story in the *Times*. But the Grace curate, Ken Swanson, suggested to one of our reporters that "the yuppy mentality" also comes into it.

"The ideal of a good citizen in American history," Swanson explained, "has always been a leader in the church and the community. I remember right after one very aggressive yuppy was elected to the junior vestry at St. Bart's, he was overheard saying, 'You know, the most important thing is it gets your name on the back of the program.'" Thomas Bowers, who moved to the socially prominent St. Bartholomew's pulpit in 1978 from Atlanta, a city the ladies believe may serve chitlings, has axed the junior group.

"I didn't mind so much when Mr. Bowers suggested a soup kitchen, or starting a TV ministry," one parishioner, Mrs. Douglas MacArthur, the general's widow, said stiffly to a friend. "But when he started referring to our President as Jimm-uh and our governor as Hughie, I had to put my foot down."

"THIS IS A VERY SOPHISTICATED CONGREGATION. THEY WOULDN'T LISTEN TO ME IF I WORE OLD CLOTHES."

The minister of an Upper East Side Episcopal parish

How much did a fashionplate clergyman earn? we wondered. Maybe $70,000?

"No one would take it for that. It's no different from running a corporation," the minister of the Upper East Side parish said, signing for our lunch at a Madison Avenue restaurant on what he characterized as a church account.

A parishioner of St. Thomas, the Fifty-third Street society church, which has an endowment of about $50 million, attended a dinner party at the church-owned eleven-room Park Avenue apartment of its minister, the Rev. John Andrew, whose salary, without measuring in perks, is $52,000 a year. The parishioner speaks admiringly of a maid, crisply uniformed in a black dress and starched white apron, of vintage French wines, and of a throng that included such room-rockers as "a bishop from London, a title from England very close to the royals, and a decorator."

"You *can't* ask," Andrew shouted.

What we had asked was how much St. Thomas received when, deciding to build a new choir school, it quietly entered into a partnership with the Fisher Brothers—the developers Andrew

Stein allegedly pitched to St. Bart's—and American Express to erect a high-rise on the old school's site. The rector finally directed us to one of his parish officials, who courteously explained that it was difficult to put a monetary value on the deal. It was having to be carefully structured, he elaborated, "so we don't lose our tax-exempt status [on the project]."

St. Thomas, which gives away $263,000 a year to charitable causes and religious education, will use the income from the tower primarily to construct the new school. "If there is anything left, it probably will be used to expand our music mission," said the church official. To put all of this in perspective, Temple Emanu-El, with about a $7.5 million endowment, disperses over $300,000 and is part of two Upper East Side coalitions that have raised over $1.7 million for social projects. Fifth Avenue Presbyterian's $200,000 in good works is supported by its $8.5 million endowment, though that church, of course, does have expectations. With St. Bart's and St. Thomas, the Fifth Avenue kirk also belongs to a midtown counterpart to the Upper East Side social coalitions. At the time of writing, this group was planning a garage sale—the first effort to raise money in its two years of existence, but, as a staffer at St. Bart's, the Rev. Judith Baumer, says, "It takes a while to get everyone together."

We incorporated our tax-exempt religious opera company, sent the forty thousand dispossessed one ticket to the first performance of *La Bohème,* and then moved smartly along and put in a call to St. Peter's, a midtown Lutheran church that had sold out its old sanctuary as a site for one of those towers, the nine-hundred-foot Citicorp Center. The church had had to build its new facility, a rough granite prism that squats at the base of the skyscraper, out of the $9 million proceeds from the deal, and it certainly wasn't well endowed. It was said to have lost $800,000 in the stock market. What we had in mind, though, was that comfortable new sanctuary. Thanks to the cantilevered seats (so ministers need not squash their billowing vestments), movable pulpit, and other innovations by a top interior design team, it was *so* comfortable that the *Times* had done a living-section write-up on it. Headline: "Feeling at Home in St. Peter's."

"We're very involved with the homeless," said Sylvia Bjornson, the pastor's secretary. "We have a Tuesday-morning hot breakfast for two hundred with a bag lunch for them as they leave.

"We have a program for AIDS victims and we reach out through three gallery spaces in the church, including one for emerging artists and two for well-known artists. And we do classical and jazz programs." The church's famed jazz "ministry," with its annual star-spangled "All Nite Soul" festival, is "very expensive," she continued. "It's a real outreach. Jazz musicians are all indigent. Our jazz vespers is free. All our services are free. . . ."

We steered the conversation back to the homeless. Perhaps we could learn what accommodations the church was offering the forty thousand?

"It's not a practical thing here. The church is not equipped," said Bjornson.

We pursued this further with Gary Sievert, the parish administrator. He said the problem was that the church's bathrooms didn't have the showers required by "city codes." So we are delighted to be able to tell him that we made a few checks on his behalf, and *this very evening,* if he hasn't already learned the good news, Mr. Sievert can program the Lord's computer to dim the sanctuary lighting. . . and swing wide the doors. For every one toilet, St. Peter's can take in six people up to a total of nineteen guests (after which, tighter state regulations come into play). No showers required.

"THIS YEAR'S FOCUS FOR RIVERSIDE IS SORT OF GAY AND LESBIAN CONCERNS. LAST YEAR IT WAS THE SANCTUARY ISSUE."

"OH, WE HAVE ABOUT FIFTY-SIX KITCHENS, SEVENTY-TWO BATHROOMS, OUR TOWER IS TWENTY-FOUR STORIES TALL. WE HAVE A GYM, A BOWLING ALLEY, A THEATER."

"RIVERSIDE TRIES TO DEVELOP FROM INTERNATIONAL, GLOBAL ISSUES THINGS THAT WILL IMPACT THE LOCAL COMMUNITY. HOUSING AND HUNGER, FOR INSTANCE, CAN BE RELATED TO THE INTERNATIONAL ISSUES LIKE ARMS PRODUCTION."

From interviews with administrators at the Rev. William Sloane Coffin, Jr.'s, Riverside Church, which has a $45 million endowment

---

As the Scourge of the Establishment, the former chaplain of Yale has been sticking it to Ronald Reagan by giving sanctuary to a refugee family from Central America. And as for the Lucky Ten North American homeless to whom Coffin Castle is affording a room at night, at least they should have plenty of choice of places to wash up.

"We only have space for ten," said Dr. Carl Fields, the church administrative officer. "There is no other livable space that would conform to city codes."

To be fair, Riverside single-handedly has solved another New York shame, unemployment. The church has 130 people on its staff, more than one-third of them involved in building upkeep. Others help man its famous assault squads on global issues such as disarmament or teach at a private church kindergarten. Some $3.1 million of Riverside's $6.8 million revenues were absorbed by salaries and employee benefits in 1985. About $353,000 of its budget—$208,000 from special Sunday collections and $145,000 in income from the $45 million endowment—was devoted to conventional good works, such as helping the sick, and unwed mothers. That was somewhat less than the $412,000 invested in an adult learning center that teaches conversational English to newly arrived refugees and immigrants. Still, it was substantially more than the $128,000 budgeted for the disarmament program— and than the $117,000 earmarked for the church's four-person "communications" office. Riverside's administrative officer, Carl Fields, conceded that the publicity outlays might seem unnecessary: "It depends on what is determined important," he said. "You could cut out newspaper advertising, but that means you might impair the number of people who come to church." Besides, should the need arise, there is always scope for more special collections: Riverside volunteers regularly solicit victuals from shoppers outside supermarkets. The church's splendid feeding and clothing programs depend almost entirely on such donations, rather than endowment income, Riverside staffers explain. Such husbandry apparently pays, because Coffin's Castle finished 1985 with a $158,000 surplus of revenues over outlays.

Trinity Church, the soaring Gothic revival pile at the corner of Broadway and Wall Street, is one of the richest religious institutions in the world, employing 350 staff, many of them involved with the upkeep of its forty commercial properties in Lower Manhattan. It also has a $50 million stock portfolio.

"We're not a real estate business that holds services," said a spokesman, disclosing the church's income for the first time. About $25 million. The London *Economist* had guessed $10 million, which is more like the amount Trinity spends on its religious payroll, grants, and programming each year. Heading the payroll, according to a diocesan official, is the Trinity rectorship (a job that at this writing was about to become vacant) at $100,000 a year, plus a home on the Upper East Side. The Trinity spokesman was unable to confirm the details of this package, but said he knew it was large: "There's such money here that you really wouldn't want the man at the top worried about money," he explained. The grants amounted to $2.6 million in 1985, including generous help to blacks in South Africa. In New York, the church supports such projects as housing for senior citizens. Trinity has pitched its theology of giving-it-all-away in an advertising jingle:

> *You can't get to heaven in a limousine*
> *'Cause the Lord don't sell no gasoline.*

The rhyme was part of the initial push to promote the new Trinity not-for-profit mausoleum. Spaces in the gracious granite building, set on a hillside overlooking the Hudson river, retail for $1,250 to a respectable $20,000. "The top levels, that can't be kissed or touched, cost less," a cemetery counselor tells prospective buyers.

"By acting now you avoid making decisions under stress and having to pay for everything in cash," urges a flier the Wall Street church has been mailing around town.

Heaven's Gate

Built in the mid-Victorian period in the Romanesque Revival style, Brooklyn's Lafayette Avenue Presbyterian Church is an exquisite example of what St. Bart's—which estimates that it needs just over $11 million in repairs—would look like if it were allowed to build the tower to help the poor and give itself a fix-up. Lafayette's Tiffany windows, towering mahogany-encased Austin organ, and muralled walls look to be in pristine condition. Yet this church also has the funds to support a thriving range of programming: Christian education classes, a Sunday school, four choirs, five scout groups, a senior citizens' group, coffee after services, occasional buffet meals for the congregation, and a shelter program for the homeless that is operated on a rotating basis with other churches in the neighborhood.

Lafayette's endowment at this writing is zero. Its $100,000 annual budget, to the St. Bart's $3.2 million, has to be raised from its worshippers. It pays its minister $9,000 a year. Plus housing, of course. We'll get to what Father Bowers of St. Barts is paid later.

"DON'T BE BROKE FOR CHRISTMAS! GET REV. IKE'S CHRIST-
MAS MONEY BLESSING."

*Mailing from the New York reverend's tax-exempt United Christian
Evangelistic Association*

The chief benefactor of God's Builders, the Internal Revenue
Service, is studiously sympathetic to the primacy of maintaining
the separation of church and state. In fact, some of the favorite
reading of ambitious New Yorkers is IRS Publication 557 (Rev. July
1985), page six. This explains that except in limited and, fortunately, ambiguously defined circumstances, houses of faith do not
even have to file a 990, the financial disclosure form required of
other not-for-profit tax-exempt organizations. You will find that
this imparts an added sense of zest to the many and varied
metaphysical ventures that are available to you in Gotham as an
alternative to erecting towers and fostering music missions.

Along with several U.N. dignitaries, we attended the Eastern
Orthodox investiture some years ago at the First Avenue United
Nations Chapel of Mario Maimone, a thirty-five-year-old former
airline hijacker.

Maimone, who had commandeered a Rome-bound DC-9 and
demanded an audience with the Pope, was arrayed for the solemn
occasion in lapidary-colored robes and a penitential headdress,
beneath which trailed a sapphire-studded pectoral cross, the
entire effect being accented by the cognac diamond smoking on
his pinkie. The stones, he said proudly, were genuine, as was his
commitment to the paths of conventional spirituality. "I have to
make a living," he elaborated. He was planning to charge a
$2,000-a-year membership fee at his new church. We ask those of
you who are also incorporating, after, of course, a conversion
experience, to study the following guidelines:

Right: Devernon LeGrand, a self-styled Brooklyn bishop, tooled
around town in chauffeur-driven flashy cars and pulled in an
estimated $250,000 a year—with the aid of maybe eleven "sis-
ters," by some of whom he allegedly had fathered nineteen
children. Attired in nun's habits and shaking tambourines, the
women manned sidewalk begging bowls. The state attorney general was unable to go through with his pledge to put the "reverend" out of business because LeGrand effectively had *chartered
his church as a convent:* its sisters were required by a nonrevoca-

ble clause in its constitution to take care of the founder (LeGrand) and his family (the nun "harem") for the rest of their earthly lives. The bishop finally did go too far, but not in a direction that would interest you. When last heard from he was doing twenty-five years to life for killing two of his followers.

Wrong: Lawrence Ranucci, the bishop of the Life Science Church, and his assistants just got too big (allegedly taking in $10 million) too fast and lost control of the "parishes" that their ministers—including more than a thousand New York City public employees, most of them cops—were registering for tax exemptions. For an initial fee averaging $3,500, the pastors received church credentials, tax instructions, and training on *how to give one's entire life (especially one's house) to God* (one would not want to leave so much as a pebble unturned, lest a local school tax collector sneak under it). But, honestly, if you were the IRS, wouldn't you have questioned the euphony of the Church of Transmission, as one overly pedantic auto transmission dealer named his house of worship? The bishop was sentenced to up to seven years and ordered to pay his back taxes: $834,000.

Right: The three-man St. John of Rila Eastern Orthodox Monastery, a former Long Island Roman Catholic church properly re-roofed with an onion dome, was registered with New York State as a not-for-profit corporation for objectives that included to provide a home for its monks and "buy, sell, own, manage and operate real property, and personal property." The monastery's archimandrite, the Right Reverend Paul Ischi was a former Episcopal minister who had left his Philadelphia diocese one step ahead of a move to defrock him that he claimed was due to a philosophical disagreement. He was listed as a director of the monastery corporation. Under his baptismal name, William Vaughn Ischie, Jr., he was registered with the same state office as a real estate broker. A firm owned by the monastery, Barnesdale Realty, also was registered with that state office—as a for-profit enterprise. It turned out to be in the business of real estate development.

"Father Paul is a very knowledgable real estate man," enthused Leon Casper, senior vice-president of Cushman & Wakefield, one of the country's leading property brokers.

Casper and a Chase Manhattan Bank executive were among the references we received from Ischie after replying to a cryptic ad that, at the time of writing, was still running in national publications like the *Times, Fortune,* and the *Wall Street Journal:* a religious corporation was soliciting donations of "hard to sell, distressed and other real estate." To be sure, there was no reference from the Philadelphia zoning board, on which Ischie had sat until his resignation amid allegations of conflict of interest (which he denied) involving property he once owned in that city. But the archimandrite was admirably forthright about his current credo: "We have a long track record of trying to structure contributions not only to our benefit but to the advantage of the donor," said his cover letter. It was attached to an IRS ruling attesting to the monastery's tax-deductible status.

The federal government being discreet about private freedoms, only the IRS, God, and the James River Dixie Northern Corporation know how much that giant toilet-paper manufacturer took as a deduction when, in 1983, it gave the monastery a Pennsylvania building it had been valuing at $2.3 million. The monastery sold the building three days later for $250,000. A Philadelphia firm did a graceful segue that involved transferring a warehouse to the monastery, taking a tax deduction, then renting part of the building back for $100 a month. According to property-tax records, the real estate mogul Harry Helmsley donated 151 acres of rural land in New York State on which Barnesdale, the monastery's for-profit arm, subsequently sought a zoning change to build 350 condominiums. Unsuccessfully, as it turned out, but fortunately they weren't starving back at the House of God. Ischie spoke of doing good works: "We've paid to bury people . . . people's rent . . . purchased food for a good number of people, paid tuition for a number of students, and published a number of books." He also conducts services that are attended by local people. "We do what monks are supposed to do," he elaborated.

As the white-gloved ushers pass the famous plastic collection buckets at the Rev. Ike's Moorish palace, a former movie theater at the far end of Broadway from Trinity, on unfashionable 175th Street, the nation's most ingenious black evangelist watches contentedly. "I'm goin'," Ike shouts, with a laugh that bubbles deep from the springs of belief, "to give you a little preview. The title of my message this Sunday is going to be '*I-I-I* Am Money."

"*Praise God!*" the crowd choruses.

We have caught a glimpse of June (*Lassie*) Lockhart in Ike's congregation on one of his telecasts, the telecasts that carry his commercials for Good Luck, and are along in the hope of getting her autograph and receiving "THE MIGHTY SNOWBALL BLESSING!"

This is outlined in the prayer treatment that a lady is selling at a table near the sanctuary door. The well-dressed couple next to us are sharing a copy, gripping it like a talisman.

"Like a mighty rolling SNOWBALL," it explains, God's blessings will become "bigger and bigger, greater and greater: blessings of GOOD HEALTH, HAPPINESS, LOVE, SUCCESS, PROSPERITY, INFINITE MONEY.... Thank you, Father! thank you, God-in-me!"

Since this science of positive thinking ("a right attitude will make you RICH in every way") has worked well for Ike, he is not bashful about talking about it. He leans into the microphone and does a little patter about his collection of Rolls-Royces.

"I've more cars than I can ride in," he chants in his rich baritone. "More clothes than I can wear, the fourteen million dollars just came to me ... oh, people, this is the kind of living that God *intended* for people. How many of *you* want to live like this?"

"Thank you, Jesus!"

Dear Commissioners of the IRS: What we like about the Rev. Ike is we can contribute to his Blessing Plan in easy installments. As little as $10 a month. We would like to share with you the experience of one couple who mailed him a $100 "love offering." They received a check that very same day for $10,000, and a brand-new gold Cadillac. We think from the Lord, though the letter from the couple that is reproduced in Ike's brochure doesn't give the secret of that blessing away.

"THE PEALES DRIVE A MAROON AND GOLD CADILLAC SE-VILLE. IF THEY CAN AFFORD IT, WHICH THEY CERTAINLY CAN, THEY DESERVE IT."

From the authorized biography of the Rev. Dr. Norman Vincent Peale, author of The Power of Positive Thinking

---

New York's best-known white positive thinker was well into his twilight years when, for those of his followers who wanted to enter their golden years with some positive *planning,* his tax-exempt Foundation for Christian Living published three special booklets. A cover letter introduced these as the answer to requests from "hundreds of friends" for an annuity program that would "protect their standard of living against inflation and unexpected emergencies, but after their passing, yield the Foundation funds to carry on its important ministry."

"I feel so much better now," declared the headline on the cover of one of the pamphlets over a picture of a smiling silver-haired woman.

Thanks to such epiphanies, the foundation, which pumps out thirty-four million spiritual messages a year from its campus in a small town outside New York, has a balance sheet that might make even William Sloane Coffin, Jr., Peale's liberal antipode at Riverside Church, jealous. In 1984, the last year for which figures are available, the organization was running a $313,000 surplus, on $11.4 million revenues. The foundation's director stressed that Peale didn't get a cent from this when first interviewed by a reporter. We thought about this for a while, then reinterviewed him. How about Peale's wife, Ruth?

"Mrs. Peale is the chief executive officer of Foundation for Christian Living. She is the administrator," the director said. He wouldn't comment on whether she is salaried.

Peale, as it turned out, was drawing a salary from *Guideposts,* his 4.1-million-circulation $6.95-a-year magazine. Being inspirational by nature, this also is a tax-exempt, not-for-profit corporation. "It is a small salary," said an aide. "He essentially is its chief executive officer." Peale's undoubted fortune derives mostly, of course, from his books and speaking engagements. The authorized biography opens with a description of a discourse that the clergyman delivered to a sales convention: "Peale is perhaps at his best when speaking to a group of sales people: he understands them and they love him."

For those who wish to make more intimate studies of the techniques for emulating the Peale lifestyle—a country estate, dinner in the good old days with Ferdinand and Imelda, house-guesting with the Chiang Kai-sheks—a $3 million addition to the Christian Living Foundation is planned. Chaired by Art Linkletter, the Norman Vincent Peale Center for Positive Thinking already has made a preemptive strike against skeptics: "Surprised at 'monument' for Dr. Peale?" says a fact sheet apparently prepared to help staff deal with the press. "Dr. Peale is humble and modest and was reluctant to approve such a project until it was made clear to him that the Center is to be a live, vital place for scholars and visitors to experience positive thinking."

Positive Thinking in Action: The school board in Carmel, the New York town where *Guideposts* is published, tried to force the enterprise onto the tax rolls. Peale retorted that if that happened, he'd fold his big top and over three hundred Carmel residents would lose their jobs. The board capitulated.

Peale's Legacy: The Venus of Abscam, Rita Jenrette, whose famous copulation with her then husband the congressman on the Capitol steps was followed by her appearance in the movie *Zombie Island Massacre,* now worships at Marble Collegiate, the Fifth Avenue church where Peale made his pulpit until his retirement. She sits in an unobtrusive balcony pew and has been spending one night a month working as a counselor at a shelter for the homeless. While we're on the subject of homelessness, when several representatives of the forty thousand held a Lenten vigil on Fifth Avenue, Peale's successor, the Rev. Dr. Arthur Caliandro, provided coffee, cake, and bathroom facilities. The doors of St. Thomas Church and St. Patrick's Cathedral remained closed.

Peale's Parsonage: Though the clergyman's Fifth Avenue apartment, across from the Metropolitan Museum of Art, has been described in press interviews and even in his own biography as the Marble Collegiate parsonage, the church did not reclaim it after he retired. Initially, a Marble spokeswoman said that was because he remained the *senior* minister of the Collegiate Reformed Dutch churches in the city. There are four of them, which doubtless explained why Peale hadn't been seen at Marble since leaving its staff. He was keeping in touch by phone, said the spokeswoman. Eventually, Dr. Caliandro cleared up the mystery. Peale had been voted the use of the parsonage for life not in return for new duties, but to honor "his service to the world."

Who took that crucial vote? We found a potential clue in Peale's biography. " . . . the finances of the Collegiate Church are not controlled by Marble, nor even Dr. Peale," it crowed, "but by the Board of the Collegiate Church Corporation. The Collegiate Corporation has the unique distinction of being the oldest institution in the new world. . . . Its charter was granted by King William III of England in 1696. As such the Collegiate Church Corporation has privileges and prerequisites [sic] no one can touch—not the city of New York, the Internal Revenue Service, or the denomination."

The corporation, which is so secretive that several officials at other denominations whom we consulted had never heard of it, is on John Street, in the financial district. Location isn't the only similarity to Trinity, the Wall Street Episcopal church: Collegiate owns twenty towers in the financial district and midtown and part of the land under Rockefeller Center.

Collegiate clerk-treasurer Robert Williams brusquely declined to disclose any financial data. "It's poor taste, vulgar to talk about it," he said. "Spiritual things are much more important than monetary things." The corporation supports its churches, including a

Harlem parish, and donates amounts—which, naturally, are undisclosed—to educational institutions and benevolent causes.

Again like Trinity?

"My job here is held by three different people at Trinity," said Williams. "*I* start at six in the morning and work until nine or ten p.m. every evening. We have five employees in this office and about one hundred and fifty altogether, including the four churches and all the real estate. We run a very lean ship here. No big salaries or extravagance. Strictly shirt sleeves. Trinity does things on a more luxurious level. We're an old church, older than Trinity. Our charter is on sheepskin. Trinity's charter came, you know, a year later."

The Collegiate official was no longer irritated.

"Probably," he said helpfully, "the Roman Catholics are number one for office buildings owned." He urged us to call John J. Reynolds, the realty firm owned by Harry Helmsley, he elaborated, that handles the archdiocese's transactions. He gave us the phone number.

Even with Peale on your side, you can't win 'em all.

The Catholic archdiocese, which pays its pastors $425 a month, has many ways of raising revenue, but commercial real estate ownership isn't one of them. It makes total financial disclosure, and John Reynolds, of the realty firm, recalled only one income-producing property of any size, the land under the Helmsley Palace Hotel. It brings in $1 million a year.

"UNWARRANTED REPETITION OF MUSICAL PHRASES, SINGING OF MULTIPLE VERSES, INSTRUMENTAL MUSIC GRATUITOUSLY INSERTED AS 'MINI-CONCERTS'—THIS KIND OF THING BOTH DELAYS THE LITURGICAL ACTION AT THE ALTAR AND DISTRACTS THE PEOPLE...AND WHILE WE ARE GRATEFUL TO SEE THAT MOST 'FOLK MUSIC' GROUPS ARE APPROPRIATELY ATTIRED FOR THE SANCTUARY, WE STILL NOTE ATTIRE, HERE AND THERE, WHICH IS MUCH MORE FITTING FOR OUTDOOR BARBECUES."

"THE PULPIT IS NOT THE PLACE FOR THEOLOGICAL SPECULATION."

"THE PRIEST WHO WILL NOT ACCEPT AN ASSIGNMENT COULD FIND HIMSELF WITHOUT ANY ASSIGNMENTS. THE

PASTOR WHO WILL NOT ACCEPT AN ASSISTANT COULD FIND HIMSELF WITHOUT ANY ASSISTANT."

What the thoughts of Chairman Mao were to the Red Guard, Bishop John O'Connor's twenty-three-page letter from which the above extracts were taken was intended to be to the Catholic priests of Scranton, Pennsylvania. Five months after it went out, the Pope promoted him to archbishop of New York.

A press photographer covering O'Connor's 1984 barnstorm through some of the farther-flung stretches of the archdiocese nicknamed him "the archduke." It was, after all, rather as if a European monarch were visiting. Carrying bouquets, gifts, and welcome banners, flustered crowds pushed into the churches and parochial schools to crane for a peek at the chief priest. In his black robes and fuchsia cap and red rose anti-abortion button, he eased himself out of his limousine to tour a women's shelter in the Newburgh ghetto. After asking each woman how she was doing, he climbed back into his conveyance and, escorted in a mini-motorcade by state police, drove the one block to the men's shelter.

"It was as if," says the photographer, "he was inspecting the troops. I was rather surprised."

We weren't. We are his troops. You are his troops. You don't have to be Catholic. The onetime Pentagon chief chaplain considers all New York his battlefield—for a war that, according to a bulletin by the *Daily News*'s syndicated columnist Liz Smith, now targets sodden socialites of all denominations as well as the ghastly lineup of Peacenik Bishops, Female Baby Murderers, and Gay Perverts. The philanthropist Brooke Astor had invited the cardinal to mingle at one of her elegant little dinner parties with folks like Felix Rohatyn, a $2-million-a-year investment banker who is the chairman of the Municipal Assistance Corporation and an outspoken critic of the circus's pervasive desire to caviar-coat its charity. Brooke was hoping to spark a civilized discussion about what could be done for the betterment of one and all in New York, wrote Smith, but this admirable goal was temporarily sidetracked by some slight stickiness about whether O'Connor or another prelate in the party, the Most Rev. John Maury Allin, at the time the head of the entire Episcopal Church, should say the blessing. O'Connor was relegated, Smith said, to the closing grace and rose to his feet to say that "he didn't particularly approve of everybody drinking, but would say that 'it was very good food'."

"I feel certain," Allin would say later, "that he was just joking..."

As those social drinkers in the crush who hadn't realized it was a joke blanched, the Episcopal bishop made some remarks about what he felt was needed to help the disadvantaged.

"Archbishop O'Connor followed by saying that all such comments were well and good and very nice, but that all the church could actually do was try to help people learn to better themselves!" Smith reported.

There has been much speculation that what O'Connor is really trying to do is wield the same absolute moral and political authority in the city and nation as a predecessor at the Chancery once did, the late Francis Cardinal "Check it with the Powerhouse" Spellman. If so, the new cardinal has a way to go.

Spellman's power was such that immediately after he tiraded against the immorality of the Broadway stage, the police raided a burlesque show called *Wine, Women and Song,* which featured a fan dancer and a comic. Consider, however, what transpired after the current Catholic hierarchy heard that a forthcoming biography of Spellman, *The American Pope,* would accuse the primate of contracting homosexual liaisons with, among others, a chorus boy from the show *One Touch of Venus.* The best O'Connor could come up with to defend the late prelate's name and hence that of the church was a deputation to the New York Times Company—at the time the owner of Times Books, the biography's publisher. Not a cop in sight. According to an article in *Forum* magazine by Eric Nadler, the deputation consisted of the former U.S. ambassador to Ireland, John Moore, and Edward Larkin, chairman of the executive committee of W. R. Grace & Co. They met with Sydney Gruson, the Times Company's vice-chairman.

By Moore's account to *Forum,* he told the *Times* official that the homosexuality charges were false and "it was quite evident [the biography's author, John Cooney] didn't have any substantiation." The allegations indeed were attributed primarily to secondhand sources—for instance, Gore Vidal, who'd known a wealthy Catholic whose East Side town house supposedly was the scene of homosexual parties attended by the prelate—rather than to firsthand sources, such as the purported lovers themselves. "[Gruson] agreed with me," Moore told the *Forum* reporter.

"That's not true," counters Gruson. "I said I wished they hadn't come because we didn't need a visit from them. We had decided well before that [to demand substantiation]."

In an attempt to satisfy those demands, Cooney located a Greenwich Village man who said he had had an affair with the cardinal and was willing to tell Times Books about it. The man evinced an impressive knowledge of Spellman, Spellman's relatives, and Spellman's apartments at the chancery, which persuaded Cooney that his story was genuine.

"[Spellman] was a nice old man. He was whimsical. He helped me get my secondhand dealer's license," the man told us tremulously.

Times Books declined to interview the man.

"It was too dicey," says Gruson. Short of someone finding some tapes, there was, indeed, no way to check the man's veracity.

Though some wags were wondering whether the Times Books History Project was about to be set up (to censor all uncheckable excesses from the life of Henry VIII), the biography would now merely state that "numerous priests and others interviewed took [Spellman's] homosexuality for granted." On the other hand, nothing else was missing from what Spellman's defenders foamed was a hatchet job. The late prince of the church was portrayed hard at work at such activities as cultivating rich old women in the hope that they would bequeath their worldly goods to the church. "Whenever he could, Spellman visited [the widow of a president of U.S. Steel] on the way home from a banquet, grabbing flowers from the head table on the way out as a present for her," the book asserted.

We assume that Gruson may not be welcome at some archdiocesan Perrier parties. The *Times* official can remedy this, however, by the simple act of expressing fealty to the cardinal: "How can you not get along with a guy who, when you say, 'Hello, your Excellency,' on the phone, says, 'Hello, your Majesty,'" as Ed Koch once glibly deadpanned. This was when reporters sought his reaction to O'Connor's ultimately successful move to kill a mayoral ban on discrimination against homosexuals in city-funded hiring.

The archdiocese has devised its own solution to the "shameful lusts" of homosexuals.

Taking the cure: It's simple, folks, really. Since, according to official church teaching, it is your homosexual *activity,* as opposed to your homosexual orientation, that is morally wrong, all you have to do is adopt the same ascetic standard as unmarried straight Catholics. Chastity. Lifelong chastity, in your instance. Father John Harvey, a moral theologian, runs Courage, a support group for Catholic homosexuals who agree to do, as the archimandrite of the three-man monastery would put it, what monks are supposed to do.

Courage chapters—which have been lumbering to life in Phila-delphia, St. Louis, Chicago, and some other cities besides New York—must be directed by priests, according to the group's handbook, and members are mandated to partake in "service to others, spiritual reading, prayer, meditation, individual spiritual direction, frequent attendance at Mass and the frequent reception of the sacraments of penance and the Holy Eucharist." Service, another booklet explains, gives a homosexual "a sense of achieve-ment and of self-acceptance which he needs." Members of the group who become "disruptive" can be expelled.

Between thirty and fifty men belong to it in New York. In 1984, organizer Harvey, who is not gay ("I think there is an advantage in being able to stand back . . . ," he says, "so I can help make a judgment"), expanded the effort, starting a separate women's group.

"CATHOLIC HOMOSEXUAL WOMEN: TO BE CHASTE TAKES
COURAGE
SPIRITUAL SUPPORT GROUP, 424 WEST 34TH STREET
CALL 421-0426"

Ad in the Village Voice *in the "Counseling" classifieds*

"We ran an advertisement for six weeks and hardly got any response," Father Harvey says disconsolately.

Nothing can interrupt the circus in New York. Well, nothing much. The forces of rectitude have scored one or two triumphs. A classified advertising clerk at the *New York Native,* a leading gay weekly, went to lunch one day, got born again, and did not come back. Sometime after this, the Unbroken Chain Fellowship, a fundamentalist Christian group whose Broadway, music, and modeling industry members include Roberta Flack's bass and synthesizer players and a former *Dreamgirls* star, Ben Harney, got word on the divine hotline that a gay porn theater, the Adonis, at 839 Eighth Avenue, was going to be deeded to it by God for a church.

Accordingly, the group laid siege to the "Male Flagship Theatre of the Nation" ("The Best in Male Erotica"). The designer-dressed faithful could be seen circling the building, murmuring prayers and stroking the walls—in a Biblical laying on of hands.

"That's how Joshua took the city of Jericho in the Old Testament," bubbled a pretty young singer. Indeed. But even though the *Native* gave the fundamentalist group an unexpected boost—grumbling that the Adonis, in whose darkened seats many types of entertainment go on, "does not offer AIDS information or safe sex literature to its customers"—the theater stayed open. "A lot of this AIDS business is a media blowup," its night manager said sourly as the born-agains kept filing past.

Fortunately, the moral minority have been getting another assist from Where It Counts. The vessel for this is Our Lady of Flushing, Veronica Lueken, a plump Queens housewife who from time to time witnesses a supernatural Mardi Gras in the skies above the site that housed the Vatican pavilion at the 1965 World's Fair in Flushing Meadow park: Michael the archangel, glorified nuns, the saints, and, regular as clockwork, the Blessed Virgin Mary and her son. As the faithful feverishly chanted the Rosary one summer's evening in 1984, Veronica knelt before the stone altar just east of the Unisphere: "And Our Lady and Jesus now—I can see them—they are coming from quite a distance, but they're both coming down together. . . . I can notice the shining crown upon her head. . . . and Jesus now has tapped her on the shoulder."

And just what did Our Lady have to tell New Yorkers?

"The children, the innocent children, are victims of debauchery. The children—many of them shall die. We shall set upon your nation, and other nations of the world, a mysterious disease. . . . Any country that allows homosexuals to roam and to seduce the young shall be destroyed."

That Lueken's hordes of followers did not take to the streets at this may be because they were confused by the BVM's simultaneous frantic tocsin to "protect your homes. I have asked you many times to bar your homes to all but your immediate family and close Shrine workers, for those who knock upon your doors will be evil, and will be sent to invade you."

ALTERNATIVES

The Salvation Army, after dallying with homophobia for just long enough to beat the archdiocese to page one of the *Times* in opposing the mayor's ban on discrimination in city-funded hiring, embarked on an exuberant new crusade. New, in religion as in all else in the Onion, is what counts. "Accompanied on stage by his wife, Rose," said an Army press release, an evangelist called Mike Warnke would describe his former life as a hippie, Marine corps medic, drug addict/pusher and *a priest presiding over a coven of witches.* As part of the Army's Friday Evening at the Temple series. Witchcraft is rather popular these days with those yuppies who do not go to Grace Episcopal. Some of them do complain, however, that the Old Religion is being commercialized by the growth in the city of such emporiums as Magickal Childe. This West Nineteenth Street store does a roaring trade in dead bats, green candles (for money), brown candles (retribution), and, for those New Yorkers requiring help from the blacker arts, $75 human skulls. Clearly, Warnke's warning was overdue. The audience, mostly young Salvationists in orthopedic shoes, screamed amen as the evangelist warmed to his message. This concluded with a musical medley, including one number with the line "I know I am but a worm/ So step on me God and let me squirm."

This sort of exhibition is not going to get you invited to Brooke's next party for the clergy. Some more realistic options are as follows:

Rescue a Loved One from a Cult

Advantages: Many photo opportunities. Rita Lachman, the former wife of the Revlon tycoon, called us after visiting her daughter Charlene during a parents' weekend at Rajneeshpuram, the Oregon town run by Bhagwan Shree Rajneesh until the feds persuaded the so-called swami of sex to leave the country. Charlene was among his followers, and Rita, who was his guest at a champagne brunch, had hit on the idea of mounting a one-woman campaign against him. Rita-style. "I'm trying to save our American children. I have exclusive pictures, rubbers," she said. "It's a *ter-ri-fic* story." The rubbers were from the guru's anti-AIDS kit. We demurred. The tale of heinous goings-on at the $100 million city had been overwritten. Not with *this* angle, Rita retorted. She produced an article about her visit that had appeared in a paper in her native Germany. "See. I am on top of the page with big headlines, about how I am the Revlon widow going to visit Charlene—naturally, I want her home." Underneath that story, in very small print, as she rightly pointed out, was a story about Jackie O.

Join a Cult

Advantages: Facilitates both your spiritual and material progress, though this can require patience. John-Roger, for instance,
the chapter two way-shower, can be seen on videotape at the 365
Canal Street center of his Movement of Spiritual Inner Awareness.
He became the physical embodiment of the Mystical Traveler
Consciousness in 1963 after kidney-stone surgery, and there's
been nothing like it since Wilhelm Reich's discovery of orgone
energy. If you ask the Consciousness to work with you, it will
gradually escort you, for a very reasonable outlay on books, tapes,
and seminars, through the physical, astral, causal, mental, and
etheric realms to the Soul Realm. You also may give up smoking,
lose weight, no longer feel jealous, angry, depressed, or hurt—and
become prosperous.

Would a way-shower produce a drought?

The most celebrated apostle of J-R, as he is known to his
followers, is probably the author and socialite Arianna Stassinopoulos. His fifty-hour "Insight" training scheme "changed my
life," she has said. She meant spiritually, of course. Still, about a
year after traveling with him to the Bronx to present Mother
Teresa with the John-Roger Foundation's Integrity Award (she
wrote up the conversation that they had en route for Andy
Warhol's *Interview*), she did happen to marry the heir to a $300
million oil fortune, Michael Huffington. Ann Getty was the matron
of honor at the St. Bartholomew's ceremony. Barbara Walters was
a bridesmaid, and the guests included Jerry Zipkin and Henry
Kissinger. Lousy photo opportunities, however. The bride had
spoken of having a cameraman, camouflaged in choir robes,
record her nuptials from behind the altar, but the plan was
dropped. "It had become a question about whether it could be
done in good taste and they were wrestling with lighting problems," says a St. Bart's minister.

Become a Buddhist

Advantages: One of the chief teachings of the many Tibetan
lamas in exile in New York is that the physical world is only an
illusion, which is obviously one way to deal with life in Manhattan. And it's rather like double coupon day at the supermarket:
two religions for the price of one, since you don't have to be
Buddhist to be a Buddhist in New York. One frequently publicized local Zen community, Greyston, which supplies breads and
cakes to Hamptons delis and elegant stores like Bloomingdale's

and B. Altman, has as its sensei, or abbot, Bernard Glassman—a former aerospace engineer who sees no conflict, says a spokeswoman for the community, in also being a practicing Jew, since the community is "interreligious" in its approach to Zen. His wife keeps a kosher home and, during holy days, a Zen rabbi conducts services at the community's mansion, the former summer home of the Dodge family. For Buddhist Catholics who are in residence, there is a Zen Jesuit priest.

Become a Moonie

Advantages: Easy entry requirements into what yet may become a circus sect of choice. While the Rev. Sun Myung Moon was incarcerated, after his run-in with the IRS, recruitment seemed to be flagging, so Moonie missionaries fanned out across the swankier reaches of the Upper East Side, attempting to proselytize at, among other silk-stocking establishments, the Church of Heavenly Rest. They were snubbed in an attempt to enlist the latter's Rev. Hugh Hildesley but promptly "tried to get my curate," he says. Poor Moon. We sent a reporter to join up at the Unification Church's headquarters at 4 West Forty-third Street. He opted for "associate membership," which requires a $10 application fee and giving as much money and energy as you can to Moon's efforts to breed a spiritual super-race. You can collect your enrollment form at the fourth-floor reception desk and may get acquainted while you are there with Dr. Mose Durst, the church's U.S. president. His office is approached through an electronically operated heavy wood door, equipped with an antijimmying guard and a chicken-wired glass viewhole.

"HE CAME TO BROOKLYN TO FIND THE TRUTH."

A Lubavitcher rabbi, after Bob Dylan was deborn-again

Despite a rumor that he was baptised in Pat Boone's swimming pool, Bob Dylan, by birth Jewish, never took the formal conversion plunge when he became a born-again Christian, says an acquaintance of the star. Indeed, some time after his repentant thunderings in "Saved" and "Slow Train Coming," the singer abruptly refused a invitation from the National Music Publishers

Association to present its Gospel Song of the Year award in New York. "He won't have time to do it," the acquaintance elaborated. "He has to be in California . . . for his son's bar mitzvah." A year later, the star moved in with the Lubavitchers, an ultra-orthodox Brooklyn Hasidic sect. To find his Jewish roots. The implication was clear—Dylan did not understand our next lesson, the *politics* of New York religion. If he had embraced the teachings of the Satmar, a rival group of dogmatists, he might have gotten a grant toward his religious tuition costs from:

The Frederick W. Richmond Foundation.

Williamsburg, the Brooklyn neighborhood where thirty thousand Satmars live in a tightly knit Yiddish-speaking community, was part of Richmond's district at the time that the millionaire Democratic congressman suffered a slight hiccup in his career. Never needlessly discreet about his preferences—"Yeah," he guffawed in a gay bar one night, "I'm a congressman, you know"— Richmond had paid a sixteen-year-old black Washington youth for a tryst. This culminated in some unpleasantness in court and raised the problem of an approaching Democratic primary in which, sure as the Torah teaches that he who sympathizes with the commission of a sin is worse than the sinner, every Satmar of voting age would go the polls.

Sin? The Satmar believe that homosexuality is an "abomination."

Atoning for abominations costs.

By the time a group of Satmar rabbis visited the congressman's district office, the Richmond foundation, which always had been as generous with the United Talmudical Academy as with the Sacred Heart Day Care Center, had perceived new need just crying out to be assuaged everywhere it looked in Jewish Williamsburg. And, of course, if Richmond stayed in office, the neighborhood would continue to act like a giant electromagnet on federal housing dollars. If Bernard Gifford, the black former deputy school chancellor who was his opponent, were to win, the money would go to build high-rises in Botswana or somewhere.

"The meeting was very businesslike," a former Richmond aide recalls. "The rabbis' attitude was 'How do we limit the damage?'"

It was decided that the congressman would apologize to key rabbis at a special meeting.

"Better a faygeleh [faggot] than a schvarze [nigger]," one of the rabbis added with a sigh of relief.

That took care of Gifford with the Jewish vote. But how did Richmond explain his tumble in the teenage hay to the district's large population of Polish and Italian Catholics?

"Fred's guy in those neighborhoods told everybody that Fred was drunk and thought it was a woman," says the former aide.

Smartass. We supposed they told the constituency's *black* voters that the kid was white?

"Every Sunday Fred was in town when he was a congressman, he would go to a black church and give a sermon," the ex-aide says triumphantly. Fred Richmond is Jewish.

Such a waste. After creaming the Gifford competition and going on to win the November election, the pol enjoyed a delightful romp with an escaped con (whom he'd placed in a job at the House of Representatives), but then had to resign his seat after pleading guilty to common-day New York activities. Marijuana possession, tax evasion . . .

Fortunately, the spirit of ethnic reconciliation that he pioneered lives on.

"Hallelujah! Hallelujah! Hallelujah!"

The man setting up the chant at the Brooklyn Tabernacle, a large auditorium on the borough's Flatbush Avenue, clasps a mike in one hand, flings his other arm in the air as he whips the capacity congregation, most of whom are Hispanic or black, into an exhausting frenzy of antiphonal adoration that will last for two and a half hours.

The man, Pastor Jim Cymbala, is white, but he knows the Holy Roll.

"Let's give God a wonderful clap!"

They lift their voices in the "blood hymns" and, after the pastor dedicates a baby—"gonna be a little beauty queen"—there is testimony from a young CBS-TV executive about his struggle to bring the Lord into an industry that "is really ruled by Satan."

The Lord does pretty well on the first two passings of the wicker offering baskets.

It is time for the third.

"We have to take a building-fund offering," exhorts Cymbala. The piano strikes up. "We are expanding down the block a little to give a little more room for the children. We signed a lease. We have to fix up the building. . . . I need a couple of hundred of you to give twenty-five dollars today . . . let the records be kept, Lord, for everyone who gives today. There are people who might make a hundred-dollar, a five-hundred-dollar offering today, Lord . . . *the angels are writing it down!"*

Let it be recorded by them, then, that the elderly lady next to us finally has found a crumpled dollar in her purse.

"Normally, we only have one collection," says a Tabernacle official.

"AND WHILE I KNOW THAT IT WAS THE PEOPLE WHO ELECTED ME, IT WAS GOD WHO SELECTED ME."

Mayor Ed Koch, in a speech at Mount Nebo Baptist Church in Harlem, April 1985

Just expressing his gratitude to the Deity, the mayor later explained. It is to God, of course, that the Rev. Thomas Bowers of St. Bartholomew's also gave thanks after he was first called to build the tower to help the poor. But with the New York Landmarks Preservation Commission voting early in 1986 to block the church's lofty plans, it is no longer putting its trust entirely in prayer. A church official, Peter Lareau, explains that constitutional specialists have been retained to argue the case all the way to the United States Supreme Court. Where, Lareau says in the most Christian of tones, the entire New York City landmarks act doubtless will be thrown out.

And then just think how many skyscrapers y'all can build.

Many must be the time that, chewing on one of his good cigars, Bowers has reflected on what a shame it all is. Here you have a church that currently can afford to spend only $100,000 out of its $3.2 million annual budget on the needy, a figure that might increase tenfold if the tower plan went ahead, and yet Brooke and Jackie are talking about preserving a heap of stone. "Do you think Mrs. Astor thinks about Harlem? Do you think Mrs. Onassis knows what it is to starve?" the pastor is said to have stewed. Since this liberal is a proud man, he is hardly going to come right out and admit what a tough time he is having at making ends meet himself. His salary is only $64,311. Admittedly, this is exclusive of $72,000 in benefits, according to opponents of the development; about $46,000, according to church official Lareau.

Bowers's Parsonage: The benefits include an allowance for maintenance costs on the rectory, a $2.5 million, thirteen-room Park Avenue apartment ($1 million, insists Lareau). *Bowers's* rectory, on paper at least. When the rector moved to New York from his Atlanta pulpit in 1978, the place was sold to him for $250,000, according to an affidavit filed by opponents of the planned skyscraper. Not that the minister actually paid over a cent of that, the affidavit adds, citing church financial records. Despite its supposedly parlous finances, the church simply took back a $15,000 demand note and gave God's Would-be Builder a

$235,000 loan at 4 percent interest. The following year, the church laid out $75,000 for "rectory improvements," the court document notes. We asked Peter Lareau, the St. Bart's official, about this. Just a shuffle of paper, he said breezily, in order to give the rector the "tax benefits" of home ownership. If Bowers should leave his job, the parsonage will be shuffled back. Not for $250,000, presumably. According to a tax lawyer, the IRS normally would require it to be sold back for its "fair market value"— which would give the priest a huge windfall profit. St. Bart's vestrymen insisted, however, that the buy-back would be for "a modest amount," as low as $2,500 a year for each year Bowers serves.

"A tax avoidance scheme," sneered the opponents of the tower plan in their affidavit. "This seems to be a new version of an old dodge," said the tax lawyer, himself a former St. Bart's official. "It doesn't generally work."

We thought that Father Bowers might like to accelerate his controversial miniature version of Fifth Avenue Presbyterian's happy real estate event, sell the thirteen-room sprawl back to the church right now, and donate his profit, if any, to the poor. Under this plan, the church in turn would unload the apartment and donate its profit in the same way, hence allowing the needy to get a jump on the income the rector will be giving them when the tower gets built. Peter Lareau said that wouldn't do at all: "He's got to live somewhere that fits his status as a leader of the church."

And there you have it, Father Bowers. Since the sidewalk outside St. Bartholomew's Church fits the status of the city's forty thousand homeless like a glove, you'll be glad to hear that you don't need to build the tower to help the poor to fix up the church and finance the TV ministry. . . and if only the vestry will let you keep the rectory for life, like Dr. Peale, presumably you'll also get to keep your tax benefits in perpetuity. Which in the end is what counts.

Let's give the IRS a wonderful clap!

5

RICH MAN, SHOW MAN

"THESE PEOPLE DON'T KNOW WHAT THEY'RE DOING, AND IT'S MARVELOUS."

A stagehand on the Broadway musical Singin' in the Rain, *which had a record fifty tons of sets and props, including a rainmaking machine, mountains with palm trees, a steam locomotive, a red trolley car, and a white Bugatti. When the show opened in 1985, to some of the worst reviews in recent memory, it had a cast of thirty-six. It was brought to you by forty-two stagehands, twenty-three wardrobe and wig people, twenty-four musicians, three stage managers, seven treasurers, one director, and three millionaires.*

Grown men have been reduced to quivering wimps by the diva sometimes dubbed The Beast of Broadway, Lauren Bacall. It would be reasonable to assume, therefore, that it was in something of a spirit of humility that the creative crew of *Woman of the Year* clustered in the back of a Boston theater to watch the star breathe life into this new musical at its first pre-Broadway tryout. The house lights dimmed, the director poised his pen to take notes, the orchestra whooped into the overture—when suddenly there was a loud commotion from somewhere in the audience. A few seconds passed, then two women were seen stalking up the aisle: Carole Shorenstein, a California property baron's daughter, and her mother. The crew recognized Carole. She was one of the show's producers and her face was volcanic with wrath, her dress swishing like a whip as she stormed toward them.

A last-minute casting dispute? A tiff over the score?

"They didn't like their seats," a *Woman* staffer gulps.

Such concerns traditionally have been accorded a low ranking among artistic priorities in the Broadway theater, but democracy—borne on the wings of skyrocketing production costs—is doing its refreshing work in what used to be the exclusive domain of a few professional showmen. With the average budget for a major new musical pushing $5 million, these professionals have begun taking in big investors like Carole as partners. No experience required. Just bring your checkbook. The Great White Way, New York's biggest tourist attraction, is now open to influence by any tourist with a few hundred thousand to gamble. About $400,000, in Shorenstein's case. That's the very respectable contribution she made to *Woman of the Year,* and the fact that her seats were not on the aisle was merely the final insult. She had expected to have input in the show, but instead, Lawrence Kasha, the show's veteran chief producer—his credits include TV's "Knots Landing" as well as other Broadway billings—had not even invited her to production conferences.

"They totally misrepresented this. I had a perfectly *horrible* time. I'm talking about four hundred thousand dollars," Carole seethes. "I'm not talking about four hundred dollars . . . We were treated like charpeople."

THE MAKING OF A PRODUCER

Synopsis of Scenes
Musical Numbers

ACT ONE

(Skip this section if you've never wondered why you walked out after the first twenty minutes of a $6 million Broadway musical after paying $20 to park, $80 for dinner, and $150 to a scalper for your tickets.)

Scene 1: Walter Shorenstein's office, somewhere in the Bay Area
          "We're in the Money" (with apologies to David Merrick)
          . . . Walt and Carole

Carole Shorenstein's father, Walter, the Sir Samuel LeFrak of San Francisco, had installed her as a San Francisco theater operator when she was twenty-eight, and there was no doubting her business acumen. She began importing "an impressive string" of Broadway hits, the San Francisco Sunday *Examiner & Chronicle* reported. But why be just an importer? Why not be a real producer? With that goal in mind, Carole *needed* to be part of Kasha's counsels, in order to learn about Broadway: "It was," she elaborates, "like my enrollment at graduate school."

Scene 2: Under the dryers at Kenneth's
　　　　　"Bertolt Brecht Loves Clairol"...The Living Theater
　　　　　School Ensemble, with reprise by Jerry Zipkin, Susan
　　　　　Gutfreund, and Tyler the Singing Pooch

Carole is one of the more serious-minded newcomers to producing. Circus luminaries have been registering for instruction in
such swarms that the production credits on Broadway shows are
becoming indistinguishable from the guest list at one of the better
dinner parties, and the bulk of them aren't in this as theater
operators: the theater is simply one more photo opportunity.
Indeed, come to think of it, instruction isn't really needed. Since
it's your moolah, you give the orders—"Dahling, ever since that
evening at the disco, I've thought that Imelda would be just the
thing for the lead in our revival of *How to Be a Jewish Mother*"—
as well as choosing what gets funded. Obviously you aren't going
to pick anything too esoteric, because you wouldn't understand
it. If you don't go for revivals, a nice Neil Simon, an adaptation
from a movie like *Woman of the Year,* or a British import—
preferably a drawing-room farce in which you can cast Lynn
Redgrave—will do equally well for the announcement of your
new career in the society columns. Do not be bashful about
responding to the critics who carp that the entire Great White
Way will soon be taken up by musicals and three or four plays, all
or most of the latter being by the amusing Mr. Simon.

What do they think the Off-Off-Broadway stage is for?

An heir to the Alexander's department store millions, Jonathan
Farkas, who for a while was billed as a producer on more
successful shows than David Merrick has had temper tantrums
(*Nine, My One & Only, La Cage aux Folles...*), put it better than
we ever could: "I like simple stories and visual desserts. I
wouldn't bring *Carmen* in if my life depended on it," he said in an
interview with the *New York Post.*

Scene 3: The dining room of an East Seventy-second Street
　　　　　townhouse
　　　　　"You're My Ticket"...ensemble, with reprise by Liza
　　　　　Minnelli and Chita Rivera

Farkas was speaking facetiously, of course, because he did help
bring in *The Rink.* "An investment in art," he called this musical
about a reunion between an estranged mother and her daughter in
a decaying roller rink, but to heck with art. What the wife of one
of the show's numerous millionaire producer-backers had set her

heart on was setting her table with its stars, Chita Rivera and Liza Minnelli. Such a delightful accent to the pink peonies and better-behaved than both the late Prince del Drago and the prize Guernsey cow that Claus von Bülow once arranged for a party at J. Paul Getty's British mansion. "We said Chita and Liza would be rehearsing, but the response was that there'd be twenty people there, all potential ticket buyers, and it would be all right for Chita and Liza to arrive late," scowls a show staffer. Jules Fisher, a professional producer and award-winning lighting designer, had charge of the tedious artistic and technical chores. These included rebuffing an attempt by Farkas to bring a TV set to the opening-night party. The producer had wanted to put it on his table so he and his friends could catch the reviews. The following morning, after the thrill of reading the *Times* panegyric had subsided ("the turgid, sour musical . . . is a curious affair," the paper's chief arbiter, Frank Rich, mused), the show's entire cast of millionaire backers crammed into a room at its advertising agency. The professionals associated with the production scratched their heads. What to do with so much good will in so small a space? How to keep these well-meaning benefactors occupied while the pros talked dollars and cents and marketing strategies? By putting them to work, of course. The task they were allotted normally is performed by a show's hirelings, people like the press agent, but no matter. The room soon hummed with happy activity as the millionaires began culling quotes from the less damning reviews for an ad campaign: "We didn't use their choices necessarily," says the show staffer, "but they felt they were having an input."

INTERMISSION

ACT TWO

Scene 1: Kenneth Greenblatt's office, somewhere in the garment
district
"Gotta Listen" . . . Ken, John, Mary, Martin, Jimmy, Hal,
Michael, Susan, and Jonathan

Another show memorable for its millionaires was *Grind,* a 1985 musical that had, depending on how you counted, seven or nine producers: Ken, John, Mary. . . They included the veteran impresario Hal Prince (*Fiddler on the Roof, West Side Story*), who also was the director, but not the line producer. That star role was reserved for Kenneth Greenblatt, a cheerful swimwear-fabric tycoon and former champion wrestler who now wrestles with lyrics and theater unions as a producer-investor. His partner is John

Pomerantz, a clothing manufacturer with strong show business connections—his company makes the *Dynasty* collection.

Grind closed after three months, losing $4.7 million.

Still, even David Merrick had his disasters. Between staccato commands to the staff at his company, a division of Guilford Mills ("Ethel, I'm going to fire the truck driver"), Ken explains what went wrong. "Fay Kanin [the writer] thought her book was perfect," he says. "And none of the producers could convince her [otherwise]. Creative people should be more open-minded. Then shows wouldn't be closing so fast."

Scene 2: Motion-picture set, near a creek somewhere in Florida
        "We're Telling You Now" (with apologies to Freddie & the Dreamers)...Maury and Loie

The chief producer of *Singin' in the Rain,* probably the costliest musical ever when it thudded onto the Broadway stage in 1985, was Maury Rosenfield, an elderly lawyer. He and his wife, Loie, are, like Kenneth Greenblatt, late but enthusiastic recruits to the joys and sorrows of show business—as witnessed by the director's chairs that they are said to have had made up for themselves for the first big venture they produced and financed, the movie *Bang the Drum Slowly,* starring Robert De Niro and Michael Moriarty. Based on a novel by Mark Harris about a dying baseball player, it was directed by John Hancock, but Maury has to get a lot of the credit for what was to become a considerable critical success because, as Loie stitched furiously at her needlepoint, he provided the pros with daily coaching. "You already have a picture," Hancock recalls him fulminating, his face flushing beet-red, as the director shot close-ups. "We have to go on to the next scene." The lawyer also threatened to shut down production, the director says, unless De Niro was given a more flattering hairstyle. *Pronto!* "Yes, but not in the middle of a scene," Hancock pleaded. Still, as our lyrics say...at least Hancock says the hairy brouhaha is why, in one locker-room shot, De Niro takes a shower. The whole experience was a bit of a cold shower for Mark Harris, who did the screenplay, since Maury banished him from the set, for reasons the *Bang the Drum Slowly* author attempted to elucidate in an article for the *Times* under the headline "Is the Only Good Writer a Dead Writer?"

Scene 3 A Broadway production office, thirteen years later
        "We're in the Money" (reprise)...Maury, Loie, Cindy, and Twyla

Delete the question mark from the *Times* essay. Maury banished

Singin' in the Rain's scribes, Betty Comden and Adolph Green, before the show even went into rehearsal. They had clashed with him and Twyla Tharp, the choreographer who was making her directing debut on the show. Since there was no shortage of dough—the production was being bankrolled to the tune of nearly $5 million by the Rosenfields and Cindy Pritzker, wife of a Hyatt Hotels and Braniff Airlines owner—why didn't Maury, the chief producer, immediately hire a new writing team? "I really didn't think that a book [script] was terribly important," Maury explained. "It's just a device to get from scene to scene." The cast were handed copies of what appeared to be Comden and Green's screenplay for the original Gene Kelly movie, and Tharp evinced a most interesting technique for translating this to the stage: she ordered the stunned actors to "just do it," they complained.

Some time after hundreds of people walked out during a preview performance of the show, Maury and Loie brought in another director to help, and, stationed constantly in the theater as the fine-tuning proceeded, they had various little recommendations themselves. Indeed, who knows how much better the critics would have reacted had Mary D'Arcy, the show's lissom female lead, not balked at the suggestion that she don a bathing suit for her wistful duet "You Are My Lucky Star"?

"WHAT IS MOST LIKELY TO BE REMEMBERED ABOUT THIS *SINGIN' IN THE RAIN* IS THE RAIN."

Frank Rich, New York Times

The extra budget, $1 million, that its three producers had to come up with to keep *Singin' in the Rain* open after the opening-night pans corresponded rather exactly to the entire budget of *Moose Murders,* a "comedy" that opened in 1983 at New York's Eugene O'Neill Theatre. Some historians consider this play the apogee of "vanity theater," and it indeed provides an excellent example of how little your producing debut can cost you. Just be prepared to thrust a pink slip into Liza's hand the moment you're through posing with her for your opening-night pictures.

Scene 4:   An oil rig, somewhere in Texas
        "Killing You Softly with Our Song" (additional lyrics by
        Roberta Flack's orthodontist)...the full company, with
        reprise by Tyler, John Simon, and Frank Rich

Moose Murders was presented by Force Ten Productions, an entertainment group whose owners include John Roach, who directed the play, and his wife, who was in the cast and whose family was rumored to have put up part of the budget. Roach was used to big productions, having been active not only in the theater but also in Force Ten's parent concern, which develops oil, gas, and real estate, explained a Force Ten executive. According to an article that a *Moose* cast member, June Gable, wrote for *Esquire,* the latest big production was well received by "friends and relatives of the playwright, the director, the director's wife..." Unfortunately, the deafening sound track of rain and thunder combined with an incessant tap-dance routine by the play's child star—Mara Hobel, formerly of *Mommie Dearest*—to deplete the ability of some other members of the audience, the critics, to follow the plot, involving as it did a quadriplegic, a neurotic, a blind man, and a tone-deaf singer. Or some combination thereof. All assembled with the Ginger Rogers brat at the Wild Moose Lodge.

"INDESCRIBABLY BAD... WHAT IT NEEDS IS A MERCY KILL-ING."

Clive Barnes, New York Post

"WILL SEPARATE THE CONNOISSEURS OF BROADWAY DISAS-TER FROM MERE DILETTANTES FOR MANY MOONS TO COME."

Frank Rich, New York Times

"SO TITANICALLY BAD THAT YOU JUST SIT BACK AND LAUGH TO KEEP FROM CRYING."

Stewart Klein, WNEW-TV

"AS CLOSE AS I EVER HOPE TO GET TO THE BOTTOMLESS PIT."

John Simon, New York

The show closed opening night. This was a shame. The great thing about vanity theater is that it is by the people for the people. The matinee ladies loved *Singin' in the Rain.* Some of them probably were even inspired to go out and start producing themselves.

"I MADE IT OUT JUST LIKE YOU TOLD ME, TO CASH. THAT'S A FUNNY NAME FOR A NEW PLAY."

Little old lady, handing a check to Max Bialystock (Zero Mostel) in The Producers, *Mel Brooks's comedy about a villainous Broadway producer who deliberately tries to create a flop,* Springtime for Hitler

Don't worry if you're still in the processs of weaseling that crucial first $10 million for your social debut. The money for your Broadway debut doesn't have to be your own. What you need are investors. Place an ad in your hometown newspaper—"Partners wanted for major new Christian musical starring Madonna and the Singing Angels"—and don't worry if it flops. It's not as if a cent of your own money will be at risk. Among the many things Broadway old-timers understand that the schoolchildren who lent you their lunch money do not is that one man's flop can be another man's fortune.

A brief terminology lesson. Under the traditional Broadway financing formula (now modified in some shows), an *investor* generally does not make any money unless a production turns a profit; a *producer,* whether or not he also is an investor and whether or not the show is making a profit, gets a share of the weekly box-office receipts. If after deducting this so-called producer's fee and other operating costs, such as salaries and royalties, there is nothing left for the little old lady who donated her life savings, too bad. Nobody said this was philanthropy. Since, as chief producer, you also will collect a weekly payment toward your "office" expenses (the Porsche parked outside with the engine idling in case you need to make a quick getaway), the incentive to keep *Tyler Takes Gracie Mansion* open is naturally somewhat stronger than your sense of duty toward the investor whose last cents you are burning up.

The above example is fictional, of course. But the fact is that this is a business in which, as Alexander Cohen—a showman known for his limo (license plate AHC-1), exquisite tastes in French champagne and caviar, and annual Tony Awards telecast—once put it, a failure can translate into a very *respectable* income: "There are certain shows which quite legally and justifiably would make the producer a hundred thousand dollars and the investor would not see his money back. It happens very often. Especially musicals," he observed.

There are two ways of assessing Cohen's own track record. He has produced dozens of shows, about half of which either have made a profit or recouped their investment. "That's above average," argues a Cohen spokesman. The other way of looking at it is somewhat less flattering:

In a 1979 *New York* article entitled "Lord of the Flops," writer Cliff Jahr figured that Cohen's clunkers—about half of all the shows he had presented—had cost his investors more than $6 million. "It is said that Mel Brooks had Cohen in mind...as a model for some of the characteristics of Max Bialystock..." Jahr wrote. "Brooks denies this, and no one suggests that Cohen is a crook. But the fact is, probably no man in Broadway history has had so many flops as Alex Cohen—and survived."

Cohen, who attributes much of his income to his successes as a TV producer, was known to be livid about this critique. The gossip created by the article in the industry was incessant, and this may have something to do with a phone call that another writer, David McClintick, received soon after the publication of *Indecent Exposure,* his exposé of Hollywood's boardroom shenanigans. The caller, identifying himself as Alexander Cohen, proffered himself as a whistleblower on *Broadway's* chisels and invited McClintick to lunch: "He said he had lots of good stories, and would be more than happy to help," an acquaintance of the author says.

Since McClintick declined the offer, P. T. Barnum's spiritual successor has had to confine his help to more conventional charity. He is a man with as big a heart as the city itself, or so an examination of his spectacular fundraisers for a nursing home planned by the Actors Fund of America would suggest. During the media blitz that preceded his first *Night of 100 Stars,* there was talk that he was being paid anywhere between $250,000 and $750,000 to produce the $4.5 million network television gala. The stars, while they were showered with perks, were performing free. Cohen, presumably looking the *Times* reporter who sought the truth straight in the eye, discussed this over a poached egg breakfast at a favorite dawn mess hall of our local powerhouses, the Hotel Dorset (the article explained that the producer detests eating at home):

"I agreed to do it for my usual fee. But then, when I was asking artists on every continent who are friends of mine to participate, I became uncomfortable that I was being paid. So I said I wouldn't accept the fee," Cohen declared.

It wasn't until some months later that the *New York Post*'s Cindy Adams reported that the showman's wife, writer-producer Hildy

Parks, who worked with him on the extravaganza, had received her usual renumeration for a three-hour TV special, $120,000.

For the second, $5.5 million *Night,* over three hundred stars were solicited to strut their stuff. From Petula Clark to Joan Collins and Placido Domingo, they once again sailed onto the stage unpaid. Cohen spoke of them being seen by two-hundred-million viewers in more than a hundred countries. This time, however, we noticed that he wasn't speaking of working gratis. Since none of the reporters who interviewed him seemed to have raised the subject, we did, and, yes, he did accept a fee this time. He had to, because the arrangements had been so time-consuming, taking a whole year. Though he wasn't saying how much he received, an acquaintance estimated it at $200,000, or "considerably less" than the $250,000 to $500,000 the producer normally commands for such a Brobdingnagian feat. Parks got her $120,000 again. The two events and another, smaller fundraiser that the showman assembled grossed about $10 million, of which around $2 million had gone to the nursing home project at the time of writing. The other $8 million was swallowed up by expenses ... the scenery, the crew, the one hundred wardrobe and hairdressing people, the cold poached salmon supper, the security guards posted every ten yards along an underground passageway used by the celebrities between their hotel and Radio City Music Hall. This was on top of such costs as the producers' fees. "Do you know how many free events stars are asked to attend? If Alex wasn't as lavish, they wouldn't turn out," says the Cohen spokesman.

"HAVE YOU HEARD THE JOKE? ALEXANDER COHEN THREW A BENEFIT FOR HIS SCHOOL WHEN HE WAS A TEENAGER, AND IT LOST MONEY."

Rival producer

"IT'S TRUE THAT IF FRANK SINATRA COMES TO THE MUSIC HALL FOR A CANCER CARE CONCERT, HE CAN RAISE ONE MILLION DOLLARS ALL BY HIMSELF. THAT'S NOT THE SHOW I CARE TO DO."

Alexander Cohen, in the Daily News

Only one other impresario in recent history has Cohen's panache, and a red-haired twenty-five-year-old tap dancer called Karen Prunczik married him. David Merrick was seventy-two at the time. The chorine murmured her vows wearing a copy of the slinky white wedding dress in *42nd Street,* the Merrick smasheroo in which she was appearing. "She was very much in love with him," a Merrick friend says. Let's go to the videotape. You'll recall that just a few months after this honeyed event, Merrick, felled by a stroke, sued for divorce and Prunczik asked a court to consider making her the manager of his $50 million assets, claiming he was exhibiting "severe paranoiac tendencies." (By now you should be familiar with the need to keep a gimlet eye on your beloved's, or ex-beloved's, competency.)

The legal experts in the producer's entourage had their money on Prunczik winning the spat. Because Merrick's speech had been badly impaired by the stroke, it seemed unlikely that he could testify in the divorce case. "All she has to do," one of the experts mused, "is sit back and wait to become the fifty-million-dollar Widow Merrick."

So money—big money—seemed the only explanation when the hoofer suddenly agreed to what was thought to be the swiftest divorce ever granted in New York State, taking under two hours as opposed to the usual minimum of eight *weeks.* It was rumored that Merrick had baited her with a settlement of $2 million down plus $100,000 a year alimony. In fact, according to a former Merrick aide, it came to about $75,000 after her attorney's fee, plus $36,000 a year for the next twelve years.

Peanuts by circus standards. Back to the videotape. Had there been reporters in the courtroom that morning, they might have noticed a former *42nd Street* star—and former Prunczik roommate—Wanda Richert in one of the pews. Raoul Felder, a Merrick lawyer, had persuaded this actress to sit inside the courtroom where Prunczik was vying for check-signing power over her husband's assets and stare silently at her old friend, says the former Merrick aide. "The message was very clear that she was there to give damaging testimony," he explains. What would that have been if Prunczik hadn't capitulated? "Oh, Wanda might not even have testified," the ex-aide says. "The whole business was a massive bluff." The drama wasn't totally over, as it turned out. A psychiatrist said in a court document that the irascible theater czar had been stuffing his pockets with cash, possibly to facilitate the "eliminating" of his ex-father-in-law. Prunczik père, the keeper of a Pittsburgh kitchen-equipment business, was rumored to have complained about his daughter's billing in *42nd Street.* A Merrick lawyer denied that his client had any such homicidal thoughts: "It's just David being eccentric. He wears a money belt."

"THE CULTURE SHOCK WAS ENORMOUS AND NEVER WORE OFF BECAUSE WE COULD NEVER SINK TO A LOW ENOUGH LEVEL WHERE ADAPTATION TO THIS SOCIETY WOULD BE POSSIBLE."

From a manuscript about Jean Harris, the headmistress who killed the Scarsdale Diet Doc, by Broadway producer Adela Holzer, Harris's neighbor in prison

There are many ways to nurse a theatrical nickel, and Merrick could teach you a few of them. Have you thought of substituting radishes for the strawberries that that overpaid poorly-reviewed actor eats in a scene? Moreover, after the stroke incapacitated the producer, a court-appointed conservator, delving into his paperwork, discovered that he had not paid out profits owed to 655 of his investors and other former associates.

"He intended to pay them," one of his longtime staffers said, as an accountant hurried to pay the debts. "But he hated to sign checks."

Since many producers suffer from such phobias, an entire chorus line of Securities and Exchange Commission and New York State regulators will have started high-kicking around your efforts from the moment you began to raise money—with the consequence that your well-intentioned efforts may end up having all the brio of a wake.

Consider *Boo.* Not to be confused with *Bodo,* a new musical with no director and no casting that was attempting to raise money around the same time (sample number: "I Love My Serfs"), *Boo* was a show that, its coproducer Anthony Moyer informed an attentive group of potential investors, would have "incredible subsidiary rights":

"A lot of people have seen possession tales," he enthused, "but in this, the demon jumps from nun to nun." Abruptly, Moyer stepped aside and a woman with red pigtails bounded to the center of the floor. One of the possessed, and aged ten, her role would be to off people with a hatchet. Another woman would electrocute her husband and comb her fingers through his cremated remains.

Boo, as the prospectus put it, melded "skullduggery with humor."

Moose Murders Goes to Salem!!!

The *Boo* company, Moyer trumpeted, reappearing to talk business, had received queries from manufacturers desirous of emblazoning the show title on party favors, and its costumes could be mass-produced for Halloween. Hadn't the work's advertising agent told him that "this show has the integrity of a *Nicholas Nickleby* and the commercial appeal of a *Cats*"?

At least, that's how the *Times* reported the pitch, in a feature that was bannered across the front page of the paper's business section. The SEC was not amused. "Investors should not rely on this article whatsoever," warned a revised prospectus that the regulators promptly obliged the show's producers to file.

The comparisons in the article to other plays, the value of merchandising and other subsidiary rights had been "inaccurate and misleading," warned the revamped brochure.

It was 1985 when two producers called John Roberdeau and Robert Geisler arrived in New York from somewhere in the southwest to present two of the most-heralded plays of the season. *Strange Interlude* would star Glenda Jackson, while *Aren't We All?* was uniting Claudette Colbert with Rex Harrison. We were at Elaine's, a popular celebrity watering hole, one evening when someone mentioned that the director Robert Altman would like to precipitate Roberdeau and Geisler into an eternal interlude. We called Altman up to ask about this and he explained that some time before the two producers vaulted into the Big Onion Ring, they had prevailed on him to direct a motion picture they were producing, *Streamers*. When he arrived at the location, he said, there was no money raised and it turned out that the pair didn't actually own the movie rights: "I said I'd go ahead with my own money." He did. Expensive mistake. The producers sued to halt the shoot, and since they *did* own the cable rights, Altman ended up having to pay them $500,000 to get off his tail. On top of which he still had to buy the movie rights. He'd started shooting early, Geisler replied, "knowing full well the money wasn't there."

A Federal Deposit Insurance Corporation judgment that was outstanding against Geisler was even more easily explained. It involved an unpaid loan from a defunct bank. "All I know," Geisler said very reasonably, "is the loan was due and the bank was gone." Then there was the matter of Gwen Gunderson, a Los Angeles typist who had extended a $3,500 one-year loan to the twosome for the Altman flick. She had met them when Roberdeau bought a used Toyota from her, and four years later she hadn't been repaid. "All the people like her were spiritually investors," said Geisler. "When and if *Interlude* and *Aren't We All?* become profitable, people like Gwen who have not been paid will get their money back." Except, perhaps, for people like Robert Zarem, the top press agent the producers had hired to trumpet their New York debut: the two checks he was paid bounced. Geisler explained that the PR man deposited one prematurely and the second was stopped because of dissatisfaction with his work.

"I WELCOME A LITTLE GLOSS AND FROTH."

John Simon, on Aren't We All?

Two producers of the musical *Annie,* Irwin Meyer and Stephen Friedman, were hailed as the icing on the cake, the cream in the coffee.

"The hot new team," exclaimed one of the columns. The men, it reported, were erecting a big billboard at Broadway and Forty-fifth Street that would belch smoke and, being committed to their images as impresarios, wore fur coats when they tootled around town in their Rolls-Royces. Curdling the cream somewhat was the suggestion that *this* pair's Daddy Warbucks was a tax-shelter scheme, one allegedly involving nonexistent coal-mining rights and marketed to investors like Elvis Presley. Meyer and Friedman pleaded guilty to conspiring to assist in filing false tax returns and were sentenced to six months in prison. "In a matter of weeks," a prosecution memorandum had charged, the scheme, involving four defendants, took in $21 million. "The four defendants received over $2 million each," the memo said.

Tax shelters, Robert Altman movies, . . .

"You have to be always pushing, pushing," as another producer, Adela Holzer, would say, cool cobalt eyes flashing imperiously as she stretched out in her sunny yellow drawing room, the light glinting on gilt and silver, granting one of her press audiences at her Manhattan town house. Its treasures included a bed in which Chopin supposedly had slept. The visiting journalists were impressed and much was written about her birth (in Spain, she said, to a wealthy family), her Broadway investments (she burst onto the scene with an investment of some $50,000 in the rock musical *Hair* that reputedly made her $2 million), and, most of all, her overseas investment ventures. She had made "fistfuls of money investing in spice, rice, sugar, butter, cement and other commodities," said a 1975 report in the *Times*.

Hundreds of investors flocked to join Adela in these ventures. But by 1979, they were baying for the $35.5 million they said she owed them: $12 million in cash and credit given to her, the balance apparently calculated on the basis of profits she had led them to expect. Adela replied that she was broke. A bankruptcy trustee requested her bank records. She couldn't furnish them, she said, because she had entrusted them to a man to take to Indonesia on a ship from San Francisco.

She was indicted for fraud. By the prosecution's account, there were no commodities: Adela had been diverting the cash to herself and her Broadway shows, it was charged. She was found guilty—and got two years. So was it all worth it? Perhaps. The authorities thoughtfully placed her in the next cell to the Wronged Headmistress, who is doing fifteen to life for accidentally bumping off her lover, Dr. Herman Tarnower (she had been trying to shoot herself, you'll recall). Aha. . . . photo opportunities! A winsome little letter appeared in the book-review section of the Sunday *Times:*

"For the last seven months, Jean and I have been sharing the same living quarters," wrote Adela. " . . . The Jean I know is so different from the one portrayed by the press or Mrs. Trilling's book [about the case] that I wonder if we are talking about the same person."

Adela readily agreed to expand on this in an interview with us for *New York.* When we arrived at the jail, she escorted us to the cafeteria, a pleasant room looking out on a square that would not have been out of place at Harvard. Harris sat nearby in matte apricot lipstick and carefully fluffed hair. A fur jacket—lent by a visitor, a guard said—was thrown over the back of the headmistress's chair. The commodities expert did the talking. "She cries for Hi [Tarnower] in private," Adela said. "She plays the music she used to listen to with him, like *Hello, Dolly!,* on a little stereo she has. . . ."

It was hard to tell whether Harris had requested this apologia or whether she had any input in the mawkish manuscript that Adela produced some time later about life as Jean's neighbor. A short extract from it somehow found its way to the *Daily News.* But we do believe that Adela's ship finally came home. No sooner had she been released than she was telling people that she had optioned the rights to, well, for some reason not to the Jean Harris Story. It was Marcia Davenport's novel *My Brother's Keeper* that was soon to be a major motion picture. Adela didn't say whether the locations would include Indonesia.

"He just fell in love with me, this tall, long-legged brunette," says Rita Lachman, relaxing here at the "small Versailles," as the Paris apartment she shared with her husband, Charles Lachman, was known. The Revlon cosmetics nabob and his bride, an ex-maid, also kept a home on Fifth Avenue in New York.

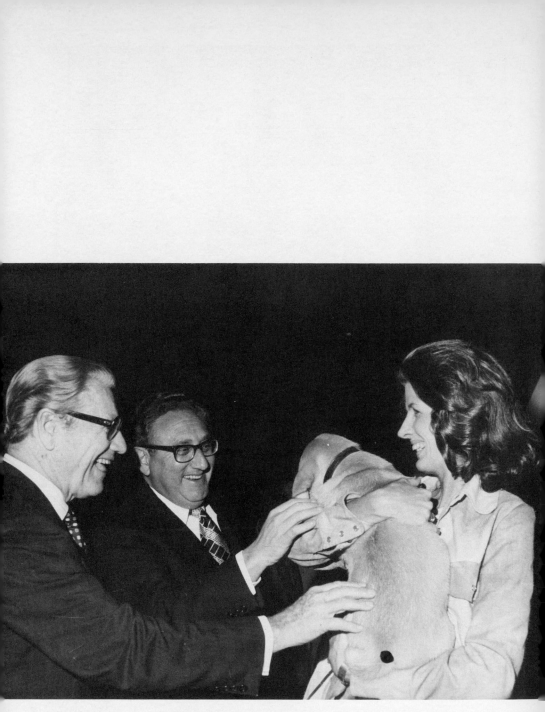

Tyler, the only member of the Cast who is camera-shy, is introduced to Vice-Presisdent Nelson Rockefeller (*left*) by his proud parents, Nancy and Henry Kissinger, during the Ford administration.

Style-setters Susan Gutfreund and William F. Buckley, Jr. She owns a "subway bracelet" with sliding steel panels concealing the gemstones. Like all the best people in the Wild East, he has a gun permit.

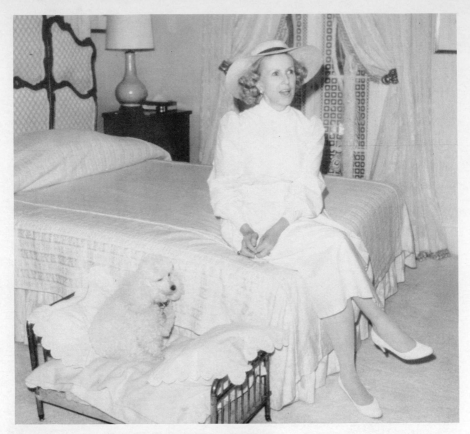

Can you spot Edelweiss's mistake? Yes, the pooch, resting with mistress Marylou Whitney, is in her birthday suit. Beautiful Dogs wear pajamas from Canine Styles, on Lexington Avenue.

He never got to build his 60-story castle with gold-leafed crenellations, but Donald Trump is forging ahead with plans to put this model of the world's tallest building (150 stories) into production.

"Wherever Pan Am goes, I go," declares cable television personality Nikki Haskell, New York's unofficial Queen of Comp.

If Barbara de Portago agrees to host an event at your restaurant, you're on the social map. She grew up in the Palace of Versailles, which, as she says, is "the hallmark of quality."

Change your name to Vanderbilt, or DuPont, and presto!... The DuPont twins, Robert (*left*) and Richard, are nightclubbing with the nation's most celebrated debutante, Cornelia Guest.

"I love to spend money. It's an obsession with me," Arthur Ringwalt "Burke" Rupley IV has confided. How much money he has to spend still isn't clear, but, living it up with escorts actress Sylvia Sachs (*left*) and Angie Best (ex-wife of international soccer star George Best), it's the company that counts.

"How can you not get along with a guy who, when you say, 'Hello, your Excellency,' on the phone, says, 'Hello, your Majesty,'" deadpanned Mayor Koch when reporters sought his reaction to John Cardinal O'Connor's ultimately successful move to kill a city ban on discrimination against homosexuals. The cardinal, in regular hat, and mayor, in funny hat, are reviewing the 1985 Puerto Rican Day Parade outside of St. Patrick's Cathedral.

"SHE'S VERY PECULIAR ABOUT THE CARPET. IT HAS TO BE VACUUMED UNTIL IT LOOKS LIKE VELVET, SO WE HAVE SIGNS UP, 'DON'T WALK ON THE CARPET.'"

Solly Pernick, the eighty-eight-year-old head property man at Broadway's Plymouth Theater, confiding one of the many reasons why he and five other union stagehands were needed to staff The Search for Signs of Intelligent Life in the Universe, *a 1985–86 show starring one woman, Lily Tomlin*

The classic story about why it always has cost more than it should to stage a Broadway show even without a rain-maker, a Bugatti, or a con man in sight concerns Marc Blitzstein, reported at the time of our tale to be an ardent Communist. It was 1937 and he had composed a magnificent operetta about the revolt of the Oppressed Workers against an Evil Steel Tycoon, scored to be played by one musician at a piano. Himself. Two days before he was to premiere at the ivories, however, a delegate from the musicians' union requested an interview, and informed Blitzstein's producer that he would be hiring. . . a nine-piece orchestra. They wouldn't have to play, of course, as long as the producer paid them.

It is unrecorded whether the shaken composer went home and burned his *Das Kapital,* but nearly a half century later, the Broadway proletariat continued to occupy a featherbed of such delicious softness that when police investigating the murder of a woman at the Metropolitan Opera House requested a list of stagehands who'd worked that night, there was an embarrassed silence.

Several of the men who were supposed to be on duty hadn't shown, said a police source, because it wasn't their "turn"— something the Met didn't want publicized since it was "in the middle of a fundraising drive." The reticence was unwarranted. Some *Singin' in the Rain* stagehands may have raked in $3,000 some weeks, but that was with overtime, installing that show's fifty tons of gimcrackery. The opera absentees would have been on a basic rate. About $800 a week. No point in being too greedy, especially since most stagehands hold at least two jobs. There is plenty of time for this, since their average backstage week totals twenty-eight hours.

Still, it has to be said that there is also something to the Tomlin's Tootsies theory of Broadway costs—costs which, of course, are reflected in Broadway ticket prices. If certain of the following stars are billed in a show, chances are that you're paying a premium, if not for their foibles—which sometimes rival their talents—then for tranquilizers for the crew.

• Lauren Bacall was reported to have gone through at least six dressers during her hugely successful New York run in *Woman of the Year.* "There were people who were promoted, who took better jobs," explains her agent, Clifford Stevens. Then there were the two weeks when Raquel Welch substituted in the show while Bacall caught some R&R. The critics weren't invited to review the curvaceous temp, but some of them bought seats—and gave Welch quite favorable notices. There were also general news stories about the stand-in. "Greatly displeased" by this wave of media attention for her replacement, Bacall sulked in her dressing room upon her return, refusing to speak to the show's press agent. Or so a *Woman* staffer perceived it. The star's agent says the breakdown in communication had nothing to do with Welch. He explains that his client is a perfectionist, not a beast: "The difficulties had to do with the way the press agent was doing his job." Certainly, an employee assigned to help Bacall find her way in the murk behind the sets each night appears to have had difficulties doing *his* job: show staffers say he hurled a chair downstairs one evening, shouting, "Betty, I wish it was you!"
• Anthony Quinn, earning a reported $25,000 a week during his lusty stage appearance in *Zorba the Greek,* naturally had to take precautions to ensure that the squealing squaws who fought for the white carnation he tossed each night into the audience were in awe from the moment he arrived at the theater. Shortly before one performance, a call came into the show's management office from someone in Quinn's entourage. There were no hubcaps on the Lincoln Town Car that had drawn up to collect him. No hubcaps, no Zorba! There was some suggestion that the omission was deliberate on the part of the rental agency, motivated by the general Climate of Fear. The Big Onion's crime statistics have been inflated by a surge of thefts of rear windows from parked cars. However, the replacement limo that was dispatched had its wheels perfectly chromed.

One appearance Quinn never did get to make was in *Man of La Mancha.* He presumably was interested because the director of this stage show, Albert Marre, recalls getting a call from him about acquiring the screen rights to the property. "My wife and I met him at a Chinese restaurant," says Marre, "and he was incredibly rude, discussing people's personal habits. We got up and said, 'Thank you so much,' and left."

• Jackie Gleason delayed the shooting of the 1985 CBS television movie *Izzy and Moe* while he agonized over the length of his sleeves and demanded a change of chapeaux. "He will not wear the straw hat," the director announced solemnly. "He says he has worn it in every scene." A staffer who accompanied the Great One on the national tour of the comedy *Sly Fox* says, his voice tremulous, "First, he redesigned *all* his costumes. Then he had to be moved from city to city by private jet and we had to pay for him to have his chauffeur with his own limo waiting for him. He had to have a house on a golf course rented at each place, except in Chicago he moved into a hotel. They had the entire floor repainted for him, but he didn't like it, so he moved out a day later. We had to back a trailer up to one theater, because the dressing room wasn't big enough for him." Yes, but surely he was an enormous crowd-puller? "He wasn't a big draw at all," the staffer says, despondent.

• Richard Gere is mostly a screen star, of course, but if he does return to Broadway—his 1982 appearance in *Bent,* a play about Nazi persecution of homosexuals was a big success—he may prove to be the only bargain ticket on our list. With Richard, producers don't have to squander huge sums on courting the press because, believing, it's said, that publicity interferes with his art, he does not enjoy talking about himself. He did consent to give Gloria Steinem an interview for a 1986 *Ms.* cover story. This went quite successfully, presumably because the feminist did not follow the line of questioning pursued some years earlier by a reporter for *Ladies' Home Journal.* When that scribe led off by asking what it felt like to be a male sex symbol, Richard responded by dropping his pants. Should you congratulate him on his performance? It's unclear. Dotson Rader's biography *Cry of the Heart* records that the late Tennessee Williams went backstage during *Bent* with a woman friend and found Gere "lounging in a chair wearing only a pair of jockey shorts." The actor listened wordlessly to the playwright's praise, his face a mask of smug ennui, Rader wrote. Williams finished his little speech. Gere still said nothing and Williams left in some bewilderment, or so he later would tell both Rader and another friend whom we interviewed.

To the contrary, contends a Gere aide: Tennessee and Richard had a most cordial talk, about how a *Bent* scene in which the star heaved rocks corresponded to a remedy the playwright once tried for writer's block.

• Elizabeth Taylor, moving with her Broadway play *The Little Foxes* from New York—where she had a lavender dressing room, with lavender tropical fish—to London, required the show's producer, Zev Bufman, to install her in a town house and rent her a Rolls-Royce. Costs rocketed and, with grosses down, the show, which in New York had turned a healthy profit, started to lose money. There was no choice in the matter, however. "What she wants is defined clearly in the contract when you make a deal with her," says Bufman, dimpling boyishly, "and she expects really big gifts." The veteran producer flew stone crabs to England for her from a Miami Beach restaurant. As her partner in the Elizabeth Theater Group, which reunited her with Richard Burton on the Broadway stage in *Private Lives,* the producer also presented her with "the world's smallest perfect diamond" and a snowy white fur cape. Her erratic attendance record, if not her ossified performance, during *Private Lives* was blamed at the time on various ailments. Laryngitis. Bronchitis. "It was all booze, huge amounts of it. That and the painkillers," says Bufman. Later that year, she quietly checked into California's Betty Ford Center to detoxify.

"ZEV BUFMAN (COPRODUCER) IS AMONG THE MOST ACTIVE OF TODAY'S THEATRICAL IMPRESARIOS."

"MARGE AND IRV COWAN (COPRODUCERS) FOR MORE THAN TWO DECADES HAVE BEEN THE CREATIVE FORCES BEHIND THE ENTERTAINMENT IN THE SHOW ROOMS AND LOUNGES OF THE DIPLOMAT RESORT AND COUNTRY CLUBS OF WHICH HE IS OWNER AND PRESIDENT.... BUT IT WASN'T UNTIL PEGGY LEE AND *PEG* THAT THEY JOINED THE RANKS OF ACTIVE PRODUCERS FOR THE NEW YORK STAGE."

"GEORGIA FRONTIERE (COPRODUCER), AMIDST HER BUSY SCHEDULE AS A FULL-TIME WORKING OWNER OF THE LOS ANGELES RAMS OF THE NFL, IS BRANCHING OUT INTO OTHER AREAS OF THE ENTERTAINMENT INDUSTRY."

From the producer credits in Playbill *for* Peg, *Peggy Lee's 1983 Broadway autobiography*

As the billing said, Marge Cowan, a Food Fair heiress, and her husband, Irv, indeed had prior stage experience. "We are *not* novices," Marge would later protest. She was referring to the money that they often had placed in big Broadway shows as investors. There was no way around it, however: the couple's most impressive credit before Peggy Lee, an old friend, persuaded them to help pay for her New York splash had to be the $250,000 wedding that they had thrown for one of their daughters at the hotel they own in the Florida resort of Hollywood-by-the Sea. The reception featured thirty waiters brandishing flaming sabers, decor by the designer who did Madison Square Garden for Mike Todd's premiere of *Around the World in Eighty Days,* and entertainment by Sammy Davis, Jr.

Like the cloud-machine cirrostratus billowing through the Diplomat's grand ballroom that evening, Lee emanated an almost magical quality when, some time later, she auditioned her proposed "musical autobiography" for a group of friends at her Bel-Air mansion. "She was lying back on a chaise in something pink and silky," says Zev Bufman. The producer had been invited there by the Cowans and came away enthusiastic enough to return for a second hearing, this time accompanied by his New York partner, Elizabeth Taylor.

The room was crowded, but as a waiter placed a drink in front of Taylor, Lee's eyes focused in like high-power microscopes. She stopped in midchord. "Would you *mind* not serving drinks when I'm singing," she barked.

About one song later, a man offered Taylor a cigarette. Still tense from Lee's implied rebuke, she accepted it and the man lit it for her. She took a puff. Lee's eyes were slits. A second puff. Lee started to cough. The singing stopped.

"Elizabeth, dear, I'm allergic to smoke. . . ."

After Bufman joined the Cowans and Georgia Frontiere on the *Peg* team, as an investor and producer, La Lee set about selecting her dressing room. The second-floor suite that Taylor had used when *Private Lives* was at the same theater was judged unsuitable—it was very *small,*" explains Lee—so an elevator had to be built to lift her to the third-floor apartments that she settled on. She says her doctor had warned her not to use the stairs. A peach bathtub was installed, antique wing chairs rented, and for her elegant Manhattan flat (supported with a per diem allowance), there was a white baby grand piano. Rehearsals did not go well, however, and, with tensions mounting between the star and Bufman, it was agreed about two days before opening night that the Cowans and Georgia Frontiere would buy him out. The veteran producer says this was after he warned them that the show needed work and the opening should be postponed, or "we're going to get murdered."

The Cowans have a different recollection.

"He never said that," says Marge.

"I still remember his words," says Irv. "He said, 'This is as good as we're going to get and we might as well go with it.' None of us were overly thrilled with [the book], but the music was excellent, to the point where people were crowding the stage every night after the previews."

The paperwork on the buyout still had to be completed when Lee, robed in sepulchral alabaster, launched into a blow-by-blow account of her saintly life. There were the childhood whippings ("One Beating a Day"), the dramatic illnesses, searing odysseys of marital grief. Periodically, the singer would make odd marionette-like gestures with her arms and cast her gaze upward, her lips embalmed in a motionless beatific smile.

"The Cowans loved it," says the show staffer. And their enjoyment, by most accounts, was not punctured. The critics had attended a preview performance and, as is standard practice, some of them had told *Peg*'s press agent what they thought. It wasn't good, he informed Bufman. Though the *Times*'s Rich and his paper have a strict policy against such prepublication leaks, "somehow, Zev also found out about the *Times*," claims the show staffer.

"THE SHOW IS MOST LIKELY TO EXCITE THOSE WHO ARE EVANGELISTICALLY DEVOTED TO BOTH PEGGY LEE AND GOD—IDEALLY IN THAT ORDER."

Frank Rich

"Zev said not to disturb anyone with the bad notices," says the staffer.

Sometime during the opening-night performance, the bailout was clinched. Bufman got back most of his original investment. He insists this was just after a consultant to the show, the composer Cy Coleman, told Irv Cowan about the *Times*.

"Maybe one of us had a lapse in memory," says Irv, "and it wasn't me."

Says Marge, "of course" they wouldn't have gone through with the buyout had they known about the pan.

"Cy never told the Cowans about the reviews," says an aide to Coleman.

The show closed after five performances, at a $1.9 million loss to the Cowans, Frontiere, and investors enlisted by Bufman. The Florida hoteliers had got together with Frontiere to reward their star with a little opening-night gift—a full-length black mink cape. "I'd say it was part of my salary," says Lee. "I worked very hard."

Bufman also gave Lee a gift, of course. It was reported to have consisted of a peach-colored glass rose. He is still active in show business. The Cowans, who continue to consider him a friend, haven't been seen on the Broadway producing scene since the show closed. But they may be back, if the right property comes along.

"It's not like we went in there as children," says Marge. This is true. There is one caveat, however: would you believe any native of the Cowans' sunshine state who told you that he did not do his uttermost to monitor the activities of the local sharks when he was taking a dip? During the negotiations on Bufman's release, Marge recalls asking the producer if maybe he did know how our local sharks, the critics, had liked that preview. "He told us he went out of his way not to have any knowledge of what was in the reviews," says Marge.

6

INSIDER TRADING

"MR. CLARK LIVES ON FIFTH AVENUE AND IS A MEMBER OF THE BROOK CLUB IN MANHATTAN AND THE PIPING ROCK COUNTRY CLUB IN LOCUST VALLEY ON LONG ISLAND. [HE AND PETER BRANT] ARE MEMBERS OF THE RACQUET AND TENNIS CLUB ON PARK AVENUE AND EACH OWNS A CONDOMINIUM AT THE PALM BEACH POLO AND COUNTRY CLUB IN FLORIDA."

The New York Times *on two men implicated in a 1984 stock scandal involving a reporter for the* Wall Street Journal

The best New York clubs ostentatiously discourage business discussions on their premises. "You'll have to check that, sir," a retainer at the Knickerbocker, an East Sixty-second Street preserve of civility, instructed a visitor who was carrying a sheet of paper. Most also ban women from their membership rosters, a combination of rules that can make these citadels of privilege a superb cover not only for your financial ambitions but also for certain of your more private pleasures. The kind that you wouldn't want the wife to hear about. That Rambo of the communications industry, the late William Benton, apparently understood this principle and put it to use in his older years.

Benton, a founder of the ad agency Benton & Bowles, organizer of the Voice of America broadcasts, and publisher of *Encyclopaedia Britannica,* was a grandfather of eight. A biography issued by his office ascribed his "physical stamina" to his boyhood exertions clearing "forty acres of rock" and working on a Minnesota iron range. However, what he really enjoyed, it can now be revealed, was *mental* exercise. Practicing the conversational arts, that is, at Les ———, an unpublicized New York club that we have decided not to identify, since some of its stalwarts may still be alive. In the club's heyday there were about twenty of them, all elderly, married millionaires, and their main activity seemed to be inviting women—singers, actresses, dancers, a writer or two—to meet them at decorous lunches in the private dining rooms of hotels and restaurants like Lutèce and "21." Though the guests tended to be half the age of their hosts, the club's last known president, the seventy-nine-year-old financier George Nelson, described this generational Delaware Water Gap as purely coincidental when he granted us an interview at his Fifth Avenue offices shortly before his death in 1985. He had a cherubic face and a wispy fringe of white hair around his pate, and looked as if he had stepped straight from the pages of Zola.

"Younger men can't afford this club," he explained, insisting that rumors that the club had become inactive because of its members' increasing infirmity were unfounded. "The meals and the ladies, both are expensive. I give a speech at the beginning of the lunch. I tell them here are the rules of the game. The ladies can limit themselves to saying, 'Yes,' 'No,' or 'Maybe.' The gentlemen say simply, 'Would you like to meet me again?' and give out their cards."

In the not-uncommon event that two tycoons were panting to meet with the same chorine to discuss the federal budget deficit, the membership committee adjudicated. The rules used to require that the fräuleins be left to make the first overture, presumably because aggressive pursuit would be unbecoming to these titans of America's business firmament. But the procedure had to be loosened, Nelson said sadly, because the women "didn't phone." His involvement with the club was limited to these little organizational matters, he added with a beatific smile, since his wife, in contrast to the "quite homely" baggage of some of the frat brothers, was a beauty. But in that case, why were a large thank-you photo of Ronnie and Nancy ("in appreciation" for contributions to the Republican Party) and a similar citation from the Republican National Committee having to share space in his elegantly wainscotted office with a disgusting eighteenth-century French drawing of a man holding aloft a buxom naked trollop? It dawned on us that we should infiltrate and send a list of Nelson's partners in lechery to GOP headquarters. He had been willing to identify only departed members of Les ———, like William Benton (a Democrat and former U.S. senator), and the investment banker Robert Lehman—so your author suggested that she join the boys for a little consommé.

Nelson's eyes panned slowly from her brunette hair to her

upper torso. "*Our* ladies," he said coldly, "are usually blond and very sportive." Sportive?

"Sports," snapped Nelson. "It makes them a good shape. The brain is not important. We have brains ourselves. You are not tall enough," he added. "I'm five foot six and I like ladies who are six feet."

While this dénouement to what could have been a peerless opportunity for a frolic in the foie gras was a disappointment, and while Les ——— may be a joy of the past, Ed Koch has vowed to inject some of its flavor into gentlemen's clubs throughout the city. Hizzoner has ordered those establishments with four hundred members or more to fall into line with a city law that says they must admit women—and has told them to adapt their shower facilities accordingly.

"Where's your husband, Gladys?"

"At his club, Brenda, taking a shower."

"WE THOUGHT HE WAS FROM BALTIMORE."

A member of the Maidstone Club, in the summer colony of East Hampton, after losing money to another member, William Parr, who turned out to be the son of a local grocer

---

The immediate question, of course, is not whether the club of your choice will be swarming with nubile nymphets but whether it will even admit you to its rolls.

If you're applying for membership in the Century Association, there should be no problem. The Century, one of the city's most prestigious sanctums, may have balked at the fiat on admitting women, but it does not discriminate against *people,* as in, says an official, "we have Jewish people, gay people," even black people on the membership register. The association first publicly demonstrated these liberal views at the close of World War II. Beset, like all clubs, by a servant shortage, it endeavored to impress on those of its employees who'd been in the services that it was an *honor* to be a menial. According to Cleveland Amory in his book *Who Killed Society?* a dinner was thrown, and, as the teary-eyed black minions were marched into the room, in full uniform, "the entire club membership rose and sang 'Mine Eyes Have Seen the Glory.'"

Since getting through the door of a number of other New York clubs can be a less than glorious experience if you are Jewish or

Roman Catholic (if you're an *Ethiopian* Jewish grocer's son, don't even bother applying), you may have to undergo the kind of genealogical surgery that we explored in chapter two. And hope you aren't found out. After one local clubman, a virulent anti-Semite, accused another—Charles*, let's call him—of receiving alimony from all five of his ex-wives, Charles did some research at the New York Supreme Court and discovered that, although his foe was listed in the Social Register under a WASP name and was a pillar of the vestry of a silk-stocking Episcopal church, he was born Goldberg.

"It appears that a member of your club, ———, is enrolled under a name which does not belong to him. His legal name is ——— Goldberg," Charles wrote in a mass mailing to the man's clubs. He dispatched similar letters to three societies the man and his wife had joined—the Mayflower Descendants, the Pilgrims, and the Colonial Dames.

The Maidstone Club, an overwhelmingly WASP pile in East Hampton where Jackie O played lawn tennis as a child, was not a recipient of Charles's communication. It was at this club that an ethnic slur allegedly was tossed out at a visiting Jewish child (chapter two), but it would be unfair to judge the place just by that episode. The establishment has some Jewish members, says its president, and, even before its landmark decision to admit single women to full membership, allowed a number of new money types—East Hampton businessmen—to use its golf links. They were given limited memberships, a technicality that prohibited them from socializing in the clubhouse and therefore would not have done at all for William Parr, an East Hampton grocer's son. Moving back to his childhood town from Baltimore, where he had been convicted of fraud, he was taken for a rich aristocrat and admitted to full membership at the club. His Cadillac, with its PARR 4 vanity license plate, stood out "like white socks with a dinner jacket" among the battered woodies in the club parking lot, reported Debra Scott in *New York*. The new member could afford to be flashy, having launched a resourceful real estate marketing scheme (the Maidstone has the usual rule against transacting business on club premises). The formula for successfully emulating his enterprise is simple to grasp: just sell the same shares in a property venture several times over. And then leave town, fast. Parr did not leave town, and after it emerged that the partners he had enlisted in his scheme, who included five of his fellow

*A pseudonym.

clubmen, owned among them 350 percent of two property projects, he pleaded guilty to grand larceny. This was unfortunate; his Maidstone membership was revoked. However, should you be keen to take up where he left off, the chances are that you too will be admitted to *full* membership at the Maidstone. The club is phasing out the discriminatory "limited pass" system and is "reaching out" to NMs and would-be NMs.

If you have an underutilized backyard, we suggest you reach out to Gregory Wulster. He may be running out of space.

Wulster, you see, has been wagging two tails, so to speak. Not only was he the president, at this writing, of the OM Tuxedo Club, in the walled New York exurb of Tuxedo Park, but, although it is unclear whether some of his fellow clubmen knew it until an unexpected turn of events, he operates a pet cemetery business. A booming business, it seems, because, around Labor Day in 1985, investigators discovered that his picturesque New Jersey hillside graveyard, with the custom headstones and discreet statues In Memory of Bonzo, had a discount adjunct: an open trench in a nearby meadow was piled eight feet deep with dog and cat carcasses.

Since New Jersey has a proud history of serving as one large illegal repository for out-of-state industrial wastes, none of this struck us as out of the ordinary. However, hundreds of cemetery customers and animal lovers from as far away as Louisiana inundated the police with calls. Some of them ordered exhumations to see if Bonzo really was resting beneath his headstone. He was. But a member of another club called us to joke that legions of G-men soon would be dragging the Tuxedo lake. The atmosphere at Wulster's clubhouse and in the surrounding mansions was said to be doggone funereal.

"This is incredibly embarrassing for the club," yelped a Tuxedo lady as New Jersey regulators first ordered a site cleanup (Bonzo, they smirked, should be treated as dirty landfill and removed to a town dump), then backtracked (pet owners were growling about making dog meat out of them). Wulster's image began to look up again, however, after his attorney, Gerald Krovatin, revealed that the trench was "not a trench" but a "common grave," where the clubman performed low-cost "mass disposal" for veterinarians. It had been left open temporarily because Wulster's backhoe was out of order.

"In places where there are no facilities like Greg's, a lot of vets sell the remains," a Wulster acquaintance whispered, "for rendering."

Another flap that grazed the Tuxedo started, according to an affidavit by a Securities and Exchange Commission official, at the Racquet and Tennis Club, on Park Avenue. Peter Brant, a thirty-one-year-old stockbroker who'd been hailed in an ad for his firm, Kidder Peabody, as an expert who could "hear of promising situations before the herd," had decided to wire himself to a human crystal ball. According to a federal affidavit, the broker met at the club with R. Foster Winans, a writer on the *Wall Street Journal*'s "Heard on the Street" stock-analysis column. The column is so influential that it can touch off a bull market in a stock—or send it into a meltdown. In view of this, "a lot of money" could be made, Brant is said to have observed, if he knew in advance just what Winans was going to be writing.

It is only proper for a clubman to share his good luck in life and Brant allegedly shared *his* with a friend and client, David W. C. Clark, a thirty-four-year-old Social Registerite lawyer. The Securities and Exchange Commission has claimed that Clark "spoke with Brant on almost a daily basis," making huge illegal profits from the tips that Winans leaked. Clark, who has denied this, reportedly had met Brant on a polo field and subsequently introduced the broker to people like former diplomat Averell Harriman's grandson, Averell Fisk, and C. Z. Guest. Though these friends said they had no professional dealings with Clark or Brant, the intent seemed clear: "David [Clark] wants to help me so that I can afford to play polo," Brant told a fellow broker.

The lawyer and the broker were fixtures at the best charity balls and clubs. They also were reported to be active in Preservation of American Free Enterprise, a tax-exempt foundation chaired by a Lady of the Club. The Tuxedo Club. Gloria Muller had been admitted to the Tuxedo roster after impressing other members with word of her good works in the *living* world. While Wulster was interring Bonzo, she was toiling away, according to a résumé circulated on her behalf by one of her club sponsors, on the committee of the "New York City Mission Gala Ferry Boat Outing" and helping to organize balls like the New York Infirmary debutante cotillion. Her son Scott was a broker at Bear, Stearns & Co., and Brant's lawyer pal, Clark, had opened an account with him after the general counsel at Kidder Peabody—Brant's firm—noticing a correlation between the lawyer's trades and the *Journal* "Heard" columns, informed him that this "ought to stop."

Gloria's foundation had nothing to do with the insider-trading scheme. Its sights were set on Higher Ideals, and its supporters were of the Highest Class. Averell Fisk was listed as its president and a New York socialite, who belongs to the Tuxedo Club, says she did some of the chores:

"Gloria hired me for a hundred dollars a month to mail things for the foundation," the socialite recalls. "And she convinced me and several of my friends in the Junior League, all lovely, respectable people, to be on the foundation committee." The mailings, according to the clubmate's files, were to Fortune 500 companies, like General Motors and TRW.

Giving Muller's East Seventy-second Street residence and phone number as the foundation contact, the pitch warned:

"There are powerful groups and organizations dedicated to the overthrow or weakening of the free enterprise system. We must resist these attempts!" Donations of up to $1,000 were suggested, but, in a shocking display of un-Americanism, the Fortune 500 refused to open their checkbooks, according to the Tuxedo Club lady who did the secretarial duties. Still, the foundation stuck to its "free lunches opposition to lefty." Guests invited to attend what appeared to be its sole function, throwing singles parties, "had to pay thirty-five dollars to get in, and pay for the drinks," says one middle-aged bachelor who was on Muller's list. "She'd call up and say you'd meet all these desirable women."

Brant pleaded guilty in the stock-trading scheme; Foster Winans, his *Wall Street Journal* accomplice, is appealing after being convicted of fraud. (Clark, sued in a civil case by the Securities and Exchange Commission, said he would "vigorously" defend himself.)

"All of us who are in the Junior League have resigned from the foundation," says the socialite who did the mailing chores.

Gloria's broker son, Scott Muller, resigned his Big Board registration even though he had not been accused of any wrongdoing in the case; he had decided, Gloria told us, to start a new career—as an actor. Her own career also seemed to be taking a slight change in direction. Her foundation's laudably anti-Communist travails had been dismissed in the *New York Times* under the headline: "Tax-Exempt Group Made No Gifts to Charity."

About two days after this story appeared, the middle-aged bachelor who'd been on the foundation's mailing list received a new solicitation. "Gloria Muller cordially invites you for 'cocktails,'" this said. "Cash Bar $35 Per Person. . . . checks payable to: Cornucopia Group Inc." At Muller's home address. Checking state records, we discovered that a lawyer for Muller had incorporated this group "to conduct a club for the purpose of having its patrons engage in recreational activity of every kind, including dancing, sports, informative presentations of current problems and vogues and other social intercourse of every kind. . . . "

We begged Muller for more information. "It's just nice people meeting nice people," she replied. We were planning to ask her if she'd thought of a merger with the shell of Les ———, which also opposed antisocial intercourse, but she put down the phone on us. We are reporting this rude behavior to the Tuxedo Club.

7

THE NIGHT FRONTIER

"PEOPLE USED TO BE DISAPPOINTED IF WE DIDN'T GET A
POLICE RAID AND THEY JUST HAD THEIR SEX AND DRUGS
AND WENT HOME TO BED. ONE RAID WE HAD, DAN
AYKROYD AND JOHN BELUSHI WERE WITH ME ON THE
STAIRS AND DANNY ASKED IF HE COULD STICK AROUND TO
WATCH."

*Paul Garcia, co-owner of the Continental, a Manhattan after-hours
club. It has closed, but there are two thousand more to choose from.*

In the winter of 1984, a disco called Area was the club of the
moment in New York. It had the crowds (a chic graffiti artist, Joan
Rivers, Malcolm Forbes), it had the decor (a "danger" motif,
including a steel-pin version of the traditional bed of nails), and,
on the evening in question, it had Jesus Christ. Walking on a small
pool of water above the dance floor.

Jesus was being played by the impersonator who earlier did the
club's Queen Elizabeth I and Quasimodo. As props for this "Faith"
theme, the establishment had installed a plastic light-up Vatican, a
Zen prayer chapel, a giant Buddha, and a mezuzah. A prayerful
scroll had been swiftly dispatched to the city's Catholic prelate,
John O'Connor, announcing this new take on heresy, and Area's
staffers could hardly contain themselves waiting for the photo-
opportunity-packed responding blast. "We'd already done a 'Holy
Communion, Corpus Christi' theme," the club's publicist, Joe
Dolce, explained, "and all the born-again types found it *highly*
offensive."

The reply arrived promptly from the powerhouse. "Dear Joe," O'Connor's secretary wrote equably, "The concept of finding the divine within the secular is indeed the beginning of holiness and peace. Please be assured of the Archbishop's best wishes on your endeavor."

Just as the Big Onion's rats have built up an immunity to warfarin, its people have acquired a steadily increasing genetic barricade against shock. This gives New York nights a special quality. The kind of feeling you'd get, dear tourist, if you would only tear yourself away from your drink at the Hors d'Oeuvrerie, the cocktail lounge atop the World Trade Center where you've spent your entire visit, and take a revivifying plunge out the window.

New Yorkers like to play the way they live. On the edge.

Sometime after Area's dalliance with religion, for instance, an establishment called Paddles began circulating engraved cards for its 140 West Twenty-fourth Street facilities.

"The Friendly S&M Club," it billed itself. A few blocks away, a store called the Noose was offering cats-o'-nine-tails handmade by the whipmaker who supplied Harrison Ford in *Raiders of the Lost Ark*. S&M appeared to be the trend of the second, since New York yuppies were learning to trot over red-hot coals at seminars given by the Learning Annex, a Manhattan school.

We put this to a Minor Media Personage who had been taking bullwhipping instruction from an Oriental. "When the S&M scene *was* at its height," she said scornfully, "we went to a bar called Dogs." She rose daintily to her feet. "I hear there's an opium den just opened downtown," she instructed a secretary. "Get me the phone number!"

"IN BERLIN, WHEN THEY TALK ABOUT EXPERIMENTALISM, THEY'RE TALKING EXPERIMENTALISM. I BROUGHT THIS GROUP TO NEW YORK FROM THERE THAT THROWS FLOUR AT THE AUDIENCE WITH COCKROACHES IN IT AND PLAYS MUSIC YOU DON'T WANT TO HEAR. VERY LOUD. VERY NON-MELODIC. ESSENTIALLY THE IDEA IS TO IRRITATE THE PETIT BOURGEOIS"

Rudolf, a consultant to the Palladium and a director of the disco Danceteria

You do not ever want to appear bourgeois, so sigh deeply the next time you're invited to, say, a foot fetish party, as though you are terminally bored. Thaasophobia, the morbid fear of boredom, is a most fashionable New York neurosis, explaining a phenomenon that the *Washington Post* has referred to as the city's "every night fever." As a remedy for your psychosis you indeed will want to be out every night. Take any two members of the Cast of This Book with you when you commence the tours suggested in this chapter. We've used Nancy and Henry, but only for convenience. You need VIPs with you to ensure you get photographed. The following are some questions we're frequently asked:

What Are We Going to Do Until the Speakeasies Open?

Certainly not go to the theater. Producing plays to get your name in the society columns is one thing but, as Rudolf, the Palladium consultant, points out, "very few people in New York want to see a play and have to follow a story. A fashion show is the maximum they can follow." Fashion is the key word here. The early hours of the evening should be spent digesting your soft-drug postprandial pick-me-ups and buffing your appearance (this takes some people all day), in order to become a *celebutant.* That's nightspeak for a person who attracts the attention of a celebrity, and the place where you're going to find celebrities, whether it's Malcolm and Princess Caroline you seek, or Boy George and Bianca, is on the club circuit. At legal clubs, such as Area, that is. At official closing time, four A.M., you can tail the celebs to the speakeasies.

What Kind of Fashion Should We Follow?

Pearls, in your nose or around your neck, are a must for either sex. Power may be an aphrodisiac, Henry, but what will work a lot better for a man of your height is an eighteen-karat gold chain, strung between your pierced nipples. Nancy probably will want to invest in a rubber dress, the kind pioneered by Dianne Brill, the young designer who appeared in an Andy Warhol music video with "hello again" stamped on her chest. Henry should slip a Giorgio Armani tux over a bedsheet (by a good designer, please), draped toga-fashion. The gold lamé dress on the fellow at the high society bender in chapter one quite eclipsed the zebra-striped jockstrap girding another guest. At the gala opening night of the Palladium, at this writing *the* place to celebutate, Boy George, done up in flame-red lipstick and wet-look police uniform, whispered sweet nothings into the ear of a zombie that had its bald cranium banded with electrical insulation tape. The one-way exchange lasted an eternity—fully five minutes—before a man in white gauze petticoats, who introduced himself as an "internationally renowned photographer" (do keep that résumé up to date), elbowed his way in and stole the Boy's attention. How was the party? "Fabulous and the greatest thing happening in New York," another guest—C. Z. Guest—told the *Times*.

What if We Don't Like the Champagne and Need to Complain to the Palladium's Owners?

Contrary to appearances, the greatest thing happening in New York is not owned by Steve Rubell and Ian Schrager. The pair are simply the Palladium's "conceptual consultants" and the club is owned, according to its records, by a group of business and real estate investors. You too may find yourself in this situation if, in your New York business operations, you adopt Rubell and Schrager's banking methods—at their former club, Studio 54, Glad Bags of cash were stowed in the rafters. Though the duo said this was just for convenience, they were obliged to spend some time in the slammer for tax evasion. That's one reason that the New York State liquor agency would have quibbled had they applied for a license for the Palladium; the other reason is spelled out in an agency memo that recalls vile goings-on at what was once the world's most famous disco. The document cites a press report about a birthday party at Studio 54 for Rubell at which a giant cake shaped like a Quaalude was wheeled in under a snowstorm of confetti and streamers: "Fifteen hundred gay voices" chorused "Happy Birthday," then "pop went the giant cake-pill and out popped [a woman]. . . . Rubell was visibly touched. He took the microphone and offered everyone a Quaalude."

Are We Going to Dance Tonight?

The most dedicated celebutants either don't dance at all (dancing creates sweat) or dance with themselves. This inspired a song by Billy Idol, "Dancing with Myself," which was a smash hit in New York clubs and led to a statement being issued by the Palladium's "conceptualizers," Steve and Ian, on parchment paper:

"There will be no blinking lights or strobes. . . . What was the 'me' generation is now the 'we' generation. People want to talk, share and be intimate."

What Are We Going to Talk About?

Yourselves. Preferably something risqué about yourselves. When Xenon, billed as "the ultimate discotheque," opened in New York in 1978, its co-owner Howard Stein made no bones about it. Sure, his Pop was a league-one loan shark who had been found floating in the city's Jamaica Bay, without his head. "There are gangster groupies," Stein explained to *New York* writer Julie Baumgold. "You say to them, 'That man's in the mob,' and they light up. It turns them on to think about me that way." Bobby Kennedy, Jr., had stared intensely into the club entrepreneur's eyes and begged, "Tell me about your dad."

Should We Go to the Palladium in Our Own Rolls-Royce or Rent a Limo?

Neither. By subway. This will give you a head start on a vital stage of any New York night, substance abuse. You'll recall that in 1984, a report was published that revealed that the hard stuff—coke, heroin, pills, LSD, and methadone—was so readily available from dealers who positioned themselves in the last cars of the IND A, CC, and DD lines, the BMT LL, and IRT Number 2 trains that customers were referring to riding in the "smoking" parlor. You also may get to party en route if you take public transportation. Vito Bruno, a young consultant to Pizza-a-Go-Go, the city's primo disco cum pizza parlor, has thrown several impromptu bacchanals on public property, including one at the Twenty-third Street subway station. As you would expect with a host whose other triumphs have included getting celebrities to sit on garbage (at a club, not the Staten Island dump), it was a blast if only because the music was provided by one of those ghetto blasters that make traveling the New York transit system such a pleasure. The racket woke up a homeless man who'd been dozing in the station, but, realizing he was not properly dressed, he quietly sat out the fun on the stairs. Bruno later found him a place in a shelter, and people who live near the city's discotheques may soon have to join this member of the forty thousand at the Sally Army. Residents of the Club Zone have tried to hang on to their homes with the aid of earplugs, barbiturates, and white-noise machines, but nothing screens out the low beat of the bass. At least so says Councilwoman Carol Greitzer, a handsome brunette who is the city's self-appointed Scourge of the Night (for her camp secret, see chapter nine). "New York is increasingly a twenty-four-hour city. You can avoid the law here for a long, long time . . ." the politician, a close ally of Ed Koch, fretted to Jeffrey Hogrefe of the *Washington Post.* "The lines bother people too. There are always lines of people . . . at three, four, five in the morning. People trying to find cabs on their way out. People trying to get in. . . . I have no idea who these people are." The following is a brief explanation. Skip it if you aren't a Greitzer constituent.

"THIS IS PUBLIC DEPRAVITY."

Paul Moore, the Episcopal bishop of New York, in a letter to the Times *about one guest's choice of transportation to the opening of Limelight, a New York club that is in a former Episcopal church. The woman was carried in on a cross, which she proceeded to dance with.*

Since the bourgeoisie's boiling point, like that of all Onionites, keeps rising, and since Xenon is now defunct, apostles of Gangster Chic are now outnumbered by acolytes of Area-style Sacrilege Frenzy. Like Area, Limelight also has secular events, of course. The highlights of these have included "I Am the Eggman," at which a woman popped eggs from various parts of her anatomy and cracked them over a briefly clad man sitting in a bathtub, and "Night of 100 Trees." Though this was a benefit for a cherished Kennedy family charity, the Special Olympics for the mentally handicapped, two of its hosts, Eunice Kennedy Shriver's son Bob and his cousin Caroline Kennedy, didn't show up when it was first held at the disco in 1983. A benefit organizer explains that Eunice was thumbing through a news magazine that contained a story about the twentieth anniversary of the assassination of John F. Kennedy when she came across a picture of the cross antics—and, like the bishop, had a fit.

"Evidently there had been some rather bizarre sacrilegious practices, but it had reached a point where it was too late to withdraw and calls were made to the club owner," says another organizer, Herb Kramer of the Kennedy Foundation, taking up the story. "We received firm assurances that [the cross] had nothing to do with the club and that the event would be conducted to our high standards." The evening raised a pile and the following year Limelight was used for what Kramer calls "a second very successful fundraiser."

Such are the pragmatic forces in the club as well as the charitable marketplace that Danceteria, a playpen with an agitprop floor (posters of Marx and Lenin), also found God. For Good Friday, this club imported the Jesus and Mary Chain, a British group that did not have its genesis at a Billy Graham revival. And after a happy couple tied the knot at a Catholic church where the priest, while stopping short of executing a gator dance, paid tribute during the ceremony to Darwin's theory of evolution, the club had everyone round to a reception. Another Danceteria hoot consisted of a reconceptualization of *Jesus Christ, Superstar* as a rite in which Christ receives forty lashes.

For its Holy Communion, Corpus Christi "theme happening," Area glued a communion wafer to the invitations. "My main objection," one of the club's habitués fumed in a protest letter, "is that you have belittled and mocked a religious symbol by using it on a club invitation and also by placing it in the same position that you placed a dog biscuit for your Pets Obsession invitation. This is not 'cool'."

Indeed it wasn't. The response gave Area's staffers the same sort of warm glow of achievement that stole over them when they sent out mousetraps to announce a Gnarly. Gnarly is California jargon for "anything twisted or extreme," and the event featured a diorama with strobe-lit electric chair and videotapes showing amputations, a hatcheting, and an exploding head. Some recipient heads exploded when they opened their invitations. "The mousetrap emitted ammonia sulphate," said Area's Joe Dolce. "It was great. It smelled horrible and we got letters from people who said they got their fingers caught in it. A pianist threatened to sue." Judy Collins had her name purged from the club's mailing list. That is because, unlike John Cardinal O'Connor, she did not understand what motivates the Night Frontier's pioneers. Perhaps the prelate was being too cynical, though. What it's *really* all about, some say, is *art* . . . .

"ARTISTS ARE THE STARS OF THE EIGHTIES. THEY ARE AS ROCK STARS WERE TO THE SIXTIES AND DESIGNERS WERE TO THE SEVENTIES

The Palladium's Steve Rubell

"BOHEMIA USED TO BE A PLACE TO HIDE. NOW IT'S A PLACE TO HUSTLE."

John Russell, chief art critic of the New York Times, *on the downtown art scene of which Palladium claims to be a part*

Yes, darlings, we know it's not the kind of art that you saw at Ann Getty's Metropolitan Museum party. But it's all out of the same theoretical school. The circus school. On the Night Frontier, anything that you can hustle for a buck, including yourself, is defined as art and becomes the subject of Serious Reviews in Serious Magazines and Newspapers.

Some Past Art Works:

The altar shooting out laser beams at Limelight's early parties; a Sieg-Heiling strut to über tapes by a singer who has cut an album on which a surfer blows his brains out (to giggles); a man tattooed with one thousand crosses (the blood spots, dripped onto fabric and numbered, were used as the preface to a tastefully bound, limited-edition book about the soirée); Delilah, a tame python, who would put her head in singer John Sex's mouth (having hogged on live rabbits, however, the reptilian beaut has outgrown this stunt and Sex has been talking of giving her to a zoo).

Moving to New York with a papier-mâché model of John F. Kennedy's brain in your luggage is the beginning of a career in art, which, when it involves you moving your limbs, is sometimes called "performance art." The brain arrived here with Ann Magnuson and was a relic from a theme party (the Kennedy Assassination) that the budding actress had thrown in the basement of her parents' home in Charleston, West Virginia. Her theme parties in New York have made her what you want to be. Famous. At one of them, she and her friends wrapped towels around their heads and pretended to take hostages at an Iran, Iraq, and Iroll night. She soon was the subject of stories in magazines like *People*. "We make [people] think," she was quoted as saying.

For some reason, though, when the *New York Times Magazine* did an entire cover story on the city's "Different Bohemia," a veil was drawn over the details of what was referred to in the opening paragraph as Ann's attitude of "affectionate mockery."

Where, you may demand, were the full-color shots of her nightclub reenactment of the Sharon Tate massacre? ("Someone fainted in the audience," she recalls.) Where were the lyrics of "Vulcan Death Grip," her affectionate parody of heavy metal? The piece did not mention the details of either of these skits nor Vulcan Death Grip's major prop—a bloody pig's head, nailed to a pole. This totem came loose during one performance at a club and bounced off into the crowd of cheering spectators. Oh yes. The lyrics. They included "Pigs Squeal in Fear" ("Now it is your turn

to die, you filthy swine") and "Holiday in Hell" ("my skin is fallin'
off and I'm wasted/I'm pukin' out my guts and I'm wasted"). Ann
dedicated another number, "Eat Shit and Die," to a Long Island
teenager who had killed himself after joining in a cult murder.

That was living art.

Sometimes art is art.

Subway graffiti art, particularly. Keith Haring, the city's best-
known graduate of the school of subterranean doodles, was
reported in the *Times*'s "Different Bohemia" analysis to be raking
in a six-figure annual income. He was among the artists brought in
to decorate the Palladium by its *art curator,* Henry Geldzahler.
Geldzahler, who used to be curator of twentieth-century art at the
Metropolitan Museum, also had an Italian painter fresco the club's
walls and ceiling, basilica-style, and employed Kenny Scharf to
encrust the public telephones in the basement lounge between the
rest rooms with plastic toys and to marabou the walls. The lounge
was one of the most traveled features on the club's opening night.
Partygoers flowed through it nonstop to check out the homage-to-
Area polysexual bathrooms. We weren't sure at first whether these
constituted art, but we were reassured by *The New Yorker*'s Calvin
Tomkins, who wrote that discos like the Palladium "may yet
produce a new academy of the baroque."

We're Not Shocked by Art Now It's Getting Reviewed by *The New Yorker.* Can't You Give Us Something Different?

We're glad you asked. You're in very good company.

"Once a trend is in full force," says Rudolf, the Palladium
consultant, "we sort of get disinterested in it. I'm turned off art."

The new turn-on may be charity. Limelight, as usual, is in the
vanguard. It staged a $15-a-head benefit in 1985 to aid a slew of
Hell's Angels, who had been incarcerated on federal racketeering
and drug charges. The racketeering statute, the so-called RICO
Act, "has been assailed by civil rights activists for being vague and
contradictory to constitutional rights," fulminated a release issued
for the nightclub by its glitzy PR firm. The event, intended to help
with the gang's defense costs, brought another contradiction to
light: "Twenty-five years ago, [the Angels] wore motorcycle out-
fits. Today, in their late forties, many of the leaders wear three-
piece suits, drive sedans and live in fashionable homes," the FBI
had instructed reporters after the arrest of the gang members.

The brutes who led a roar past the Manhattan federal pen to Limelight were wearing full leather regalia and driving Harley-Davidsons.

What the feds meant to say, of course, was that Angels are not yahoos. They did not dance—though this also may have had something to do with the fact that several of them were on crutches, having fallen off their Harley-Davidsons.

"We don't rape our women. We don't share our women. The club is like an Elks Club," an Officer Angel grunted into a mike. "Like what we believe in is freedom. We love America." One of their all-American motorbikes had been wheeled into the Limelight foyer. A placard announced that it cost $5 to have your picture taken with a gang member. This is an angle that other media hounds in these pages—we name no names—should learn from.

"I'D SAY THE SHAPE OF THINGS TO COME IS BREWING IN LONDON. YOU GLUE CORNFLAKES, PAINTED RED AND YELLOW, TO YOUR SKIN, SO IT LOOKS AS IF YOU'RE BEING EATEN ALIVE BY THE PLAGUE AND HAVE PUS COMING OUT."

Rudolf, the Palladium consultant. While we interviewed him, Chrysis, a transvestite secretary, was assembling some instructional artifacts for us, like program notes for the 1985 premier presentation of a gig called "Mermaids on Heroin" at Danceteria, his other club.

"The trendy set is always looking for something new," sighed an undercover narcotics detective, showing us the New York Police Department's latest revised (1985) five-hundred-word glossary of "Common Drug Terms." From this document it was apparent that our local sheriffs are laboring under the misapprehension that Timothy Leary is still at Harvard and the magic mushroom is a toy sold at F.A.O. Schwarz. One entry under B in the glossary was "Boo Hoo—A leader of the Neo-American Church, an organization which considers hallucinogens to be sacraments." Other entries included "Catnip—An animal stimulant; either smoked alone or used to dilute marijuana" and "Hippies—Persons believing in a way of life based on love and beauty."

For what's really the latest belief on this scene, the police, of course, only needed to look to California, where Leary now lives. After a neighbor called the police to complain that the sixtyish former Harvard prof and his wife were fighting, Leary revealed that actually they had been "making loud love...We regularly take extremely strong aphrodisiacs." The "cocaine" the cops confiscated from him was ketamine, he explained. Street name, "special k." That was in 1979. Like ethyl chloride (pronounced "ethel" and breathed from rags), ketamine now can be purchased from some dealers who work New York's gay clubs and, though it has yet to make the police list, clearly is a drug on the rise. Since it is manufactured by Parke-Davis as a general anesthetic ("It used to be used in childbirth," says a New York gynecologist), special k has an effect that is perfect for your long Gotham nights: it prevents pain while leaving the eyes open. Moreover, Parke-Davis elaborates in a leaflet prepared for physicians, "the psychological manifestations vary in severity between pleasant dreamlike states, vivid imagery, hallucinations, and emergence delirium."

"Sometimes," says Mary, a Manhattan noctambule who uses it, "you do black out."

A note to club owners about etiquette in the "crack" age:

Right: Offer your guests a giant cake shaped like a coke spoon.

Wrong: "Limelight when it opened was a big scandal, because it tried to attract the crème de la crème and employees were walking around knocking joints out of people's hands. They had to be told they couldn't do that," says John Howell, editor-in-chief of *High Times*. Just as the *Wall Street Journal* carries stock market tables, this New York-based magazine caters to a somewhat overlapping readership with a monthly dope price list. It also offers an "adviser" service. How else could "Rose of Bloomington, Indiana" find out whether she should continue smoking pot daily during her first trimester? ("Even though grass is known to ease morning sickness, cramps and 'bitchiness' in early pregnancy, we do counsel against smoking it in the first months," replied a Howell staffer.)

"I TEST FOR THE MIDDLE-CLASS DEALERS. THE ONE I'M MOST FAMILIAR WITH IS A CONSULTANT FOR HUD."

Justin (not his real name), a former mail-order entrepreneur, who now lives on a bench on Houston Street in Lower Manhattan and tests heroin and cocaine for small-scale dealers by injecting himself.

For those of you in Bloomington who are unfamiliar with the financial opportunities as well as the pleasures available in a city where illegal drugs are estimated to be a $45-billion-a-year business, which is somewhat over half the combined profits of the entire Fortune 500, here is a digression. The writer Nicholas Pileggi calculated in an article in *New York* that drugs do more for the New York economy than retail trade ($24.5 billion), manufacturing ($14.6 billion), or the service industry, including your hotel ($13.9 billion).

"At a time of widespread unemployment," Pileggi added, "the drug trade is notably labor-intensive." It employs between 100,000 and 300,000 part-time workers (teenage hit men, baggers, "steerers" who flag down your car) and about 10,000 bosses (the Lucchese family and the Sicilian-based arm of the Gambino Mafia family largely control the heroin; Colombians run the coke). In 1982, the New York rag trade had 141,804 workers. The New York construction industry had 83,936. Another way of looking at it is that so much money is made at the top end of the narcotics trade that weigh scales are used to count it, and dealers sometimes forget where they hid the booty.

"I had one guy who lost three hundred thousand dollars he buried somewhere upstate, and another guy I represented stashed some loot in a basement closet for six months," a defense attorney told Pileggi. "When he went to get it, he found that mice had eaten about forty-eight thousand worth."

In the middle echelons of the industry are the retailers who operate out of elegant brownstones or hi-tech SoHo lofts. One has a price card—"minimum purchase $500"—on the polished mahogany dining-room table, a reminder that since sustaining a habit is expensive, some of the circus's nighthawks deal on the side. An apartment in a West Seventy-sixth Street town house owned by Nik Cohn, the writer whose magazine article was the basis for the movie *Saturday Night Fever,* became the hub, according to lawmen, of a jet-set heroin and coke ring that catered to other writers and rock musicians. Traffic on the street gridlocked, federal agents were told by people in the neighborhood, as celebrities swept up in their limousines to do their "shopping." "Hyperbole!" retorts Cohn, who was arrested in the case, explaining that he had rented the apartment to a friend. "I never saw any limos, but a hockey player lived two doors away and he may have hired one." The apartment's tenant confessed to leading the drug operation and the government agreed to drop most of its charges against Cohn in return for his pleading guilty to possessing a small amount of cocaine. He was fined $5,000.

Traditionally, the low end of the narcotics market has been catered to by low-key dealers—small stores on the Deuce, a block of Forty-second Street in the Times Square area, that sell "vics" (dolts) phony drugs such as coke that is really incense ("whack"), or diluted dope ("beat drugs").

Sell whack to a vic, and you have given him a "whack attack." Brownish-yellow flakes that are supposedly THC, the active ingredient in marijuana, are also available, at an exorbitant price—and only when you take that first snort and burst into uncontrollable sneezes will you realize that you got sold a bunch of horse tranquilizer. As you try to rid your mouth of the taste of rust, you should fill these detumescent moments by reflecting on one deuce of a chemical fact, which is that there is no commercially feasible method of extracting pure THC from grass.

At least your fix will be smartly packaged. In the early eighties, the Mafia's salesmen started embellishing their heroin labels with Madison Avenue style cartoon artwork. The initial logos included little sketches tagged "Ayatollah's Best" and "Jimmy Carter," followed by "E.T." and a variety illustrated in honor of Mr. T.

At an end of the market that you probably never will see, there is always some "shooting gallery" that will charge $5 to give a junkie whose veins have collapsed a shot in the last firm part of the body left, the neck.

On a rainy fall night in 1979, Robert Kennedy's son David tooled up in his sports coupe to the ramshackle Shelton Plaza Hotel in Harlem on a drug-buying foray and was set on by three muggers. This was no surprise to a narcotics detective who worked undercover at the Shelton and another hotel on its stretch of West 116th Street. A photo in his files shows a sign at one of these hostelries:

RENT

Rent must be paid on a daily basis because we have a lot of Mother fuckers who want to be here for nothing. this hotel owes nobody Nothing
Friends if you are dealing with a white man it is so easy for him in his place of business but, when it comes to a Blackman trying to make it you want him to Kiss your ass
YOUR RENT WILL BE PAID ON A DAILY BASIS OR GET THE FUCK OUT!

"There were so many dealers in the rooms at those two hotels that guys there were charging visitors an entrance fee to go upstairs," says the detective. The young Kennedy's drug-induced death eventually occurred in a more fashionable hotel, in Palm Beach.

While Justin, once a highly successful businessman, has been on a similar decline, he is fussy about his dealers. He tests drugs for the kind who drive up in natty BMWs or Mercedes convertibles to his position on Houston Street. He used to own a mail-order jazz record company, but at forty-four, addicted to heroin, he has come to terms with living on a bench: "Diogenes," he says, carefully removing the tattered insoles of his filthy boots to check them for infestation, "lived in a barrel." He paws at his scalp. Most of his hair, once a carefully oiled triple pompadour, fell out one day when he was chewing raw gum opium. "I'd sweated it out," he says, gently inserting a syringe into an arm that has the spongy texture of raw liver. He is testing one-tenth of a half-gram of "cocaine" for purity. Later, he'll shoot another one-tenth of the grainy powder, the residue constituting his "payment." Fifteen minutes or so later, the surface of his face erupts into a boiling, streaming field of pustules.

"That's because what this is is *synthetic* cocaine," Justin says, mopping the water that has begun to drip in a steady rivulet from his nose, "and the chemicals are eating up the heroin already in me. What you look for with shootable cocaine is the flavor of fruit bubble gum, because that means it's been through the best processing. With good heroin, you get a warm glow."

He buys the few nondope necessities of his life with his Social Security check.

"I get one once a month for being terminally ill," he says. How long has this "illness" been bothering him? Ten years, he says.

"IT WAS REGULAR DISCO MUSIC. IT WOULD HAVE BEEN BETTER IF THEY'D PLAYED DRUG MUSIC, LIKE JANIS JOPLIN."

David, a drug connoisseur, of his visit to the Nickel Bag, the city's only known opium den

---

The Nickel Bag was—and maybe still is—a movable feast. When David caught up with it, in mid-1985, it was on East Sixth Street. Its outer chamber consisted of a rudimentary bar and dance floor, where well-dressed women and their escorts clustered, waiting for a young servant, his head shaven like a Buddhist monk, to usher them up some steps, past a bouncer, through the heavy drapes screening off the Dispensary.

When David's turn came, he sank into the comfortable pillow cushions that had been arranged around a hookah pipe and paid $30 for his gram of opium. Mein Host the dealer was a youngish man, in a dead-end kid's wool cap and glasses. Since most of his customers had never tried anything more demanding than coke or ketamine, the proceedings took on the temper of a seminar.

"You don't smoke it like hash or pot. You heat it and smoke the fumes," the dealer lectured.

"The best way," said David, interrupting him, "is to insert it anally."

After that icebreaker, everyone felt more at ease. The dealer poured mushroom tea from an orange-juice pitcher, to keep up the spirits of those waiting to use the hookah, and when he eventually ran out of opium, he cranked up the pipe with free hash.

"It was," recalls David, "a nice community thing, a party atmosphere."

"I'VE NEVER HEARD OF THEM. ARE THEY IN QUEENS?"

Deputy Inspector Leonard Kaplan, an enforcement official at the New York City Police Department, when the author asked him why the Mine Shaft and Hellfire, Manhattan's two raunchiest unlicensed taverns, were being allowed to stay open

---

It's nearing dawn—time to move on to the speaks. Unlike Nickel Bag, these illegal New York institutions specialize in sex or booze or both, and any drugs are a mere sideline. As in "If you rub your finger along the bar at ———'s you get a free line of coke," jests a young socialite. No need for you to be any less bold than Dan Aykroyd during that raid on the Continental after-hours club. There is no law against being a guest at such establishments. Nor should you expect too much in the way of help from the law if you run into any trouble during this stage of our tour. The *Daily News* reported that on average, fifty people a year are murdered at these bars:

"They drag the bodies out and insist that it didn't happen inside the club. By the time we get the call, the floor has been mopped to clean the blood. . . . We can't go in to search the place," a police officer, we assume keeping a straight face, told the newspaper.

With friends like these, the clubs keep about as low a profile as the mounted cop whom we watched mating with a hooker one summer's night. He'd hoisted her onto his steed and they were going at it on a well-lit street near Times Square. When Galaxy 21, a West Twenty-third Street after-hours club, was closed because of a dispute with its landlord, men stood outside the building on a frigid January night handing out leaflets that implored Galaxy patrons to protest by contacting television stations.

At this writing, Tory's, a luxurious three-level after-hours haunt at 119 East Twenty-seventh Street, teems with more bluebloods and celebrities some dawns than Mortimer's on a good lunch hour: a millionaire florist, expatriates from Andy Warhol's Factory, Madonna, fashion designers. Even a flunky from the Court of King Koch. We assume that it is because Tory's possesses a liquor license (which does not allow it, of course, to serve outside licensing hours) that the club feels securely enough placed to become perhaps the first establishment in its line of business to advertise:

"SPEAK EASY, open 7 nites 3A.M. till . . ." says the glossy little brochure about it that is distributed around town. The classical facade of the building was bathed in white floods the night that we visited, and at four-fifty in the morning, as a police car shot past, the florist's Rolls-Royce was parked out front. The club's elderly landlord, Gilbert Kiamie, a former silent movie star (stage name Don Gilbert Alonzo), has protested that this was not at all what he expected when he rented the premises out. He had been under the impression, his attorney, Joel Bernstein, explains, that the plan was for "an 1890s English-style club, where they discussed literature and fine art and sipped sherry." We mentioned the Rolls-Royce. "Some nights," Bernstein said, "you have *six or seven* limos parked outside and hookers plying their trade in them. You can see the springs rocking." After making increasingly frantic pleas to the authorities to shutter the place, Kiamie decided to prove definitively that Tory's wasn't the Algonquin Round Table: he put a private eye on the case. The sleuth submitted his report. He'd been "approached by transvestites which proceeded to place their hands on the private parts of the operative's body." A few minutes later the ace discovered that his wallet was missing.

"There were a couple of summonses for after-hours sales, and they were dismissed on the defendant's motion," says Mike Linn, a lawyer for the owner of Tory's. "They stay within the confines of the law."

"Cops and firemen are welcome here," gloated a Tory's staffer the night we visited. "They love it." Off-duty, he meant. It's unlikely that many cops are demanding payoffs from the illegal clubs. The memory is too fresh of that unfortunate melodrama in which the Continental, the late John Belushi's as well as Dan Aykroyd's after-hours pond, turned out to be harboring an FBI undercover operation. The club's co-owner, Arthur Weinstein, would tuck a transmitter under his natty white dinner jacket and black cummerbund, so the feds could hear what was going on.

In a trial that grew out of these best-dressed-list techniques, Weinstein testified that one summer night in 1982 he was sitting in his limo outside the club, counting receipts, when a squad car pulled up and an officer got out and "climbed into the back seat with me.

"I said, 'Hi,'" the club owner told the court. "I knew what he was there for. I paid him three hundred dollars and that was it."

The casual police attitude toward illegal bars that is reflected in Deputy Inspector Kaplan's comment to us about the Mine Shaft (gay after-hours sex) and Hellfire (mixed after-hours sex) clubs is ascribed to lack of manpower by department insiders. Accordingly, speakeasies should be high on your list of financial opportunities. Unless you decide to get a liquor license like Tory's, no city codes to obey and no taxes to pay, because officially you don't exist. Or you can avoid taxes quite openly: the Mine Shaft and Hellfire were registered with New York State as not-for-profit corporations. Presumably none of this was a total surprise to local regulators, if only because an informer was mailing in regular reports to the police about the after-hours scene.

"You missed a fun week at the Shaft," said one of these missives. It was dated October 23, 1979. The report went on to claim that a staffer at another sex club, the now-defunct Chateau————, was pimping children, to customers such as a politically connected Rhode Island millionaire. "Also one way to help close Chateau," the stoolie added, "is to get ——— on taxes for the club or even personal income. Well he hasn't paid any and Chateau has been open over one and a half years." The Koch administration subsequently conceded that it had learned about the Mine Shaft's tax gimmick and started to investigate it and other illegal clubs around 1982. But the probe was discontinued because it wasn't producing "a large enough financial return." The city was more interested in chasing "the bigger fish," Ed Koch elaborated. The Mine Shaft finally was ordered closed in 1985, because of the AIDS epidemic, and the Hellfire shuttered itself, under heat from the authorities because of the public health crisis. Not because of any pressure from the guardians of the Big Onion's finances.

Another famous after-hours establishment also has undergone some changes. Page Six, a bottle club and disco at West Houston and Varick streets, suddenly was renamed Houston-on-Hudson and, where drinks one week were being served from a gleaming brass-railed bar, a few days later they were being produced from a hatch in the wall. Explained Lt. Bill Shannon, of the police club squad, precisely because manpower is short, when an illegal saloon's number finally does come up, the hope is not to have to raid more than twice: "The second visit, we call Emergency Services to help. They come in with chainsaws and axes and cut up the bar, which we take with us as evidence in case the judge wants to see it. We cut up the bar at Page Six *and* we took their leather couches."

CLUB 62
CORDIALLY INVITES YOU FOR YOUR GAMING ENTERTAIN-MENT
BLACKJACK & POKER
IN COMFORTABLE SURROUNDINGS ON MANHATTAN'S UPPER EAST SIDE
FOR YOUR PLEASURE COMPLIMENTARY DRINKS & FOODS ARE PROVIDED
24 HOURS A DAY   FREE PARKING   7 DAYS A WEEK

Invitation mailed in 1985 to Upper East Side gamblers, on the back of an imitation $100 bill, from a casino at 1122 First Avenue (212-752-4724) that, at this writing, has changed its name but has the same address and phone number

---

After the after-hours clubs, many New Yorkers like to celebrate the new day with a throw of the dice. Though charitable "Las Vegas Nites" are the only form of gaming that's legal in the state, the Big Onion has more casinos than Las Vegas and Atlantic City combined. Invariably, these operate around the clock, and many bartenders and limo drivers can give you their addresses. Getting on their mailing lists is more difficult. All you used to have to do was subscribe to a gaming magazine or sign the book at a New Jersey or Nevada casino. But our local gambling lords have

stopped buying lists from publishers and the out-of-state competition. Too much riffraff was coming in, explains an associate of the
legendary Johnny Mac.

Johnny, a Century 21 real estate broker, appears here under his
nickname. He is a leading advocate of legalizing gambling in the
state and, to hasten that day, he runs several of New York's nicer
casinos, guarded by freestyle wrestlers. For instance, the associate
says, Johnny was behind a Bronx haunt that advertised "gambling" on an illuminated marquee and accoutred its croupiers in
shirts lettered "For Your Gaming Pleasure."

"Maybe they're testing the gambling laws," said the police
lieutenant who interrupted the party.

Not testing them. *Using* them. It is not illegal to gamble in New
York State. It is illegal to operate or work in a casino, but the
offense is a misdemeanor, and arrests customarily result in fines of
a mere $50 to $500. "When you get busted, you're supposed to
roll over and die," says the Johnny Mac associate, "but Johnny
looked at the law and opened up again three hours later." Since the
cops are permitted to confiscate the scratch during raids, certain
defensive measures do have to be taken. Women employees at
Johnny's casinos have been known to pose as patrons. When the
police arrive, they're sitting demurely, clutching their purses, the
bills hidden away in their hairspray cans.

The real estate man, who was born in Britain, sports a coat of
arms (dice rampant) at his current flagship casino, on East Eightieth Street. It offers nonstop blackjack and Johnny personally
selected the high-quality wallpapers. The establishment used to
be called the Erin Society, "but we had too many Irish guys, so we
took the name away and right now it has no name," says Johnny's
associate.

The Trump Club, not one of Johnny's, has changed its name.
This two-floor spread at 227 East Fifty-sixth Street (212-319-0430)
was called Bridge & Games East when we visited, and was
offering one of the few nonfloating poker games in New York.
Color photos of people playing games—though not of them wager-
ing money—were displayed by the street entrance. We took the
elevator to the club's first level, a huge open area where maybe
twenty senior citizens were playing Scrabble and bridge and
backgammon. For $1 an hour, said a sign near the coffee (50 cents
a cup) dispenser. After Eddie, a young Sicilian wearing a gold
crucifix and a Korem medallion watch, checked our bona fides
(say you're rich tourists), he escorted us up a back stairway to the
well-worn baize gaming tables, in a locked, windowless room.

"You get a bunch of cutthroats playing there," an acquaintance of ours, who is a professional gambler, said angrily when we told him where we had been. "Little Red, this Italian guy, said could he borrow fifty dollars from me because he'd lost and he'd give it back to me the next day, so I went there the next mornin' to get my money and I said, 'Where's Little Red?' Eddie said 'He's not here no more.'"

That may be how it was. Under the Trump Club regime, "The club is not responsible for your gambling. There's not supposed to be any gambling on the premises," said a staffer. He added that poker and Eddie were both still around.

A third category of casinos in the city are run by the mob, whose front men can be quite disarming. One place was managed by several ancient mariners. "We went to handcuff them—one was an eighty-year-old—and they showed us their scars. They'd all been in the Victory Memorial Hospital [Brooklyn] coronary unit," says Capt. Jerome Piazza of the police department's public morals division.

The five New York Mafia families aren't interested only in illegal gambling. They are devoted to the Catholic church, so they often are involved in Las Vegas Nites, raising money for religious causes and other good works. Sometimes, to be sure, they do get their beliefs a bit mixed up. A young sprig of the Lucchese family was arrested for promoting gambling at "Kol Jacob Hall," in Brooklyn's Sheepshead Bay area. The plush, wood-paneled room had been touted as a Jewish neighborhood center, but the police became suspicious when an angry husband complained that his wife had blown $3,000 there in a single evening. In Queens, there were complaints that "Congregation Kol Israel" was staffed by uniformed dealers and croupiers, and was not holding services.

There have also been *Gourmand* Vegas Nites. One of these, near Kennedy Airport, featured a pig with an apple in its mouth and was really a recruiting drive, says Lt. Remo Franceschini, an organized crime expert. He explains that when his men walked in on this feast, airport employees, who might be needed in future heists, were being encouraged to sign markers by henchmen of the Luccheses.

It was the Genovese family who introduced the gourmand's game of chance, a card game previously monopolized by European nobs, to New York—baccarat. One of the family's soldiers initially ran the play, in a loft decorated with ultramodern paintings and sculpture.

Sophisticated stuff. Still, there was an excellent response to those fliers that went out to a thousand federal fugitives notifying them that they were the lucky winners of a free "Gem Tours" outing to the Sands Hotel and Casino in Atlantic City. *With a $50 cash bonus!* Twenty of the crooks dashed to the appointed Brooklyn place to take the bus, where federal marshals—wearing green Gem Tours T-shirts—welcomed them aboard for the short drive to the holding cages. "A lot of them said it was the first time they had ever won anything," said a federal agent.

"THE DANCERS AT A LICENSED PREMISES CAN SHOW THEIR BREASTS AND THEIR NIPPLES SO LONG AS THEY ARE ON A PLATFORM AT LEAST EIGHTEEN INCHES HIGH AND SIX FEET FROM THE NEAREST PATRON."

Spokesman for the New York State Liquor Authority, explaining the law

---

Obviously, dear visitor, you want more than a long-distance view of mammaries once you have persuaded the wife to go linen-shopping at the midnight sale you've heard is on at the Queens branch of Gimbels. You're going to the ballet, you've told her. Anyway, a balletic performance at Dreams, a heavily advertised emporium ("25 Nude Dancers...Happy Hour Daily...Bachelor Parties") at 225 East Fifty-fourth Street (212-644-0779).

Dazzled by the spectacle of the five unclothed lovelies who were undulating on the stage and periodically bending over in such a way that a gynecologist could perform a full internal examination, our reporter quickly parted with the $10 "membership fee" that was requested by a Dreams waitress. "You get three free drinks for that," she explained, "beer, wine, or champagne." A skimpily attired B-girl slipped into the seat across the table. A waiter promptly appeared and, placing a large champagne glass in front of the lady, filled it with the contents of a small gold-topped bottle.

"Twenty dollars, sir," he said.

The lady introduced herself as Lynne.

Our reporter introduced himself as a British businessman.

"We have private lounges," said Lynne, coyly regarding him from under her lashes, "where for two hundred dollars for one hour or one hundred and forty-five dollars for thirty-five to forty minutes we can have some fun. It includes all my cocktails and a bottle of champagne."

The waiter reappeared. "We take all credit cards and traveler's checks," he hissed in the reporter's ear. "Your receipt will show as a restaurant."

Lynne's champagne glass received a refill, and since he was now down $55, with tips, in twenty minutes, our reporter departed.

Around this time, a bar employee invited an undercover cop to "get to know" another of the jezebels, Renée, for $200. The cop bargained it down to $150 and handed over the moolah, but the "private" lounge turned out to be almost as public as the Dreams dancers' more interesting parts. It was behind a partition, next to the stage. "I then asked her where was the private viewing area where I could 'get laid' and she responded by saying that she would stroke my penis for forty dollars, plus tip," the officer said in an affidavit.

"We also did tests on the 'drinks,'" says the police department's Captain Piazza. "They're basically grape juice. They're not licensed to sell liquor, so that's basically the one thing they're doing right."

Dreams used to be called the Gotham Discotheque, and its management seems to have become intrigued by the vitamin potential of juice after a police raid that uncovered what the department described at the time as a "drug supermarket."

At this writing, though a judge had ordered the removal of the partition that ruined the cop's $150·enjoyment, Dreams was still selling its reveries, protected by the First Amendment against attempts to shut it down by the city fathers—who do not seem to understand that dreams are the currency of the entire New York night. An example. Leaning against the deejay booth at Studio 54, Andrew Wainrib, the owner of the city's Kangaroo Club, was enjoying Lorna Luft's "live" performance on the catwalk. "All of a sudden," Wainrib recalls, "Lorna croaked. Someone accidentally banged the tape to which she was lip-synching and there was this sudden silence."

Nor are such illusions anything new. When the original *NEW YORK: Confidential!* was published, in 1948, the owners of the city's burlesque bars were revealed to be preserving their customers' probity by demanding that they pay *before* being admitted into a room supposedly writhing with naked kittens. In fact, the girls' "generously proportioned panties and bra (which always remain on) are constructed," Jack Lait and Lee Mortimer wrote, "of material thick as carpeting, and as opaque."

Still, there always are exceptions, and the unrequited wolf will find some of them for an $8 admission at the Harmony Theatre, at 205 West Forty-eighth Street. It used to be called the Melody Burlesk, but was renamed following the disclosure in 1982 that one of its then owners was an assistant state attorney general (his specialty was worker's compensation and other labor law cases). Though we didn't get to meet the current management, the White House (202-456-1414) probably can put you in touch—posted on the wall in the Harmony lobby is a letter from President and Mrs. Reagan—thanking one of the bosses for an LP record, *Angela.*

"You were kind to remember us in such a thoughtful way. We look forward to enjoying your gift," the letter says.

The lyrics are unavailable, but we hope they reflect the Harmony's spirit of camaraderie. It was "Mardi Gras" time when we took our seats. For $1-a-minute, women in G-strings plopped onto the laps of the affluent-looking men sprinkled around the stage and allowed them to suck on their pendulous breasts. The prettiest girl in the room had her ears firmly attached to a Sony Walkman.

Just be careful if you decide to put *your* daughter on the Night Frontier stage that she doesn't use the New York talent agency that allegedly is controlled by a viceroy of the Genovese crime family, Matthew "Matty the Horse" Ianniello. The *Times* reported on the experience of a young woman who applied for a job at the agency, which supplies much of the city's topless and bottomless flesh. She was interviewed by a manager whose office was decorated with stickers that advised, "Help Prevent Rape—Say Yes."

"We treat our girls right," the manager said, "if they behave." A dancer who had transgressed, Suzy, was seated in the room, wearing a padlocked dog collar around her neck. Handing out doughnuts to other women in the office, the manager placed a large bone in front of Suzy. "Until that collar comes off," he said, "she can't leave New York State, date more than once a week, or miss an appearance in a club.

"If she does," he added with a grin, "she'll never work again."

___

"THEY HAVE CHAMPAGNE AT FIFTY DOLLARS A GLASS."

One of the many versions of what it's like at Club Forty-eight (there is no evidence that it exists)

The only constant in the descriptions that for years have made the rounds in certain sectors of chic society about what is supposedly a necrophiliacs' bar on West Forty-eighth Street is that none of them contain an address—and all of them appear to be based on secondhand information. Generally this hip conversation starts between spoonfuls of raspberry sorbet at literary dinner parties on the Upper West Side or in Brooklyn Heights. Still, it was a surprise when, in his biography of Tennessee Williams, *Cry of the Heart,* Dotson Rader wrote that the late Truman Capote actually attempted to persuade him and Tennessee to go to the club: "Its chief attraction, Truman claimed, was a real dead body. . . . Truman seemed confused by our objections. 'Disgusting?' he said. 'But they change the body *every day!*'"

Where did Capote get this amazing information?

"Truman said he was told about it by Claus von Bülow," says Rader.

We asked von Bülow, the Danish socialite who was acquitted of the attempted murder of his heiress wife, about this. He never even met Capote, he insists—and never heard of any Club Forty-eight. He *was* aware, however, that his name was being linked to the beepees' most nauseating little fantasy. "It started as a bad-taste joke in Capri in 1948," von Bülow says. He had arrived in Italy from London, and was so pale that Prince Dado Ruspoli, a Latin playboy, jested that he *looked* like a necrophiliac. "It was a crack at dinner and we live with it forty years later," von Bülow adds calmly. "It has been useful in the last four years for people who had it in for me."

"THE THING THAT I CAN'T STAND ABOUT THIS CRISPO CASE IS THAT THEY USED AN INCREDIBLY CHEAP MASK."

John*, a New York-based federal bureaucrat, on the sadomasochistic slaying of Eigil Vesti, a Norwegian fashion student, by a sidekick of the socially connected Manhattan art dealer Andrew Crispo

---

John, an avid practitioner of S&M, was joking, of course. Still, the grisly discovery of Vesti's corpse, his head zippered into a black leather mask, did not do much for the image of the bureaucrat's hobby in New York. The young man had been killed in a frenzy of violence that allegedly was the culmination of numerous

* A pseudonym.

S&M sessions involving Crispo, his sidekick Bernard Le Geros, and other youths at the dealer's East Fifty-seventh Street gallery. Accordingly, a certain note of evangelicalism creeps into John's voice when he gives lectures on S&M around the country to groups like medical students. *True* S&M is consensual, he tells them. "Mummification, for instance, is a nice little skill. It takes about fifteen minutes to mummify a person in stretch elastic. Some people enjoy having it done in adhesive tape," he adds thoughtfully, "because it hurts more when it is ripped off."

John's bosses in the Reagan administration know about his interest in the inquisitional arts because the matter came up when the Secret Service gave him his security clearance. Prudential-Bache, on the other hand, probably did not know that one of its stock-dividend managers was helping to open up an S&M "art gallery" and an S&M club—using some of the loot, federal prosecutors said, from a scam in which the executive and several confederates whipped nearly $19 million out of the brokerage firm.

While such capers are hardly the norm, this does go to reinforce the impression that Marquis de Sade complexes are concentrated heavily among the middle-to-upper classes in New York. The men and women who meet Monday nights at the Eulenspiegel Society, an East Fourth Street S&M consciousness-raising group (212-477-6588), are mostly yuppies or middle-aged professionals with a leavening of faded themes who appear to have wandered in from an Area party, including an emaciated young man with a luxuriant beard who likes to recreate the Crucifixion for a nonsexual spiritual high. "He sounds quite rational," murmurs the Harvard-educated management consultant who introduces us to him.

Named after a German folklore character who liked to schlepp heavy loads up mountains, the society was founded by Pat Bond,* a masochist—or, to use the preferred term in this scene, submissive—who was having problems finding a suitably incongruous mate. By definition, whether or not they're into Torquemada scenes, most New Yorkers share Bond's "s" tendency (submissives always refer to themselves in the lowercase). The city's sadist population probably numbers under one million, and is confined for the large part to certain stars of the circus, non-English-speaking cab drivers, sports-team owners, and chefs at celebrity restaurants. None of whom were available for Bond, a schoolteacher at the time.

"I married a woman I thought would be dominant," he says,

---

* A pseudonym.

"but it turned out she just wanted a regular relationship."

He is much happier these days, however, as he has learned word processing and become a secretary. "I wish this had happened much earlier in my life," he says. "One of my bosses is a woman and she's kind of interested in me a little, though I don't know if she'd go for S&M." For a time, the group did have a first-rate dominant as its president. Jack ———, while married, maintained a female slave on the side who got her kicks by pretending she was a horse and being led around on a bridle and bit. "When people imagine S&M, they think of a few nuts out there going around hitting each other," as Jack once said.

Control of the society these days, by all appearances, is back with the submissives. Normally, its meetings begin with a panel or lecture. How to tell your mom you're into S&M; "S/M Without Pain"; "Ethnic S&M"; or "Flirting in the Scene" (it is rude to ask Mistress Blondie to let you lick her boots on a first date). This is followed by "the circle," a sort of combination public confessional/personal ad in which each partcipant says, "Hi, I'm ———, and I'm into..."

But the evening of our visit, the society is having a "social." Small tables are set with munchies and candles and the bar is serving juice and soda. A thin woman in black is wandering the room with her slave, a ruddy-faced business executive in a pad-locked dog's choke collar, while several dominatrices, garmented in evening dress or black satin underwear, mill around the emcee. He is a beige-faced man in an unfashionable heavyknit sweater. "Fellows," he says nervously, "these are very nice ladies. They will help you act out your fantasies."

The dominatrices spank the members and some of the members spank each other. In this listless atmosphere, the only purposeful action is provided by a college professor who orders Kimberley, the pouty brunette who has accompanied him into the room, to open up the smart black leather attaché case she is carrying. It contains a paddle, and he thwacks her soundly with it, then offers us a back massage.

If this tepid scene hardly rates after the aggressive displays that made the Big Onion's S&M clubs a topic of awed gossip among the beepees in the seventies, that's because of the AIDS epidemic. Though you can't get AIDS from a whip, your consciousness-raising efforts can be embargoed if they get too explicit under state regulations designed to combat the disease that, in one early instance, were enforced by city food store inspectors. Though it was doubtful whether these sleuths could tell a ball gag from a cheese ball, they were assigned to investigate the baroque mysteries of the Mine Shaft. "They had a thorough clinical briefing," explained a spokesman for the Department of Consumer Affairs.

In the old days, you didn't need any briefing to understand some of what you were seeing. "At the opening night of Chateau ———," the informer who used to snitch on S&M bars to the police says whimsically, "a Long Island man nailed his girlfriend's breast to the wall and, when someone screeched, she said, 'It couldn't have been that bad. I did climax.' It was a sterile hypodermic needle."

In that halcyon era, the Hellfire Club, a fetid, stone-walled cellar, was what Tory's is today to the beepees. The bugle-beaded lovelies and their dates would cluster around a hammock affair in which men of various ages and shapes reposed while having fists—male or female, the club being ecumenical—thrust up their anuses. Removable tattoos (sold on the premises) decorated the women's décolletage; rented whips ("$5 plus deposit") dangled from their escorts' belts. Then the crowd would surge en masse to the murkily lit booth area, where maybe an Urban Cowboy would be anointing his sweetie's skin with hot wax from a black candle. Or to the stained bathtubs where flabby men, who all seemed to look like small-town bankers, lounged in hope of receiving a "golden [urine] shower"—the Real Thing, as distinct from the warm ammonia squeezed from a rag onto dupes as they lie back, eyes obediently closed, at some of the city's more expensive brothels. In later years, as the socialites retreated to more conventional clubs, or began to spend long evenings nibbling $50 pizza dinners, a new crowd descended on the bar—a crowd of victims of Portnoy's Complaint. Mostly they were from New Jersey and they would wander the room, playing with themselves.

"No fighting/Decorum/ . . . Join scenes only upon invitation," said a board in the lobby where guests were required to sign the Night Frontier's most realistic declaration, testifying they were not present "*on duty* as a police officer" (our italics).

Deprived of such meeting places, Mr. Fixit types now pore over a manual by David Barton-Jay, the Big Onion's Enema Master, that explains how to conduct this "renewal and cleansing" ritual with no outside help except the strains of Robert Fripp's "Let the Power Fall" on your stereo. Since the brownstone with electrified water in its elevator shaft also has gone out of business, you might consider booking the Onion's Electric Shock Master to come to your home to administer a revitalizing dawn jolt. Just the thing for when you get back from Paddles, a club that is perhaps the last repository of the original Hellfire esprit. Entire suburban families—matrons in floral print dresses, their husbands, their daughters—mingle with the salesmen in tartan jackets, professional dominatrices (one has to go somewhere on one's night off), and tourists from Boston at the club that prides itself on "friendly" S&M. You can borrow equipment from owners Michael and Donni. "I try to provide what they're going to enjoy,... whips, nipple torture, cock torture devices, a box of rope for cock bondage..." Donni says. She also gives instruction: "I tell people not to do a caning until their aim is perfect with a riding crop." But the big draw is the cabaret. Wearing a smart SS cap, Jack the Stripper suspends the near-naked Lady Leah from a cross over a bowl of leaping blue flames, and after she has let out a few shrieks, ignites two torches and tenderly rolls them over her body, to a tape of David Bowie's "Putting Out the Fire with Gasoline."

"The fire department sent some guys to watch me and gave me a certificate that the naphtha mixture I use is safe. The trick is to keep the torches moving very fast, so you create a hot wind, and don't touch the skin more than four seconds," Jack says. **Lady Leah's Beauty Secret:** "I use a good cream, like Clinique, once a day." The fire also saves her money on depilatories. She and Jack are available to entertain at private parties, and at bar mitzvahs. "For those I sing 'Little Me' or 'Mame' or 'Dolly' and then do a classical dance, tossing the torches, to 'Chariots of Fire,'" Jack says.

The former beauty parlor owner Belle de Jour and her hardworking girls are to pain what the Mayflower Madam and her employees were to love. A one-hour session giving or receiving torture at Belle's facilities at 192 Third Avenue (212-505-7817) can be had for about the price of a pair of theater tickets, and there is a show, Paddles-style, Sunday nights. Once you're past the demure little sign, "B. D. Jour," on the front door, you're plunged into an ambiance that is a most skillful blend of the English country house touches popularized by Mario Buatta with early auto-da-fé. "I did all this room myself," Belle declares proudly, showing us the chamber with a monkey cage, which clients reach by scaling a ladder. A copy of the latest *Architectural Digest* is lying on a nearby couch. "And this is the wheel that turns," she says. The contraption creaks authentically as she demonstrates it. She snaps at Bobby, a lean man with crooked lips who is her House Slave, to empty the cigarette butts and stops to tidy a cluttered bondage bench. "And this," she says finishing up the tour, "is the reception room where the ladies sit." There is a sign on the mirror. "Start Thinking. Stop Littering."

One of the ladies, Anne Pierce, did think about it, and has gone into the S&M business for herself—in a suburb that was once the territory of a friend of hers, "Baroness" Monique Von Cleef. Monique's pain parlor was the subject of a landmark 1967 obscenity case. After a shrink testified that photos from this dominatrice's establishment showing men being whipped were "deviant in the biological sense that no children would issue from them," Von Cleef was found guilty. The Supreme Court overturned the conviction, but the feds, after discovering that the Baroness kept a little black book filled with the names of military officers, fretted that since the lady was no lady, she might be a Soviet spy. After investigations by the Office of Naval Intelligence, the CIA, the FBI, and other agencies, two Lovers of the Lash—the commander of a Polaris submarine and a colonel in the Strategic Air Command—were among those forced to take less sensitive jobs or quit, according to John Noonan, who prosecuted the case.

Anne Pierce, Monique's geographic successor, can be reached by writing P.O. Box 26, Belleville, NJ 07109.

Note to the Cashiered Strategic Air Command Colonel:

You may have found your flying career unpleasantly comfortable, but we know you won't be disappointed if you try Anne's hang-glider harness. A friend of hers, a champion sailor, copied it from the rig in which the maidens tormented their boss in the film *Nine to Five*. She charges by the scene, not the hour, or you can pay her in kind. Roger, a foreman for an electrical-equipment company, is into "mild asphyxiation," so she creams him with an industrial lubricant and squeezes him like sausage meat into a full bodysuit, in return for which he does chores like installing her room air conditioners.

A Day Frontier Digression: Time to make restitution for that secret evening at Dreams by buying the wife a piece of jewelry at Erotics Gallery, 64 Spring Street (212-219-1028). Doug Johns, who runs what claims to be "the only gallery in the world uniquely devoted to erotic art," sells sweet little phallic pendants and miniature vaginal lips. He also created AT&T's Arthur W. Page trophy, which the telephone giant presented each year, until the breakup of the system, to the member company that did the best public relations work. The award depicted Golden Boy, a statue at AT&T's New York headquarters famed for its naturalistic gonads—to the dismay of one of the first honorees. "He was worried," an AT&T official explains, "about the effect the trophy would have on his secretaries." Doug also has been hewing a bronze, "Evolutionary Ensemble," for a southwestern tycoon, one of the Forbes 400. It shows the three stages of arousal of a Texan-sized penis, but Doug is not optimistic that you will see it on display at the ranch: "Although what I'm doing is an intellectualization, most of the people who collect things like this can't get beyond the basic and keep them under lock and key," he says. "Since they want to be totally anonymous, I can't even get any decent publicity."

The longest-running Off-Off Broadway show (nearly ten years) did not have that problem. *Another Way to Love,* being about just that, included a skit about a man whose sexual kinks were related to his wish to become a chicken. Featuring a segment from the show on NBC-TV, Tom Snyder scratched his head. "Do people really do those things?" the presenter implored his millions of viewers. Produced in a SoHo loft by a not-for-profit group, The Project, the show is still available on request to college human sexuality classes. For information, phone 212-226-7600.

The city's other long-running S&M teach-in, the Castle, consisted of a demonstration by a husband-and-wife team, Jay and Diane Hartwell, that stirred D. Keith Mano to espouse a new theory in a 1985 *Playboy* essay: "The family that flays together stays together," he urged. Jay performed naked except for a leather jock and a gun holster containing his torture hardware; Diane would appear in Opium perfume, a lacy garter belt, leather wrist cuffs, and bare buttocks. Angie, the couple's eldest daughter, wore jeans and a T-shirt. She did not perform, but helped with the chores. She was mixing the nonalcoholic punch and setting out a fruit and cheese buffet when we arrived for our heartening final stop on the Night Frontier.

"We are truly your middle-class American family. We vote, we raise our children. The Castle is incorporated and pays its taxes. No booze. No drugs. You probably won't run into more conservative types than myself," said Jay, a small, anxious man with a manicured beard.

Angie came over to him, dragging a pile of chains and manacles. "Mom took the sugar," she said.

Mom bussed Dad on the cheek.

"Diane's the most famous sexual submissive in the world," her husband said.

On stage at the Castle, he would dangle a pound of fishing weights from Diane's pierced nipples. Sear her skin with a whip as she hung from a hoist mechanism. Clamp steel clothespins to her breasts. But first, an introductory pep talk. Jay would perch on a sawhorse, a straw hat tilted back on his head, the urban farmer in the Big Onion Field, and tell the audience how accommodating his yen to "tie ladies up" saved their marriage.

"It's fun, folks," he burbled later, giving his wife an affectionate hug between gigs. "It really is."

THE NEXT FRONTIER

Once it's fun, it's time to move on. The Castle vanished soon after the *Playboy* encomium, apparently of its own volition. And, while Anne Pierce, the Belle de Jour alumna, still has a thriving whip-tease business and devotes some time to art (poetry, short story writing, and body painting her Dutch-born slave), this princess of pain is striking out in what we do believe is a new direction. "I'm researching tea ceremonies," Anne explains, "because I want to formalize some of my relationships." Though it is too soon to be sure, therefore, you may want to try substituting "special t" for the "special k" (ketamine) at your next dinner party.

8

LIBERATING FORCES

"WE OFFER A SEX-POSITIVE, COMFORTABLE, NURTURING ENVIRONMENT WHERE WOMEN HAVE ACCESS TO THE TOOLS OF PLEASURE. THAT'S WHY WE SELL VIBRATORS. WE VIEW THEM AS 'LIBERATING APPLIANCES'..."

From the "Dear Sisters" letter in a brochure for Eve's Garden, a feminist sex boutique at 119 West Fifty-seventh Street

New York probably has more liberation movements than the whole of Central America, and the most high-profile of them, evincing a foaming quality reminiscent of Melvin P. Thorpe's tirade against the Chicken Ranch in *The Best Little Whorehouse in Texas,* have to do with one of the city's largest industries. Sex.

Unfortunately, since the Fortune 500 does not address such statistics, no precise measure is available of the value of the tsunami of depravity that has been lapping at the circus's doorstep and traditionally has provided a quiet rental income to certain of the ladies' husbands. For a rough flood gauge, however, you could add the pickings from the Times Square flesh palaces—one estimate is that a billion dollars is spent in them each year—to the earnings of the Big Onion's prostitutes. Its galaxy of whores is generally regarded as the biggest in numbers, as well as other statistics, in the United States and, for an idea of how they're doing, you only have to watch a rather common round-the-clock drama on several local thoroughfares.

Eyes popping in anticipation, driver after driver slams on his brakes on Kent Avenue, in a Brooklyn industrial neighborhood that is a mecca both for working girls and for hotdog salesmen who service the cars and limos as the johns await their turn. The cacophony of johnlock is intensified in some quarters of Manhattan by the thrum of other mechanical aspects of the oldest trade. Predictably, this led to an early manifestation of the yen that many New Yorkers have to be liberated *from* the sex business: a Federal Communications Commission squad rushed to the rescue of a tenant in an apartment building who wailed that the use of a vibrator in a brothel upstairs was interfering with her television reception. After a spate of complaints that as many as eighteen streetwalkers at a time were brawling for the patronage of each customer in another area, it was local cops who galloped to the rescue, barricading part of Twenty-seventh Street to late-night traffic. Perhaps it was because such actions constricted their marketplaces that a number of transvestite hookers (you can tell them because they tend to flag down cars with their skirts) have been supplementing their earnings with a modish practice known as "yoking." Reported by the *Times* to be the absolutely latest fashion in mugging, the sensation of two hairy arms sneaking up your back, prior to grabbing you in a headlock, is quite delicious, and the vermilion-stained talons that then reach around into your jacket, to feel for your wallet, are the epitome of elegance.

With the sex industry offering this sort of thrill-filled potential to both practitioners and customers, it's hardly surprising that some New Yorkers prefer the perspective of Eve's Garden, the feminist sex boutique, on what constitutes liberation. *Their* fight, as will be seen, is for a piece of the action. Though they seem to be succeeding, in deciding whether to side with them in the Struggle, you should weigh the Risks of Being Caught. Unlike Eve's Garden, most sectors of the industry are illegal. Technically illegal, that is. The police public morals division's Captain Jerome Piazza puts it this way when asked to explain his perenially understaffed squad's enforcement philosophy: "It depends on the number of complaints. If only one person complains about a prostitution situation, you're probably not going to get any action. It's when ten people complain, twenty people, that's when you're going to get action."

Moreover, in the unlikely event that you do get caught, it really can be rather pleasant. Hizzoner's sentencing procedures commonly are predicated on the belief that a hair shirt is something to share with the socially disadvantaged strumpet who's before the bench. If you're lucky, he'll even share the bench. In one famous case, Lester Evens, a criminal court judge and sometime law partner of Mayor Koch, ordered a hooker who was waiting to pay a fine in his court to pull up a chair and sit next to him for several

Archimandrite Paul Ischi, aka real estate broker William Vaughn Ischie, Jr., said of his three-man monastery, "We do what monks are supposed to do." A firm owned by the monastery turned out to be in the business of real estate development.

Here comes the bride! Arianna Stassinopoulos marries Michael Huffington at
St. Bartholomew's, the church that has been such an inspiration to God's
Builders. Arianna is a best-selling author and socialite who has said of her
experience with a training scheme marketed by a California cult, the
Movement of Spiritual Inner Awareness, "It changed my life." Huffington is
an heir to a $300 million oil fortune.

Barbara Walters (*left*), Lucky Roosevelt (*center*), and Arianna's sister Agape (her Greek name is also an early Christian name for noncarnal love) were the bride's attendants.

Above left: Mother Teresa, of AIDS shelter fame, with John-Roger, the Movement of Spiritual Inner Awareness "way-shower." This photograph of the nun and the sage accompanied Arianna's *Interview* magazine powwow with him. Mother Teresa was meeting with John-Roger in the Bronx to receive his foundation's Integrity Award; the Calcutta backdrop is a photographic special effect. *Above right:* Richard Gere, who once gave a practical demonstration of what it felt like to be a male sex symbol.

Opposite: You need discipline to enjoy New York's Night Frontier, and Belle de Jour will administer it. *Above:* Gloria DeMann with her husband, Lawrence, the chiropractor to the stars, in costume at the reception for an AIDS benefit at their Fire Island summer home. Gloria runs a Star Track restaurant and also may be one of this book's more liberating forces.

Zev Bufman presented the divine Elizabeth, his Broadway production partner, with "the world's smallest perfect diamond" and a snow-white fur cape. His next star, Peggy Lee, declined to use Liz's former dressing room. "It was very small," La Lee explained.

John Gotti, the new Godfather, bristled when the media estimated the cost of his suits at one thousand dollars apiece. "These suits cost me eighteen hundred," he is reputed to have said.

Artist Sandy Straus hoists a toast to "Recent Crimes." The painting in the background represents the slashed wrist of Donald Manes, the Democratic party heavyweight who killed himself after being implicated in one of New York's biggest corruption scandals. "I was looking for something that would be a documentation of our culture and would be sensational," Straus said of her decision to mount this and similar works in a show at a Manhattan gallery.

While some of his former political colleagues have proved themselves adept at plucking the Apple, Ed Koch so far has stuck to milking cows as mayor of what probably will be the nation's last surviving family farm, the City of New York.

hours. "To keep her from sleeping in the courtroom," the jurist explained. Another judge informed a convocation of municipal leaders that she did enforce the prostitution laws—but was more lenient if the girls obeyed certain ground rules, like confining their work to after midnight.

---

*"IN OUR HOMES THERE'S NO ESCAPE
FROM VIOLATION, FEAR OR RAPE."*

*From "Protest Song," published in Women Against Pornography's
spring/summer 1984 newsletter*

The battle was initially joined in 1977 with the launch of a campaign called Stamp Out Smut. As its name implies, this sought to liberate the citizenry from the clutches of for-profit libido and took the form of a march past the Times Square flesh palaces by the saintly, who were marshalled by Ed Koch's predecessor as mayor, Abe "I'm mad as hell" Beame. The protestors strutted through the streets, blue noses quivering, to the refrain of "God Bless America" and "When You're Smiling," blasted out by the Staten Island Musicians Society, and speeches were given. Memorable among the orations was the call by actress Tammy Grimes for "an investigation of the sex business by a special grand jury," and baseball great Bobby Thomson's pitch for a return to the days when "ballgames were enough for entertainment." Mayor Beame, for his part, had drawn himself up to his full five feet two inches in the preceding weeks and personally commanded raids on a topless bar called Jax Three-Ring Circus and Show World Center, an emporium advertising "the hottest live sex acts in America."

"For years," Beame fumed, "the courts have thwarted our attempts to clean up this spreading blight . . ."

In New York, one man's blight can be another man's fortune, even if you're on the side of the angels.

Should you be a developer, for instance, obviously you're eager to join the Head Blue Noses in administering the latest penalty for smut: capital punishment. In seeking to level thirteen acres of the Times Square area and replace its frowzy entertainments with four granite office towers, a merchandise mart, and a 750-room hotel, Comstock's Builders—an alliance of city and state planners—point to their desire to exterminate "crime and frightening street life." Since much of this street life is concerned with ripping off tourists, just why bringing more tourists (the hotel) and more out-of-town businessmen (the mart) into the neighborhood will be a deterrent is a little unclear. In 1977 there were 121 sex businesses in the Times Square vicinity; by 1983, a municipal cleanup drive had lopped this to sixty-five. That same year, while robberies in the area decreased, murders doubled, to fourteen from seven, and there were forty-five rapes, to the previous year's twenty-four. The trend elsewhere in the city was for serious crime to fall. A less ambiguous statistic, from the point of view of the real estate industry, is the price tag on the Times Square redevelopment—$2 billion, to which figure you should add the usual gargantuan tax incentives and zoning breaks that go with this kind of scheme. Still, only someone who did not understand the selflessness of a New York politician would suggest that Ed Koch's enthusiasm for the plan has any connection to the fact that George Klein, the property sultan immortalized in the mayor's memoirs as "at the very top of my list of campaign contributors," has been tapped to develop the Tower Quartet. Such generosity does not influence him "in any way," the mayor has said. Obviously, it's simply that he wants visitors to the city to have the sort of fun that is unavailable anywhere except, maybe, in downtown Moscow. Just think of the thrill of sightseeing at the newsstands in the new skyscrapers, window-shopping in the mart (which will only deal wholesale), then repairing to your comfortable suite in the new hotel, safe from putschs by the hooligans who will have been zapped by the Women Against Pornography. This feminist cleanup group, whose unpaid toil is much appreciated by the mayor's office and the developers, conducts tours of Hades. Just to emphasize the need for the death sentence.

Setting the scene, the WAP excursions begin with a pep talk in a room decorated with a poster of a *Hustler* cover of a girl being fed, head first, into a meat grinder and emerging as hamburger.

The lecture presses all the right panic buttons. For instance, women in the New York porno industry are predominantly "third world" ("Absolutely not," says a surprised police expert. "The industry is white middle-class America") and some of them are being murdered by producers of "snuff" films in order to get footage of these rites. What the talk doesn't mention is that one of the few points of agreement between police and sex industry operators is that *Snuff,* the porno flick that gave the genre its name, was faked, and that there is no evidence that any of the other "murder" movies are genuine.

"That's what the police say," snaps the Women Against's Evelina Kane. Her group also seeks to discourage Madison Avenue from producing ads that "degrade and promote violence against women"—by zapping offenders with small plastic pig awards. Hanes Hosiery got one for a commercial in which a professional woman, finally gaining entrance to a men's club, is ogled by its members because of her "smooth and silky" legs rather than her "assertive, successful, autonomous" spirit.

Such demeaning, commercially motivated material in no way should be confused with the collected works of Women Against's own photo opportunity: Linda Marchiano, née Linda Lovelace. Born again as the Happy Housewife, following her nuptials with a cable-television installer, Linda has been urging a boycott of *Deep Throat,* her internationally renowned swallowing feat. She was forced into her performance by her previous husband, who had "learned hypnotism in Honduras and . . . exotic sexual practices from the Japanese," she explained in *Ordeal,* her graphic best-selling book about these years of bondage. Marchiano has disowned her old pseudonym. "She is another person," she told an interviewer. You couldn't find *Ordeal* under "Marchiano" at the local library? She wrote it under the name Linda Lovelace, silly.

"IT WAS A TIME WHEN WOMEN WERE STARTING TO SEE THE ECONOMIC POSSIBILITIES OF THEIR BODIES."

An ex-patron of the Fifth Season, on West Fifty-seventh Street, which bills itself as "a unique environmental health club for men & women"

Traditionally, the prostitution industry in New York has been controlled by men—male pimps, male bordello owners—while it has benefited the mob and some of the more buttondown members of the Cast of This Book.

• The Mob provides brothels with protection. Against the mob. Should you be unwilling to pay weekly tribute to one of its enforcers, a call goes in to 911 from a gangster who, identifying himself as a Concerned Passerby, screams that your House of Ill-Repute is going up in smoke. Since having firemen troop through the building upsets the johns and dirties the rose shag carpet, you soon pay up. This arrangement, beneficial though it is to all concerned, was disrupted temporarily by the FBI. After one of its

Finest posed as a whorehouse owner and was threatened with violence by a gentleman called Butch, who was demanding protection payments, the government wielded the Hobbs Act at Butch's boss, Salvatore "Sally Crash" Panico. Argued the feds, they had jurisdiction in the case because the whorehouses were shopping across state lines for "plastic trash bags, baby powder, mouthwash, paper towels, prophylactics, detergents, bar equipment, and brass beds." It took two and a half years for the lawmen to catch Sally after he was convicted at the subsequent trial. He hadn't turned up in court, which perhaps was fortunate. On trial in an earlier case, alongside the Bonanno family crime don Carmine Galante, he had to be gagged and shackled to his chair after vaulting into the jury box.

• The Cast of This Book provides much of the real estate for the brothels and the rest of the sex industry. Unwittingly and unwillingly, of course. This began to emerge some years ago when Edward Finch, a relative-by-marriage of Richard Nixon—his nephew was the husband of First Daughter Tricia—was revealed to be the landlord of Peepalive. This Forty-second Street emporium's specialties included a coin-operated window that, for a quarter, slid back to reveal a floozy who, dressed only in fishnet stockings, was poised most un-Tricia-like on a small revolving stage. Finch issued a statement: Peepalive would close that *very day.* The Bankers Trust Company balance sheet was discovered to include the former Ripley's Believe It or Not theater, which was showing such epics as *Last Days of Porn.* A bank spokesman responded that these *were* the last days of porn—the property, operated by a tenant, was being held as an investment for pension funds and would become the site of a large hotel.

Such gentrification is combining with the FBI's onslaught on organized crime to weaken the grip of both the mob and the Cast on the sex business. For the fact that prostitution continues to flourish, therefore, we have to thank various women. Liberated women. "It seems," muses *Screw* magazine publisher Al Goldstein, "that a lot of feminists have found their true calling." The trend is most apparent in the outer skin of this sector of the Onion's skin business: many hookers either have dumped their pimps—or consigned them to kitchen duty. "When we went to arrest a pimp not long ago, we found him baby-sitting for his girl," says the police department's Jerome Piazza, sounding slightly wounded for his brother. One indicator of how well the girls are doing: the Teamsters want to organize them. The union's New York boss, Barry Feinstein, sent a top aide to pledge to do this just as soon as (citing an enduring concern of Teamsters everywhere) prostitution is legal.

Who cares about legal? Among the many women who have been setting up happy houses that are not at all the kind that the former Linda Lovelace now minds, Sydney Biddle Barrows, the Mayflower Madam, allegedly was among the more successful. Yet, pleading guilty to promoting what police initially estimated was a $1-million-a-year-call-girl operation, she was even luckier than the hooker who got to sit on the bench. She was fined just $5,000. No need to reveal the names of her clients, who doubtless were a Who's Who of the circus. Before this understanding deal was cut, Sydney had faced seven years in jail.

"I have been given to understand that a lot of concerned and prominent people contacted [the DA's] office," she said primly.

"She's really milking this for all it's worth," responded Robert Morgenthau, the Manhattan district attorney.

Before you start milking it for all it's worth, make sure you understand the following guidelines:

Right: Being in any kind of fashionable legal trouble in New York is as good as being called Vanderbilt. So many people rallied to help Sydney get back on her feet that sometimes it was difficult to distinguish her from a billboard. Limelight, the club that threw a benefit for the Hell's Angels in chapter seven, staged a black-tie party for her defense fund. Our invitation was accompanied by a publicity release announcing that Sydney would be wearing a strapless pink taffeta gown by Tracy Mills "accessorized with some of the Biddle family jewels" and "blonde hair and understated makeup . . . courtesy of Louis Licari and by Jennifer Lawrence of La Coupe." The stretch limos were courtesy of Royal Coach.

Wrong: Several hundred people, most of them strangers, paid $40 each to shake the alleged $1 million hand. Probably they all then went home and reread their tax filings to make sure they hadn't underpaid on their $25,000 salaries.

Right: Sydney was a risktaker, which is how you build your growing business. "She booked clients that other agencies had blacklisted," says Kathy, the madam at a rival call-girl service. The blacklist includes a Paramount executive who got himself a freebie with an Australian crumpet by telling her she'd got the lead role in *Flashdance*. The job, of course, was not forthcoming.

Wrong: Like many of the New Breed madams, Kathy wastes time and dollars nurturing her employees' welfare where Sydney, a stickler for Old School discipline, simply would have ordered them to shave their legs. Kathy is especially proud that she introduced one sixteen-year-old slut to Literature: "I gave her Baudelaire, Montserrat, books on symbolism and decadence, and she's reading *Ulysses* now. Things like that make this business worthwhile."

Right: Kathy checks up on each girl during the $135-an-hour sessions by phoning after the first fifty minutes. (Most Manhattan escort services will only dispatch to clients whose numbers are listed in the directory or who are staying at hotels.) "If anything goes wrong, like a client is refusing to pay, I call the cops," Kathy says. "Nine-one-one has been very good to me."

If You Are Korean: Tell your husband to polish his own apples at the family's produce markets—and open a geisha house. There has been a boom in these establishments in the city, probably because their protocol makes them more difficult to bust than the massage parlors that dominated the prostitution business in the seventies. While a masseuse would make a few desultory passes with the rubbing alcohol, then get down to the basics, a geisha goes through time-consuming dramatics: a drink is served, a sauna is indicated, then a body shampoo and a shiatsu massage. Suppose the entire neighborhood gets together and comes up with the requisite twenty complaints for a raid? "The Orientals create a real difficulty for us," says the NYPD's Captain Piazza, "because they do give you a massage first and they will not tell you what the cost for sex is in advance. It could get a little hairy if we put an undercover guy in there because they're going to touch his private parts before they make a deal."

There are more of these oases opening every week.

"You want special massage?"

At the Oriental Star Health Club in Queens ($30 admission, plus a "tip" for the girl), Miss Kim paired our reporter with a skinny Korean lass. After the long, arousing preliminaries, the femme fatale finally led him to a soft double bed.

"What are your hobbies?" she said, peeling off her leotard.

Our reporter assumed she meant carnal hobbies and replied accordingly.

"I like golf," she said shortly. "But usually I work six days a week at this so I don't have time for it."

The You and I Oriental Health Club, also in Queens, began taking couples. "Somebody with his wife, that's all right," its Miss Min told us. "We give them massage...." To understand what next transpired, you have to realize that the burghers of Queens, while wise in the ways of politics (see chapter twelve) are new to the notion that threesomes can enhance sex. Accordingly, they sent Mayor Koch an SOS. "They were upset," an administration official says, "that the sex industry had invaded residential neighborhoods." Like "Mad as Hell" Beame before him, the mayor intervened. "Ultimate" legal measures were invoked to put Miss Kim, Miss Min, and other operators in the borough out of business. A few days later, we were glancing through the *Village Voice* when we noticed that much of a page was taken up with ads for the openings of parlors that clearly would be resolving the unemployment problems of Miss Min's and Miss Kim's ladies. Since they were located in the heart of Manhattan, the only problem was deciding which to send you to. "Chopsticks," a friend at *Screw* magazine said without even hesitating.

GRAND OPENING!

NEW
CHOPSTICKS
ORIENTAL HEALTH CLUB

ad in the Village Voice

At this writing, the club was on the fourth floor at 138 Fifth Avenue (212-989-8779/243-9051). "For admission, $120. Tip is extra," a girl there told us. "We take couples."

Still, most women prefer more straightforward careers and relationships. Gloria DeMann runs Café Pacifico, a Star Track (see chapter eleven) restaurant. She is the wife of Dr. Lawrence DeMann, a chiropractor whose patients have included Baryshnikov, Jacqueline Smith, and Xavier Guerrand-Hermes, the silk-and-leather mogul, and she exudes theatrical panache. The reception that she hosted for an AIDS benefit at her starkly elegant home in Fire Island Pines, a Long Island summer colony, began with a drum and bugle corps playing "New York, New York." Gloria, reported the *Daily News,* was in a pink sequined dress "so skintight that she had to shuffle." Later in the evening, everyone moved to a nearby disco for entertainment by Peter Allen, Anne Meara, and Dorothy Loudon. That much about Gloria is well known. Perhaps less well known is that a Gloria DeMann signed as president of a company that took out a ten-year lease renewal in

1975 for the Fifth Season, (corporate name, the Tower Health Club.) The lease had begun in May 1966 on this "environmental health club," which, as the mailing for it that we obtained says, indeed may have its "unique" aspects. It is located in a luxury apartment building at 315 West Fifty-seventh Street. A staffer called Jim Stromberg told us that "Gloria" would have to answer our questions when we called (212-245-6161) for information on what is rumored to be the most exclusive brothel in New York. Café Pacifico's Gloria? So former patrons of the Fifth Season say.

The doctor's wife never did get back to us, but since the law defines prostitution as exchanging sexual services for cash, the rumor appears to be false. The Fifth Season's health-seekers—a cross section of the circus with an infusion of New Jersey salesmen—pay annual membership dues and a door charge, but, according to a former patron, vulgar subjects like money are never discussed when they make their selections among the scantily clad maidens who frolic around the swimming pool. In 1972, four cops posing as affluent businessmen managed to get into the place, but the prostitution busts that they made were dismissed in court. The police had hoped to infiltrate again in 1984. This time, says a law enforcement source, they were unable to procure the code that has to be punched in to open the door.

The best little house in town has not always been such a fortress. It evolved from a nudist health spa, the same nudist health spa where screenwriter Aaron Latham once visited with a fashionable group that included Gay Talese and a masseuse named Amy. Latham reported in *New York* magazine that the author of what was then a work in progress, *Thy Neighbor's Wife,* had been distracted from the club's barbells when Amy made a grab for his penis:

"I'm going to tear it off," she told Talese.

This odyssey is not mentioned in *Thy Neighbor,* Talese's seminal chronicle of the sexual revolution, which is a shame because, according to the former Fifth Season patron, that same revolution explains what the spa became. Many of the club's hostesses were impecunious aspiring actresses, dancers, and singers, and when the management assigned a couple of them to give massages—the sort of massages a doctor might prescribe—they got ideas, the ex-patron surmises.

"I don't think anyone *told* them to give anything more," he says. "This was a class of women who weren't hookers, and that's what made the Fifth Season so incredible." A member of the old health club, a female CBS-TV executive, agreed that it was *incroyable.*

She seethed in a civil court case that she'd been confronted by one nude man in what used to be the women's shower and by another in the women's sauna. The judge calmly ruled that she should get her membership fee back. The club's massage tables were replaced with water beds and couches, recalls the former patron, and a disco floor rose in place of the gym. The food and the wine were free, and there was no pressure to get acquainted with the women. It was just that they were there when needed. Two of the nation's sex media lords, *Screw*'s Al Goldstein and *Hustler*'s Larry Flynt, were joined by some other friends and at least *seven* damsels for what Goldstein understandably recalls as a "frenzied" party. It was held in the King's Room, which was painted pink and had a king-sized Jacuzzi, and champagne was served. While we're on the subject of *Screw,* yet another major distinction between the Fifth Season and cathouses is that the Fifth Season does not advertise in the Goldstein publication. But then, what cathouse promotes itself in membership mailings as a "corporate activities center for your guests and clients"?

"You can go to the Fifth Season just for a business meeting," says the former patron.

"TRY TO IMAGINE MEN IN THESE POSES."

Women Against Pornography

"Our whole industry," frowns Kathy the escort-service madam "is the end result of men being so repressed that they don't know how to have a relationship. A lot of the guys who use us are relatively young, good-looking, they do all the right drugs, have got good jobs, live in the best neighborhoods, but they don't want a relationship. They'll ask for the same woman from the service on a regular basis and then, when she is really in love with them, they simply pick up the phone and book another woman. I've seen that happen over and over again.

"There should be a man's movement."

There is. It's called Men Against Pornography, and we're going to one of its New York workshops. Right, class, we're handing you this *Playboy* centerfold of a Beautiful Virgin who was forced by the maniacal Hef to be garlanded in pink ribbons and arranged on a piano. Such tyrannical oppression of women has "nothing to do with any honest kind of eroticism," according to MAP founder John Stoltenberg. So we want you guys to just slip the ribbon over your left nipple, drape your right leg thataway over the keyboard . . . Regular practice at this exercise will help "retrain" your filthy thoughts and perhaps even set you on the way to earning one of the Women Against's cherished Ms. Liberty awards (the converse of the porker that's conferred on Male Chauvinist Pig advertisers).

"WE LUSTED AND WANTED TO BE LUSTED AFTER."
From the introductory leaflet for Sexaholics Anonymous

Suppose you want to set up your own liberation movement? The techniques for incorporation are explained in chapter twelve, and obviously what you're going to liberate the masses from is sex—sexual *addiction.* The statistics in favor of a move into this remarkably unexploited corner of the market are startling. An article in the *New York Times* cited estimates that as many as one in twelve people "use sex as a psychological narcotic." The only real competition that you'll encounter in New York is from a chapter of Sexaholics Anonymous, a California-based group whose appeal perhaps can be assessed from its Lust Test. Ask yourself, it urges in its introductory leaflet (a complete handbook costs $7), such questions as:

• Do you have to resort to images or memories during sex?
• Does an irresistible impulse arise when the other party makes the overtures or sex is offered?
• Although your spouse is sexually compatible, do you still masturbate or have sex with others?

The group's rehabilitation program is based on the Twelve Steps of Alcoholics Anonymous. And just as AA members give up drinking, SAs aim at sexual sobriety if they are unmarried. That includes you, Portnoy. Nonlustful coupling *is* permitted with one's lawful spouse.

"*For the sexaholic,* any form of sex with one's self or with partners other than the spouse is progressively addictive and destructive," explains the SA handbook, which bulges with resourceful maxims ("Lust is the athlete's foot itch of the mind") and lacerating case histories (like the "recovering sex drunk" who "before age eight" was sexually aroused by Azura the Queen of Magic in a Flash Gordon comic strip).

The group's anonymous founder will not give press interviews until he finds a "Jack Lawrence" (Lawrence's *Saturday Evening Post* paean made AA a household name). But write him at Post Office Box 300, Simi Valley, CA 93062, and he'll provide you with a contact for the New York group. It holds meetings five nights a week. Eric Nadler, a writer for *Forum* magazine, attended some of them and gave a report:

"Hello, my name is David, and I'm a sexaholic," said a tall, well-spoken man in his mid-thirties.

"Hello, David," chorused the group.

David said he was confused because he had made tender, albeit nonlustful, love to his wife the previous night. Was this a good thing or not? His fellow addicts were unable to reach a consensus. Roger, a gaunt, bearded man, ambled over to Eric to share the news that his wife had left him because he was molesting his twelve-year-old foster daughter. He worked as a junior high school teacher and was relying on SA to curb his obsession with young girls.

"WHAT WE ARE IS A CIVIL RIGHTS GROUP."

David Thorstad, a cofounder of NAMBLA, the North American Man/ Boy Love Association

---

Members of NAMBLA, which mails out its literature from New York, are obsessed with young boys. They say that their group's sole aim is to push for the legalization of homosexual affairs with them, by repealing age-of-consent laws.

Child molesters' lib? Much classier stuff than that. NAMBLA supporters include veterans of several other noble struggles. Such as Allen Ginsberg. The group's cofounder, David Thorstad, is a former luminary of both the Socialist Workers Party and the Bertrand Russell War Crimes Tribunal and, unlike Tim O'Hara, the oily, cigar-chomping mouthpiece of California's heterosexual Guyon Society (motto: "Sex by the age eight or else it's too late"), the NAMBLA official propounds his case in the national media in measured tones: "If I ever knew of any member of NAMBLA who kidnapped a boy, I would report him to the police," he instructed the *New York Times.*

A Massachussetts political scientist and NAMBLA activist, Tom Reeves, took up this theme in a letter to the *Village Voice.* The prof owned to having "a dozen boys between twelve and twenty" frequenting his house. But this was only for the young people's *own good.* The dozen "breathe easily," explained the letter. Indeed, the group's literature suggests that such in loco parentis arrangements, far from constituting child abuse, are a palliative for what NAMBLA portrays as a failure of "American society [to] . . . love its children."

"Baby Is Scalded, Put in Hot Oven," says a headline reprinted from a daily newspaper in one of the group's leaflets.

For those, including many gay activists, who doubt whether making Baby a concubine is much of an improvement, an article in the NAMBLA newsletter had this to say: "About the same proportion of boys grow up straight, or bi, or gay, who have had the [man-boy] experience and who have not! The difference is that those who have had it are in a better position to make up their minds." For that matter, some NAMBLA member may have information on your kid tucked away in his files. Items about boykind in general are culled from other media and reproduced in the newsletter. We're omitting the boys' names. NAMBLA does not: "Queens music prodigy ——— ——— , 10, has a brother, ———, 7, . . ." said one such dispatch in 1985.

NAMBLA officials insist that the group plays no role in facilitating liaisons with such little plums. The organization's meetings and social events are designed solely to provide "legal and other help for men and boys involved in interage relationships," they say. A sergeant who was heading the New York City Police Department's pedophile unit, Phillip Tambasco, was skeptical, so he had a gay informer infiltrate the group. In due course, the undercover agent was invited to one of those "legal" klatches. It was called "Christmas Balls" and, just as some of the gay activists had suspected, many of the adolescent guests enjoying the mostly middle-aged gentlemen's warm hospitality (cheap jug wine and pretzels) turned out to belong to a support group for troubled gay youths. No question, though, that NAMBLA was there with the Helpful Hints when that was what was needed.

Martin Swithinbank, a fifty-four-year-old Harvard-educated Long Island real estate salesman and NAMBLA steering committee member, was arrested for sodomizing several ten-to-fifteen-year-olds. (He subsequently pleaded guilty to two counts.) His activities, NAMBLA said in a newsletter, had nothing to do with the organization. Still, members should "expect the worst," warned a long advisory:

"One must... *assume* tapped phones, brutal interrogation of boys & parents, surveillance of homes.... Prepare the boys for questioning by police. Explain to them that police will lie to them about you, that police will threaten the boys with arrest and other troubles, that boys need not ever say anything at all about their sexual lives, that they need not go with police or answer any questions.... Considerable discussion—maybe even role-playing—is necessary to prepare boys for this situation. Obviously, if you have a good relationship with the boys, there is no need to tell boys that they can't see you if 'anybody finds out'...." Another dispatch in the mailing urged, "We must be more careful in our own judgments on other simple matters (telephone calls, use of alcohol, marijuana, leaving boys alone at home, neglecting relationships). One boy close to the arrest of a NAMBLA member was found crying outside the man's house...."

Such precautions probably weren't necessary for pedophiles whose residence was New York City. According to Phillip Tambasco, the police pedophile unit was regarded as a dumping ground for misfits when he headed it. He was assigned just seven officers. "The brass treated pedophilia like gambling and prostitution when it came to enforcement," he contends. "I wanted to do a total investigation of NAMBLA, with a grand jury, but nobody would even listen."

The sergeant resigned after repeated clashes with his superiors. The fights did not only involve NAMBLA. For instance, one time he received several complaints that a figure at the Metropolitan Opera was molesting boys.

"I wanted to at least do some interviews, but they wouldn't even go that far," Tambasco recalls. "The captain said, 'Think what will happen if you're wrong.'" We asked around the department about this. Other detectives suggested that Tambasco brought his problems on himself by annoying his bosses with an attempt to infiltrate the child-porn industry. The pedophile unit chief and three other detectives had set up a porn film company as a sting operation. Hiring a crew and talent (all adult), they shot three "loops" but, just as they were ready to distribute their handiwork, the department canceled the project. The police commissioner, it was explained, had been "morally outraged" because one of the female detectives who was working on the operation had watched the X-rated scenes being filmed.

"We've investigated NAMBLA pretty thoroughly. It's exactly what it says it is. It's no big conspiracy to break the law," said Sgt. Arty Swanson, Tambasco's successor. At the time we interviewed him, the squad had been expanded to twelve—to deal with citywide child porn and prostitution.

Talking of porn, how was the department going about investigating that aspect of the industry, in the lee of the porno sting "outrage"? Swanson replied that there no longer was a professional child porn industry. With the law considerably harsher than in Tambasco's day, porn merchants are so scared of it, he said, that *Teenage Hussy* invariably turns out to be an anorexic twenty-two-year-old in pigtails and clip-on braces. This is possible. Many things are possible in New York. During an early crackdown on smut, a handmade "Jail Bait" sign over a peep-show booth in Times Square that described sex with a "14-year-old teenaged girl, blonde hair and blue eyes" was amended with a Magic Marker— "18-year-old . . ."

"PART OF THE REASON I GOT INTO PORN IS THAT ALL WE TALKED ABOUT IN MY HOUSE WAS RACISM AND THE RENAISSANCE, AND NOBODY EVER TAUGHT ME A DAMN THING ABOUT MAKING MONEY. OUR FEMININE ENGINEERING IS A POWERFUL ASSET."

Lisa Be, the feminist daughter of prominent New York intellectuals, who became a porn star and performer in live sex shows

---

Lisa Be was endowed with her pseudonym to distinguish her from another Lisa, Lisa A, when she worked at America's busiest porn parlor, Show World Center, at Forty-second Street and Eighth Avenue. She was cast in one of the live sex shows that so disgusted Mayor Beame; after a short interview in which she wasn't asked to remove her clothes, she went on stage with no rehearsal to do a lesbian act (she was not a lesbian) with a woman she'd never met. During our visit to the center, a shapely young lady in a coral-pink swimsuit was working a shift in a red-lit room with a pudgy older woman who was nude. The pair could be spied on through a window for thirty seconds for a quarter. Coral Suit was busying herself folding a Sears imitation patchwork counterpane while Pudgy lay back on a dais and scissored her legs. Coral Suit had just finished this housekeeping task and the legs were just showing the first flash of vagina when our time was up and a shutter slammed across the window.

New York efficiency at its best. The emporium is owned by Richard Basciano, an associate in other businesses of Robert "Dee Bee" DiBernardo. DiBernardo has been described by authorities as a major domo of the Mafia. This was being denied by his attorney as recently as mid-1986, when, shortly before his indictment on federal racketeering charges, Dee Bee vanished—a victim, the FBI suggests, of internecine mob violence. Still, no one can deny the outstanding ethics of New York's Coney Island of fast sex. Basciano bans prostitution on the Show World premises, which are illuminated by glaring lights, disinfected regularly by attendants with mops and buckets, and policed by barkers who mitigate against loitering by keeping up a constant chant of "Check it out! Check it out! Ch-e-eck it out! Pussy, pussy, pussy..."

Federal auditors were somewhat nonplussed when they did check it out and discovered that the Show World owner had obtained a $65,000 loan from a Small Business Administration program. But the money, you'll be glad to hear, was used to renovate offices in the building, not the booth showing *Three Cocks for Carol*. Besides, the return on the taxpayer's capital presumably was several points higher than from the gold mine, co-owned by Richard Nixon's nephew Donald, which, because he was a Vietnam veteran, qualified for a $45,000 boost from the same program as a "minority" enterprise: a male porn star who worked in Show World's acts recalls coming across fifteen men sitting at a long table in the building—adding the takings, he says.

"When we go in there and make arrests, we get the assistance of their security and they note the time the girls leave so they can maintain their records," says the police department's Captain Piazza.

"DO YOU THINK THAT A BANK WOULD HAVE GIVEN ME THE MONEY?"

A porn publisher explaining why he allowed Robert DiBernardo's Star Distributors to produce as well as distribute his magazine. The publisher says he did not make much of a profit.

Robert DiBernardo, or Dee Bee as the controversial Basciano associate is sometimes called, reportedly was active before he went missing as an operator of Star Distributors, the largest pornography distribution outfit on the East Coast. The firm is headquartered at 150 Lafayette Street, in Little Italy. Apparently, it has been outgrowing its quarters, though, because at the time Geraldine Ferraro was seeking the heartbeat-away position, a Star adjunct called Bonate Distributors was said to be storing literature advocating other positions—Star's best-known title is *Screw*—on two floors of a warehouse at 200 Lafayette that was co-owned by the vice-presidential candidate's husband, John Zaccaro.

The nature of Star's business was hardly a secret in this Little Italy neighborhood. The firm's 150 Lafayette Street offices had been invaded by federal agents in a 1980 episode that received widespread press coverage when another of the raiders' targets, a porn tycoon called Mickey Zaffarano, dropped dead of a heart attack as the dragnet descended. Doubtless he feared the feds were going to confiscate his only remaining copy of *Debbie Does Dallas.* The heroine of this film, which Mickey produced, peeled off a costume resembling that of the Dallas Cowboy cheerleaders, before engaging in contact sport with the proprietor of a sporting goods store. The cheerleaders, their reputation irrevocably enhanced, sued to have Debbie banned. A judge called a hearing. The columnist Murray Kempton reported that whenever a question got too close to the knuckle, Mickey responded, "I *embrace* the Fifth Amendment."

Since not everyone reads everything in the newspapers, there is no reason to believe that John Zaccaro was prevaricating when he expressed surprise at his tenant's activities. The Zaccaro real estate office—where Gerry worked as a lawyer for a time before her election to Congress—was all the way down the block from Star Distributors, at 218 Lafayette.

The vice-presidential candidate issued a statement saying that now her husband had been alerted to the pornographer's presence, Dee Bee's outfit was being turfed out. Bonate had been notified that its lease would not be renewed when it expired on January 31, 1985.

In June 1985, Bonate was still ensconced in the warehouse. The lease *hadn't* been renewed, Zaccaro's lawyer, John Koegel, told us. But a concession had been made—Bonate was being allowed to stay until Gerry's husband got another tenant. "He is close to what he thinks is a new tenant, and they've been told to find something else," Koegel said rapidly.

November 1985. Maybe the new tenant was engrossed in catching up with his back issues of *Screw* and had forgotten to move in.

Koegel expressed amazement that Bonate was being so laggardly. The lawyer hadn't known until we called that the firm had stayed, because "John said it was taken care of." There again, he did recall that back in the summer, the company had asked for "a little time to move out, and when somebody says that, you think it's like an extra week or two."

A month later, nothing had changed.

"[Bonate] says they haven't found another space yet," Koegel explained. "John gave them a little bit of time...." But we thought the firm was being evicted? Koegel said he'd have to check with the boss and reported back that he'd been mistaken—Dee Bee wasn't getting more time. The Star subdivision, the nurturer of Lord knows what publishing talents, was being taken to landlord-tenant court. "Who else can people with an interest in publishing porn go to in this society but people like DiBernardo?" the man whose magazine was produced by Star said mournfully when we told him about this reactionary move.

"THESE ARE PEOPLE FROM THE LOWER SOCIAL LEVELS WHOSE GRAND OPERA IS GROUP SEX."
Philip Nobile in Penthouse *magazine on the sociology of Plato's Retreat*

This book is not intended to help the underclass get above itself. Still, as Nobile pointed out, there was something rather seductive about the arias at Plato's Retreat, America's first swingers' bar. When not attending the theater at the Hellfire Club (chapter seven) or participating at gay burlesques (chapter nine), the glitterati poured into the viewing stands. The holy of holies was the mat room, of course, but the chaises by the pool afforded an untrammeled view of the peasants performing "weights only" (watery constitutionals). Sammy Davis, Jr., Margaux Hemingway, Richard Dreyfuss, Buck Henry, Jill St. John, George Hamilton, General Motors heir Stewart Mott, and an equerry to mobdom's Matty the Horse were among the most celebrated spectators.

That was the heyday. Enter, yet again, the feds. Unimpressed by the absence of Studio 54–style Glad Bags in the club attic, they accused Plato's owner, Larry "King of Swing" Levenson, of husbanding *his* money by maintaining two sets of financial books, one of which showed taxable income of a modest $377 for an entire year, the other suggesting an indebtedness of more than $200,000 that annum to the IRS. This banking scheme backfired, the government said, when a Levenson employee turned over the real records to IRS auditors, whom she mistook for the club's bookkeepers. Convicted in 1981 of skimming $2.3 million in receipts from the club, the King, who pleaded his innocence to the end, set up his court in exile among the many other nobles staying at the federal pen in Allenwood, Pennsylvania—former U.S. Senator Harrison Williams, former U.S. Congressmen Fred Richmond...

"Larry ran the club from jail," says his manager, Moish. "He gave us instructions daily."

Shortly before Levenson was released, the swing club's newsletter carried an article on what it had been like doing hard time:

"No, there aren't any slot machines [at Allenwood], just automat-type food machines. Larry feeds those machines as if they were slots. With his arms filled with a frank, veal patti [sic], hamburger and ice cream he sits down for his feast."

Soon after the King was released, the city had a judge close Plato's Retreat. Patrons were said to be indulging in public anal sex and fellatio, in violation of the new anti-AIDS regulations.

"It's over. The First Amendment is over. The whole movement now is toward Jerry Falwell," snorted the King.

At Acquiesce, a dingy, dimly lit duplex swing club that has been the preference of rich Arabs, trade was down 70 percent. One of the operators of the establishment, David, assured us, however, that we should relax our inhibitions—because he banned gays and bisexuals. He could tell Them just by looking, he elaborated evenly. He was unconcerned by the studies showing heterosexuals could transmit the disease. "Looking at it rationally," David urged, "we're doing a service. We put juice into people's marriages and we give them medical reminders."

It was becoming rapidly apparent that you would not be requiring the phone number for Acquiesce. Maybe a nice vibrator? Jo Jo Hughes stocks one with a fake foreskin and sperm at the Underground, at 390 West Street. She no longer runs swingers' weekends at the Rocking Horse Ranch, a family resort in the Catskills. "Any sex today is a risk," sighed Jo Jo. She was planning a swingers' convention to discuss the problem.

Deux Plus Duex (sic), a rambling old inn near the Catskills village of Woodstock which is owned by two swingers, Shelli and Stuart, still hosts weekends for like-minded members of the "Couples Movement"—"one of the nicest things is at four in the morning, after they've done all they want," Shelli says, "they'll all get together naked in one room and sing songs. It's like being at camp." The inn (914-586-3182) is diversifying, though. Its "Bohemian" retreats for artists and writers have been advertised in *The Nation* and *New York Review of Books*.

"I DECIDED WHY BE EXPLOITED BY OTHERS? NOW I EXPLOIT MYSELF."

Robin Byrd, whose late-night show on Channel J of Manhattan Cable opens to a shot of her in a bikini, shimmying to her own recording of "Baby Let Me Bang Your Box"

Daniel Lander used to be a pastor—a pastor of the Lexington Avenue Church of Sharing, which was dedicated, said a large sign over the door, to the belief that "God wants all humanity to survive, be happy and to have a sharing, loving and respectful regard for all human beings." Like certain other institutions operated by God's Builders, the denomination was pragmatic in its interpretation of its motto—"religion in action"—and imposed admission charges ($80 for single men; $15 for unaccompanied women) instead of an offertory. It even issued its own version of the Ten Commandments—"It is okay," one precept declared, "to ask anyone present at the club to do anything." After a pretty detective who applied to join Lander's ministry was told she could work either as a "naked hostess" or a "party sex girl," the police busted the pastor for promoting prostitution. He pleaded guilty, but only, he says, to avoid the cost of defending the case. The church "was a swing club," he explains.

Let other ex-swingers have their Bohemian sleepaway camps, their nostalgic causes. Lander can be seen regularly on Channel J, hosting a sort of nude version of the Dick Cavett show, "Interludes After Midnight." Channel J is sometimes called the city's "porno station." Resulting from the nation's most liberal, and legally impeccable, public-access statute ("*Very* off-the-record," a cable-company source murmurs, "I will say that there are some programs out there that we would sooner be carrying"), the channel is available, on a first-come, first-served basis, to anyone who wants to put on a show.

Any show. *Screw* magazine's Al Goldstein is the impresario behind "Midnight Blue," which once treated viewers to a "Sperm-athon," starring a nondescript brunette who made love (so far as could be told from the camera angle) with eighty-three members of the invited audience. Sorry, Tyler, though. The ad that aired on the show for a "Cathouse for Dogs" was, despite the storm of protest from animal protectionists, a joke.

With the program claiming to sometimes outdraw Johnny Carson in cable households, the cable company does its best to protect the public weal, periodically censoring the footage. "In place of the deleted material, we put up a picture of Ronald Reagan riding his horse," says "Blue" executive Steve Gruberg.

The company's one resounding victory against the Tide of Filth involved "Ugly George" Urban, an amateur Svengali who, shouldering a camera, prowled the city's streets, inducing busty girls to take their clothes off. His "Ugly George Hour of Truth, Sex and Violence" was first bounced off the air when Manhattan Cable grumbled that he had aired a different tape from the one he'd shown its censors. He was allowed back on a month-to-month contract forbidding him ever to enter the cable company's Twenty-third Street premises (he lives next door to the studios). In the early eighties, he mysteriously vanished again.

"Manhattan Cable was owed money by him, so he was thrown off," a spokeswoman tersely told us. Ugly, who paid $150 a week for his airtime, seemed unperplexed. He showed us a prospectus for a magazine he hopes to start, called *Mammary Lane,* which will feature women with extraordinarily large bosoms. Tokyo electronics companies will sponsor him, he said, when he returns to the Manhattan airwaves. "I am not aware that he is returning," said the cable-company spokeswoman.

For Ugly's ex-fans (his audience was estimated at 150,000) and frustrated ex-swingers everywhere, New York has a new industry, porno *phone*. The city's seven aural sex services sprang up, like cable porn, as the unforeseen protégé of a government regulation. The Federal Communications Commission, in ruling that companies like New York Telephone had to lease out their "dial it" lines through competitive bidding, had in mind encouraging a flood of applications to set up services providing information on fat stock prices, hurricanes, that sort of thing.

High Society magazine's living centerfold "Hotline" provides recorded information on sex acts. Breathily described by ladies with names like Serena and Holly-O, the data enables subscribers to "get off over the phone," explains a business card showing two blondes baring their behinds. The spooks of the Defense Intelligence Agency found this enormously, well, handy, since they were able to achieve in fifty-seven seconds with Holly (212-976-2828) what had required long, exhausting sessions at home. Hence they could devote more time to analyzing naughty Soviet troop movements. However, after some two-star eunuch took exception to the estimated $43,000 a month that this was costing taxpayers, the Defense Department had electronics specialists put a block on the number.

"HE WAS MY AGE, A STOCKBROKER. WHY SHOULD I BE NICE AND GIVE AN HOUR TO SOMEONE I'M NEVER GOING TO SEE AGAIN?"

A New York yuppie, who moonlights from her career as an advertising account executive as a call girl with Kathy's escort agency. She gave the john twenty minutes for his $135.

In the guerrilla theater of New York sex, allegiances are constantly shifting. For instance, shortly after NAMBLA's David Thorstad was reported to have asserted at a 1984 conference of his "civil rights" group that "there isn't a boy out there who doesn't need a blow job right now," a twelve-year-old (at least the publication said he was twelve years old) columnist for the NAMBLA bulletin announced he was quitting. "NAMBLA is not a political support group for boys and their pedophile lovers," the pseudonymous columnist charged in his valedictory screed, which apparently was overlooked at police headquarters. "NAMBLA's sole function of late has been to organize pedophiles for social activities. . . ."

Screw publisher Al Goldstein is also reinforcing the ranks of the abstemious. Abstaining that is, from the dating methods propounded in his publication's ads, he has been advertising instead in *New York*'s personal columns for the perfect mate and has registered with a video-dating service. Since he is "not talking sex, I'm talking relationship," he has in mind a "beautiful and intelligent high-fashion model, lovely actress, leggy stewardess, ballet dancer, age 21–32."

And John Zaccaro can breathe easy again: pornography is going respectable. In fact, Candida Royalle is just the new tenant that the Democratic Party's favorite real estate man needs. While she made her name as the star of such porn flicks as *Ultra Flesh* (in which she was lowered three stories on a rope, landing gracefully on her costar's erect qualification for membership in the Men Against), Candida now runs Femme Productions, a Brooklyn company that makes "feminist porn."

That's no closeups of genitalia, no cum shots, but lots of afterplay in which the Great Lover doesn't go to sleep. "I see all that is wrong with porn," Candida says earnestly, "but banning it is never going to happen, so I want to show what can be done to add some respectability and responsibility to this industry."

For instance, the throbbing action of *Femme II: Urban Heat* builds climatically to a scene in—the kitchen. We thought kitchens were reserved strictly for New York's pimps, but then, the outcomes of revolutions always were hard to predict.

9

CAMP SECRETS

"WHAT IF THEY BECOME INSURANCE AGENTS?"

Senator John Glenn to aides who argued during his short-lived entry in the 1984 presidential sweepstakes that he should reconsider his opposition to gay rights legislation rather than alienate New York City's one million homosexuals

Who cares about alienating homosexuals?

On March 18, 1986, in an op-ed essay in the *New York Times,* William F. Buckley, Jr., suggested that AIDS victims should be tattooed on the upper forearm ("to protect common-needle users"), and on the buttocks ("to prevent the victimization of other homosexuals").

Some social history.

Before the AIDS epidemic started to wipe out young men in New York with the erratic virulence of shells dropping onto a World War I trench, avowed male homosexuals were considered quite the cutest ornaments by many in Mr. Buckley's circle.

With famous hostesses vying for the favor of the most beautiful couples, etiquette arbiters like Letitia Baldrige trotted out helpful advice about how to introduce John and Jim to your friends. When you weren't fishing for gays for your table, you would be on a field trip, gawking at gays at their clubs or taverns. *Out*: Harlem jazz. *In*: the Toilet and the Anvil. The trend, while brief, was memorable in that it included some of the circus's few acts of genuine spontaneity. At one establishment, a princess, carried away by the pounding music and pulsating lights, is said to have wrenched off her rings and publicly pleasured a homosexual Paramount Pictures executive. At another, a woman relative of the Guinness family made a beeline for a go-go boy who was indulging in an autoerotic act. Truman Capote loaded an entire bus with beepees, including Jacqueline Kennedy, and whisked them to the East Village to watch a transvestite troupe, the Cockettes, whose plumed, spangled, and rouged performers included a look-alike for Mamie Eisenhower.

"It was like a combination of Radio City Music Hall and an acid trip," says the Beatles biographer Steven Gaines, who observed the safari as the *New York Sunday News*'s Top of the Pop columnist.

Mr. Buckley probably would not have enjoyed the trip.

Senator Glenn certainly wouldn't have.

"He was obsessed," reported a gay Democratic district leader, Tom Duane, after a meeting with the ex-astronaut during the 1984 New York primary race, "over the question of why we are homosexuals—are we born that way, is it something in our development, or was it the influence of a gym teacher?"

It might seem that Mr. Buckley's wife, Pat, *would* have had a good time. Though Mrs. B is a lady of such magnificent bearing that she has been compared to the Spanish Infanta, it is said that she does not share some of her husband's prejudices. Dotson Rader's biography of Tennessee Williams, *Cry of the Heart,* listed the columnist's wife as among the revelers at a SoHo party celebrating an underground film in which an adolescent boy made love to a hole cut in a honeydew melon.

At this frolic, the singer Jim Morrison lay on the floor, his fly open, masturbating between slugs of beer, and Edie Sedgwick, the Warhol protégée, was discovered on her knees in the bathroom before another girl.

"That *disgusting* party!" exclaims Mrs. B., who says she only attended at the invitation of a movie director who was a Rader pal. "I took one look inside that door and left." These days she would not have to leave.

Fashions having undergone one of their refreshing makeovers in the social ether, scenes involving Jill and Jane are now *in*. And, pending the tattoos, John and Jim generally are assumed to be *out*. "Do bring your *friend,* dear," cooed a socialite to a lesbian feminist she hardly knew.

But you never can tell in the Big Onion Ring. Some of the ladies are now turning up at AIDS fundraisers. Here are a few pointers to what, if like them you reach out beyond prejudice, you will find.

"ONE OF THEM SPECIALIZES IN SYNTHESIZER COMPOSI-
TION."

*A pal of Wally Wallace, manager of the Mine Shaft, talking about the
off-hours hobbies of the bartenders at this now defunct gay S&M palace,
which reputedly was founded by an associate of the Gambino
organized-crime family*

At a downtown discotheque, Paradise Garage, Interchain, an
international fraternity of gay leathermen, is cosponsoring an
AIDS benefit, the Mr. Leather New York contest, on a wintry night
late in 1985. The group encodes its roster to protect members like
Arabs who might get crucial digits chopped off if they were
identified, so the anticipation is intense as the beefcake reveals
itself, ambling across the rose-lit stage in bikers' boots and strategically placed sadomasochistic harness. Hundreds of men in the
audience let loose with catcalls and quips. "We're looking for
someone very good-looking, with a great personality and naturally not too effeminate," beams an organizer whose mother has
written a supportive letter reproduced in the program. So here's
Gerald, muscles like marble, placed third in a recent Slave and
Bondage competition, being announced by the emcee, oleaginous
as Bert Parks at a Junior League dinner. "You're married, very
much in love . . ."

With Wally Wallace, of the Mine Shaft.

The little man in Gerald's life, off-duty for a few hours from his
toil among the slings and chains, is running the second round of
the contest, in which the hulks are urged to demonstrate their
"safe-sex" talents. As it transpires, safe sex, while it can't spread
AIDS, may not be totally suitable for a cover story in *Modern
Bride,* which probably explains why, after the investigation by its
food store sleuths (chapter seven), the city closed the Mine Shaft,
declaring it a menace to public health. It is a relief to report,
therefore, that life goes on for the leathermen who used to
frequent the tavern. Some of them meet in private now every
Sunday afternoon, for a party at Wally and Gerald's apartment.
Bring your own bottle if you join them. And you may want to
brush up your knowledge of Mendelssohn, a little Fauré, some
Kreutzer violin études—just so you can hold your own with the
two Juilliard graduates who once tended that famous bar. "There's

the one who does synthesizer and the other is a Texan who always had to leave work early on Sundays because he plays the organ at a Queens church," confides a Wallace pal.

"I'D HAVE MOVED TO SAN FRANCISCO IF I'D WANTED TO BE A FULL-TIME HOMOSEXUAL."

A New York public relations executive

Some of them already are insurance agents. And bankers, Broadway producers, bureaucrats, physicians, real estate developers, publishers, politicians... Achievement is denominated in some of the same terms in the gay community as everywhere else in the circus—money, the power that comes with money, and looks. But to those three factors, add a fourth that sets the community apart: pleasure. A potent status symbol in smart gay circles, this may be as conventional as a synthesizer concerto. Or as practice with the gay softball team. However, in the early years of the gay liberation movement, the trendiest pleasure was sex— vast quantities of it—and fitting this in between the scramble up the corporate ladder (money), the missions to Bloomingdale's (looks), the concerto, and the softball required considerable organizational skills. The apotheosis of this is still to be found at this writing at 1 Maiden Lane, right across from Merrill Lynch.

Entering a nondescript office building, the horny stockbroker can ride the elevator on his lunch hour to the eleventh floor, stow his three-piece suit and tie in a locker, and seek a quickie in the sack with a stranger in one of the tasteful bordello-red rooms of the Wall Street Club (formerly the Wall Street Sauna). Of course, there aren't many seekers. Gay men know what spreads AIDS. But this bathhouse is a useful little reminder of that era when some of the heterosexuals who are now churning out nostrums about the wages of promiscuity were greedy for a front-row seat at *all* the action, not just the gay clubs. While only the Paramount honcho's favorite princess may have understood the full significance of the booming sales of canned Crisco, the ermine and pearls set swept into the Continental Baths to hear Bette Midler, accompanied by Barry Manilow, at the famous floor shows at "the Tubs," as the

establishment was monickered. "There's a certain feeling of definite decadence," one woman guest said primly as she mingled
with the bathhouse's towel-clad regulars. The decadence—
impersonal intercourse between often lonely, quite often
drugged-out men—would get underway again as soon as the
heterosexual thrill-seekers had trooped out. One twenty-eight-
year-old AIDS victim would later reminisce that he spent Christmas Eve at a bathhouse, singing carols.

Bars offering similar facilities in their back rooms covered the
New York waterfront. The most architecturally innovative of these
was a two-story honeycomb, the Glory Hole, devoted almost
entirely to the pursuit of oral sex. Through partitions. A SoHo
gallery mounted "Glory Holelujah," an exhibition of photographs
of glory holes in public rest rooms, and a novel was published to
wide acclaim about the discotheques that synthesized this carefully codified whirl. It was by the pseudonymous Andrew Hol-
leran. *Dancer from the Dance.*

Dancing. Now that didn't sound too threatening. One-two-
three, one-two-three . . . you could almost hear the refrain echoing
down Madison Avenue in 1982, that year in which money in the
heterosexual economy was tighter than a transvestite's corset at
the old G. G. Knickerbocker Club's Barnum Room ("Le Freak,
C'est Chic on Forty-fifth Street," declared a *New York* article about
that watering hole of the beepees.) While no one would want
homosexuals endorsing a product, it couldn't do any harm to get a
few more of Them as customers, could it? Marketing men could
be seen on the five twenty-five back to Scarsdale, noses buried in
statistics about guppies, gay upwardly mobile professionals. Oh,
you gorgeous *recession-proof* beasts! Free of the burden of supporting a family, your annual median income, according to one
survey, was $30,000, or about $8,000 above the average for all
men between thirty-five and forty-four.

It was at this moment that the Calvert Distillers division of the
liquor giant Joseph E. Seagram & Sons proposed celebrating the
premiere of the movie *The Pirates of Penzance,* starring Kevin
Kline, by paying for a blowout beneath the dome of New York's
largest gay disco, the Saint. "The dome is bigger than at the
Hayden Planetarium and they can put on a star show," enthused a
spokeswoman for the company.

It certainly would be a unique sight. Normally, the Saint
writhed through the night and day with shrieking, sweat-soaked
male bodies that periodically detached themselves from the tangle

on the dance floor to take a reinvigorating whiff of Essence of Ethel from a rag clamped between their teeth. This scene was overlooked by a balcony missing only the slaughterhouse props (slings in which a gentleman could hang like a carcass, feet up) to make the constantly changing conjugations of limbs as Balthusian as in any back-room bar. Moreover, the Saint threw some pretty fabulous parties itself with no help from the American service industry. One invitation announced a Circumcision evening, though the club's owner, Bruce Mailman, later said that he was kidding. At least the Seagram women would feel special. There were just fifty of the tender sex on the disco's membership rolls, to 2,100 men. They were not allowed to wear dresses, heels, or perfume. Other ladies could be admitted by prior arrangement as guests. The passes stamped FEMALE OK that they were handed made them feel as warmly welcome as at any uptown gentleman's club.

Pirates's coproducer Joseph Papp thought awhile about the Calvert Distillers' plan, consulted one of his gay staffers—and sent his regrets.

"When you have a movie with characters like the Pirate King, you could just hear the play on words, and this was a family movie," the staffer said.

Though Gilbert and Sullivan never did have a Pirate Queen added posthumously to their repertoire, the United States Army nearly recruited a few operatic major generals.

For this, the Pentagon has to thank Steve Cohn, a New York party promoter whose seventies triumphs included a series of gay Sleaze Balls—sample invitation: "Wear tonight what you'll burn tomorrow"—and Steam, a party at which guests, entering a room full of just that, were thrown towels by bodybuilders and told to check their clothes. Like a flash it came to Cohn that what his followers really needed was a "Maneuvers" party—subtitle "the ultimate military fantasy." A pier jutting into the Hudson River was rented for the occasion (piers, and trucks parked in the wholesale meat market, rivaled the bathhouses as trysting places in the Gay Seventies), thousands of men were alerted to polish their military drag, and a casting call went out to the army. "We told them we were doing a fundraising benefit to raise money for little pocket parks," Cohn says. By some omission, the promoter did not tell them the nature of this charitable event's guest list.

"They brought in a full reserve unit from New Jersey, they set up a recruiting booth with a film, and brought in two tanks, jeeps, trucks, and a giant howitzer cannon," Cohn grins. "It took them about three hours to set up. At about midnight, we said, 'Don't you know this is a gay party?' and this colonel blew a whistle and talked into a walkie-talkie. It was like the evacuation of Saigon. It took them about six minutes to pull out."

Cohn claims the army hushed the episode up. This was no great loss to history, however, because the *New York Times* already had wrapped everything there was to say about life in the gay fast lane into a single story of dazzling breadth. The piece ran as the lead in the newspaper of record's Sunday, April 6, 1975, travel and resorts section.

"The All-Gay Cruise: Prejudice and Pride," by free-lance writer Cliff Jahr, chronicled a cruise on a French luxury liner to Mexico with three hundred homosexual passengers aboard. The article was so replete with the fact-a-second detail they teach in Journalism 101 that you could understand why nine other publications, including *Playboy*, had rejected it. The cast this time, in order of appearance, included a lesbian ex-showgirl whose lei got blown down a funnel and a Manhattan decorator who, appearing in $20,000 worth of diamonds, elaborated, "They're always just sitting in the goddam vault." Of course, no event involving au fait New Yorkers would be complete without an Animal Interest. This one had Debby Sue, a chicken, whose sexual awakening occurred after she got wafted with a popper, "a drug inhaled to rescue waning ardor." The fowl thereupon engaged in a "lust-crazed tussle with a Gucci carryall." There was some insightful description of men making bedroom eyes at each other and an interlude at an S&M fashion show that had a soundtrack of someone being savagely beaten. At dusk in a little Mexican port, we learned, fifty boys did the Bump on the main deck to the strains of Patti Labelle's "Voulez-vous coucher avec moi, ce soir?" blasting from two speakers the size of steamer trunks.

Sad to report, this formidable documentary received little public comment when it appeared. But many years later, *Forum* magazine—part of Bob Guccione's *Penthouse* empire— examined it in an analysis of the *Times*'s coverage of the fleshly weaknesses. According to the magazine's Eric Nadler, *Times* publisher "Punch" Sulzberger and his mother, then in her eighties, had not found Jahr's essay at all amusing.

"Punch, darling, who *is* this Debby Sue?"

Editors were hauled on the carpet, by Nadler's account. He wrote that the resulting contretemps was the origin of a ban on the use of the word "gay," which nowadays is only allowed in Punch's paper in a quote or formal name. A *Times* spokesman, Leonard Harris, insists, however, that it was coincidental that "gay" was first prohibited in the paper's 1976 stylebook. The proscription, a continuing sore point with gay activists despite the *Times*'s otherwise excellent coverage of issues like AIDS, was instituted, Harris explains, because the word is slang.

Among those who have learned a little about the true meaning of gaiety from firsthand observation is Elizabeth Taylor. While starring in *Private Lives* in 1983, she materialized like a Fellini vision on a yacht in the harbor of Fire Island Pines, the largely gay New York vacation community whose Islanders Club had arranged the Mexican voyage. The visitor was equipped with bodyguards, ready for the riot of adoration. Pines already had its celebrities, of course. *Little* celebrities. The resort is where Calvin Klein, Gloria DeMann (see chapter eight, Liberating Forces), and Tommy Tune keep their modernistic beach houses and Dorothy Loudon, Claudette Colbert, Rod McKuen, Twiggy, Lynn Redgrave, Peter Allen, Jerome Robbins, Valentino, Halston, Elton John, Grace Jones, Bette Midler, Diahann Carroll, and the President's dancer-journalist son, Ron Reagan, scamper from time to time across the white sand beaches or lounge by oceanside pools. In due course, the *big* celebrity left the yacht—and as the divine pair of violet orbs fluttered over a drink at tea dance, a wharf-front gay disco ritual, the bodyguards seemed set to need another job. "People just went on dancing," explains one of the real-life "dancers from the dance." "The face was beautiful, the nose was perfect, but it was very boring, to be truthful."

The female queen of the Pines that summer was Barbara Ross, a former singer who is married to the chief executive officer of Ross Bicycles. A frequent visitor to the resort, she would hold regular teatime court from a captain's chair on the deck of her yacht, the *Barbara,* anchored so close to the dance floor that the sinewy youths in codpieces and the drag queens with red light bulbs flashing on their strap-on breasts could lean over and touch the prow. With her hair stacked into a Dolly Parton beehive, fingers glimmering with diamonds and emeralds, and a gold-and-diamond Ross Bicycle pendant lapping her neck, the boat's namesake made a majestic spectacle as she began tossing Ross Bicycle beanies to the revelers one evening. Suddenly, she slipped and crashed to the dock, breaking her ribs.

That is the only time the music in the Pines is known to have stopped. "That's how I'm loved here," said Ross.

Even Congressman Gerry Studds passed like a ship in the night

in this resort. The Massachusetts Democrat had prepared a digni-
fied parchment fundraising card after he was censured by his
House colleagues for a homosexual affair with a teenage Congres-
sional page:

REPRESENTATIVE
GERRY E. STUDDS

A congressman of extraordinary wit, charm and courage

The message was wedged in the doors of Pines homes, and
residents were urged to join this political bonbon for cocktails and
hors d'oeuvres. The household where we were staying that weekend declined and instead went to a costume party that was kicked
off by a dazzling creature who, gowned as a British monarch,
warbled an address from a balcony to the stoned guests. "People
[in the Pines] are passing Quaaludes and iced vodka or Tuinals and
Scotch," Edmund White, the Boswell of urban gay America, had
remarked in his travelogue *States of Desire*. It was *not* comme il
faut, he noted, to mix these combinations and do, say, Quaaludes
and Scotch.

Dear Gerry,
In a continuing effort to keep out day trippers, we the people of
the Pines have made a major contribution to public policy, by
refusing to clutter our pristine environment with rest rooms. We
do hope your stay was comfortable in our exclusive summer
camp for grownup homosexuals.

Love,
Queen Mary

"IN ENGLAND, I RECEIVED HALF A DOZEN CALLS A DAY
SAYING, 'YOU'RE QUEER. I'M GOING TO KILL YOU.' I'VE NOT
RECEIVED MORE THAN HALF A DOZEN HOSTILE CALLS IN
ALL MY TIME IN MANHATTAN. YOU SEE, IN NEW YORK, IF
YOU LOOK ODD, YOU'RE THOUGHT TO BE ADVERTISING
SOMETHING."

Quentin Crisp, the flamboyant author of The Naked Civil Servant, *on*
why he moved to New York in his seventies after a desolate life being
persecuted for his homosexuality in his native Britain

The American gay liberation movement began late in the evening of June 27, 1969, when police raided the Stonewall Inn, a gay bar near the corner of Christopher Street and Seventh Avenue in Greenwich Village that, as a low-key predecessor of the Mine Shaft, was suspected of washing its takings more frequently than its glasses. Instead of slinking away like good little sissies, pantywaists, queers, fags, all the other slurs, the patrons scooped up their skirts (many were in full drag) and gave battle. The Stonewall Riots infused enormous self-confidence into the community. Yet, at the time of writing, nearly seventeen years later, Manhattan, in which, by some calculations, homosexuals represent 20 percent of the voting population, does not have a single openly gay elected official.

"It's the nature of New York," the president of the Lambda Independent Democrats, a gay political club, has observed of the eclipse of the movement's early militancy by such concerns as Andrew Kopkind's existential agonizing in a *Village Voice* essay over the riddle "What makes a hamburger gay?" (Answer: A restaurant in which "even the plants are well hung.") "People tend to be individual-oriented . . ." said the Lambda club president.

In 1985, David Rothenberg, a soft-spoken, conservatively dressed gay PR man who had founded the Fortune Society, a rehabilitation group for ex-cons, sought to remedy this. He challenged Carol Greitzer, a four-term city councilwoman, in the Democratic primary. Though Greitzer, the scourge of the Night Frontier (chapter seven), was touting a fact sheet listing no fewer than fifteen pro-gay initiatives for which she took credit, we deduced that she might be embracing the Cause for the usual reason that motivates New York politicians—opportunism. The late *Village Voice* columnist Arthur Bell quoted her as once telling a gay activist, "I really don't have your problem." No problem. She trounced Rothenberg.

In March 1986, a bill banning discrimination against homosexuals in housing, employment, and public accommodations did succeed in passing the city council. This ended a fifteen-year battle. During those fifteen years, at least two thousand gay men, led by activists such as the Democratic Party's Allen Roskoff, had been screaming at the recalcitrant council—about a thousand less than the crowd on a good night at the Saint. Maybe it's time to give the boys some consciousness-raising lessons.

"THERE'S A WAR GOING ON BETWEEN GAY MEN AND LESBIANS. LESBIANS ARE JUST TREACHEROUS BEASTS. NINE OUT

OF TEN GAY MEN WILL HIRE A GAY, BUT LESBIANS WILL ALWAYS HIRE STRAIGHT WOMEN. AND THEY ALWAYS HAVE THESE VICIOUS DOGS ON LEASHES AND TAKE UP THE WHOLE SIDEWALK."

A well-known gay New York novelist and commentator* to the author

---

There are some crossover nodes, of course, between the men and the distaff wing of the community. Virginia Apuzzo, a former nun, is probably the best known, heading the National Gay Task Force, at the time a New York–based lobbying group, for just over two years. While the men were practicing their peacock imitations—headdresses of silver-tipped black feathers were *in* on the gay disco circuit some time before the lady in chapter one adapted them—Apuzzo was successfully pushing for the inclusion of a gay rights plank in the Democratic Party's 1980 and 1984 presidential platforms. The only other noticeable confluence of the sexes is at the interdenominational services of the New York Metropolitan Community Church, probably the city's largest homosexual organization. It is led by two women pastors, but, interviewing a male church official, we discerned that he was keeping two card files—green, labeled "Women," and gray, for "Men."

"Men and women lead different lives, and it's no good to pretend otherwise," the official said, explaining that the congregation separates along lines for prayer meetings that would not be unfamiliar in an Orthodox synagogue. Men in one room, women in another. "Men's spirituality is very conventional. We sing old gospel songs and use traditional language for God. The women do a lot of work with healing and laying on of hands and they'll sometimes speak of God as 'she' and 'mother.' "

During the seventies, there was a valiant attempt at Columbia College to organize a conference at which gay men and women would exchange ideas and share experiences. The workshops were put in place—themes like Politics of Fat—and the great day dawned. It would have been easy to tell the men from the women even if they hadn't seated themselves on opposite sides of the auditorium for the opening perorations. "The men had the bodies of a model, their clothes were neatly pressed, their jeans were the next best thing to the immaculate conception," a lesbian who attended recalls. "The women looked as though they were ready to spend the next eight days in a paddy wagon." Future conferences were organized like the prayer meetings.

*Afraid of the Vicious Hounds, he asked not to be identified.

As often has been pointed out, lesbians have more in common with straight women than gay men, primarily because, like straight women, they earn on average 62 cents to every dollar made by a man. In the seventies, this politicized them, just as it politicized many straight women who became their allies in feminism. "Of course, you would get to know other women while you were practicing your politics, and between the discussion you might go to bed with one of them," says the lesbian alumna of the Columbia conference.

Not for any haphazard old action between the sheets, though. As an extension of your politics, the hijinks had to be Politically Correct. What would later become the cult of the G-spot was roundly condemned in this period in a pamphlet entitled "Vaginal Orgasm as a Mass Hysterical Survival Response." To ensure the sisters got the message, a New York lesbian psychotherapist issued a set of instructions for "Enjoying Snuggling" and advocated exercises for learning how to masturbate ("Pick a time of day when you're relaxed and feeling good about yourself").

Some of the sisters channeled their energy into poetry readings. Friction broke out at one recording session when Audre Lorde, a poet who read with such zeal that her nostrils would flare, was asked to remove her bracelets. The clunking was drowning out the words, another woman politely ventured. Lorde tossed her head. "The bracelets are my music," she said. An enigmatic figure at some of these get-togethers was Honor Moore, the writer daughter of Paul Moore, the Episcopal bishop of New York. "You couldn't make her out, because she had humility and she dressed in knit jackets and pants, like she just got off a train from Connecticut," another poet says. Moore, who in the mid-seventies lived with Venable Herndon, writer of the screenplay for *Alice's Restaurant,* subsequently has given some of her work, including a volume called *Poems in Four Movements for My Sister Marion* and an anthology of women's theater, to the Lesbian Herstory Archives, a New York collection of lesbian materials.

"A WOMAN NEAR THE FIRE SAYS, I HAVE FOUND LOVE THIS WAY BETWEEN WOMEN: A SEE-SAW, ONE UP"

Honor Moore, *"Poem: For the Beginning"*

"My poetry speaks for itself," the bishop's daughter says of her sexual identification. "I identify myself as a feminist writer, which

I always have been, and a woman-identified writer, which is what I always have been, no matter whom I am sleeping with."

A number of these literati overlapped with a group that has survived, if in attenuated numbers, into the eighties. The Man-Haters. In his introduction to *The View from Christopher Street,* a collection of journalism from the New York gay magazine, its associate editor, Michael Denneny, observes that the publication's hopes of gender parity were shattered when one of the women editors informed him one day that "she actually didn't read any of the pieces by men."

As a founder of the WOW Café, a downtown women's performance space, said, one didn't mind men attending one's shows, but one was *not* interested in their opinions. She went on to express her amazement that some of the sisters who used to rail against the capitalist patriarchy and relish penury were putting on skirts, taking jobs on Wall Street, and applying for gold credit cards. This indeed has been an accelerating trend. But the city for a long time has had a lesbian at the helm of a major department store, lesbian-owned manufacturing companies, even a lesbian bookie with a thirty-phone operation and real estate holdings—as a laundry for her gambling gains. "I think all the downwardly mobile dykes," one recruit to the corporate life said with a smug grin, "are going to end up living in the hills. They'll never afford New York."

MALE CO-PARENT WANTED
To create a baby w/single female. No marital obligations.

Ad in the gay newspaper New York Native

The female separatists unleash their highest-decibel ire at the increasing number of lesbian couples who have been retreating to Brooklyn and the suburbs to create babies, generally by artificial insemination and occasionally without medical help, resorting instead to the so-called turkey-baster method. The reason for the anger is that when the progeny that result are male, the proud moms frequently refuse to do the politically correct thing— genocide, exile, anything rather than keep the diapered little oppressor on the premises, "thereby making their sons *more important* than the wimmin who don't want ANY MALES in wimmin's space!" storms a 1985 article on the subject of "lesbian ethics" in a New York lesbian newspaper.

One form of women's space that has been in increasingly scant supply in Gotham is the lesbian bar. At least six of these establishments have closed during the last few years, leaving a grand total of maybe three sympathetic watering holes. Some had their licenses yanked after refusing to admit men. One taproom complained of Mafia harassment—though in fact the wiseguys have always been homophiles. "Tony Ducks" Corallo, the Lucchese family's reputed kingpin, is said to have owned an interest in an East Side homosexual establishment where the annual dues of $120 included free legal aid for members busted on morals charges. Another female saloonkeeper spoke of *fire-department* harassment: "We never paid people off, so they started bothering us at two, three in the morning," said an owner of Ariel, a lesbian bar that finally expired in 1985—after a dispute with its landlord. Not that there isn't persecution. It's just that most of it seems to be inflicted by the sisters themselves.

Peeches Three, a crowded Seventy-second Street lesbian spot, advertised itself as "New York's Gayest & Most Charming Upper East Side Snuggery" and hosted such intimate events as a lesbian marriage (bride in white dress and veil, groom in white tie, and "Congratulations Gloria and June" on the cake). Suddenly, the place metamorphosed into the Spaghetti Western Saloon. Same management. No more female exclusivity. "Women don't support you," owner Joanne Ruvelas explains. "We had a five-dollar door charge. They complained, so we dropped it, and after that they'd just walk in, say they didn't want to order anything to drink, and walk to the back and start dancing. Nine years of that was enough." At the Women's Coffeehouse, a seventies Greenwich Village haunt, the sisters would stride in, lugging their own food and drink—or even demand that they be fed for free. As if they were Vanderbilts. "Why do you charge?" one of them asked.

There is one success story. The cheerful pine-and-brick Cubby Hole, on Hudson Street, has withstood what owner Elaine Romagnoli characterized as harassment by the local *community board,* which she said had filed complaints against the bar with the city and police. We did wonder whether there might be some special circumstance involved in Cubby Hole's victory. Romagnoli used to manage Bonnie and Clyde's, a now defunct lesbian bar–restaurant in Greenwich Village owned by Louis Corso, a Little Italy padrone who is friendly with a gentleman called Matty the Horse (see chapter ten, Mobbed Spots). In 1976, when the state liquor agency balked at renewing the Bonnie and Clyde's license—the tavern allegedly was among the establishments that discriminated against men—it was the Horse's lawyer who successfully defended the case. Though Corso has no involvement in the Cubby Hole, his wife, Luba, does happen to have become the chairperson of the local community board's sidewalk café committee. Did she help call off the heat? Mrs. Corso sounds puzzled at the question. She says that she has no idea why the opposition to the bar died down.

Since the men rate pleasure the way the women rate politics, there are hundreds of bars for gay men in New York. And you have to give the brothers credit. Despite some New Leftist cant immediately after the Stonewall uprising about joining the universal struggle of the third world, peace movement, black people, and socialists, the fellows have done a spectacular job of preserving no fewer than three of the distinctions banned on the masthead of *Womanews,* a New York feminist newspaper: there is a gay bar for every racist, ageist, and classist taste.

At Uncle Charlie's Downtown, on Greenwich Avenue, a line of preppies stands, backs to the bar, sizing up the surrounding designer labels. At the uptown Wrinkle bars, this process is continued by gentlemen of substance in their mid-fifties: the one we visited, identified by a small brass plaque on a door down some steps, was orderly and subdued at two in the morning, with patrons in Shetland sweaters and dark suits, their faces smooth as the velveteen upholstery in the tactful lighting, making small talk amid oil paintings and bowls of calla lillies. The pianist, in a necktie and black cardigan sweater, was plinking something discreet when, all of a sudden, a basso voice discombobulated from some district office of the British Empire rumbled to its husky sixtyish companion:

"How did she know whether it was a Hindu or a Moslem that raped her?" Long hee-haw. "Because he was circumcized."

Such humor may drive one in search of another phenomenon that has no precise duplicate on the female circuit—attractive boys, or Twinkies. The Killer Fruit, as the city's rich gay lawyers, businessmen, and designers are called, keep retinues of the lads, and one political heavyweight dresses them as waiters when he has parties at his country home and uses them as front men on property that he wishes to hide from the IRS. Should you require one of these luscious seedlings just temporarily, say for an hour, a visit is in order to one of two places, a society restaurant or a hustler bar. An elderly German nobleman, who married a radiantly beautiful young woman in order to breed heirs, sometimes can be seen lazing over a table at Mortimer's, the Reaganauts' favorite bistro, while his wife spots talent for him. Espying a Vanderbilt there one day accompanied by two Vanderbilt sons, the young woman dabbed a hanky to the powder icing her nostril hairs, adjusted her Chanel suit, cast a long look across the room, and simpered, "Look at those pretty boys! I'll get them over for you. You must be *introduced.*"

Hollywood and record-industry executives traditionally have recruited young companionship at Rounds, a slick East Fifty-third Street restaurant and bar. One film and music producer arrived with a personal pimp.

Producer to Pimp (eyeing Andrew, a grade A oven-stuffer in skintight jeans): "Tell him who I am. Tell him I'm a famous producer."

Pimp to Andrew: "Do you want to meet the record tycoon ——? He has —— —— on his label."

Andrew, dreaming of his first platinum, treated his swain to a complimentary session. You should normally budget $50 for dinner for two, with wine, at Rounds and $100 or more to take your selection home with you—though, as the evening wears on and the crowd thins, the price drops to under $50. Just remember that that coquettish young thing in Jordache may be a KGB agent in disguise. Investigators for the state senate's Select Committee on Crime testified in 1982 that boy prostitution rings were sneaking on their tricks to the Soviet, British, and Israeli intelligence services:

"Comrade Lenin? How y'doin'? This chick says he got a new album on his label that's so bad it's number forty with the parachute."

In the New York gay politburo, the one thing that is totally taboo, that can make you so miserable you take Courage (chapter four) as the only way out, is fat. In gay life, "the body as well as the soul" may be elected, as Edmund White once observed, but there's only one size on the ballot. A group of chubbies were denied entry to a Fourteenth Street gay bar because of "size discrimination," storms Ernest Harff, a cofounder of the Girth and Mirth Club. Its members, some of them a breathtaking four hundred pounds, others scrawny chubby-chasers (admirers), meet to chew the fat at monthly socials. "In a wine cellar atmosphere," says a blurb for a club brunch, "dig in [sic] the sumptuous buffet of cold salads, egg, sausage, potato, ham, vegetables, do-it-yourself waffles, assorted cheeses, fresh fruits and, of course, the chocolate fondue for dessert. Don't forget the pound cake, the brownies and other goodies." Thus energized, amours are fostered by the Penpal section of the *Fat Apple Review,* the club newsletter. A word of caution, however, should you find yourself cuddling up to a member: "Keith, who once cracked a 'petite' partner's ribs with a simple hug, says more people need to come out of the closet where their weight is concerned," counsels an article reprinted by the club.

Now for matters of color. Just think of this as the gay extension of the circus: Jews may be everywhere, "chocolate drops" spreading, but the real danger is the invasion by *Tupperware* fiends. . . . Though some New York guppies belong to a sort of gay version of the Kiwanis that throws covered-dish suppers, at which scrumptious cold pastas and molds are arrayed in jel-n-serve sets and kracker keepers, there is a fine distinction to be observed: white homosexuals always cook with fresh apricots. "The gay Asians who frequent Twilight [an Upper East Side "Rice" bar] are very Tupperware-oriented. Many live in Jackson Heights, Rego Park and Flushing. Their apartments are nicely turned out and they cook when they come home from work, preferring recipes from *Family Circle* (like hamburger meat with canned apricots)," wrote the *Voice*'s Arthur Bell. Weep for these poor peasants. Even when they are among their own, groused a dejected Asian computer operator, "Orientals never make the first move; they're taught not to be aggressive. And . . . Oriental gay men never, ever go to bed with each other." The *Native* made an honorable attempt to remedy this by publishing a special supplement, "Coming Out Yellow." This included a guide to Oriental astrology that revealed we were in the Year of the Ox, a beast of burden who makes a good lover because he is "tender and faithful. . . . The best trust and partnership for an Ox is with a Cock." The guide also listed some people who were born in ox years: "Gary Cooper, Paul Newman . . . Johnny Carson . . . " and gave a rundown of gay Asian bars and restaurants, such as the Big Wok, on Washington Street, which we heartily recommend for your first date with Carson. A key at the head of the latter chart read as follows: "AAA—Predominantly Asians, AA—Many Asians, A—Some Asians."

"IF WE ALLOW OUR CITY TO TURN INTO ANOTHER SODOM, G-D WILL MOST CERTAINLY SEEK JUSTICE."

New York politician Noach Dear, warning against gay activism in the Jewish Press. *Running for city council, Dear subsequently was endorsed by Mayor Koch.*

While the lesbians fight the gays and the gays count Asians, several celebrities and politicians have been evincing remarkable solidarity on the issue of homosexuality. For those of you who are gay, here are some indicators of what the Big Rams think about you:

• At a 1982 Los Angeles engagement, Frank Sinatra warmed up by slamming television gossip Rona Barrett as a "bow wow"—and then launched into a scathing attack on Rex Reed, the New York entertainment critic. "He said Rex Reed had finally come out of the closet [untrue], and it was about time. Then he did a lisping, mincing impression of Rex reviewing a movie," reported a man who was in the audience. "And then he said, 'I hope the guy sues me, because then I can punch him in the mouth.'" This may have been out of revenge, not prejudice, however. Reed, transported by the sight of daughter Nancy Sinatra's boots and bewitching mascara, had once compared her to a "pizza waitress."

• Mail poured into the *New York Native* saying that the born-again singer Donna Summer was admonishing audiences during a 1983 concert tour with such profundities as "AIDS has been sent by God to punish homosexuals." Summer termed her fans' reports a "terrible misunderstanding," saying that the epidemic was "a tragedy for all mankind." But what precisely was the statement that precipitated the misunderstanding? "I can't help you," said an assistant to the star.

• When Abe Beame was running for mayor of New York after winning a hotly contested Democratic primary, he sought the help of Robert Abrams, then the Bronx borough president and·a leader of the reform wing of the party, and now state attorney general. Beame invited Abrams and an aide to outline their agenda of issues. They raced down the usual liberal list, according to a City Hall insider. "Another issue," the aide added, "is gay rights." Beame, a diminutive accountant, stared blankly. "Gays, *homosexuals,*" said the aide. "Oh," replied the candidate. "Well, we can't have *that* in New York." The aide, who is gay himself, gulped. "We do have it in New York," he said. "I know what you mean," Beame suddenly said, his face flushed in triumph. "They want to come into the schools and teach wearing dresses."

• During Mario Cuomo's losing 1977 campaign on the Liberal Party line against the bachelor Ed Koch in the mayoral election, posters appeared on Queens lampposts imploring, "Vote for Cuomo, not the homo." In his autobiography *Mayor,* Koch accused Cuomo of complicity in such attacks. The mayor cited a press report that said that Michael Dowd, a Cuomo campaign director who later would become a whistleblower in the 1986 city corruption scandal, had hired a private eye to "conduct an investigation into my sex life." Cuomo's Brooklyn coordinator reportedly had a "security consultant" doing a similar probe, wrote Koch, who repeatedly has denied being gay. In fact, there was no proof linking the man who is now governor of New York to these dirty tricks and Cuomo has barred discrimination against homosexuals in government. On the other hand, his administration's most talked-about gay initiative has been the anti-AIDS measure invoked against the Mine Shaft. Anti-AIDS to the extent, that is, that it banned public displays of the only ways two men can copulate. It was silent on the subject of vaginal coitus, despite growing evidence that this also spreads the disease. Shortly after this, there was another announcement: the governor's liaison to the homosexual community, Peter Drago, was moving to a new post and would not be replaced, since his duties were being reassigned to a "broad-based group." At the time of writing, the governor, under heavy pressure from the gay community, seemed to be having second thoughts about this. But no one was expecting any dramatic positive initiatives on gay rights from the politician, who has made it no secret that he has an eye on a move to the White House. Says a Democratic political consultant, "The number one issue with Mario is his presidential candidacy and he is concerned that the AIDS epidemic would be one more negative on top of all the other negatives that traditionally are associated with New York."

• Both Cuomo and the veteran United States senator from New York, Daniel Patrick Moynihan, have consistently declined to join other pols, such as former Vice-President Walter Mondale, on the podium at the nation's largest benefit for gay rights, the Human Rights Campaign Fund dinner, which is held each year in New York. The senator did tentatively agree to appear at the first dinner, but backtracked—and it initially seemed that this was because he didn't want to upset one of his campaign contributors, the designer Mollie Parnis. Parnis's son, Robert Livingston, had been the city's first openly gay appointed official before his premature death from cancer, and an award was to be presented in his name at the dinner. The senator's wife, Liz Moynihan, is said to have visited an organizer of the event and claimed that Parnis had broken down in tears at word of this plan. The designer, whose clients have included five First Ladies, had been traumatized when her son first came out of the closet, so this didn't seem far-fetched, according to a political insider. He says that the senator's wife frantically told the benefit organizer, "I can't let Pat do this." Moynihan soon needed a new excuse, however: Parnis's misgivings about her son's declaration of his sexuality had caused a rift between mother and son, but this was mended before his death, recalls a Parnis friend. Sure enough, the designer sent a check for $1,500 to the gay rights benefit, and has contributed every year since. A Moynihan aide says the senator has stayed away simply because of scheduling problems. Other Democrats suggest, however, that he is among a number of politicians who, despite an unblemished record of support for homosexual issues, feel uncomfortable around gays. Failing to grasp this, a contingent of gay activists visited the senator on Capitol Hill. He stared absently around the room and meandered into a monologue about the decline of the Soviet empire. The average Soviet woman had between six and eight abortions, the economy was stagnant, the male death rate was soaring: "It has to be alcoholism," he mumbled, according to the *Village Voice*.

"THE MAYOR IS NOT GAY."
"OH, COME ON, BLANCHE!"

From dialogue between a character based on a Koch aide and a homosexual activist in The Normal Heart, *a play by the New York gay writer Larry Kramer*

When *The Normal Heart,* a bitter satire about the lack of response by the government and other institutions to the AIDS crisis, first boiled into an auditorium at Joseph Papp's Public Theater in the spring of 1985, the renewed innuendo about Ed Koch's sexuality might have seemed in poor taste. Except that, blink, and you surely would have missed the handful of dollars that the mayor was flinging at an epidemic that, if it continued at its present rate of infection, would kill tens of thousands of Americans over the next five years, as many as one third of them in New York.

The city, as Kramer calculated it, was earmarking just $41,000 for AIDS-related services that year. San Francisco, with about three times fewer victims, was budgeting $7.6 million. "Outrageous!" screamed a Koch aide when we asked him about the playwright's onslaught. "There is no other mayor who has such a terrific record on the AIDS crisis." He directed us to a flunkey at the city health department for details. The $41,000 didn't include the cost of keeping AIDS patients in hospitals, the flunkey said brightly. Neither did San Francisco's $7.6 million. There was a pause. "Originally," said the flunkey, "we printed public health education brochures in English, Spanish, and Haitian dialect, over one hundred thousand of them. We then decided a better form of education was face to face." Senior flunkey, taking up the refuse-nik banner: "The information has not changed very much since we did the brochures. There is very little more to be said."

It indeed could get tedious tossing around the same old comparisons and statistics. For instance, the primary source of education and support for sufferers from the disease in New York has always been the Gay Men's Health Crisis (GMHC), a group formed by Larry Kramer and some friends. Its San Francisco counterpart was receiving 60 percent of its funding from the city and county. GMHC, said a fact sheet prepared for the audience of the Kramer play, was having to raise 80 percent of its money privately; most of the remaining funds were provided by New York State. About three weeks before *The Normal Heart* was due to open, the mayor hastily convened a press conference to announce some $6 million in new AIDS initiatives. Anything less might have been embarrassing in a city election year, though Kramer persisted in his contention that what really embarrassed the mayor was spending money on an illness that, while it strikes straights as well as homosexuals, has been nicknamed "the gay plague."

"Koch," the playwright said, "has been afraid to help AIDS victims because he is gay—and terrified of being perceived as gay."

Playboy: Are *you homosexual?*
Koch: *No, I'm not.*
Playboy: *Have you ever had a homosexual experience?*
Koch: *I'm not going to discuss my private life with you . . .*
            Ed Koch to interviewer Peter Manso in Playboy

A prominent Democrat, who is gay himself and is a longtime political ally of the mayor's, insists that Koch is gay—but suggests that, whatever Hizzoner's sexuality, it has nothing to do with his early apathy to the AIDS issue. As the Democrat points out, the mayor has been highly supportive of gay causes such as anti-discrimination measures that don't require spending city funds: "If I was to be very cynical about it, I'd say he hasn't done more on AIDS because he's very worried this could be a bombshell to chew up his budget."

Larry Kramer, a writer-producer who won an Academy Award nomination for *Women in Love,* had expected that GMHC at least would draw support from the entertainers, producers, and designers, straight and gay, who were his friends. Would David Geffen be a director of the AIDS service group? No. Would Michael Bennett help with fundraising? No. Kramer dropped off a presentation, appealing for funds, at Calvin Klein's apartment. The designer didn't even respond, Kramer fumes.

The writer recalls mentioning this to his doctor, Kevin Cahill, a New York specialist who also treats Klein.

"Kevin said Calvin was very nervous about being perceived as having AIDS," says Kramer. There had been speculation in the press, subsequently denied, that Klein was dying of the disease. Was the designer afraid of being associated with GMHC? A Klein spokesman flew into a rage when we asked him this: "The guy is *not* homosexual, he is not homosexual, period. . . . I'm his business associate and the man happens to be partner in a five-hundred-million-a-year business," the designer's spokesman shouted. Perhaps Klein had been helpful in other ways? Perhaps he had given GMHC cash? The spokesman said it was a matter of policy not to disclose such things in view of Klein's $12.5-million-a-year income: "Here you've got a guy who . . . technically could be tapped for every charity on the face of the earth." As of early 1986, we were able to find one $10,000 contribution to AIDS programs in Klein's name, but with the death toll mounting, Seventh Avenue's heavy guns finally were planning a benefit. The "World's Largest Photo Session," as it was being called, would raise money for the American Foundation for AIDS Research, a group pulled together with Elizabeth Taylor's help after Rock Hudson fell victim to the disease. Foundation board members included David Geffen. Klein again was conspicuous by his absence, until, that is, about two weeks before the event, he agreed not only to underwrite the entire evening, but to cohost it with La Liz. Ed Koch also showed up for the glittering fundraiser, and was among several guests who remarked that the fashion industry had been tardy in joining the battle on the deadliest syndrome in modern history.

"It would be nice if it had happened earlier, but I'm not looking back." Hizzoner told the *New York Times.*

"NOW TIME IS AVAILABLE (INDEED IS REQUIRED) TO ELABO-
RATE THE ARTS OF COURTSHIP."

Edmund White on the impact of AIDS on gay lifestyles

The most drastic prophylactic theories involve giving it up.
"Homosexuality is a bad aesthetic choice," asserts a spokeswoman
for the Aesthetic Realism Foundation, a controversial New York
group that claims its consultations have set nearly 150 men and
women on the straight and narrow, including a dentist and a
Methodist minister. The foundation has received only patchy
media attention: David Susskind had its representatives on his
show once—and refused to have them back, the group complains.
It teaches that the purpose of everyone is to "like what is different
from ourselves. A man liking another man isn't different," says its
spokeswoman, who presumably hasn't seen some of the odd
couples parading along Christopher Street, the West Village's gay
arterial boulevard, on Halloween.

Another kind of odd couple aired their tale on "Real People"
and Phil Donahue. A tale of the *miracles* of transsexual surgery.
Sheila, who used to be Harry, was married to Gene, who used to
be Jean. Viewers were not made privy to the fact that, as sometimes happens in these casual sounding swaps, Sheila had been
effectively neutered, perhaps permanently, by internal scarring.
Nor that an estimated 50 percent of the applicants for the
surgery—which aims to help people who believe they are trapped
in the wrong sexual anatomy—are Catholics. Many of whom,
according to one expert, may be resorting to the knife as a
"defense against homosexuality." The knife flashes too easily,
some critics of the procedure contend.

The New York State Health Department has been considering
charges that a Park Avenue plastic surgeon, David Wesser, performed sex-change operations on five ill-prepared men, one of
whom allegedly killed himself soon after. "You've already been
medicated," another Wesser patient, a thirty-year-old social
worker, claimed he was told by a hospital employee when he had
second thoughts as he was wheeled into the doctor's operating
room, "and therefore you are not in a position to make a rational
decision." That patient killed himself, or herself as he had become,
seven months later. Wesser, who has denied all the charges, is
continuing to offer the surgery, says his lawyer Deyan Brashich.

Brashich called eleven expert witnesses who argued that surgery is the only option for a "true" transsexual. Besides, "a certain philosophy of personal freedom is involved," Wesser once observed to us.

A word here about freedom for straights. Michael Salem has just the wardrobe for you if you want to take a vacation from conventional masculinity. Salem, whose family used to run a business that supplied delicate hosiery to clients like Jackie O and a Rothschild grande dame, now operates a transvestite boutique on a very elegant block of Fifty-third Street, appealing to heterosexual as well as gay cross-dressers. A paunchy man in a shimmery polyester shirt and aviator glasses, he carries a portable telephone with him at all times, so he can fill emergency orders from his 150,000 customers, who include one of John Glenn's colleagues in the Senate, a judge, and a football player. "Usually, it's our rubber chest with breast pieces they want, but padded girdles and waist cinchers are big sellers," he says. He stocks a full line of beauty preparations, and it could be deduced that this prefaces a serious *androgynous* trend, since not only do some men now wear dresses to haut monde parties, but several New York designers are employing men as models for their women's clothes. The gray silk dress in which Jane Lapotaire collected her Tony award for *Piaf* was created on the best-known of these man-nequins, Kevin Boyce. The son of a Philadelphia railroad worker, he has the same sleek proportions as the country's top female fitting model, Margaret Donohue, and applies just a layer of Lancôme foundation over his beard when he poses for illustrators who sketch him for ads that appear in publications like *Harper's Bazaar* and *Women's Wear.*

Among the gay men who have taken a vacation from *un*conventional masculinity is Jack Wrangler, the gay porno star. He fell in love with Margaret Whiting, the sixtyish recording artist ("Moonlight in Vermont"), several years ago, and lives with her in a Manhattan apartment in which the atmosphere recalls the third-act domesticity of Harvey Fierstein's drama of homosexual life, *Torch Song Trilogy.* There is a rabbit hopping around, a silver cake stand laden with frosted cookies, and a Steinway piano on which Whiting's father composed "Ain't We Got Fun" and "On the Good Ship Lollipop." The song that is Wrangler's life owes something to an ability to mix-and-match—he still plays gay discos, though he has given up porn (his work included some straight X-rated movies) because of AIDS—and perhaps something also to our advice in chapter two as regards résumé innovations. He has repeatedly described his father, Robert Stillman, including in his highly publicized autobiography, *The Jack Wrangler Story,* as the executive producer of the long-running TV series "Bonanza." Not so, according to his dad and David Dortort, the man who really had that job. Dortort created the series and brought in Stillman, an NBC executive, as his assistant. Stillman says he was mortified when he discovered that his son had given him a promotion.

For most gay men in New York, as the leathermen's Sunday salons suggest, *gay* life goes on, even if some of the gaiety has gone out of it. "One of the things that bothers me most about this epidemic," the Saint discotheque's owner, Bruce Mailman, moped when AIDS first hit, "is that we're taking five backward steps into boys wearing pink shirts and dating." Mailman owned a posh bathhouse as well as the disco. The bathhouse has been closed by the city and, with more and more of the boys not just dating but staying at home to do it, the Saint has started admitting women several nights of the week. "The insularity of the gay community was necessary to get a focus, to know that you were gay, but the new generation of gay kids don't see their sexuality as a defining force," the club owner said, happier after instituting his new policy.

All forms of gay life go on, thanks to some minor technical adjustments. Should you not want to curl up with Tuna the Cat and a beau to watch "I Love Lucy" reruns, you can experience the newest, safest, funnest development yet in Communal Sex: masturbation clubs.

"We put out fliers the other day all over Wall Street," says Jeff, an official of the JOEs (Jerk-Off Enthusiasts). Members meet regularly for sessions at which a "fluid patrol" of safe-sex monitors stomps the room in navy uniforms and jackboots. "We've had a few straight men call and women who asked if they could bring their vibrators," Jeff adds, proud as a turkey-baster father.

Yes, sexual liberation lives. Reinforcements for the movement have been eagerly acquiring their first leather, latex, subscriptions to porn magazines, whips—and dildos. Nice dykes, you see, are now into Politically Incorrect Sex in all its filthy, inegalitarian, outlandish declensions.

The Power Exchange, "A Newsleather for Women on the Sexual Fringe," is available in plain brown envelopes at New York gay bookstores. And a group called the Lesbian Sex Mafia has been sending out invitations to its S&M discussion meetings. One of these get-togethers was entitled "Exploring the Male Side of Ourselves."

The mailing for it was signed, "In struggle."

10

MOBBED SPOTS

"JOE'S FAMOUS FOR HIS MORNING-GLORY MUFFINS AND HIS COFFEE CAKE."

Al Nahas, the "landlord" of Nightfalls, a Brooklyn restaurant, on its weekend pastry chef, Joe Gambino, the son of the late mob chieftain Carlo Gambino

"Big Paul" Castellano, the elderly ex-butcher who succeeded Carlo Gambino as the ruler of the Gambino family, the most powerful organized crime network in America, was a man of gargantuan appetites and peerless stealth. Yet even during the years in which his mansion, a replica of the White House crowning a Staten Island hilltop, was under constant surveillance by everyone from the FBI to prying neighbors, he never sought to conceal his modus operandi with as much as a dollop of pizzaiola sauce.

Sweeping through the gates in his Cadillac, flanked by his sons, Joseph and Paul Jr., or his flashy bodyguard and protégé, Thomas Bilotti, the don would head for a restaurant in the quiet middle-class Brooklyn neighborhood where *Saturday Night Fever* and *Staying Alive* were filmed. Perhaps Martini's Bay Ridge Sea Food Restaurant at 8616 Fourth Avenue. What heinous purpose, you may well have demanded, watching the mobster stride to his table, his eyes hidden behind tinted tortoise-shell glasses, was this eminently respectable fifty-five-year-old establishment being used as a cover for? A sitdown about waste disposal? The feds never did turn up the body of Castellano's ex-son-in-law, who is believed to have met his maker in a most unpleasant way after cheating on Big Paul's pretty blond daughter, "Princess" Connie. A meet about one of the family's many white-collar enterprises? These included foreign trade. That's exporting stolen American automobiles to more prosperous nations, like Kuwait.

"Baloney! He never was a wiseguy," snorted the restaurant's owner, Angelo Martini, a longtime Castellano friend. Besides, a fellow has to be able to go someplace to eat where nobody will bother him. "He likes fresh seafood, period," explained Martini. "Nothing fancy on it. No sauces. He's a very plain eater. Wonderful man. Wonderful wife."

"THEY GIVE YOU THE BEST QUALITY, THE BEST PRICE, AND THE MOST WONDERFUL SERVICE. YOU CALL UP ABOUT A FEATHER AND THEY GIVE YOU ALL THEIR ATTENTION."

Al Nahas, explaining why the restaurant Nightfalls buys from Dial, a meat and poultry distributor owned by Big Paul's sons, Paul Jr. and Joseph

---

When it's time to eat for the sake of eating (not social engineering, not celebutanting), committed gourmands know there is only one course to take—and since you understandably may be shy about soliciting the uomini rispettati for their marketing and restaurant recommendations, we made some inquiries for you with these dedicated chowhounds. Dominating the wholesale end of the entire East Coast food industry, they generally settle for nothing less than Grade A quality whether they're eating out at a "rug joint" (fancy restaurant) or having a quiet little snack in the office.

"Oh no, not those!" some mob front men were heard to groan on a police wiretap when a secretary preparing their lunch reached for a pack of the adulterated hotdogs they were pumping into the nation's supermarkets.

• *You want fish?* Nina Castellano, Big Paul's widow—he was gunned down in 1985 in an apparent mob power battle—has been spotted making her selections at the fish store that Angelo Martini runs next to his Bay Ridge sea food restaurant.

• *You want meat and poultry?* Al Nahas has the idea. Any brand distributed by Dial, the firm owned by Big Paul's sons. It is said that Frank Perdue, the chicken czar, did not have the idea, and that his marigold-"yeller" birds never seemed to go on special at one retail chain in the New York area. He subsequently added Dial to his distributors. The firm, of course, is a totally legal enterprise.

• *You don't want to cook?* Not long before Big Paul's death, an investigator sampled the lemon sole at Angelo Martini's restaurant. Broiled in herb butter, the way the godfather liked it, the dish was so blissful that it is understandable that another epicure rispetto, Ed Koch, is among this Brooklyn restaurant's patrons. For reservations, call 718-748-0504.

• *For a light lunch,* Big Paul would drop into another Bay Ridge spot, Nightfalls, a palatial shrine to postmodernism at 7612 Third Avenue that seems rather out of keeping with its homey Brooklyn neighborhood. Moreover, as at a number of other institutions we have visited in this book, the management structure of this restaurant is complicated: Nahas describes himself as the landlord; a man called David Naman is the owner; Joe Gambino, the late Cosa Nostra boss's son and a partner in one of the largest trucking companies in the city's allegedly mob-dominated garment district, does the weekend pastry duties at the bake oven. After all, you can't eat management structures. John Travolta had the chicken with pistachio nuts and rosemary. Delicious! Sly Stallone nearly didn't get to eat. He sauntered in, "accompanied by four goons," grumbles Naman. Hollywood's highest earner was swathed in a fur coat which he refused to check, protesting that it had set him back $12,000. "We took the coat off him. We don't like to have people eating in coats," says Naman. Then Rocky had steak. Yummy! For reservations, phone 718-748-8700—and ask to sit near the Epicure Rispetto. The mayor, a close friend of Nahas, has eaten here at least six times, and Nahas murmured something to us about the delightful evening that he and Ed and Joe and David had sitting around trading "ethnic jokes."

Like Nightfalls and Martini's, all of the restaurants and taverns in the following list are owned and operated, unless otherwise indicated, by law-abiding citizens with no connection to organized crime. Some of these restaurateurs aren't even aware that their provender has received glowing reviews from uniquely sagacious trenchermen. Those locations that are asterisked (*) have attained the New York equivalent of a Michelin rating—enough ranking wiseguys on the premises at some point in time to warrant a wiretap or other electronic surveillance. [Again, unless otherwise indicated, there is no evidence of any connection between these establishments' owners or employees and the mob.] Bon appetit!

MANHATTAN

"WITH THESE SUPERMARKET CHAINS, YOU KNOW HOW TO DO BUSINESS WITH THE BUYERS? YOU WALK IN THE OFFICE, HE OPENS HIS DRAWER, YOU DROP THE ENVELOPE IN, HE CLOSES THE DRAWER, YOU GOT THE ORDER."

Transcript of an FBI tape of an employee of a food supply firm talking to Anthony "Fat Tony" Salerno, reputed acting boss of the Genovese crime family, as reported in Newsday

We'll go north to south, beginning in the old Italian section of **East Harlem,** where though the residents are now mostly desperately poor and black or Hispanic, they have not been forsaken by some of the original colonists. An internal New York City Police Department report has described Fat Tony as a staunch upholder of affirmative action, employing "many black connections" in his multimillion-dollar Harlem policy rackets. One of the chief targets of the ongoing federal attempt to put the mob out of business through a series of catch-all indictments, this reputed gangster lives on a manorial country estate that would do justice to a scene in "Dynasty." It even has an indoor riding arena that he constructed to enable his privately educated children to work on their dressage in inclement weather. Still, federal agents say that some of his vassals, and even Fat Tony himself, may still be found discussing good works on their old Harlem turf. You may run into them, for instance, at the Palma Boys Social Club,* at 416 East 115th Street, which is handy to these four neighborhood restaurants.

RAO'S
455 East 114th Street   212-534-9625

Down a few steps from street level, this clubby ninety-five-year-old bistro used to be fondly referred to as "the hole" by habitués, who ranged from cops to certain gentlemen who would have Swiss-cheesed anyone who got between them and the food. Gilding Rao's legend was owner Vincent Rao's brother, Joey, who once gave the restaurant as his address (police denied that he lived there) in the era when he was an acolyte of Dutch Schultz, that connoisseur of great beers. Joey subsequently enjoyed a profitable liaison with a Mafia kingpin who testified that he attended the underworld's 1957 Appalachian crime summit in the mistaken belief that it was a buffet luncheon.

Joey is now deceased, and Rao's has a new nickname these days—"the new *Elaine's*" (see chapter eleven). Among its steady patrons: Jimmy Breslin, John Chancellor, Vic Damone, Neil Diamond, Melvyn Douglas, Mia Farrow, Woody Allen, Elliott Gould, Rocky Graziano, Harry Guardino, Mayor Koch, Shirley MacLaine, Mary Tyler Moore, Jack Nicholson, Anthony Quinn, Sylvester Stallone, Jill St. John, Barbara Walters, and Frank Perdue. All of these names, and more, appeared on a list submitted to the New York State Liquor Authority by Vincent Rao's lawyer when the agency threatened to yank the restaurant's license in 1981.

This was over what Rao and a relative, who, jabbing a large unlit cigar at us, did most of the explaining, angrily characterized as a "grossly exaggerated" episode, involving a minor celebrity whose name was not on the list, Ralph "the General" Tutino. A reputed henchman of the Lucchese family, one of the five New York crime dynasties, the General had diversified from what was said to be his principal occupation, large-scale heroin dealing, into helping out strapped businessmen with loans at an interest rate somewhere over 52 percent a year. "I am going to fucking throw you in the river. I am the fucking gangster, not you," he allegedly told a man who was two days late with a repayment.

Tutino had borrowers make some of their payments by checks written to cash—and Rao did the cashing, prompting the Bronx district attorney, Mario Merola, to suggest that the new Elaine's was being used as a "laundry." But there was no proof that Vincent knew that the money had been obtained illegally—"If you come to me as a friend, am I going to give you a hundred questions?" said his relative, gesticulating violently—and the elderly restaurant owner, who has cashed checks as a favor for cops in the past, pleaded guilty to a misdemeanor. Even that could have jeopardized his license, but his lawyer, a state senator, persuaded the liquor regulators that the restaurateur really was not guilty, having chosen not to fight the rap simply because he was in "grave health."

The General went to jail, never even having gotten to try Vincent and his wife and co-chef Anna's famous clam zuppa, because, the couple glower, he is not their type of crowd. In truth, the feeling is mutual. Could you see a Genovese underling feeling comfortable talking shop in a booth that's all done up with photos of its regular Monday-night denizens, publisher Michael Korda and his wife, mounted on finer horseflesh than Fat Tony will ever afford?

"On one of our wiretaps," confides Assistant United States Attorney Charles Rose, "a man was heard saying, 'We'll meet at Rao's,' but then this other voice drawled, 'Nah, nobody goes to Rao's no more. There's too many people there.'"

PATSY'S PIZZERIA
2287 First Avenue   212-534-9783

The mushroom-and-sausage pizza is so mouth-watering here that for years some people just couldn't stay away, like Frank Sinatra. By some accounts, it may also have had an expansive effect on Fat Tony's poundage. "We don't want to have anything to do with gangsters," said an employee. "But you can't lock the door, right?" he added. "It's unconstitutional to bar people, so I guess they all came." Despite rumors in law enforcement circles that they still breeze in, the employee insisted that the neighborhood is now too "unpleasant" for them, and everyone else too for that matter, so the place really only stays open as a hobby for the owner. Then he handed the phone to someone he introduced as a relative of the owner, who said Patsy's *never* entertained a wise-guy and, confusingly, caters to a "downtown" crowd.

ANDY'S COLONIAL TAVERN
2257 First Avenue   212-410-9175

When the city police department's Organized Crime Control Bureau compiled a confidential Top One Hundred of bookmakers, policy operators, loan sharks, cigarette bootleggers, pimps, and other "public morals major violators" in 1979, Andy's was noted to be a favorite of no fewer than three of them, including Fat Tony, the reputed Genovese kingpin, and Frank "Farby" Serpico, a pudgy Genovese soldier whose income from gambling and "shylocking" was estimated at $5 million a year.

Confidential police reports do tend to exaggerate, but "Andy has never changed. Almost everybody from the Genovese family goes there," enthuses a detective. "The food is unbelievable." This is as it should be. According to state records, Andy's owner, Salvatore Medici, used to be the chef at Rao's. It is tragic, therefore, for us to have to tell you that Fat Tony, entering his autumnal years, seems to be off his grub. He was reported to be "toothless" when, a cigar dangling over his jowls, he sullenly produced his $2 million bail after his 1985 arrest in the federal "commission" case, which charged that he sat on a sort of mob board of directors that governs the five Mafia families of New York. Andy's manager said that the don hadn't been in for his macaroni in a while.

DELIGHTFUL RESTAURANT
2258 First Avenue   212-876-6224

This literally delightful, if unpretentious, spot features Beautiful Italy paper place mats and floral chintz curtains. The cash register is right by the door, yet even though the Delightful is open twenty-four hours on a street that has something of a Wild West ambiance, the staff seem admirably unconcerned about their safety. When we walked in, there were only three other customers, two of whom were glimmering like Christmas trees at Tiffany's in plum-sized diamond rings, layers of gold necklaces, and bracelets trimmed with precious stones. The menu is basic diner, but with a few specialties. Like the $5.75 Chicken Italiano, and a tasty veal-and-beef cannelloni, for $6.75. A nice touch on our tuna salad platter was the black olives. Popular with visiting banditos? A manager said she didn't know what we were talking about because she didn't live in the neighborhood.

Ever since the era when Lucky Luciano took up residence at the Waldorf-Astoria under the name of "Mr. Charles Ross" and went shopping uptown for silk jockey shorts, the Mafia's more suave luminaries have mingled unobtrusively over les rigatoni aux truffes et foie gras with certain stars of the circus on the **Upper East Side.** Four decades ago a Tammany Hall leader observed of Lucky's top lieutenant, Frank Costello, "If Costello wanted me, he would send for me." These days, companies connected to organized crime make campaign contributions on the books and some well-known hoods even have been going into business partnerships with city officials. Not that it's all business. This is a great neighborhood for grocery shopping, because you never know what's going to be available on the menu besides the buffalo mozzarella.

Praised in a 1970 *New York Times* review as a "small, new Italian restaurant" that was "increasingly interesting and international," the fare at Alda's, an East Eighty-sixth Street restaurant, eventually became so cosmopolitan that, according to undercover agents, by 1985 it included generous helpings of high-grade heroin, thankfully not swimming in the joint's famous marinara sauce. The agents claimed to have bought the stuff on the premises on one occasion from the owner, Anthony Raimone, and on others from his son, Dominick. Dominick pleaded guilty in what was purportedly a $5 million conspiracy, after being nabbed at a social club (it is not advisable to enter a New York social club like the Palma Boys unless you are invited). Anthony pleaded not guilty. His case had not come to trial at this writing, but Alda's has closed. For mystery buffs, therefore, we recommend Nicola's at 146 East Eighty-fourth Street (212-249-9850). Yes, we know it looks like just another of those star trackeries (see chapter eleven). Carroll O'Connor, Henry Ford, Warren Beatty, Mary Tyler Moore, and Mia Farrow have an unfortunate habit of hogging the front tables. But this is where Howard "Buddy" Jacobson, once the nation's principal horse trainer, ate regularly, strolling across the street from his apartment at 155 East Eighty-fourth. He was particularly partial to the Lobster Pescatora, which has a garlicky fresh tomato sauce, but was torn away from it by the necessity of putting in twenty-five years to life in the state pen for clubbing, shooting, and stabbing his charming young neighbor to death in a love-triangle case, then packing the chap—a drug smuggler—into a storage crate. Nicola's sophisticates do just adore to pack, which may be why the affair is still a subject of nostalgic gossip in these parts. "Buddy was a seafood man," the chef, Claud Lorang, says reverently.

RUSTY'S*
1271 Third Avenue   212-861-4518

The Met's star pinch-hitter, Rusty Staub, a prodigious cook and consumer—he generally weighs in at 240 pounds and his marinated barbecued ribs, redolent of applejack, at only somewhat less—owns this trendy restaurant in the East Seventies, which is popular with customers like Brooke Shields and Howard Cosell. For a time, according to court records, Rusty had a partner, Carlo "Carlos" Vaccarezza, an alleged associate of the Gambino crime family who—unknown to the Mets star—seemed to prefer recipes with mathematical ingredients.

"He says you got tonight's game 3?" a caller queried, according to a transcript of a 1982 federal wiretap on the restaurant phone. "Yeah, I got 3 and I got 38.... Do you want any games for tomorrow?" replied a voice identified by lawmen as that of Carlos. "Oklahoma is two and a half and 38."

The caller rang off after placing his bet.

In a sweeping 1984 racketeering indictment, the government charged that Carlos's eclectic interests also included helping to collect the moolah in the most sophisticated, and ethnically integrated, loan-sharking scheme that the FBI had ever encountered. After all, if Chemical Bank could advertise that it had capital available, why shouldn't Dr. Jesse Hyman, reputedly a onetime money man for Meyer Lansky in Atlantic City, follow suit? The doc was credited with being the brains behind the operation. Though he was said to be a deft hand with his dentist's drill, the brawn allegedly was provided by stalwarts of no fewer than four Mafia crime families. And by Chaim Gerlitz, a cantor at a temple in Great Neck, a posh Long Island suburb. The capital, according to the feds, came from the underworld and Teamsters pension funds.

"You gotta remember," Hyman observed during an electronically intercepted palaver at a table at Rusty's, "we got money from people . . . who can blow your fucking head off."

Among the recipients of the loans were Wings (a hip SoHo restaurant) and a dress shop.

A thug attired in jeans and a T-shirt appeared regularly at Wings to collect the vig (weekly payment), distracting some diners from their boneless braised duck in raspberry vinegar. When the owners lagged in their payments, a mobster called and left a polite message for the manager: "I would appreciate it if he gets hold of me," he said, or else "people will be taking out the silverware, the glasses, things like that." Wings closed. The ring shuttered the shop, to sell off its frocks, and the owner, who was going to testify in the case, was killed in an accident involving a speeding tow truck.

Hyman and Gerlitz were found guilty. Though Rusty Staub's co-owner, Carlos, was among the defendants who were acquitted, the case presumably was a bitter blow for him, since Rusty gave him the boot before the trial even started, at the prompting, says a prosecutor, of the FBI. In so doing, the sports star may have lost a valuable line to the unions. "Every union guy knows one another," the voices were heard saying at Rusty's on a federal tape. The agents had assumed this was a reference to mob infiltration of unions, but Carlos's attorney explained that his client had simply been offering to help remove pickets at the restaurant at a time when its staff were being targeted by union organizers. For some reason, the removal methods weren't specified.

GIAN MARINO
221 East Fifty-eight Street   212-752-1696

This restaurant has attracted the mob equivalent of Earl Blackwell's Celebrity Register over the years, but the owner, Giovanni

DiSaverio, especially remembers Anthony "Little Augie Pisano" Carfano, an aging Al Capone lieutenant and organizer of the butchers' union, whose last meal consisted of Marino's pasta e fagioli followed by shells with broccoli and zucchini stuffing and the piquant Veal alla Casa, with its basting of egg, lemon, and white wine.

The squat, potbellied gangster was accompanied that evening to the restaurant—then located at a different address—by a former Miss Jersey. Later that night, she and "Gus," as Little Augie liked to be called by the ladies, were shot dead by gunmen who raced alongside their Cadillac. A handwritten recipe for Marino's clam sauce was found in the racketeer's pocket. Little Augie was always punctilious about important details. He is said to have been marked for death because, among other annoyances, he had called Vito Genovese, the Genovese family's then CEO, to whine that one of the don's aides had stood him up on a date to play golf.

"We are famous for our shells," DiSaverio says thoughtfully. "Some dishes are immortal. They never die."

Genovese's underboss, Anthony "Tony Bender" Strollo, had also been in Marino's that fall night in 1959, sipping on the restaurant's velvety Amarone Polla. Tony Bender was a regular here—until he vanished after assuring his wife that he didn't need a topcoat because "I'm only going out for a few minutes. Besides, I'm wearing thermal underwear." Underworld informers surmise that he was compacted in a junkyard car crusher on Genovese's orders, perhaps in furtherance of a longstanding grudge. Don Vito's wife, Anna, had become a partner in a Greenwich Village club that was a hangout for female impersonators and lesbians. Complaining that Tony Bender should not have allowed Anna to associate with "undesirables," Genovese knocked her teeth out. After the couple divorced, their bed was sold at auction, along with the giant mirrored headboard and the sensuous Genovese peach satin quilt.

"Tony Bender was a nice gentleman," DiSaverio says mournfully. "Trippa alla Romana [tripe with Romano cheese] was his favorite. You know, Frank Costello came in here three days before he died. He was with an official of the postal workers' union."

Virgil Alessi, a discreet, gray-haired narcotics violator still visits the restaurant, but not with union leaders and only when he isn't in jail. He and seven other men are said to have devised the $73 million heroin heist from the New York City Police Department property clerk's office that inspired the movie *The French Connection.*

"His favorites are the fried calamari and the Clams Posillipo, a Neapolitan dish," says DiSaverio, perking up. "We do it with a parsley, garlic, and white wine sauce."

Salvatore Gravano, whom authorities describe as a young turk of the Gambino family, was a fan of another Fifty-eighth Street spot's regional Italian cuisine, which included such delicacies as Cartochio—macaroni steamed in a bag with succulent chunks of lobster and clams. However, the menu is in the process of switching national loyalties (to Indian), and anyway you wouldn't be interested in meeting Sal. Though he reputedly has become one of the most trusted aides of John Gotti, the family's new Godfather, Sal's lawyer says he is in the construction business, not organized crime. And in property deals? He collected a $690,000 down payment on the sale of a building he owned that houses a popular Brooklyn disco, the Plaza Suite. In cash. You can't beat liquid assets when you want to move fast in real estate. But, since the money allegedly traveled to him from the building's buyer, Frank Fiala, a distinctly self-made millionaire, via a string of bank accounts (starting in Austria) before being delivered by a Scorpion armored truck, the government jumped to the ridiculous conclusion that this was out of some sort of dislike for the IRS.

Gravano's lawyer set the record straight. He assured a jury at Sal's subsequent trial that, "Even though I have my American Express, Diners Club, and MasterCard, cash is still legal in America."

Happily, therefore, Sal was acquitted of tax-evasion charges. The building's buyer, Fiala, had not been available to testify. He had been on a roll (the drug industry has never been healthier, as we explained in chapter seven), having accumulated a helicopter, two twin-engine Cessnas, a Rolls-Royce Silver Cloud, a stretch limo, a Mercedes convertible, and a yacht (for which he paid $180,000 in cash), and had been eager to buy the Brooklyn property because he intended firing the disco's help. They had not given him good service, Fiala said pensively. But two masked gunmen approached him outside the place and executed him by shooting out his eyes.

Though most of our local wiseguys try to prolong their sadly precarious existence by watching their health, a few of them still overindulge in foods high in cholesterol, and if you come across any of them at **midtown**'s famous steakhouses and delis, we beg you to impress upon them the virtues of switching to a high-fiber diet. Paul Vario, Sr., a capo in the Lucchese crime family, had steak delivered to him five days a week while he was in Long Island's Nassau County Jail (fellow prisoners cleaned and swept his cell and made his bed). His gluttony once was nearly his undoing. He and two other hoods were hauled before judges and asked what they had been digesting over the groaning platters they had ordered up at the Palm Restaurant, a powerhouse at 837 Second Avenue (212-687-2953). "They all ate here at one time or another, but we never became a hangout," says the Palm's Paul. "You sort of ignore them, instead of catering to them." It's just that sort of rude New York attitude that led a clutch of refined associates of the Gambino family to vow to do it the way the Miss Manners columns say when they put together a new heroin ring. The drugs were presented, prettily gift-wrapped, across the tables at some of the city's best restaurants to buyers who, sadly for the development prospects of Latin America—the ring had intended using the dough to finance a heroin-processing plant in the Dominican Republic—were in the employ of the Drug Enforcement Administration, not AID. We do not recommend using the Hallmark approach at any of the following eateries.

JIMMY WESTON'S
131 East Fifty-fourth Street   212-838-8384

Owner Jimmy Weston is a former member of New York's finest, so let him know if the boisterous good old boys at the neighboring tables—Richard Nixon, Howard Cosell, Frank Sinatra, Bob Hope, Lee Iacocca, and George Steinbrenner—try to mess with your prime ribs. John Gotti also had taken to coming here by the time he succeeded Big Paul as the Gambino family's godfather. His lawyer declined to ask him for his menu recommendations, but we can tell you his reported choice of role models—Albert Anastasia, Murder Inc.'s Lord High Executioner. John has been overheard on a police wiretap advising a subordinate, who hadn't returned his phone calls, to shape up: "Listen, I called your house five times yesterday," the don screamed, "and if you disregard me and my phone calls, I'll blow you and the fucking house up . . . this is not a fucking game!"

Gotti rose to power as a protégé of another Jimmy Weston's customer, Aniello "Mr. O'Neil" Dellacroce, the head, before his death in 1985, of what Brooklyn's federal Organized Crime Strike

Force chief Edward McDonald calls the "leg-breaker" faction of the Gambino family—loan-sharking, extortion, gambling, hijacking, and murders as opposed to Big Paul's string of white-collar businesses. Dellacroce was nicknamed "the Polack" by some of his minions behind his back, but he preferred his Irish alias and sometimes would masquerade as a priest, "Father O'Neil," on travels to adjudicate contretemps between Mafia clans.

The "father"'s Manhattan pied-à-terre at 232 Mulberry Street was in a Little Italy tenement owned by a family company of Geraldine Ferraro's husband, John Zaccaro. The building was conveniently situated across the street from the Ravenite Social Club, at 247 Mulberry, the Gambino family headquarters. When Dellacroce sallied across the street to the club, his bodyguards would pull out in automobiles to block the road to other traffic. "If it was raining, a little guy with an airline umbrella came out and held it over him as he walked," says Nicholas Pileggi, a journalistic expert on the mob who detailed some of its other vanities in *Wiseguy,* a book about the $6 million Lufthansa Airlines heist.

Let's pause from our meal to look at some characters who, had that presidential campaign gone differently, might have become part of White House history: Philip Zaccaro, Gerry's father-in-law, was a partner with Salvatore Profaci, reputedly a top underworld figure, in a clothing-manufacturing firm in her hometown, Newburgh, sixty miles north of New York City, and in a Little Italy realty company. Philip acted as a character witness for Profaci's pistol permit—a deed that led to his own license being revoked and that also didn't do his colleague much good. After Profaci unexpectedly passed away (his cabin cruiser exploded while he was sailing off the New Jersey coast), the realty venture he had owned with Zaccaro was dissolved. Zaccaro folded his assets into the P. Zaccaro property firm, reported the *New Republic.* Gerry eventually would list herself as this firm's vice-president on a state insurance form. She owned a one-third interest in the company but described her involvement in its affairs as minimal.

Dominic Ferraro, Gerry's father, was arrested on Long Island on bootlegging charges, revealed Sidney Blumenthal in the *New Republic.* It probably was after his arrest that *he* began working in Newburgh, where he was associated with Michael De Vasto, a local crime kingpin, according to an investigation by *New York Post* reporters Guy Hawtin and Jeff Wells. A Newburgh lawyer told them that Dominic was initially a driver for a De Vasto rum-running operation and then managed a De Vasto nightspot. Although Gerry, denying this, huffed that the most he drove was a "wet-wash laundry" wagon, De Vasto's son conceded that his dad gave the vice-presidential candidate's dad "protection." He may have needed it: he died the day he was to appear in court, charged, along with Gerry's mom, Antonetta, with operating a numbers racket. Following his demise, the charges against Antonetta were dismissed.

Nicholas Sands, a former union official, had been convicted of federal labor law violations when he became Gerry's fundraiser after she was first elected to Congress. Some months after a successful gala, "An Evening with Geraldine," nine bullets were aimed at Sands and his Mercedes. Fortunately, the former labor leader, who denies reports that the feds believe his local was mob-controlled, survived. During the 1984 presidential race, a Mondale-Ferraro campaign aide said that Gerry hadn't had an inkling of Sands's background until the shooting, at which point she stopped using his services. Sands had been a campaign coordinator for New York Governor Hugh Carey and was active in charities, "especially involving the handicapped," a Mondale-Ferraro statement elaborated.

Michael "the Baker" LaRosa, one of Gerry's contributors, had borrowed some $250,000 from the Zaccaro family when Philip Zaccaro was alive. He subsequently was convicted of labor racketeering. "I've known Mr. LaRosa. He's a businessman in New York and beyond that I'm just not going to comment," said Gerry.

Lawrence Latona and three other buyers were represented by Gerry when the Zaccaro real estate company sold them the tenement where Aniello Dellacroce, the Gambino chieftain, had his pied-à-terre. According to a report in the *Wall Street Journal,* Latona was an incorporator of the Ravenite, the Gambino clan's headquarters across the street, and managed its building. The foursome in turn sold the tenement a few years later to Joseph "Joe the Cat" La Forte, Sr., a reputed Dellacroce subordinate. La Forte also snapped up two Little Italy properties that were being managed by John Zaccaro, for just $60,000. The old owner, a physician, grumbled that he had been pressured into this deal. "Dr. Tse, you must take this offer because I will never get another buyer like this," Zaccaro had written him, reported the *Philadelphia Inquirer.* La Forte resold the buildings nineteen months later, for $200,000. Asked about this during the 1980 presidential race, a Ferraro aide explained that Zaccaro did not know at the time that

La Forte was the buyer, since the offer had come from Lawrence Latona. From Gerry's old client, in other words, the reported incorporator of the mob HQ.

Once you have digested the above, you can continue your meal.

STAGE DELI
834 Seventh Avenue   212-245-7850

Forget ethnic stereotypes. This internationally renowned stronghold of the *Jewish* whopper—three-decker sandwiches named for patrons like Warren Beatty, Raquel Welch, and Billy Martin—was once a port of call for "the Genovese crew, mostly narcotics violators," says a police department expert. Nowadays, for some reason, he says, these characters prefer to hang out on nearby streets. Checking the menu, we were disgusted to find that nothing has been done about memorializing such loyal former customers as Ralph "the General" Tutino, the moneylender who embarrassed Rao's restaurant, and Milton "Miltie" Wickers, a bookie who made the police department's Top One Hundred with an estimated gross income of $25 million a year. Miltie is now said to be retired in Boca Raton. You'll be eating the *same cheesecake,* by the way, as Amy Carter when she was First Daughter. Jimmy "Lust in the Heart" preferred the Swiss-cheese omelette. It was at this deli that he delivered his greatest ecumenical epithet: "And we wouldn't come here," the president quipped, baring his teeth, "without having some lox."

"21" CLUB
21 West Fifty-second Street   212-582-7200

When he reigned as the union boss of the Brooklyn waterfront, Anthony Scotto, the dapper consort of socialites and presidents (LBJ and "Lust in the Heart"), contributor to New York Democrats and husband of the former Marion Anastasio (her uncle was the Lord High Executioner of Murder Inc.), tailored his image as carefully as his boutique suits. But it wasn't until his sojourn in the slammer, after being convicted of racketeering, that the longshoremen's leader, who has denied allegations that he is a Gambino family member, finally showed himself in his true lights. While having his teeth fixed up at government expense, he whiled away the hours by tutoring the jail's medics on where to eat.

"The places he sent them were terrific," a friend of one of them says. "And they always got wine on the house."

The government charged that "21" was a meeting place in the racketeering scheme that was Scotto's undoing. The longshoremen's leader raked in payoffs, it was said, from waterfront executives in exchange for cutting down on compensation claims by members of his union. "21" certainly has the ambiance for such shenanigans. It's a former speakeasy and its brick-armored wine cellar is now a repository for the Cast of This Book. Richard Nixon has a magnum of 1961 Dom Pérignon stowed there, and will uncork it when Tony joins the GOP. And Elizabeth Taylor is so taken by his angular physiognomy and brooding blue-gray eyes that she is keeping a precious '64 Bordeaux from a Rothschild château in the bins for that very special occasion.

We should warn you, however, that there is a doppelganger at this restaurant, a spirit of a bootlegger departed that possesses patrons and forces them to behave like slobs. We were upstairs at a private dinner party there for the Italian ambassador to the United States when, after imbibing rather too many glasses of bubbly of a much superior voltage to the Screamer's, Baron Ricky di Portanova lurched to his feet. As his wife, the Baroness Alessandra (the former Sandy Hovas, of Houston, according to *Texas Monthly*), tugged at his arm in an apparent attempt to restrain him, he staggered to room center. "To Ee-ta-lee," the baron declared jubilantly, lifting his glass. "That shee-tee little country." Quite out of character. Ricky is a maternal grandson of the King of the Wildcatters, Hugh Roy Cullen. The noble title reportedly came when his mother, who ended up as a Times Square bag lady, married an Italian actor and this baron is normally the least pretentious of mortals, investing his $1.2-million-a-month pocket money in practical ventures. Like air-conditioning his mother-in-law's backyard.

There was also the spring evening when "21" treated a group of boxing fans, including Senator Ted Kennedy, to supper. The guests proceeded to Radio City Music Hall in a genial mood, for a screening of a title fight, but when one of them, Nathaniel Kramer, a young scion of a Wall Street investment family, stood up to greet a friend, Senator Kennedy, who was right behind him, is said to have barked, "Sit down!" The columnist Liz Smith reported that although the event hadn't begun, a hulk accompanying the senator enforced the order by grabbing young Nat, ripping "his coat up the back." The terrified fellow's mother pleaded with Ted's brother-in-law, Steve Smith, to explain what was going on.

"You tell your son to cool it, because this man with Teddy is famous for pulling guys out of cars and killing them, and your son's going right over the railing!" Smith answered, according to his eagle-eared journalistic namesake. (A Kennedy aide later said that the Tarzan, a former FBI agent, simply "put his hands on Kramer's shoulders and he sat down.")

When the Kramer and Kennedy entourages repaired to "21" for a nightcap, the brawl recommenced. Spotting Steve Smith and Senator Ted approaching, young Nat's dad, Irwin Kramer, was so enraged that he had to be restrained by six men. Or so his son told the tabloids. "I came up behind Steve Smith and put the death grip on him," said Nat. "I never met the young man [before]" retorted Smith, "but as soon as we got [back to "21"] he grabbed me by the lapels. His father was pointing an umbrella."

We rest our case.

We next proceed to the **wholesale meat district,** stopping in on the way at Sparks, the 210 East Forty-sixth Street steakhouse beloved by *New York*'s food supremo Gael Greene ("the best sirloin around"), prime ministers, presidents (the United Nations is down the street), and Big Paul. He and his aide, Thomas Bilotti, had just drawn up at the restaurant in a limousine when they got whacked. This put an end to a string of little setbacks for the godfather. On trial at the time in the Kuwait car export case, his gourmet image had been trashed by the testimony of underlings like the gay hit man, Vito Arena, who described sending out for *pizza* while dismembering two victims' bodies. Arena also had demanded cosmetic surgery (see chapter one) and dental work for his lover, a convict, in return for his testimony. The Final Straw is, perhaps, reflected in a tape from a bug hidden in Big Paul's mansion by the FBI.

"I don't even get a drink," the godfather complained of his reception at Sparks, where he is said to have been a regular customer.

"Makes you pay him?" asked a restaurant union vice-president.

"Hey, I don't even get a drink," the godfather repeated. So take your wallet. For reservations, call 212-687-4855.

OLD HOMESTEAD
56 Ninth Avenue   212-242-9040

The attractions of this meat-market institution over the years have ranged from the largest lobsters this side of the Galapagos to the men's room. In *Vicious Circles,* an exposé of the Mafia in the marketplace, Jonathan Kwitny records a meeting here between a meatpacking executive and Sol Steinman, brother of an executive of Daitch Crystal Dairies (now the Shopwell supermarket chain). Apparently something untoward was required of the packing firm, because as the executive and Steinman were standing at adjoining urinals, Kwitny wrote, the executive suddenly "felt Steinman's hand in his pocket. His first stunned thought . . . was that Steinman must be some kind of pervert. Within seconds, however, he realized that bills were being inserted. He says he pulled a couple of $100 bills out of his pocket, returned them to Steinman, and got out of the restaurant as fast as he could." Old Homestead owner Mark Sherry insists that that sort of thing doesn't go on anymore, because the meat industry has become "much more" honest.

PONTE'S
39 Desbrosses Street   212-226-4621

While you are on the Lower West Side, this restaurant, another alleged meeting place in the Anthony Scotto case, will allow you to appreciate the advantages of extraordinary food and solitude. Its off-the-beaten-track location has been a magnet to everyone from Kirk Douglas, who recommends the linguine with white clam sauce, and former Mets manager Joe Torre (striped bass Marchiare) to elder statesmen of the Genovese family like Matthew "Matty the Horse" Ianniello and the late Thomas "Tommy Ryan" Eboli, the family's sometime underboss. Eboli, by some accounts, assisted in the cream-cheesing of Tony Bender, the hapless Gian Marino customer, in that junkyard car crusher. If he did, it was fitting, since Tommy Ryan, before *he* was murdered, wielded an iron grip over something without which those important New York delicacies, lox and cream cheese, could not exist: the East Coast bagel market. His old bagel company vanished after getting into the Securities and Exchange Commission's bad books over irregularities in the sale of its stock to the public. According to *Vicious Circles* the firm was "replaced" by Bagel Nosh, a fast-growing national franchise that initially featured two ex-cons as officers who had been involved in the Eboli operation. When a reporter, James Drinkhall, started investigating this in 1978, a telephone receptionist at the company told him the pair had resigned and were now just "consultants."

The commodities under discussion these days at Ponte's may be less tasty than in Tommy Ryan's time. The restaurant is where garbage carters have met to set rates for hauling away demolition debris, according to testimony to the New York State Senate Select Committee on Crime. Ponte's owner Angelo Ponte, a private carter himself, was described to the committee as "a member of organized crime" who had "always controlled the demolition part by muscle." We asked one of Angelo's brothers, a Ponte's co-owner, about this charge: "It's a lie," he responded. "We're working people. We've worked all our life. We can't stop people [like the carters] coming in here." The *Village Voice* took a look at someone else who had been coming into the restaurant. It revealed that Angelo was a partner with Mayor Koch's transportation commissioner, Anthony Ameruso, and a corrupt judge in a secret property deal. Ameruso, who resigned after his agency turned out to be at the center of the Parking Violations Bureau scandal (Introduction), was a regular at Ponte's. "Our information was that Ameruso met with city contractors in the back room," an investigator told the *Voice*. At this writing, however, Ameruso was not accused of any wrongdoing—and what counts in the back room as everywhere else, of course, is the food.

Despite what the tourists think, Umberto's Clam House, at 129 Mulberry Street, where Crazy Joe was gunned down over the seafood combination (chapter one), is not the sine qua non of dining in **Little Italy.** Its uncluttered decor making for excellent sight lines, Crazy Joe was picked off with humane dispatch—but, after he staggered out to the street to die, the establishment came under the scrutiny of a reviewer who discerned that its sauce repertoire included Del Monte ketchup and a cellophane-packaged substance by Kraft. Umberto's is owned, on paper, by a brother of Matty the Horse and in practice, say the feds, by Matty himself. Following his conviction for skimming over $2 million of cash from the place and other bars and clubs, things do not seem set to get any better—the feds have been making noises about confiscating the restaurant. Should Ronnie be presiding in the kitchen when you visit, hasten immediately to:

BENITO II
163 Mulberry Street   212-226-9012

A bit of a long shot, this one, because we don't know that any organized crime figures have ever been *inside* and the sight lines leave much to be desired. Thus, no one eating at the time saw nothin' when mob enforcer Salvatore "Sally Bugs" Briguglio, a

Teamster official who was a suspect in the disappearance of the union's leader, Jimmy Hoffa, was obliterated with a volley of shots on the sidewalk outside. The Horse and a reputed Genovese family colleague, Anthony "Tony Pro" Provenzano, who was Sally Bugs's boss in the Teamsters, were having dinner down the street. So presumably they didn't see nothin' either. The feds speculated that Tony Pro, who also had been linked to the Hoffa case, had feared Sally Bugs was going to rat on him. One hopeful sign so far as the prospects at Benito's go is that Ed Koch, Big Paul's restaurant disciple, has identified it as one of his "ten bargain restaurants." Hizzoner favors the linguini in garlic and oil and the chicken alla Scarpariello (garlic and lemon).

District Attorney Robert Morgenthau is another regular, and though the Horse may not get to coming here for a while, thanks to his legal difficulties, when he does we are hopeful that he will observe the normal courtesies. "Hi, chief!" he bellowed when the DA strode into another place where he was at the manger.

RUGGERO
194 Grand Street   212-925-1340

The slender, classily dressed, gray-haired man who sometimes takes a table in front of the bar is Joseph N. Gallo, the Gambino family's consigliere, say investigators. According to a 1982 study released by State Senator Franz Leichter, Gallo is influential, like the film in which Nightfalls pastry chef Joe Gambino is a partner, in the garment industry. We wouldn't suggest using Leichter's name as an introduction when you buy the fashion-plate consigliere a drink. Brandishing a polka-dot polyester dress in the air, the senator claimed that the mob's participation in its manufacture had doubled its price, to $25. Leichter said his staff had bought this abomination on the name of the Mafia at Sears.

FERRARA PASTRIES
195 Grand Street   212-226-6150

Reputed Colombo captain and loan-shark Benedetto Aloi, who was among those acquitted in the case involving Rusty Staub's co-owner, has been spotted here. Newcomers to the city probably will want to get some self-defense tips from him. A Cosa Nostra brute was once overheard instructing him in this skill: "People . . . worry about their face when they are getting hit, instead of their stomach, liver, and kidneys. . . . dopey. . . . What's the face? . . . What's important about the face? . . . I got a stitch or two."

ANGELO OF MULBERRY STREET
146 Mulberry Street   212-966-1277

An organized crime prosecutor was in Angelo's one day when he noticed a group getting up to leave. One of them, a Gambino capo, pulled out a *green* American Express card to pay the check. But maybe it was borrowed. In any event, at least one person of gold-card stature has guzzled here. The $45 repast for two is named in his honor on the menu. "The President R. Reagan" consists of "The Continental Hot Antipasto, Homemade Fettucine alla Matriciana, Veal Sorrentina with Fried Zucchini and Potato Croquettes."

CAFFÈ PALERMO*
148 Mulberry Street   212-431-4205

The fresh-faced young proprietor of the café is John DeLutro, or Baby John, as he is dubbed on the matchbooks that were still being given away to patrons some months after he was accused of heading a $150 million dope ring. Since he pleaded guilty to a lesser but still serious charge in the case (he claimed he was just a customer of the ring, doing a little resale on the side), he may not be around when you visit the café. But the cappuccino should still be heaped with enough cream to make you believe you are in heaven. A pious note is also struck by the photo of a burly priest which flanks the portraits of Baby John's children. "That's the late Father Vincent, who founded Cabrini Medical Center," said a motherly lady, beaming as she collected our check. We did feel that $5 for two coffees was a bit steep, but, mindful that the feds had turned up what they called "truly astonishing" weapons caches at the homes of alleged members of the ring—twenty-nine rifles and handguns, seven of which were loaded, and a silencer— we decided after a few moments' contemplation not to protest. And later we were gladdened by our gesture, because we learned that the federal raiders had also walked off with the ring's housekeeping money, $4.8 million.

Baby John comported himself, we are pleased to report, with dignity throughout these rigors.

Right: Late one evening, there was everyone at the café worrying about where he had got to, when he phoned to say, according to a wiretap, that he wouldn't be coming in because he had "pupils like a fucking ogre."

Wrong: Baby John's father, a reputed Gambino family soldier, raised him well, and maybe it is because *he* wasn't around much—

he has been doing twenty-five years in Lewisburg on narcotics charges—that Baby John sometimes got snappish with his staff. "You're not my friend, you're just my worker," he told an alleged lieutenant in the dope ring in another monitored conversation. "You can't sniff with me no more."

S.P.Q.R.
133 Mulberry   212-925-3120

A glossy brochure they hand out here explains that the restaurant shares its monogram, Senatus Populus-Que Romanus, with ancient Rome. It is located in a former tile factory and its etched glass, brass rail, classical statuary, and mahogany paneling are picturesquely accented by a big mural in the rear. This depicts, one restaurant reviewer enthused ("S.P.Q.R. spells elegant"), the family of S.P.Q.R. owner Louis Corso as "villagers." Lawmen have suggested that Corso, a husky former bicycle salesman, has a backer. The Horse.

"I wish I had a partner like Matty," Corso says, denying the charge.

It is, he explains, no partnership, just an old family friendship. The Horse has eaten here a lot—though he apparently declined to be an extra when the restaurant was used for a scene in ABC-TV's Mafia soap, "Our Family Honor"—and the don held court, a former S.P.Q.R. staffer says, at a Fourth of July party at Corso's home. The entertainment at this included a Houdini act. "A man was chained up and jumped in the pool," says the former staffer.

We timed our foray to S.P.Q.R. for a few hours after the feds corralled some of the bigshots of the Gambino family, and were pleased by the establishment's enduring sense of humor. An accordionist hovered over us, belting out Rogers and Hammerstein, as a waiter directed us to the little cards advertising a forthcoming $89.95 per person, five-course banquet celebrating Marvelous Marvin Hagler's bout against Thomas "Hitman" Hearns. We also could not help noticing that although the place is not Mafia-owned, it appreciates the importance of chemicals; the use of chemicals in the meat industry was one focus of Kwitny's *Vicious Circles*. "Question: how to serve wine by the glass without incurring significant amounts of spoilage . . . " said an S.P.Q.R. leaflet. "Now there is a unit available that solves this dilemma. . . . The system operates on a nitrogen displacement system, whereby nitrogen, under low pressure in a tank, is passed through tubing into the bottle of wine, as the wine is drawn off through the spigot on the top. The void thus is filled with nitrogen which, being an inert gas, has no taste and no effect on the wine."

So for a bargain $11, you too can savor a two-ounce glass of Château d'Yquem—and maybe learn a little more about how New York works. Or how to work New York. The *Village Voice* has reported that when our acquaintance from Ponte's, Anthony Ameruso, was the Koch transportation commissioner, he was quizzed by "wired agents" about a decision to grant S.P.Q.R. two coveted NO PARKING ANYTIME signs on the street outside, hence treating the place like a church. "The contractors asked for the signs in 1979 when the building was under construction," says Corso. "They went in 1982 when the construction was finished." But the restaurant was open by then? "The restaurant *partly* opened in 1980," says Corso, "but construction was not finished."

CASA BELLA
127 Mulberry Street   212-431-4080

Styled CaSa Bella, this ritzy spot is said to have been named for Michael Sabella, a reputed Bonanno family gangster who, police believe, was the original owner. On paper, the owner was a Sabella pal, and the place then was sold to the current management, Alfred Polizzotto, a lawyer, and Anthony Bottone, a urologist. It has been rumored that Albert "Kid Blast" Gallo, Crazy Joe's surviving sibling, also has an investment in the restaurant, which, of course, would be much more appetizing to talk about over dinner than cystitis. "Anyone can claim anything they so desire," responds Polizzotto. His clients include Kid Blast, "on civil business. I don't do criminal cases," he says evenly.

PASTA POT
30 Mulberry Street   212-962-9249

Customers at this pasta restaurant range from lawyers, judges, and detectives (it's in the shadow of the courthouse) to ranking members of the Bonanno crime syndicate. The restaurant is within easy reach of the Fulton Fish Market, which handles much of the seafood sold from Maryland to Canada—and fish is to the Bonannos what meat used to be to Big Paul. A union official allegedly connected to another Mafia family, the Genoveses, Carmine Romano, was sent on vacation at federal expense after it emerged that he was providing wholesalers in the market with a protection service. He is sorely missed because security there always has been a problem. For instance, after Carmine's uncle was rebuffed in his attempt to acquire a bar-grill in the market for $35,000, (a married couple had come in with a slightly higher offer, $120,000), some thugs gave the eatery that fashionable rubble look—in broad daylight, said a prosecutor. Understandably, therefore, when Carmine was convicted of racketeering, John Hightower, at the time the president of the South Street Seaport Museum, petitioned the court to be lenient, lauding Carmine as an "enormously positive force" in stemming vandalism and break-ins at the prestigious seafaring collection, which shares the market area. "I can only assume," Hightower elaborated to the *Wall Street Journal*, "that he told members of the union not to break into the museum."

CAFFÈ ROMA
385 Broome Street   212-226-8413

The original owner of this corner café, Eli "Joe the Baker" Zeccardi, also ran the day-to-day operations of the Genovese family. From the café, says Remo Franceschini, the police lieutenant who is a veteran mob-buster. The Baker was kidnapped while driving to the Roma in his diamond cufflinks and white Caddie in 1977, and has never been seen since, so the café is now operated by his son, Vincent, who, being a law-abiding citizen, doubtless wouldn't even recognize many of the old customers. Like "Cocky ———," a 260-pounder who perhaps became fond of the place because its nibbles contain no artificial preservatives. Preservatives can make you nervous, which wouldn't have done at all in one of Cocky's suspected professions, contract killing. "What happened in the past," Vincent says tersely, "has nothing to do with the restaurant."

PATRISSY'S
98 Kenmare   212-226-8509

In Little Italy at least, the government may be winning its war on the mob. For years, the dons of the Genovese family would wine and dine their wives and girlfriends, mostly the girlfriends, at Patrissy's. Some of them still do to this day, or so one police veteran maintains. "There's not as many of the old-timers now," owner Danny Patrissy replies, somewhat glumly. "They're dying out or moving away. We get a lot of yuppies from Wall Street now." He's even had to change the menu for them: "We started out Neapolitan, but we got kind of sophisticated. The yuppies go for mad lobster." Mad lobster? "We call it Lobster Arrabbiata, but that means 'mad,'" Danny says. "It's a fried lobster, cut up and no sauce. It's $45 for two."

BROOKLYN

"THIS [U.S. ATTORNEY] GIULIANI, HERE'S A GUY WHO WANTS TO CRUCIFY NICE PEOPLE...THEY ARE NO WORSE THAN THE PEOPLE WHO RUN THIS COUNTRY."

J.B., of Bamonte's restaurant, on Giuliani's war on the alleged employer of two of his best customers, the mob

The aroma of the quiche lorraine ovens of Brooklyn Heights wafts, on a clear day, into the bustling blue-collar neighborhoods where hundreds of Sicilians settled before the turn of the century and began to perpetuate a heritage that, mob boss Joseph Bonanno was told as a boy, began in 1282, when a French soldier raped a Palermo virgin on her wedding day. The girl's mother was said to have dashed through the streets, screaming "Ma fia, ma fia"—my daughter, my daughter. The incident was, perhaps, "highly romanticized or exaggerated," adds Gay Talese, recounting this history in *Honor Thy Father,* his biography of the Bonanno clan. The same caveat applies to one much-publicized Bonanno shrine that we visited in Brooklyn. Joe and Mary's, the Italian restaurant at 205 Knickerbocker Avenue where a subsequent Bonanno family boss, Carmine Galante, was rubbed out in 1979, was, judging from contemporary news reports, positively arboreal ("grape vines" hung near the table in the "quiet, sunlit garden" where he was sitting, said the *Times*). But it is now the Kok Kei, a Chinese takeout, and though it is one of the few restaurants in the city that features wall-to-wall indoor graffiti that is not by Keith Haring, we are omitting it from our compendium.

In the borough's **Greenpoint** neighborhood, which is now mostly Polish, the Hi-Way Lounge,* at 362 Metropolitan Avenue, was in transition when we stopped by—a menu offering Sicilian scungilli salad was still in the window, but the place was in the process of being sold, very privately, probably to "some Orientals," who were expected to go the Kok Kei route, said a local realtor. The lounge should have been designated a landmark, since the Genovese family's James "Jimmy Nap" Napoli used it as his base when he was running what allegedly was the country's most lucrative illegal gambling operation: one estimate of the annual take flooding in was $150 million. Indeed, should Geraldine Ferraro ever return to public life, Jimmy would be an excellent replacement for the hapless Nick Sands.

"[I] ran a big affair for [Representative Mario Biaggi] out in

Brooklyn," Jimmy once bragged in a remark relayed over a bugging device. "He says to me, 'Jimmy,' he says, 'I never seen so many people in my life.'" Though the controversial New York congressman has dismissed this as "name-dropping without fact," Jimmy's public-spiritedness is undeniable. Those of you who want to appeal to it should take the short drive from the Hi-Way to one of these well-known restaurants:

CRISCI'S
593 Lorimar Street   718-384-9204

Jimmy Nap and one of his alleged gambling lieutenants, his son, James "Lefty" Jr., are longtime customers, and since the judges who are also regulars have sometimes dislocated their necks while craning to see what is on the pair's plates, we consulted owner Pete Crisci.

"The father's a good eater, the son about the same," he said. "Their favorite sauce is the pomidoro, fresh tomato with prosciutto, and they like a lot of greens. They like a veal chop, sirloin steak, and their pasta cooked al dente, usually rigatoni or tagliatelle. A little wine, not too much, usually a Riservo Ducale." That's a chianti. "They don't drink no hard liquor," Pete added. We decided it would not be tactful to ask about the jurists' drinking habits.

BAMONTE'S
32 Withers Street   718-384-8831

You may come across Jack Nicholson, Mario Biaggi, a sports star or two, the Napolis here . . . but probably not Rudolph Giuliani, the ambitious United States attorney who has declared war on the mob. "Jimmy Nap is a nice, nice man. He'd give you the shirt off his back. He's helped countless people. He's a personal friend of mine," fumed a restaurant staffer who asked only to be identified as J.B. when we brought up the subject of the prosecutor's campaign.

We persuaded him to break off from this tirade long enough to tell us what Jimmy père eats here.

"He likes the pasta e fagioli [beans and macaroni], calamari with shrimps in a sauce, and he has peppers and eggs," said J.B. "Fried peppers and eggs. They're not on the menu but we make them for anybody that wants."

Near the murky Gowanus Canal, at 451 Carroll Street, you'll find Monte's Venetian Room (718-625-9656), a gathering place for movie stars, powerbrokers, Tony Scotto—and, say investigators, the heavies of the Brooklyn mob, though a member of owner Jo Monte's family says *he* doesn't know any wiseguys, only "perfect gentlemen." When we put this to the lawmen, they said they could only hope that one of the gentlemen, the reputed consigliere of the Colombo crime family, Alphonse "Allie Boy" Persico, would appear among the judges at Monte's next spaghetti-sauce tasting. Allie Boy got permanently lost, according to his wife, while he was making his way to court to be sentenced on a 1980 loan-sharking conviction. His brother, Carmine "the Snake" Persico, the family's alleged boss, also hasn't been sighted at Monte's in some time. He was convicted of racketeering in 1986. Shortly before he and ten associates went on trial in the case, on an indictment that alleged his syndicate controls the key union locals in the city's construction and restaurant industries, a lawyer who has done work for the Colombo clan had a parley with a PR man, saying she wanted to retain him to buff the Persico Eleven's image. She removed the notes the PR man took of the conversation—"Don't think I'm paranoid," she said, burning them with a candle. He declined the job, and the attorney is said to eventually have tackled the campaign herself. The *Daily News* "People" page was alerted that Carmine's cousin and codefendant, Andrew Russo, had undertaken a daring rescue at sea:

"Russo, according to police, dived into the water and battled rough seas" off Long Island to save two fishermen who had capsized, the gossip column informed its readers.

Next: Blasting the *QE II* out of the water and sending in the Snake? That won't be necessary. Carmine, who was once charged with nearly strangling one of Crazy Joe's brothers with a length of rope and a tire iron in full view of the other customers in a Brooklyn bar (the charge was dropped after his victim had a memory lapse), is said to be hoping that the feds will start calling him by another nickname. His boyhood nickname—Junior. Instant image lift!

The South Brooklyn neighborhoods of **Bensonhurst, Bay Ridge,** and **Sheepshead Bay** are a paradise for mob-watching, especially if you are a paid-up member of the Kiwanis. Several civic-minded hoods acquired high office in the Mill Basin–Georgetown chapter of the club, according to a federal informer, holding their meetings regularly at a local restaurant, the Georgetown Inn. The agenda was a welcome change from those stuffy patriotic hymns and the Pledge of Allegiance: "They were using the club to hold sitdowns," says Assistant United States Attorney

Charles Rose. One of these involved a huddle between the reputed Colombo family underboss John "Sonny" Franzese—who was on parole from a fifty-year term for bank robbery—and Carmine "the Doctor" Lombardozzi, who, as the Mafia's reputed liaison with Wall Street, presumably was urging the virtues of nonviolent monetary policies on Sonny during what Kiwanis officials described as a ladies' night. Though Sonny went back to jail, for a parole violation, and the Georgetown Inn is no longer with us, Carmine has remained as loyal as ever to his Kings Plaza Kiwanis branch. "He has invited his probation officer to go with him to meetings," says Rose.

TOMMASO
1464 Eighty-sixth Street   718-236-9883

John Gotti's second-in-command Frank DeCicco was a "very good" customer of this Italian restaurant, according to owner Tommaso Verdillo, until he was blown up by a car bomb across the street. Another alleged Gambino family princeling who may not be in for a while is Anthony "Nino" Gaggi, the "vice-president" of the Kuwait car export caper: he was sentenced to five years in the case. He's also the fellow suspected of taking a hand in the elimination of a Gambino hood, James Eppolito, Jr., who allowed himself to be photographed with Rosalynn Carter while she was First Lady—at a charity luncheon arranged by a con man who was a government stoolie. Mob bosses were enraged when Eppolito began brandishing the picture around. Frightfully bad form! So they saved the Justice Department a heap of trouble and had him and his sixty-four-year-old dad, Jimmy the Clam, snuffed. Nino was captured in a shootout with a cop that night and charged with the killings, but then acquitted. Sometime later, one of the leading prosecution witnesses at his trial was found shot to death.

VEGAS DINER
1619 Eighty-sixth Street   718-331-2221

This ultramodern Greek-owned diner is another Nino favorite. Its specialties include moussaka, Boston scrod, and fifteen vegetables of the day.

MY-WAY LOUNGE
343 Avenue U   718-372-9530

We have avoided sending you to bars, but this cocktail lounge is in a neighborhood that is just so exceptional. The night we were there, young men were nonchalantly parking their Mercedeses and Cadillacs outside in enough numbers to make it look like a dealer's lot, and it is a testament to the unusual solidity of the community that people feel it is unnecessary to lock $60,000 vehicles. Under different owners, the tavern was a hangout for the late Bonanno boss Carmine Galante. Another regular was Charles "Moose" Panarella, recognizable by his bull neck and propensity for music. So anxious was this reputedly high-ranking don of the Colombo family to acquire title to his very own jukebox, that he allegedly helped hold down a jukebox salesman at a Brooklyn restaurant while another tough beat him. The salesman testified to the United States Senate that this was amid a running fire of demands that the merchant take them in as his "partners." The gentle Moose was said to have twice stopped the beating to order coffee. He tipped a revivifying shot of it down the entrepreneur's throat, wiping away the blood from his ears, mouth, and nose. The chances of seeing any action at the My-Way these days are slim. An investigator says that the mobsters who still sometimes mix inconspicuously with the locals at the tavern are just "kids." What would these kids happen to do for a living? "Drugs," says the investigator, "cars..."

MICHAEL'S
2929 Avenue R   718-339-9288

A Gambino family gunman, Roy DeMeo, used to treat his workers to meals at this southern Italian restaurant—"Roy *always* paid when he took his people out," says a lawman—and he was said to have carried out other favors for his colleagues, like tracking down and killing the government's key witness against "Nino" Gaggi in the Eppolito case. But even though Nino was acquitted of the Eppolito murders, poor Roy's generosity boomeranged, and in January 1983 his frozen remains were found stuffed in the trunk of his new Cadillac. Police said he had been beaten before being shot many times, including twice in the face, it is suspected on the orders of crime bosses who feared there might be some ulterior motive to his ostentatious big-heartedness. A cover, maybe, for snitching to the feds on Big Paul.

VILLA SIXTY-SIX
6602 Fourteenth Avenue   718-236-9470

Gerard Papa, the gangster-nephew of Vincent Papa, a reputed French Connection mastermind, was rubbed out here, allegedly by Roy DeMeo, as he arrived for a late breakfast. The Villa is also a

Moose pasture, according to the police Top One Hundred, and specializes in inventive combination crops. Veal with shrimp. Veal with eggplant parmigiana. Veal with shrimp and eggplant parmigiana. . . .

GROTTA D'ORO ON THE BAY
3206 Emmons Avenue   718-646-4300

Carmine "The Doctor" Lombardozzi, the banking expert, more than once has been voted "Kiwanian of the Year" by his local chapter of the organization, which holds its meetings at this restaurant. Whether he's visiting to meet, or just to eat, the Doctor customarily parks his vanilla-and-brown Rolls-Royce on the sidewalk. "He's big for the rigatoni, very very al dente," said Grotta D'Oro co-owner Tom Faga. "We cook it much shorter for him than for anybody else, seven minutes, and the chunky tomato is his favorite sauce. He's very Italian that way. He's very thin. Very in shape. He drinks nothing but white wine." Preferably the Fontana Candida Frascati. "I tell you," Tom said admiringly, "he's not a Dom Pérignon and lobster eater. It probably goes back to his poor youth."

If certain undercover agents get that hollow-stomach feeling as they read this, they should think themselves lucky that the Doctor never prescribed them any of that special mob medication. They tried to *trick* him as he ate with them at the Grotta, chuckling to themselves that he would soon be cooked better than a well-done steak at Sparks. They claimed he had loaned them the princely sum of $2,000, at a 130 percent interest rate, for a gambling parlor they'd set up as a sting operation. Video-game machines, rigged to pay out quarters, had been installed at the Rainbow Yogurt Shop.

But was the man whose financial prowess is suspected to have inspired the mob to take over entire stock issues, even entire brokerage houses, going to allow himself to drown in a cup of Dannon? After his attorney explained to the jury that Lombardozzi was innocent, the Doctor was acquitted in ample time to go around to the Grotta for dinner. Just the usual bottle of wine, and veal scaloppini with his rigatoni. Nothing special, said Faga, because he'd "had nothing to be nervous about. I tell you, when you try to frame somebody, it's very difficult to get a conviction."

Daily News city editor Arthur Browne was interviewing Al Nahas, the Nightfalls landlord, one evening about the mayor, for *I, Koch,* a biography the newsman coauthored with two other New York reporters.

The garrulous restaurateur strayed from the topic to reminisce about how two men, who identified themselves as envoys from the Doctor, had tried to muscle in on the Brooklyn brasserie, which boasts Carlo Gambino's son Joe as a pastry chef.

"Nahas said he called Koch to tell him about the problem," says Browne.

At the mayor's suggestion, according to Nahas, the Nightfalls landlord looked for somebody to "help out"—and settled on Joe Gambino. Next time the hoods walked in, Nahas said, he put them on the phone with the chef/trucking executive, who apparently proved to be his father's son, because before long Nahas heard them stammering, "Oh yes, sir, Mr. Gambino . . . yes, we'll pay our check."

Browne steered the interview back to what interested him. Nahas's old friend Koch. Some time later, Gambino walked over and the subject of the feds' onslaught on the mob came up.

"Joey [Gambino] kept insisting to me there was no such thing as organized crime," Browne says. "I said, 'Let me tell you about this story Al just told me.'"

He recounted the anecdote about the Doctor.

"Joey said he was surprised Al had told it," he recalls. "He pretended his hand was a gun and mimed firing it at Al."

OTHER BOROUGHS

The Bronx

"I DON'T UNDERSTAND HOW YOU CONVINCED YOUR ATTORNEY TO PRESENT THE DEFENSE THAT YOU WERE SIMPLY INVOLVED IN GAMBLING, ONE OF THE SILLIEST DEFENSES I'VE EVER HEARD IN MY LIFE."

Judge Richard Owen, to "Sonny" Guippone, who was convicted in a federal narcotics conspiracy case. The attorney, Paul Victor, is one of the most powerful Democrats in the Bronx and the son of Albert Viggiano, who was listed as a bookmaker in the police Top One Hundred list.

A 1985 national survey identified the Bronx's tightly woven Arthur Avenue neighborhood as the safest place in America, but didn't mention the reason, which is that it shelters certain businesses that require a peaceful environment. And should their owners get into any trouble, why they can just call up a lawyer with links to the political system. This a proud tradition in the Big Onion.

For instance, Sonny Guippone's attorney, Paul Victor, is probably the second most important Democratic Party official in the Bronx. He made the key decision that allowed Stanley Friedman, the politician implicated in the Parking Violations Bureau scandal, to take over the Bronx party organization. According to a Victor law partner, the attorney's previous clients include Mike Clemente, one of the Onion's waterfront rackets bosses. The *Village Voice* asked Victor why he agreed to represent Sonny. Preserving an Arthur Avenue heroin business presumably wasn't high on the wish list of the Bronx Democrats. Victor explained that he took the case at the urging of Sonny's wife, "a woman who is close to being a saint." Sonny got thirty years.

Dominick's, at 2335 Arthur Avenue (212-733-2807), was a favorite years ago with top gangsters and the sturdy Italian food here is probably the best value in town. Served family-style, at long tables covered with oilcloth, under an autographed photo of Bronx Borough President Stanley Simon, a huge meal of spaghetti, salad in a fragrant oil dressing, veal scaloppine, and wine (Gallo Hearty Burgundy, by the mug) will run you just $23 for two.

Queens

"GEE, THAT'S A VERY GOOD AIRLINE."

What Jimmy Breslin, the Daily News *columnist, says Jimmy Burke said to a blond Lufthansa stewardess*

Breslin places the above conversation in Queens, at Pep McGuire's. Whether or not the exchange occurred, it certainly makes historical sense: James "Jimmy the Gent" Burke, a hijacker and mob enforcer, was the suspected mastermind of the $6 million Lufthansa heist in 1978 that inspired Nicholas Pileggi's book *Wiseguy.* Pep's closed. In due course, The Gardens opened at the same 120-20 Queens Boulevard location. Lieutenant Remo

Franceschini, the mob-buster, works across the street in the Queens district attorney's office, and he was curious about the new restaurant. Fashionably decorated, with a flowery menu and Manhattan prices ("Three Musketeers," $11.50), it seemed rather out of character for the man who was listed as its owner, Frank Ocello, a retired sanitation department lieutenant. Franceschini says the real owner appeared to be Pasquale Catalano, a reputed associate of the Colombo family, whose pertinent qualifications for the hospitality industry include once hijacking a load of whiskey.

"I've seen him in there," said the detective, "giving orders."

Maybe that was because Ocello was away, though, doing the prison stretch to which he was sentenced, rather awkwardly, shortly after the restaurant opened. He'd been learning the industry from the ground up, it seems, conspiring with other cops in shaking down illegal drinking clubs, and he was busted in the Continental sting (chapter seven). The Gardens was still his place, not Catalano's, "to my knowledge," retorted Ocello's lawyer, Anthony Lombardino. There was one fact in this restaurant's history that nobody disputed, however: one of its best customers, career mobster Anthony "the Gawk" Augello, had gone absent for good. Distraught because he had introduced a man who, unknown to him, was a federal agent to a Colombo family heroin distribution ring, the Gawk killed himself with a shot in the brain, first phoning his wife and, of course, his *lawyer,* to say his farewells.

"He did the right thing," another mobster sighed in a conversation recorded a day or so later by the FBI at a Long Island marina, "right to the end."

Not quite. The place he selected for his leavetaking was a Burger King. The Gardens closed and was replaced by Tony Roma's, a rib house that is part of a Dallas restaurant chain.

ALTADONNA
137-01 Cross Bay Boulevard   718-843-9228

The new godfather, John Gotti, has been an enthusiastic patron, say investigators, of this Sicilian restaurant where the specialties include fresh fish, presented raw on a tray for your approval before it is cooked. Don't confuse the godfather with Charles Bronson, who took a liking to Altadonna while he was on location nearby for what we understand is one of John's favorite movies, *Death Wish III.*

PRUDENTI'S VICINO MARE
51-02 Second Street, Long Island City   718-729-7572

It was here that Raymond Donovan, when he was a Schiavone Construction Company executive, allegedly witnessed a payoff by a colleague to an officer of a union reportedly under the sway of the Lucchese crime family. Donovan, under indictment at this writing in a $7.4 million fraud case involving a New York tunnel project, was quite understandably cleared of the payoff charge while he was President Reagan's labor secretary: a special prosecutor, Leon Silverman, found that there was "no credible evidence that the [Prudenti's] lunch ever occurred." Nonetheless, there are a few reasons why we are advising you to visit. The obliging nature of the help, for instance: Silverman noted that at the request of a Schiavone official, a waitress had destroyed records of lunches that Schiavone people *had* enjoyed at Prudenti's. Not that these records would have been relevant to his investigation, the special prosecutor reported, because the waitress said they were not for the appropriate year.

And since the one bankable skill that Virgil Alessi, the controversial customer of the Manhattan restaurant Gian Marino, definitely has is *obtaining* things, it made absolute sense when his probation officer told us that the reputed real-life French Connection star was working as the Prudenti's food purchaser when he was picked up for a parole violation in 1984. "He's a friend of somebody's here, not mine, and he needed a job," said one of the restaurant's owners, slamming down the phone.

THE FINAL COURSE

"THEY BURIED HIM IN THE BACKYARD AT ROBERT'S, UNDER A LAYER OF CEMENT RIGHT NEXT TO THE BOCCIE COURT."

Henry Hill, a Jimmy Burke partner, in Wiseguy, *the Nicholas Pileggi book*

Lamentably, we have reached the end of our trail, the moment at which those of you who are not fortunate enough to live in the world's most family-oriented metropolis must leave for home. From **Kennedy Airport,** if you're smart, because, as columnist Murray Kempton has observed, the nation's biggest air-freight terminal is also "the largest inspiration to the criminal impulse within our geographical limits."

We had been planning to have you hoist a farewell libation at Robert's Lounge to the men who have made your stay here so eventful and inexpensive. Just minutes from the airport, at 114-45 Lefferts Boulevard, this saloon was the scene of two interesting archaeological digs in 1980. The first was conducted by the bar's former owner, James "Jimmy the Gent" Burke. His properties were suspected to include part of the Lufthansa booty, though he denies this through his lawyer (who also represented the Gardens' Frank Ocello). Members of the airline stickup gang had been busy wiping each other out, on the logical premise that few means more, and the FBI had been tipped that two of the corpses were stored beneath the Robert's cellar.

"The toilets were overflowing," smirked the Gent, chugging a beer, when Jimmy Breslin asked him why he started digging before the federal agents arrived. The crestfallen official excavation team had to console themselves by trying to figure out why the only bones found were those of a horse (someone suggested it had been trucked over from another local attraction, the Aqueduct racetrack, and replaced with a ringer), and by locking the Gent up for life for another murder involving storage (the body was on ice, in a refrigerator truck).

Stored in the Robert's window when we looked in was a large cutout of a lady in a sari and a sign saying this was now Ram Thakrat's place, specializing in real estate accounting and insurance. So, for your final meal, we are advocating the Villa Russo, at 101-12 Lefferts (718-849-0990). Villa owner Frank Russo was pleading not guilty to sales tax evasion charges at this writing, but it was business as usual at the restaurant, which includes Il Palazzo, a catering section reminiscent of a Disneyland castle.

"[Queens D.A.] Santucci has done parties here. We have the bishop's dinner, and all the priests come to it, and Frank Sinatra has our food sent to him quite often," said Russo's son, Frank Jr. "My uncle takes our homemade cheesecake down to him in Vegas."

We wondered what John Gotti, another fan of the place, would recommend off the wine list, which is really rather magnificent, with its $16.50 Gattinara, "known to the ancient Romans during the period of Campi Raudi." "Those things I won't answer you," said the junior Russo. D. A. Santucci couldn't help either. He stopped visiting the Villa after being tipped to its popularity with the Godfather. Before you sit down to eat, therefore, we suggest you stroll over to Gotti's office, at the Bergen Hunt and Fish (not social) Club, and ask him yourself. It's at 98-04 101st Street and if, for any reason, he has gone away at government expense or to join Big Paul in a happier place, someone else there should be glad to help you. You don't need to lock your luggage if you're leaving it in the trunk.

11

STAR TRACK

"MRS. ONASSIS, WITH ALL YOUR MONEY, YOU SHOULD BE ABLE TO AFFORD A GOOD WATCH."

Owner of an Upper East Side restaurant to Jackie O when, arriving fifteen minutes before her reservation time, she politely asked if she could be seated

Were this Hollywood, the time would have come to sell you a brightly colored map, load you on a bus, and whisk you off on a tour of the barricades around the bunkers of the celebrated ones. Since this is New York, a city that affords no one privacy, you will champ your fodder within julienne distance of great circus stars at famous restaurants—probably without paying, because, as a straight-A student of our little primer in la nouvelle fakery, you now pass as a star yourself. Swagger into the room, draped in the ranch coyote you procured without paying sales tax (any Gotham furrier will tell you how), and seat yourself at the best table. Slough off any objections by the headwaiter by pushing mucho moolah into his palm and murmuring the following incantation:

"I haven't seen ——* since I got back from staying at Jerry's darling little beach house in Bali with dear Princess Caroline."

If the dining room has a glass window to the kitchen, the preferred parking spot is right in front of it. That way, as other customers admire the modish spectacle of an untrained chef whipping up 50 cents' worth of pasta ingredients to sell at $12, their eyes inevitably will pan to you. Otherwise position yourself near a door, to the restaurant or the rest rooms. The challenge then is to confuse Ann Getty into thinking she knows you, by

---

*Insert the maître d's first name here. (All information in this chapter was current at the time of writing, but staff change. So do some detective work on the phone, just to be sure, before you make your dramatic entrance. Simply ask whoever answers when you call if "dear *Henri*" is still the maître d'...)

kissing the air and emitting hysterical little shrieks of affection as she scurries past.

Should there be tourists in the room, taking pictures, you're really in business. Startled by the pop of a flashbulb as he lunched at the Four Seasons, a midtown potency palace, the late Yul Brynner demanded that his waiter confiscate the film "of me" from the shutterbug's Polaroid camera. As the picture developed, the King saw to his chagrin that the "I" was nowhere to be found: immortalized was not his shining pate but a cake on the dessert trolley with rather more topping. Unlike Brynner, you will not return the photo that you order impounded—*before* it develops, rip it into shreds, grind it with your heel, and loudly inform the maître d' that you will be consulting your lawyer. That way, Ann Getty pleads for your autograph and you get a free meal.

The Elaine's Test

How grand an appearance do you make? At Elaine's, 1703 Second Avenue (212-534-8103), you can give your skills a dry run by inviting George Plimpton, William Styron, Diana Ross, Bruce Jay Friedman, Cheryl Tiegs, a Wyeth or two, Dick Cavett, and Ben Gazzara to join you at the bar to discuss your new production, *Tyler: The Movie*. Walk over to Woody, who'll be working on his cringe act, squeeze Mia playfully on the cheek, and ask him for a taste of his tomato-splattered mystery (he sometimes orders the Pasta Segretto).

It is considered tacky to inquire the prices of the wine or the specials here, and anyway, you do not want to skew the meter reading—"It's like being in a cab," A. E. Hotchner has observed of proprietor Elaine Kaufman's unusual billing techniques—because the final total will give you an instant computation of your status.

"When I was unknown," a well-known author explains, "no matter what I ate, no matter how many bottles of wine I ordered, the check always came to thirty-five dollars. As I started getting on the covers of magazines, the check escalated to forty-three dollars. When I began to go on TV talk shows, no matter what I ate—it might be the veal chop or chicken and three bottles of wine—it was sixty-eight dollars."

Elaine protests that these sums sound a little high to her. In the past she has allowed many undiscovered scriveners to run up tabs. So, once your test is complete, come back another evening with some dog-eared file folders protruding from a Pathmark shopping bag. Your first Best-seller-in-Progress. "Writers need to get out of the house," Elaines says, rising, protective as a mother fish, to the bait word: Literature. She is that rarest of restaurateurs, Gay Talese marveled in a twentieth-anniversary essay on her saloon in *New York,* one who actually reads books and welcomes their authors, hence "elevating them from the status that most of them had occupied since the 1920s, when George Orwell was washing dishes at the Ritz."

EAST SIDE

At 1621 Second Avenue, Elio Guaitolini, who was Elaine's first waiter, operates Elio's, a groupie Eden that has been compared to a nonstop cocktail party (772-2242). *People to meet here:* Lauren Bacall, Walter Cronkite, Tom Brokaw, Peter Jennings, David Letterman, Neil Simon, John Irving, Norman Mailer, Shirley MacLaine, Gregory Peck, Diane Keaton, Bianca, Anjelica Huston, Madonna and Sean Penn, Anthony Quinn, Richard Gere, Kate Hepburn, Bob Hope (at a big round table in the rear), Peter Fonda, Kirk Douglas, Treat Williams, and Cathy Lee Crosby (lapping up milk at the bar). *Places to sit:* Tables one through five, by the window, or the "power section" along the northside wall. *Talking points:* The late Perry Ellis, one of New York's most glamorous designers, was another regular. He would scan the throng's finery, head swiveling like a satellite tracking dish, and once sent a dumbstruck out-of-town woman a note, complimenting her on her taste and, says Elio's manager, Bob Sheridan, "good looks." Unless you're a glitter fish, peak-hour reservations are tough to get here. But those "good looks" or a "special occasion" should get you a degree of preferential treatment, says Sheridan. Ask for Anne or Elio, who is his own maître d'.

The starting lineup at Oren's (734-8822), a 1497 Third Avenue locker room, bulges with aggressive simians from the Rangers, Knicks, Jets, and Yankees. Reggie Jackson used to double-park his white Rolls-Royce out front, where it would be plastered with billets-doux by swarms of young women while he refueled. When the player eventually tripped out to retrieve these testaments to his virility, the panting sirens would jump him and have him tattoo his signature on their arms. *Talking points:* Reggie has been traded, but the Ranger's Ron Greschner and his lady, model Carol Alt, who met here, are still regulars. One year when the Islanders won the Stanley Cup, a player lugged it to Oren's, where LeRoy Nieman, who happened to be by that evening, knocked off a quick painting of the celebrations. You want to know the maître d's name? You some kinda pantywaist? Try Sam's Café down the street, at 1406 Third Avenue (988-5300). It's co-owned by Mariel Hemingway's husband, Steve Crisman, and his brother Eric, and the crush is Basic . . . Basic Bill Blass, Basic Lauren Bacall, Basic Euroroyals.

Jim McMullen, who, as an Eileen Ford model, used to be the pearlies in the Close-up toothpaste ads, runs an Ed Koch favorite, Jim McMullen's (861-4700), at 1341 Third Avenue, where Nancy Reagan's mentor, Jerry Zipkin, has said he "always has the chicken pot pie." After customers at that other Zipkin port of call, Mortimer's, at 1057 Lexington Avenue (517-6400), were ordered to flatten themselves on their stomachs by gun-toting bandits, owner Glenn Bernbaum allowed that he was glad that it hadn't happened the next day, when the Aga Khan and his English daisy, Sally, would be in for brunch. Probably the city's most immaculate arbiter—he used to be president of a chain of shirt stores— Bernbaum targets a "nice balance" of the "right people": Mike Wallace, Pat Lawford, Gloria Vanderbilt, Zipkin ("chicken paillard and the house coleslaw") and his girls, Bill Blass, Oscar de la Renta, Claus von Bülow, Andy Warhol, Geraldine Chaplin, Ray Stark, Bianca, George Hamilton, and Claudette Colbert. The designer Carolina Herrera threw a saturnalia for the Queen of England's little sister, Princess Margaret, in the private dining room. *Places to sit:* Tables one A, B or C. *Talking points:* Bernbaum's help has included an English lord, an English lord's son, and a Greek greeter, Stefanos Zachariadis. The bistro owner had brought Stefanos and his family here after meeting him during a cruise he was taking through the Greek islands with Bill Blass, according to a famous story by the columnist Taki. In a fit of appreciation for the Greek's fine work as a maître d', Bernbaum said he was leaving him and two other staffers the place upon his death. The Greek was led away by police after trying to accelerate his inheritance by hiring a hit-man who turned out to be an undercover cop. Call Bernbaum for reservations—and lots of luck. *W* caught him in deep debate with Robert, a Stefanos successor, over the fate of a lady who might not be a lady because after having her booking accepted she had phoned back to ask if she could bring in *her own birthday cake.* "I just knew I shouldn't have said yes when they booked, I just knew it," the restaurateur moped. "Who even knows this woman? What will that cake look like?"

J. G. Melon's has three locations, but the restaurant at 1291 Third Avenue (744-0585) is best for enlisting subscriptions to the Bahamas subdivision you're selling as a tax shelter. If Warren

Beatty doesn't bite, nail an Auchincloss. Many rich young unknowns also like the V&Ts here. This translates as *"Vodka and
Tonic.* Gets you smashed fast," says *The Official Preppy Handbook,* which listed J.G.'s as a wunderkind pond. *Talking points:*
The latest affectation in the city's preppy crowd is "A," confides
partygiver Baird Jones, a prototype prep himself. "That's asexual,"
he explains. "For instance, Gwynn will say, 'Is ——— A, or is he
into girls?'"

At Petaluma, 1356 First Avenue (772-8800), the dressed-for-
success female yuppies can be distinguished from the males by the
women's habit of disdainfully raking the topping from their pizza.
Despite a survey indicating that, just as Baird Jones's comment
suggested, 61 percent of New York women would rather eat out
than have sex, that is purely because eating out offers more
opportunities for display. One doesn't pay Petaluma prices to end
up looking like the dough on the menu. Feign indifference and
have Andrew, the maître d', plunk you down next to John
Chancellor or Harrison Ford.

At lunch one day in the Westbury Hotel's Polo Restaurant, 840
Madison Avenue (535-2000), a regular called Richard Nixon
showed his moxie by engaging two wenches at an adjoining table
in clever banter. One of the women, a Scandinavian, had been
toying with a drink while waiting for her friend.

"We thought she was trying to get picked up!" quipped the
Screamer, who was lunching with a former aide, William Hyland.
"New York is cold, vicious, dirty, but never dull," the ex-President
advised the Scandinavian. Seizing the moment, her companion
remarked that she was acquainted with former First Daughter
Tricia, and asked, "Do you know any terrific men for ——— [the
Scandinavian]?"

Nixon studied the Blond Viking. "How old are you?" he asked,
scribbling down her name. As he and Hyland got up to leave, he
glanced at her again and, as other diners gaped, remarked porten-
tously, "She only gets one more drink. She's had four already."

"In Europe, he's very well loved," the Scandinavian said.

Le Relais (pronounced, in lockjaw French, LO-RO-LIE), down
the street at 712 Madison Avenue (751-5108), was a location for
the movie *Perfect.* Among the perfect *People to meet here:* Calvin
Klein, Prince Albert and Princesses Stephanie and Caroline of
Monaco, Shirlee Fonda, Mick Jagger, Liza Minnelli, David Brenner,
Richard Harris, Raquel Welch, Carol Burnett, and Mary Tyler
Moore. *Places to sit:* In summer, the most coveted spots are the six
sidewalk tables. During cooler months, aim for the banquettes or

the big round table behind the bar. *Talking points:* Whether you're straight or a camp secret, this is one of *the* places for finding a rich South American husband. Just remember the house rules—dress smart and eat fast. An out-of-towner, resplendent in a persimmon-and-emerald polyester jacket, turned up for dinner. "How dare he come in here wearing that!" Le Relais co-owner Albert Hacko recalls exclaiming as he shooed the lamebrain and his wife out into the street. On another occasion, two ladies from New Jersey lingered over their coffee for an excessively long time, then disputed the check and refused to budge. Albert instructed a waiter to remove the table, and after staring at each other's knees for five minutes, the shrews took the hint, paid up, and left. The maître d' here is Philippe.

At Le Cirque, 58 East Sixth-fifth Street (794-9292), you'll be hugged by Henry (Kissinger), bussed by Nancy (Reagan), and jostled by an (Arab) prince's bodyguards. That's on an average day. Other *people to greet here* over the world-famous crème brûlée: Donald Sutherland, Michael Caine, Elizabeth Taylor, Barbara Sinatra (toying with chichi restraint at a diced-chicken salad with imported mozzarella), Zubin Mehta (an extra-hot chili powder is stored for him in an initialed silver box by Le Cirque's management so he can orchestrate his meat), Robert Wagner, Malcolm Forbes, Barbara Walters, Jill St. John, John Hurt, and the discriminating Jerry Zipkin (who generally sips at a balloon of iced Sanka, perhaps with some cold bass). "Jerome is different . . . ," Diana Vreeland has said. "He is that rare species: a man of leisure who is an American." *Places to sit:* Whole essays have been composed on this, but owner Sirio Maccioni (ask for him or Bruno) describes "the Right Rectangle" as the section at right as you enter, near the windows and extending to the rear banquettes. The acoustics in the section are especially to be recommended to would-be extortionists, since the dishing and deal-making at the other tables is transmitted in a "tunnel effect" right into your twitching lobes. Table twenty-six confers Extra Élan on its occupants, since it is barely visible and leads people to believe you are important enough to have something to hide.

You'll catch up with Warren again at Safari Grill, Third Avenue at Sixty-fifth Street (371-9090), where he hides in "the cheater's corner," a front-room nook camouflaged by a column. To exchange scowls with Yoko Ono, try Gino's, at 780 Lexington Avenue (758-4477). For a true paella of powerful richies and glitzies, however, have a member of Le Club, 313 East Fifty-eighth Street—maybe Al Pacino, George Steinbrenner, or the Maharaja of

Jaipur—squire you to this exclusive spa. *Talking points* in the event that another Clubman, Donald Trump, will bring you here: that familiar High Society hobby, kleptomania (the soap rosettes kept vanishing from the powder room five minutes after being set out, so they were replaced with ordinary soap dispensers), and aerobatics. Le Club executive director Patrick Shields says the editor of a top fashion sheet and a former governor of New York used to swing Tarzanlike from the chandelier over the dance floor in the main dining room when they had had a tipple too many. Another time, a sports magnate and a pal were caught trying to remove the twelve-point antlers from a European elk that stares down on the dance floor. "When I intervened, ——— [the sports magnate] gave me a flying tackle," says Shields. "We have had to remove the antlers ourselves to discourage this pillaging."

On a good evening, the decibel level at Prima Donna, at 50 East Fifty-eighth Street (753-5400), almost rivals that at Xenon, the disco that owner Howard Stein ran before he discovered the job satisfaction of dotting wafer-thin pizza with caviar and truffles. *People to see here* through the heaving sequins of shoals of Eurotrash: Bob Fosse, Anthony Quinn, Diane Keaton, Jim Dale, Sly Stallone, Christopher Reeve, and Marsha Mason. At P. J. Clarke's, a 915 Third Avenue saloon, broods of young Kennedys and movie would-bes hide in the airholes in the yuppy crowd.

For the price of a hamburger at the Four Seasons, at 99 East Fifty-second Street in a crook of the bronze-and-glass arm of the Seagram Building, you could put your scion through college. As for reservations, take several Valium and dial 754-9494, while repeating after us the following mantra: Oommamoooomaletem-cancel. Ninety percent of the lunchtime customers are regulars, some of whom only call the magic number on days they're *not* going to be hogging *their* pews. *People to see here:* Consult your *Times* for who's au courant in the publishing world, buying a company with junk bonds, or Carrying the Flag into Communistic Jungles. This is where Henry, without even first treating Tyler to a hiya, nice-to-be-back bowl of Purina, lunched, the Managua mud still crusting his shoes, with David "the Chase is on" Rockefeller—*before* briefing Ronnie on his fact-finding whistlestop through Latin America. Do not confuse this episode with the time that Richard Stone, another presidential missionary just back from down south, briefed the board of Chase Manhattan, the Rockefeller bank. "I'm sure he'd have gone to Citibank if they'd asked him," an aide to the envoy assured us. "They certainly weren't trying to find out where they should lend money. He gave an exposition to the board on Central America and he was given a rather nice lunch in return." Chase, at the time, was said to be a major lender in the region.

Positano, at 250 Park Avenue South (777-6211), is owned by director Bob Giraldi, who made Michael Jackson's *Beat It* video. Since Giraldi was quoted by the restaurant critic Gael Greene as not regarding his restaurant as a lifelong dream—"It's another production"—we suggest moving briskly on to One Fifth Avenue (the address as well as the name of the restaurant). There is a definite whiff of Hollywood East here. It is where some scenes for *An Unmarried Woman* were shot, and Richard Gere, who lives very nearby, Susan Sarandon, and Brian DePalma are among the celebs who will try to avoid you by eating in back. For reservations, call 260-3434. Luci is the day floor manager.

The circus's tame tiger, Mayor Koch, eats as often as five times a month at the Bridge Café, 279 Water Street (227-3344). The six-seater table in the center is kept vacant for him weekday lunchtimes, while the kitchen awaits his coming with all the joyful anticipation of a nation on nuclear alert. Explains a staffer, the chef, Bruce Frattini, grudgingly prepares one of Hizzoner's favorite medleys, softshell crabs or sauté of salmon with *garlic* meunière sauce. "A tradition," our informant stresses, that goes against custom and taste, but "that started before Frattini began working here."

WEST SIDE

When Café Pacifico, at 384 Columbus Avenue (724-9187), was called Café Central, *People* magazine calculated that it rivaled the Hayden Planetarium, across the street, for star counts. Central subsequently changed hands, and the new owner, Gloria DeMann (see chapter eight, Liberating Forces), has perked it up with fiberglass camels (reminiscent of the life-sized herd on the seawall of her summer home in Fire Island Pines) and pink-and-silver-striped upholstery. "We're going to do a new theme every two months," she declared, "like Area." For instance, six-foot-long blush-pink plastic teardrops for Valentine's Day. "It'll be for lovers only. If you don't have one, I'll get you one," she told a reporter, who was unaware at the time of her possible involvement in the practical side of the lonely-hearts industry. Police had to be called when a feminist group threatened to lob a brick through the window at Pacifico's silver statue of a nude man towering over an upended female torso, and Women Against Pornography seethed that the grouping glorified rape "in the name of male machismo." *People to meet here:* Stacy Keach, Harry Belafonte, and Yoko Ono. *Places to sit:* The best table is just to the left of the stairs as you come in, but if that's unseizable, go for the back platform. *Talking points:* Brooke Shields's mom, Teri, rushing to get to this white-hot spot one evening, slipped and wrenched her ankle, which was resuscitated by a soaking in a bucket of the specialty of the house, Pink Pacifico. Roy was the first maître d'. Competition for his favor was so intense that one hopeful arrived with a Rambogram (New York's answer to other cities' stripper messenger services) to threaten him. These days, you should muscle his successor, Todd.

Out-of-town rubes will be impressed by the "Dynasty" and jambalaya flavoring of Memphis, 329 Columbus Avenue (496-1840). Try a balcony table for a catbird seat at this restaurant in which Al Corley (formerly Steven Carrington) is a principal owner. *People to see here:* The Big Chill generation of actors.... Treat Williams, Kevin Kline, William Hurt, Dustin Hoffman, Faye Dunaway, Kathleen Taylor. *Talking points:* This is where Tatum O'Neal got her purse jammed in the toilet, and wrenched off the lid, some believe in a subconscious effort to escape her escort of the evening. Could he have been John McEnroe? Book tables for the weekend seven days in advance or, if you're a desperate Linda Evans fan from Des Moines, go through your hotel's concierge. Memphis's manager says he tries whenever possible to accommodate tourists who work it this way.

Psst! Do you know where your fur is?

At one restaurant frequented by Jackie O, Treat, Mick, Boy George, and Cyndi Lauper in this neighborhood, we charted the progress of the customers' king's ransom of fleeces from the checkpoint (at the door) to the subterranean kitchen, where they were bundled onto a rack next to a stack of greasy caldrons.

Though we frankly consider Tavern on the Green, in Central Park at Sixty-seventh Street (873-3200), a tourist trap, a publicist for the restaurant blithely assures us that Yoko Ono is a *daily* visitor (even if neither George Washington nor Chopin has slept here in a while). Don't blame us. Call the showman who operates the place, Warner LeRoy, if the Crystal Room isn't wall-to-wall with: Lily Tomlin, Shelley Winters, David Frost, Burgess Meredith, Kenny Rogers, Maria Shriver and Arnold Schwarzenegger, Sally Struthers, at least one princess, and Peter Falk. *Talking points:* Pearl Bailey got hung up in traffic on her way to kick off a charity press conference here one Christmas, so Dolly Parton was yanked from her table to calm the impatient hacks. *Very confidentially:* The Democrats who control the city's permanent government hold cocktail soirées here, which are easy to infiltrate if you need their aid while Plucking the Apple (chapter twelve).

Lunches are the most fertile hunting time at Café des Artistes, 1 West Sixty-seventh Street (877-3500). Faye Dunaway and Gloria Steinem both like the corner privacy of table thirty-eight, unlike Paul Newman, who ostentatiously stations himself up front. Le-Roy Nieman, Zubin Mehta (the café stashes a special bottle of sauce labeled "For Indian conductors..." for him), former New York mayor John Lindsay, and Rudolph Nureyev scuffle for table two. Although jackets are required after five, owner George Lang (ask for him or Stephen) waives the rule for the émigré ballet star, who likes to prance in in a polo-neck sweater and leather coat. Prime-time faces like Harry Reasoner, Ed Bradley, and Diane Sawyer line the bar. *Places to sit:* You can monitor most of the activity from table nine. Failing that, anything front right, facing the windows. One customer got up and quit for Tavern on the Green, across the street, after he was seated near the entrance to the kitchen, under the café's famous mural, "Spring." This features seven unclothed soubrettes, one of whom the patron recognized as his mother. "She'd been an artist's model and he was here with a girl on his first date," Lang explains. Sounds just like the plot you were seeking for *Tyler: The Movie.* To scrape together some names—"I'd like you to meet our leading man"—for the party you're throwing for the schmucks who'll be investing in the project, wander over to Chipps Pub, at 150 Columbus (874-8415), a playpen for soap stars from ABC's nearby studios and for some of the younger spores from programs like "Good Morning America." The tube continues in ascendancy at Alfredo, 240 Central Park South (586-7975), where Dan Rather fusses about his figure and allows Ary, the maître d', to choose his provender, generally a light pasta and veal or fish combination. Walter Cronkite, resigned to his contours, has the linguine with four cheeses. Mascarpone, Gorgonzola, Parmesan, and Romano. *Other people to see here:* Luciano Pavarotti, Candice Bergen and Louis Malle, Billy Joel and Christie Brinkley. *Places to sit:* Tables one through four, twenty-three or twenty-four. "Walter Cronkite will sit anyplace," adds il padrone, Gianni Minale. "He is a very humble man."

The mink banquettes at Petrossian, 182 West Fifty-eighth Street (245-0303), probably the western world's first caviar snack bar, showcase Billy and Christie, a smattering of Rothschilds, Vincent Price, Irene Papas, Christopher Plummer, and Ann Getty. Joining them will cost you a minimum of around $30, for fifty grams of sevruga, so you might want to scram before your order arrives and move to Eleonora's, just to the east at 117 West Fifty-eighth Street (765-1427). The night we checked out what is Robert Duvall's pet restaurant, Robert De Niro was wolfing the Caesar salad and stuffed veal chop. Carol Burnett is another regular.

Despite all the hype, the Hard Rock Café, 221 West Fifty-seventh Street (489-6565), is a gamble. Even if one of the owners, Dan Aykroyd, is around, finding him in the noisy postadolescent crowd is about as probable as having a regular like Cyndi Lauper come rock your clock. The manager, Yul "Rock" Brynner, is the late actor's son, and inherited his dad's stake in the restaurant. *Talking points:* The young staff recognize John Kennedy, Jr., Sting, Tina Turner, Julian Lennon, those sort of regulars, whether or not they're Hard Rock gold-card holders (the card saves you standing on line like a sheep at the Heinz's chapter two birthday supper). But when Lauren Bacall swept to the door for the March 1984 opening party, the doorman turned her away, says Eric Crisman, the Sam's Café owner who used to be Hard Rock's general manager. Another Hard Rock employee, realizing the error, admitted the miffed Great Female One and her party— Roone Arledge, Adolph Green, and Phyllis Newman—to where she thought she belonged.

Face it. Mel Brooks and Anne Bancroft may have the karsky shashlik airlifted to Beverly Hills when they can't get to the Russian Tea Room in person, but you aren't visiting this Polo Lounge East, at 150 West Fifty-seventh Street (265-0947), for the blinis. Since honesty will launch you straight into the RTR's upper-level Siberia, where you will have a superb view of fellow no-bodies, best adopt a name at random from *Daily Variety,* don your Pilar Crespi designer shades—Cazals are too risky because the city's street hoods have taken to snatching them for the gold-trimmed frames—and divebomb one of the bar booths. Table-bopping is how RTR regulars get their exercise. Take your pick between Frankie, Calvin, Omar, Elizabeth.... or selling *Tyler* to Sam Cohn, the superagent. He and Warren both like booth forty, but Warren always defers. As has so rightly been remarked, a fellow never knows when he's going to need the sort of pitchman who can pull down $9.5 million, which is what Cohn secured for the screen rights to *Annie* at this very table. *Talking points:* Sylvia Miles used to sit on a phone book to make herself look taller when she lunched in a booth, but now she has graduated to her own table in the center of the dining room, so she no longer requires the extra elevation.

The savvy network star who suspects a silver stiletto is about to be inserted between his vertebrae creeps into the clubby dining room of the Dorset Hotel, 30 West Fifty-fourth Street (247-7300), for breakfast. CBS officials plot on the west side, ABC execs on the east. Howard Cosell is probably the only regular you'll recognize. He apparently understands the politics of his industry well, because he always asks for a table near the door.

The savvy stage star periodically renews his acquaintance with mortality by dropping into Joe Allen, 326 West Forty-sixth Street (581-6464), where the walls are smothered with posters from Broadway bombs. In line with this, you'll see ten unemployed actors for every Lucie Arnaz. Sardi's, 234 West Forty-fourth Street (221-8440), is a traditional venue for opening-night parties and *some* show people. Brenda Vaccaro, Jack Lemmon, Rita Moreno. Sardi's landlords, Bernie Jacobs and Gerald Schoenfeld, who pilot the Shubert Organization, one of the Great White Way's two major theater chains, had been perceptibly absent from the chow for a while when we asked a Schoenfeld friend what was up. "Vincent tried to sell the place to some guy who ran a deli in Brooklyn, without even having the courtesy to tell Bernie and Gerry," the friend said. He also said something about the food, which we won't repeat. "The Shuberts *are* very particular who I sell to," said Vincent, explaining that he was in the process of closing a deal with two new buyers, both producers, indicating that restaurant ownership may be the trend of the future for chapter five's rich men, showmen. *Talking points:* Should you just happen to roll in here equipped with an Actors Equity card, you get to eat at a 50 percent discount.

When Rock Hudson was alive, the Market Diner, 572 Eleventh Avenue (244-6033), was one of his feeding grounds, as it has been over the years for everyone from the late Herschel Bernardi to Jane Fonda. Frank Sinatra, whose presence on the New York foraging scene has a certain mythic quality, came by, despite many stories to the contrary, only once. However, David Bowie is said to swear by that Zipkin staple, the chicken pot pie.

To sell the rights to the theme song from *Tyler,* look in at Jerry's Bar and Mesquite Grill, 565 West Twenty-third Street (807-6261), which is owned by Carly Simon's ex-manager, Jerry Brandt. *People to meet here:* Duran Duran, Billy Idol (who had the windows blacked for his birthday carousal so guests wouldn't be disturbed by the rising sun), Keith Richards, Ron Wood. Also Tony "Taxi" Danza, Timothy Hutton, Al Pacino, and, to dangle from your arm on the Night Frontier, Ford models. *Places to sit:* Tables two or four or by the window. Table eighty-six is good for larger parties. *Talking points:* The men's room was evacuated so that

Evita star Patti Lupone, an antiques buff, could take a tour of the circa 1890 porcelain urinals. "We do that for women who are very curious," says a staffer. Moving slightly southeast, the Empire Diner, at 210 Tenth Avenue (243-2736), ladles chicken soup into Geraldine Page's bowl. Paulina, the *Sports Illustrated* cover girl, keeps her swimsuit filled by trekking here with Ric Ocasek, lead singer of the Cars, for chili sundaes. *Other people to greet:* Once more, Warren (according to a manager at Café Luxembourg, one of the actor's uptown hasheries, he propositions waitresses zealously on his travels, so you might want to consider this in your dress planning). Also Kathleen Turner and Michael O'Keefe. *Places to sit:* Table one or the counter. The place starts hopping around one in the morning, with the pre-bottle-club set.

La Colonna, at 17 West Nineteenth Street (206-8660), has an eclectic air, imparted by Lee Radziwill, Mick, and marriageable Greeks who own ships. Odeon, 145 West Broadway (233-0507), started as a status-confirmation shrine for the smashed-plate school of artists, but it's cool, if you are a trendy like the mayor, to come here to ogle them. *People to see:* Bruce Springsteen and Julianne, his 34/22/34 wife-model (he bolts the crispy roasted duckling and an apple turnover while she picks at a vegetable plate), Andy, Paul Simon, John Schlesinger, Calvin, and Meryl. Koch comes for lunch, a chicory salad with his favorite dressing. *Places to sit* (let's hope out of range of the mayoral garlic breath): the tables by the window are best for scoping, but they tend to be assigned to artists, so unless you're a look-alike for Jean-Michel Basquiat, settle for a booth. Sightlines roomwide are pretty clear. *Talking points:* Funky pairings are the order of the day at this former cafeteria. Whoopi Goldberg munches with Tim Hutton, Cher with young Tom "Risky Business" Cruise. Espying Drew Barrymore, another patron invited her over to swap wisdom on the raptures and pitfalls of being a child headliner. Elizabeth Taylor and the *E.T.* starling imbibed Shirley Temples and schmoozed for two hours. David is the lunch maître d'; ask for Bruce or Stephen in the evening.

OUTER BOROUGHS

Glenn Scarpelli, the teenager in "One Day At a Time," ingests cheeseburgers at the Colonnade Diner, 2001 Hylan Boulevard, Staten Island (718-351-2900 for directions), where the more sporadic celebrity visitors have run the gamut from Raquel to Ricky Schroder. Telly Savalas and Colleen Dewhurst snack at the Forge Diner, opposite the law courts at 124-18 Queens Boulevard (718-261-2800). Ah, courts.

If music be the food of love...lady justice is sweet as a muskrose to a machine sachem. When he was the boss of Brooklyn's Democratic apparatus, the portly Meade Esposito summarized his philosophy of government for Jack Newfield and Paul Du Brul, as reported in their classic book about New York government, *The Abuse of Power:* "I pick every fuckin' law secretary in Brooklyn Supreme Court. . . . If any guy I send over to a judge turns out to be a rotten apple, I tell the judge it's okay to fire him. Only I get to pick the replacement. I keep pickin' 'em until one guy works out."

Now pastured out from these hallowed halls of patronage, Meade the septuagenarian was the subject at this writing of another of those federal probes into the nuances of New York politics. But he denied any wrongdoing, as did another reported subject of the inquiry, Nicholas Sands, the chapter ten helpmate to Hugh and Gerry. Meade's real dream was to do something for the people of New York—open a chain of Italian gourmet takeout shops. "This seems like a bleeping good venture," he guffawed to a reporter. In a scene not in the least reminiscent of Nightfalls (chapter ten), De Boss sometimes has been found in a chef's hat, overseeing the cuisine for one of the testimonial dinners thrown from time to time in his honor. His most confidential plan, however, involves "prostitute sauce." Known in more cultivated circles as salsa puttanesca, this delicacy was invented in Naples by hookers "because they could make it quickly while the pasta was cooking between tricks," Meade tells us. He is planning to market it. His probable advertising slogan? "Without Meade, you got nothin'," he chortles.

12

PLUCKING THE APPLE

"WE HAVE UNDERTAKEN TO WRITE SOMETHING ABOUT THE GOVERNMENT OF THE CITY OF NEW YORK, AND YET WE HAVE FALLEN INTO A DISCOURSE ON STEALING."

Article in the North American Review *of October 1866, quoted in* The Abuse of Power *by Jack Newfield and Paul Du Brul*

As you slice away at the obstacles between you and the Big Onion's delightfully elitist, necessarily secretive, so very sweet-smelling core, you sometimes will get tempted to stop. Do not.

Yes, it's wearying to have to come up with a new animal a month to decorate your little buffets for eighty. Of course, it's vexatious that you haven't even bumped into Jackie O's *chauffeur* yet on your daily visits to Encore, the ladies' favorite Manhattan resale shop. And we truly were sorry to read that you lost your entire $8 million investment in *Tyler's Song* after Frank Rich called your new musical a dog. But stick to your course. It will get easier—because of the exponential expansion in photo opportunities, financial opportunities, and, above all, opportunities for thievery that will occur as you advance.

We're not talking just about stealing the other guests' hampers at the April in Paris Ball, though obviously every little bit helps. What we have in mind is your increasing access to the political tribunes who mind the cash cows on what probably will be this nation's last surviving family farm. To turn this access to your advantage, think of the public weal as an extension of that filet mignon you purchased in chapter two. You'll know you've arrived when, as one of God's Developers, Wall Street's Pharaohs, or simply a team, Pharaoh and Wife, you get to snap, "Gift-wrap it,

Koch!" (Or, if he's on a boat en route to exile in Ireland by the time you read this, his successor. Just send another $20,000 campaign contribution.)

This system is as immutable as it is sagacious, so there is absolutely no point flying into spasms of good-government rage and burning this book. *Bind* this book, by all means, in leather-look plastic. Dab some gold paint on the edges, fake the author's autograph, and sell it for $300 a limited-edition copy in Podunk. Rage is a symptom of powerlessness, and what we have been endeavoring to teach you is that the first step toward a happier state—getting the access, getting to be seated at a free dinner at Regine's between Brooke and Mick—is as easy as learning to conjugate your chosen new name. Du Pont, du Pont, DuPont . . .

This chapter is for those of you who may have been stalled in the second step: Getting Your Hands on the Gravy. The gravy for starting up. Frankly, most native New Yorkers find that accumulating capital at other people's expense is second nature, and they seldom run out of people to victimize (convicted of fraud, one phony aristo you met in an earlier chapter is now bilking his fellow white-collar prisoners). Still, maybe marrying up hasn't been smooth sailing despite your sail to the Caribbean with Koo, Michael Deaver, the entire Reagan administration and the Cast of This Book on the *Nabila IV.* Maybe you weren't able to afford a platoon of lawyers and media-relations specialists to help you wheedle a $100 million contract to rebuild the Brooklyn Bridge. Maybe, in short, you'd better introduce some elasticity into your thinking.

Consider, for instance, what, with minimal ingenuity, you might have made out of the municipal corruption scandal—the one involving the Parking Violations Bureau—that sent 1986 off to such a rousing start. Admittedly, as scandals go in the city, it initially seemed a disappointment. A million dollars usually is considered the rock-bottom goal for New York political extortionists, this being the sum involved in an earlier scheme masterminded by a Koch Administration official. This time round, a bill-collecting company was said to have greased its business relationship with City Hall by handing a parking bureau official $5,000 in the men's room of Hisae's Place, a downtown Manhattan restaurant. Soon, however, so many law enforcement agencies were on the tail of so many related ill deeds that you could have *pulled down* the Brooklyn Bridge and sold it for scrap and no one would have noticed. The feds alone were busy subpoenaing enough documents to fill a subway car.

Some New Yorkers quickly sized up the situation and derived

priceless inspiration from it. Some of them didn't even find it necessary to *commit* a crime in order to turn a profit.

Leaping into the culture gulch with the most daring gimmick since Marylou Whitney's brougham, a painter called Sandy Straus opened "Recent Crimes," a show at a fashionable SoHo gallery that had as its centerpiece a huge painting of a slashed wrist streaming blood. "Donny Manes' Wrist," shouted the accompanying text. Manes was a prince of the New York Democratic Party through his dual role as party leader and borough president of Queens. The borough has an almost unblemished record of public sector thievery and by all accounts Manes had not let down the side. His Hamptons beach house was acquired at a bargain price from a reputed mob money-launderer with whom he often jaunted to Atlantic City in a helicopter. And, after he was found with the knife wounds that inspired the work by Sandy Straus, following a botched apparent suicide attempt, evidence began to emerge that he had been sharing in the plunder from the parking-ticket collection racket—to the tune, claimed the feds, of over $270,000. Just one more piece of proof that it's more fun at the top in New York. Straus's exhibition paid tribute to the lot of inhabitants of the Onion peel with a portrait of a dismembered body lying on subway tracks, memorializing one of the numerous incidents in which waiting passengers have been hurled to death or disfigurement by criminals or crazy persons. There also was a picture of a corpse clad only in a bondage hood, based on the sadomasochistic murder of Norwegian fashion student Eigil Vesti (chapter seven) by a sidekick of Andrew Crispo, the socially connected Manhattan art dealer. The work was accompanied by a graphic textual description of the killing.

"I was looking for something that would be a documentation of our culture and would be sensational," Straus gurgled.

Since her bold brushstrokes evinced the same straightforward quality as the men's-room encounter, they were not beyond what you might aspire to. The series was priced at between $250 and $2,500. But more important, since the long term is what you should be considering, it put her up there with Ed Koch in terms of photo opportunities. (The biography *I, Koch* reported that the mayor regularly regales guests at Gracie Mansion with a propaganda film of himself, *Doin' My Job,* sponsored by Merrill Lynch, the investment house located across from one of our Camp Secrets.) Television crews were arriving to tape the artist. Newspaper columnists were panting to give her ink. The exhibition was still running when Donny Manes finally did succeed in killing himself, plunging a knife into his heart. The morning after his death, Straus's publicist said the painter would proceed with plans for a series of dinner parties at the gallery—to promo her take on mortality with luminaries of the circus's art branch.

So she has cleared the starting gate. The following is a short, and by no means exhaustive, list of alternative game plans, with a few rules for weathering the inevitable little falls from grace that will stud your raid on what, as the 1866 article quoted in the Newfield-Du Brul book so thoughtfully observed, is a most "fruitful and ill-fenced orchard":

PLAN A: NESTING PRINCIPLES

Steven Spielberg and the ex-wife of Timothy Hixon, the Texas oilman, can bypass this one. We have nothing but admiration for their sacrifice in plunking down, by one calculation, $3 million and $9.7 million respectively to roost in Fifth Avenue's Trump Tower. We rather fear, though, that you're one of those $50,000-a-year nebbishes who pores over the articles that regularly appear in our local press about how the baby can sleep in the bathtub in the one-bedroom Lower East Side snap at $1,600 a month. Not to forget the incredible advantages of moving to welfare hotels, the Bowery (where the bodegas have begun to stock Perrier), Harlem ("This is not Harlem, my dear. This is the Upper West Side," a woman insisted to the *Washington Post,* advertising a one-bedroom sale on 111th Street for $100,000), even the South Bronx. While the latter neighborhood, plagued by poverty, may look like a movie about the world after a nuclear attack, it was advocated in a *Times* writeup under the headline "The Appeal of Living in the Bronx."

Of course, the fact is that Tyler will not be by to do his duty on your stoop if you move so much as a block north of Ninety-sixth Street or south of SoHo. With this in mind, we have devised the following low-budget housing plan for you. Though we say it ourselves, it should earn us a medal from Ed Koch since it will help both you and those mayoral best friends, the real-estate corsairs. Having forked over as much as $2,500 a plate to attend Hizzoner's famous sixtieth birthday party in 1984, many of them are now desperate to make a quick killing before the bubble bursts by unloading their remaining rental apartments as co-ops.

Here's how it works.

State law generally requires the approval of 51 percent of the tenants in a building before it is converted to a cooperative. This is commonly obtained by hiring highly trained professional vacating companies—like the crew of junkies, hookers, burglars, and other thugs who drove around town in a rented U-Haul truck. Once the last old lady withholding her vote has been terrorized into a nervous breakdown and carted off to Bellevue, the landlord faces a new problem: the law stipulates that no more than 10 percent of the apartments can be vacant before the building is sold off. You don't have to be a property genius to understand why, if you're willing to be the stooge who offers to take Grandma's place for a few months, you may not even have to pay rent.

Or you might try calling Robert Marceca, of RKM Enterprises (212-593-1122). He doesn't harass tenants, but he does have space. "EXCELLENT POTENTIAL FOR CONDO CONVERSION. 9 + Apartments Delivered Vacant," says a circular from his company offering two limestone mansions on East Sixty-fifth Street for sale. After tenants protested conditions in these buildings a couple of years earlier—no trash pickup, no cleaning, no elevator, and, often, no heat or hot water—some of them received anonymous notes, decorated with a picture of a black widow spider or a skeleton and warning, "Move or you die soon." A Marceca staffer assured us that the threat did not come from RKM and explained that the problems with building services were "inherited" from a previous owner. Consequently, RKM is appealing a court decision that awarded the tenants damages. Conditions at the mansions are now back to normal, so you won't find them uncomfortable. What's more, the firm seems to have other vacancies from time to time. RKM once offered a British newcomer to the city a short-term lease on a former S&M bar, the basement of a residential building in Greenwich Village. "And this could be the bedroom," an RKM man said, confiding that the building soon would be sold off and gesticulating at a room with walls strung with interesting formations of chains and shackles.

Clearly, once you have moved into one of these bargains, some rapid cosmetic surgery will be called for by one of those society decorators from chapter two. While he is at work, you should be sprucing up your wardrobe and jewelry collection, ideally making your purchases out of state, because, in line with your new policy ("If only you were called Vanderbilt") you won't be paying for many of them. Your creditors eventually will obtain judgments against you, but if you don't have a job, they can't garnishee your earnings, and retrieving their assets would be impossibly expensive. For example, say you go to Burke Rupley's old stamping ground, Miami, to do your shopping. The stores will sue you there—but the paper will be meaningless unless your pursuers retain a New York lawyer to have it rubber-stamped by a local court. In the unlikely event that they bother, move to New Jersey. They'll get the point.

For that matter, it probably won't be necessary to go on the lam—because once you're fixed up in your Princess Katalin gowns, nutria upholstery, and Diane Von Furstenberg tissue boxes, you are going to be ready to land that $300 million spouse.

Since you will need a sponsor to make the introduction for you, put in a phone call to Ann Getty at the New York office of Weidenfeld & Nicholson, the publishing house in which she is an investor and partner, and invite her to a little dinner party that you are having catered. By a Washington, D.C., firm, of course. It was Getty who hooked up her great friend Arianna Stassinopoulos with oil heir Michael Huffington. Should Getty's books be full, pick another mentor at random from Suzy's column and say that ———,* whom you house-guested with in Vienna, told you to give this personage a call. If the phone number is unlisted, any astute New York private eye can get it for you for a small fee. We normally use Marvin Badler, at 718-698-0003.

Now, let's be honest about it, your affianced may not have you hyperventilating. Two courses are open to you. A preppy, slender blondine landed the scion of a local clothing dynasty, moved into his spread in a tower that is almost as good an address as Trump's, refurbished her wardrobe with his credit cards—and stuffed on fried Brie and Häagen-Dazs until, just four weeks before the wedding, she was indistinguishable from an eggplant in shape. Stupefied by the sight of so much flesh, her beloved called off the event. She drove away in the Alfa Romeo Spider he had given her, lost weight, and started dating his best friend, the scion of a local cosmetics dynasty.

Or you can go through with the vows. Just establish a second identity (one superlawyer who looks like Clint Eastwood calls himself Mr. Ho**), and rent an apartment under this moniker where you can attend to your lovers. Or meet them at the New York Hilton, Sheraton Centre, or Vista International. These hotels are popular with cheating spouses because they not only extend 50 percent discounts for daytime guests, but have the room ready promptly at ten in the morning. You don't have to be out until six.

Like Al Goldstein, more and more New Yorkers are resorting to advertising to find the perfect mate (chapter eight), and, being

---

*Insert the name of any well-known nonresident of the United States.

**An ethnically appropriate pseudonym for his pseudonym.

New Yorkers, they go about this with mathematical precision. Lynn Kesselman, a wife-hungry forty-five-year-old real estate investor, placed an ad in *New York*'s personals for a "loving lady entrepreneur" who wanted to "share the good life." Nearly five hundred women replied. Lynn invited fifty of the most appealing to meet him at a party, so he could winnow the field to perhaps five in a single evening. He estimated the ladies' average annual income at $100,000 and charged them $35 to attend the function, which was manned by him and twenty-two of his bachelor chums.

Suppose that even this doesn't work, and the corsair is telling you the time has come to move out of the apartment you took over from Grandma? Have you never heard of blackmail? Refuse to leave—you legally were entitled to a one- or two-year lease—and he will have to buy you out with a handsome settlement. Don't accept a cent under $200,000. Should he balk, or try to send in his goons, twit him by dialing 212-488-4141. That's the state attorney general, Robert Abrams. This plan has been tested successfully by an acquaintance of ours.

Or buy the entire building from him. Get a loan from the first wiseguy you find at one of those mobbed spots, then go missing, because you won't be able to keep up the vig. Since the building immediately will start to deteriorate (you'll have sabotaged the heat and hot water and fired the doorman and super), the tenants will go to court, and the judge will install an administrator to run the place. "I call it taking a vacation from your responsibilities," chortles a lawyer who recommends this plan to real estate speculators, like the physician who is trying it with an apartment complex on Seventh Avenue. Once you think your building has appreciated enough for you to repay your Mafia bankers *and* realize at least a $1 million profit, reappear and demand it back. The $1 million will buy you a new Upper East Side apartment in the sought-after early shoebox style. Balloon shades will hide the view of the airshaft.

Another option. If you are black, tell the cabbie to drop you at the Palma Boys Social Club, that reputed hangout for partisans of the Genovese crime family, and request a big enough loan to put a deposit on a co-op at any of the Fifth Avenue or Park Avenue buildings that just *adore* minorities. For your interview with the co-op directors who must approve your purchase, forge a statement showing your net worth at $50 million (this will not work at one of the gilt-edged buildings that uses private investigators, so hit up the second tier), wear two-tone shoes and a salmon polyester jacket, and say you practice voodoo. Since state law prohibits co-ops from discriminating on the basis of race or creed, when they reject you, sue for damages. The only possible snag is that His Honor may order the building to admit you, so pretend that because the case has dragged on for months, you have accepted an offer from the NAACP to become its field director in Iowa.

People in places like Iowa often think that New Yorkers have no reverence for history. Far from it. Smart New Yorkers know that investigating the many historic homes in the city, or within commuting distance, that have director-custodians can pay even bigger social dividends than polo. In return for various formal responsibilities, you can get to live *rent-free* on the extremely splendid premises. For instance, Robert Porter, a former private school headmaster, and his wife occupy an eight-room house attached to the Van Cortlandt Mansion, where as the "mansion director," he arranges tours and activities suitable to the Georgian pile's past. It was a base for George Washington during the Revolution and is a charming place for parties. The Porters have held large gatherings amid the antique Dutch and English furnishings. All of these plum residences are currently occupied, but it's worth putting in an application, because the market shows signs of loosening up. The society that administers the Old Merchant's House, an East Fourth Street Victorian gem, is contemplating buying an adjacent building, which will have a curator's apartment. For a complete list of all the possibilities, contact the Metropolitan Historic Structures Association, at the Dyckman House, 4881 Broadway, New York, NY 10034, and suburban preservation groups, such as the Society for the Preservation of Long Island Antiquities, 516-941-9444. The society owns a manor house near the shore where one young couple started out their married life.

PLAN B: TOURING THE TOWN

It can be cheaper than you think.

Presenting themselves as Michael and Diane, a hardworking Oregon farm couple, two young people stoically told reporters that pickpockets had left them penniless the day after they arrived here for their honeymoon. Diane added that she had pawned her diamond wedding ring to buy food, rather than accept charity. Impressed by the pair's "good old American" values, the streetwise cops at the Times Square precinct made some calls in their behalf, a hotel gave them two free nights, and they left town with free Greyhound tickets home to the West Coast—via Florida, because they said they wanted to see Disney World. They planned to sell a cow, they said, so they could reimburse the hotel and the bus company. "Subsequently," reported the *Times,* another Oregon woman heard about this lachrymose tale on the news "and said that the couple were not honeymooners." And that *she* was married to Michael. The truth remains blurred, but the moral shines through, clear as the smirk on the face of the Statue of Liberty when she emerged from her multimillion-dollar federal spring-cleaning looking almost as filthy as ever. A variation on the honeymoon theme for older tourists is to call any New York radio station and say, between sobs, that you saved all your lives to visit the statue, in memory of your immigrant mother God-bless-her-soul, parked your car at the ferry dock, and returned to find the trunk jimmied and your luggage and American Express card stolen. Such stunts are pulled successfully by at least two visitors to the city every summer.

If you need to stay more than a few days, and are from far enough away—Europe, maybe, or Alaska—pay a visit to any peripatetic socialite in your hometown and filch her address book. A young Londoner spent six months in New York without paying a single hotel bill after pulling this trick. She would phone a millionaire at random from the pilfered pages and sigh, a carefully bashful note in her voice, "I just arrived at Kennedy and Helene said she was sure you wouldn't mind if I asked a really big favor of you . . ." This ingénue might still be shunting from town house to yacht to Hamptons hacienda had she not, in a moment of conscience, wanted to give something back to one of her hosts. "Helene says she so much hopes you will look her up when you get to Europe. She'd love you to use her house in Italy."

If you have to foot your $200-a-night room bill yourself, have a stiff drink at any local gin mill on us. A wizened old man used to prop up the bar at the Algonquin, sorrowfully declaring, "Well, this is my last drink as a single man . . ." It worked for years. A hardened Washington journalist presented him with a rotisserie as a wedding gift.

PLAN C: PRIME TIME

Remember how all good things come from being a Vanderbilt? Or any celebrity? The quickest way to become a celebrity, of course, is to get your name in lights—*television* lights. Primetime, a San Francisco–based firm that employs a network of former ABC, CBS, and NBC producers as consultants, says it can do this for you easy as billing you by the results. $11,500 for a spot on the "Today" show, $40,000 for "60 Minutes" . . .

The firm is at 415-383-3311. Now allow us to teach you to do it yourself. For no cost. Anita Sarko, a deejay at the Palladium, suppressed a giggle and brought tears to countless viewers' eyes when she went on cable and told all ("It was really beautiful, it was unbelievable") about her "affair" with the late John Lennon. Choose any dead celebrity or live politician (nobody believes politicians, and they find it harder to collect for libel) and have a pal, describing himself as your agent, contact the bookers at the show of your choice. He might want to open the conversation by saying that you have just clinched a $500,000 contract with Crown Publishers to write your memoirs about your years as Jimmy Carter's Secret Bimbo. It's not a bad idea to instill a sense of competition by having a second friend phone the same booker. "Hi," he says, "this is Pete from the morning show. Listen, between us, Anita Sarko's agent keeps calling us and we've booked her for next Tuesday to talk about her affair with Carter, but we want to be sure you don't have her."

Since you will want something to remember your network debut by, get in touch with your favorite couturier:

"Hello, this is Anita Sarko, Jimmy Carter's ex-mistress. Darling, I don't know how to say this but I just love your clothes and I don't have a thing to wear on 'Good Morning, America'. . ."

By the time your benefactor asks for the gown back, you will be back home under your old name in Flushing. Or groan the following line into the phone, "Darling, I don't know how to say this but that horrible little man in makeup spilled L'Oreal all over the collar when he was touching up my roots."

One other tip. Always think what you can do to help a journalist. Hedy Klineman, a New York painter, has gone into "fashion portraits"—portraits of famous people's clothes. For instance, Andy Warhol's tuxedo and eyeglasses. And, as it happens, the duds of several famous *media* people, the kind with columns that mention her. "I asked Michael Musto [*Village Voice*] for a pair of bellbottom trousers and I wrote one of his columns on the canvas," she says, "and Dinah Prince [*Daily News*] gave me a headpiece she wore at a party at Area and a pair of black gloves, and I'm hoping to do Anthony Haden-Guest [*New York*'s "Fast Track" cartoonist]."

PLAN D: LENS MASTERS

You're off to the beach, as the new Hamptons stringer for any foreign glossy cousin to *Town & Country* magazine. Since high society loves to be chronicled, you'll be invited everywhere. The chap who last tried this one kept it up for three years, though he did employ a few props, waltzing into parties with a glamorous girl on his arm, who kept popping off the flash on her $150 camera, and assiduously mailing out notes taking credit whenever anyone he'd met really *was* mentioned in the magazine. He was last heard from riding the Orient Express, free.

However, for the finest treatment, here or abroad, you really should equip yourself as a TV Personage. Thanks to the miracles of shrinking electronics, you can pose as a network cameraman by renting an industrial-quality Sony—it looks like a pro's Betacam—from a supply house like Ferco (212-245-4800), for just $750 a week, or $7,225 to buy for a lifetime's use. No one will know if it breaks. Invite two of your pals to come along for the ride—the ugliest of your trio should be the Important Interviewer and the other two, the crew, must wear aqua jackets—and the world's your Oyster Rockefeller. Before you catch the Concorde to Paris to do a special for "Entertainment Tomorrow" on the miracles of Air France, celebrate by calling Petrossian and offering to tape a segment on the uses of leftover caviar. Restaurants like this do not like to have apes with cameras barging in, (*impromptu* photo opportunities can be dangerous, because you never can be sure who's lunching with whose husband), but they do like publicity. So the management will urge you to stage a private party with your friends posing as customers. And don't forget to contact an expensive clothing store that is doing badly and propose loading up the plane with its fashions for a shoot outside Dior's window. When you fail to return the gear, the owner will be delighted, because she'd never have sold it, and can lie about the value of the loss on her tax. *Extra, Extra! Double Indemnity!* Shortly after Richard Burton's death in Europe, someone made reservations for Elizabeth Taylor and her then fiancé, Victor Luna, on Pan Am flight 120 from Los Angeles to London. A bureau manager for the West German magazine *Gong* was elated when he was tipped to this by an American paparazzo. With images of a world exclusive of the ex-wife weeping at the bier scudding through his mind, the manager thrust a $2,800 round-trip ticket at the eager lensman. As did the *Star,* the American celebrity tabloid, images of a . . . well, anyway, it had been delighted to hear from the paparazzo. Skulking through the bushes, some informer alerted the *National Enquirer* that a scoop was brewing, so it put a reporter on the plane, which, with word spreading fast, was met by ten more news hounds and a TV crew in London. Not a sign of Liz or Luna. "The only person I recognized getting off was [the paparazzo]," said a photographer for the London *Daily Mail.* Liz's press agent claimed she knew nothing of any Pan Am booking. Still, the *Star* and *Gong* agreed to go halves on the paparazzo's expenses, so everyone was happy. "There are no clear-cut rules in this business," the *Gong* bureau manager remarked. Indeed, should *Gong* ask to see any of your work when you offer to cover Princess Diana's clandestine romance in Monte Carlo, clip any paparazzo's shots from the pops and have Lew, the free-lance illustrator with the CBS News card (chapter three), forge your byline on them.

You wouldn't want to arrive at the airport on the bus, so send the same tearsheets to one of the big car manufacturers and you will be entitled to a press rebate, generally 5 percent, on any new model. Most working journalists are forbidden, because of the post-Watergate ethos, to accept such favors, so the manufacturer's public relations office will be overjoyed to hear from you. Or say you're the automobile columnist for the *Podunk Herald* (have a friend waiting at the phone to snap, *"Herald,"* when they call to check), and ask to borrow something zippy for a short evaluation. A man who had had a piece about taxis published in the *Village Voice* wormed a champagne-colored 300D out of Mercedes-Benz for a week using this tactic. We notice the fear in your face. No, of course you aren't going to have to pay $20 an hour to park. Just have two portable NO PARKING signs concocted, like those Diana Ross's staff have been known to erect to partition off the spot where the star's limo draws up outside her East Sixty-third Street office. Or select any illegal zone where cars already have been ticketed. Take the ticket off one of them and slip it under your wiper blades. The meter maid will reappear shortly and slap the vehicle you denuded with a second summons, but other people's problems are never your concern in New York.

Limo Logic

Being a permanent poseur may not be your style, but while we're on the subject of travel, unless you're on a drug-buying spree (chapter seven), why risk turning up sprawled across a Straus subway painting? Put it another way. Would you really turn down a chance to leave the party in a limo? Someone else's limo? This tango takes two. First your accomplice sidles up to the drivers who are leaning on the hoods of the gleaming monsters triple-parked outside the function. "My girlfriend really fancies him," she simpers to one chauffeur, pointing to another man who's a few cars down the line. "What's his name? . . . Who's he working for?" Once it is established that it's the Gutfreund (you pronounce it Good-friend) Jalopy, driven by————, your move. Stride up to him and bark, "John and Susan said you'd take us back to Pelham Bay." Have him drop you a block from your house, just to be certain Les Bons Amis never find you.

PLAN E: ON HER MAJESTY'S SERVICE

There's nothing the circus likes better than a title, and, should you be shy about making one up for yourself, you can always exploit someone else's. A Britisher who applied to join a very snooty New York PR firm was asked to submit a detailed account of one of the shindigs that, according to his résumé, he'd arranged for the Queen of England. The Brit rushed to the out-of-town newstand on Forty-second Street. Yes, there they were, the London tabloids with blow-by-blow accounts of HM's latest Buckingham Palace Garden Party . . . he strolled back to his walkup studio and composed his Running Order. The Scottish salmon (sliced gossamer-thin because everyone knows HM's hubbie is a real tightwad), the beach umbrellas flapping in the teeming rain, the silver platters of Milk-Bones for the Royal Corgis. We are pleased to report that he got the job. Also that the trip to London for Princess Di's wedding that was touted back in 1981 by a Manhattan travel agency went swimmingly. The "British Aristocracy House Party"—$9,000 (excluding airfare) for two weeks, or $5,000 for one—attracted about a hundred people, who were promised they'd hobnob with almost enough nobles to fill the World Trade Center. This did seem to be news to some of the bluebloods. "We are not on public view," huffed the Duchess of Wellington, who, with her husband, the duke, was listed as a "preliminary" tour host. "This kind of thing is not on."

Moving Stories

As the wedding trip—and the wedding jackets (chapter three)—demonstrate, names can make the difference to both your business and your personal prospects in New York. Here are three more examples:

• Nice Jewish Boy with Truck, a New York moving company that has attracted considerable Jewish custom and counts John Lennon and Yoko, Marlo Thomas, Andy Warhol, Jane Curtin, and Kathleen Turner among satisfied past clients, turned out when we investigated to be owned by two Jewish-born members of the Church of Scientology, Leslie and Steve Simon. According to affidavits filed in a National Labor Relations Board case, the firm at one point had twenty believers from the L. Ron Hubbard cult on its staff of seventy. "People try to point out the contradictions [between Judaism and Scientology]. There are none," says Steve, who has ascribed his "million bucks a year" success to Hubbard's teachings. "It makes me a better Jew."

• Yankees owner George Steinbrenner was advertised as a "charter member" of a "country club" to which Tom Carvel, the New York emperor of ice cream, was trying to sell $5,000 subscriptions. "George denies this flatly," growled the sports tycoon's attorney, Roy Cohn. A Steinbrenner pal took a drive past the club's acreage and was unable to detect the "several ballrooms," theater, and recording studios promised in Carvel's solicitation, but a Carvel spokesman explained that "video" and "recording equipment" and "partitions" would allow a barnlike building on the site to be used for these purposes.

• Calling himself a former CIA agent, Andrew Topping, a Manhattan man whose last known job was driving a cab, approached General Daniel Graham, the former head of the Defense Intelligence Agency—about putting together an attempt to oust Iran's Ayatollah Khomeini. Graham apparently was impressed by the ex-cabbie, whose résumé includes an alleged plot to kill Richard Nixon (the charges in that case were dismissed)—because he arranged for him to meet with one of the DIA's top Mideast officials. The two caucused twice, but in the end no mission came out of it for the Big Onion's own James Bond. "The whole thing sounded a little cockamamy, but you never can tell," said Graham.

Once you're back from your unsuccessful attempt to overthrow Fidel Castro (you cashed in the first-class ticket that the DIA bought you and went to Saint-Tropez economy-class instead), it will be time to do something for your friends in New York.

How about getting twelve of them, all unknowns, into Palladium tonight? No door charge. Confides Rémy Blumenfeld, a young New York reporter for WPIX-TV's Independent Network

News, "I call up and say can I bring Omega Timex, Cartier Seiko, Mercedes Ford, with Laams Wool of the *Vogue* Norwegian bureau, and then I say, 'Oh, and you know the Princesa Anorexia di Nervosa from Madrid?'" Since labels are the only thing that New York discaires read, and since no New Yorker is ever going to admit he doesn't know a princess, the free-drink tickets descend like confetti as your group sweeps through the door.

PLAN F: A RESTORATIVE

After several months of real estate dealing, world travel, and partying, you're In Distress. Fire ants are gnawing at your spine and your skin has erupted in shingles; if you're a man, your blood pressure is racing into the stratosphere; female, and you have terminal menstrual cramps. What you need is a Dr. Feelgood. Most of the physicians who provide rejuvenating blasts of dope to rich New Yorkers use amphetamine but, since this narcotic is no longer even as fashionable as heroin, we don't recommend it. The feds have been know to crab that speed injections don't constitute legitimate medicine, and the risk of seeing the doc marched off between two detectives before he has time to rub alcohol on the track marks on your bottom is just too great. For totally legal and remarkably inexpensive relief ($25 a visit) instead, hasten to the Park Avenue office of the octogenarian Dr. Milton Reder. He will alleviate your shingles, high blood pressure, menstrual cramps, in fact, "any kind of pain," by inserting a small amount of a cocaine mixture up your schnozze. The mixture, on occasion twice as concentrated as some street cuts of the drug, is placed on a swab. When our reporter visited, half a dozen patients, including the receptionist, were standing around the doctor's office, some with as many as five swabs protruding from their noses. The remedy depends on the swab touching a nerve center, so that the drug "interrupts the nerve reflex," the doc says. Adherents to the therapy—which is exempt from federal regulation because of a legal technicality—include several millionaires and celebrities. Lew Rudin, one of New York's biggest landlords, says he was treated successfully by Reder for excruciating back pain. "It's a magic formula," enthuses the real estate man, adding that he doesn't know what Reder gave him. The late Yul Brynner was a regular and testified for the doctor when a housewife, Hildegard Kurland, filed a malpractice suit against him and a psychiatrist who also gave her cocaine, saying she had become addicted. The docs denied her allegations and the case was settled after the psychiatrist, who used a stronger mixture than Reder, agreed to pay Kurland $202,500. "I've yet to see anyone get high on my treatment," says Reder, who obtains his supplies from a pharmaceutical company. "It's not habit-forming."

PLAN G: WITH CHARITY TO ALL

We know you're impatient to toddle off to Gracie Mansion with the Crucial Campaign Contribution, but it will feel so much better if it's not your own dough. Turn back to chapter two. The key line reads as follows: "Get yourself a charity." Referring to helping the arts, the diseases, and your status, of course. But let's change the emphasis just slightly.

The canon then takes on, we think, a rather stirring ring: "Get *yourself* a charity."

Religion, as we have seen, is the ultimate way of making a contribution to your spiritual exchequer (we define spirituality in the literal sense, because what are spirits if they don't lift up the Whole Person, including your net worth?). But whatever type of not-for-profit organization you incorporate in New York State— educational, patriotic, philanthropic, scientific—you should be sure to simultaneously set up a for-profit company. Maybe a real estate company such as the St. John of Rila monastery's subsidiary in chapter four. The monastery is in business as God's Builder, of course. You're in business to do some fast asset shuffles. New York State has some of the least zealous regulation of such matters in the nation, since regulation is deemed "antibusiness" by the lawyers who dominate the state legislature. So your for-profit arm doesn't even have to reveal its directors, who, of course, will coincide precisely with those of the not-for-profit, which does have to disclose its board. All that the for-profit enterprise has to disclose is its incorporators and an address where creditors can serve judgments. The company owned by Geraldine Ferraro's family-by-marriage that was landlord to a mob boss was listed to a dead lawyer's address at the time the congresswoman ran for vice-president.

Now you're up and running, let's outline a few fields into which you may wish to expand:

Poverty

Our mouths water as we write that golden word. So much suffering. So many government grants. Ramon Velez, the South Bronx entrepreneur crowned the "king of salsa poverty" by the *Village Voice*'s Wayne Barrett, controls a dozen community groups with a $16 million budget. His annual income from them has been estimated at over $220,000. Public funds don't come for free, of course. Velez's ability to deliver votes in return to the white political establishment can be assessed from the fact that his patrons include Ed Koch (who hugged him three times during a press conference) and Ronald Reagan (who invited him to the first state dinner after the 1984 election). Do take the time to research the history, or purported history, of this povertician's empire. Then ask yourself:

• Have you stocked up with pads of blank bills that can be used as vouchers to account for your expenditures of public funds? It was suggested during an investigation of Velez's agency that that was the purpose of certain stationery found at his not-for-profit fiefdom's offices, but Velez dismisses the probe as a political "setup." He was not personally in charge of the bookkeeping, he says, so he has no idea what the blank bills were for or indeed whether any were found. "I have accounted for every penny given to my agency," he says.

• Have you identified a vacant lot where you can dump the school lunches that your agency is being paid $312,000 to distribute to malnourished youngsters? A TV crew claimed to have captured just that happy scene in some 1976 footage about a Velez program, but the King of the South Bronx explains that that also was part of a "political conspiracy" against him.

We wondered whether reports of his annual earnings were exaggerated? Nope. "I work for it," says the plutocrat, whose personal real estate holdings have been valued at over $1 million. "I hope one day to make a million a year. What I do is worth that."

Perhaps he's already on the way there. Just as we would have recommended, he has established a *for*-profit real estate and consulting corporation. Its office is in a building owned by one of his nonprofits, a building rehabbed, reported the *Voice*'s Barrett, at government expense.

"Yes," Velez says politely. "Anything else you want to ask?"

The China Syndrome

Count Lanfranco Rasponi, the late public relations man who was the circus's arbiter, used to represent the Renaissance of Italian Youth Foundation. How we miss its annual Night in Venice Ball! How joyous the news that you are reviving its charter! The organization, which gave hope to countless six-year-old goatherds in the Tuscany hills, was dissolved by the state supreme court, following charges that its promoters had pocketed 85 percent of the funds collected, reported the *New York Times*.

Officials of the sine qua non of society fundraising galas, the annual Boutiques de Noël Christmas-gift sale, announced that this charity was going out of business in 1984 after a squabble in which some of its patrician board members accused others of exploiting the organization for personal profit. Mais oui. How else are you to afford your Mottahedeh dinnerware? A shipment of this WASPy china was said to have been billed to Les Boutiques, hence entitling the mysterious purchaser to both a 50 percent trade discount and a charitable sales-tax exemption. "It was bought from Mottahedeh by women who paid Les Boutiques for it," said the organization's president, decorator Richard Hare. Society women still run another annual sale, for the physically handicapped. Not that the ladies look particularly handicapped as they grab armfuls of fur coats and Paris originals as they're donated and give them to their chauffeurs to load into their woodies, sometimes depositing $30 or $40 in the charity's books for appearance's sake, though usually they don't pay anything at all.

America the Beautiful

Don't even think about going into competition with that $230 million federal campaign to restore the Statue of Liberty and Ellis Island. The effort, which gives companies like Kellogg's and United States Tobacco the right to use the Lady's lamentably still-dirty likeness in advertising—in exchange for sponsorship pledges—has been touted as one of the first full-blown demonstrations of President Reagan's commitment to replacing government involvement in such projects with "volunteerism." Yet the president has been surprisingly reluctant to allow at least one citizen to volunteer. Tony Campaigne, a former Republican Congressional candidate, had his own foundation—the Foundation to Rebuild America—and it wanted to help the official foundation, it seemed.

It mailed out over thirty thousand letters, imploring citizens to contribute to the Lady and promising that their names would be "inscribed on the 'Statue of Liberty Roll of Honor.'" A White House lawyer said this was "misleading": there was no official honor roll. The lawyer fumed that Campaigne also had been using Reagan's name to drum up money for a "National Day of Prayer and Fasting."

Though fasting certainly won't sell in New York and the statue is off-limits, there is a patriotic alternative. Appear at any of our local parades in an American Legion cap and, mumbling to yourself as if bomb-shocked, jingle quarters in your hand while sticking flag pins in the lapels of the crowd. "Dingers", as these phony collectors for veterans' organizations are called, easily make $500 on a good day. Should the skies open, they start purveying umbrellas.

Relative Values

As your public-spirited dominion grows, you will find room in it for your family. When New York Senator Al D'Amato first ran for Congress, his campaign kitty had to pay for the TV ad that showed his mother, Antoinette, walking up the steps to her house lugging a heavy bag of groceries and muttering about the ravages of inflation on the middle class. But when Al headed Reagan's reelection drive in New York State in 1984, he took $40,000 from the presidential campaign treasury in order to put Mom back on the screen. The cameras followed her this time to the produce section of a supermarket, where she spoke of how far we had come since Ronnie's accession. Or was it since Al's? "He found a legal way to shamelessly use Reagan-Bush funds for his own benefit," snarls a former Reagan campaign official.

Show Business

Now for your overtly for-profit ventures. Call Ed Koch immediately to see if he needs a backer for his sequel to *Mayor,* the musical based on his eponymous first book. He gets 1 percent of the gross from the New York production. The lion's share of its budget was put up by Imelda's New York front men, Joseph and Ralph Bernstein—who, besides looking after the Evita of the Philippines, had their hands full trying to negotiate a deal to acquire prime development rights from the city. The Koch administration said it was powerless to do anything when the *Daily*

News revealed that the city was owed more than $1.1 million in taxes on the East Sixty-sixth Street house where Imelda danced. Not a quid pro quo for the contribution to the mayoral show, as it turned out—to get away with this one, you don't have to give a cent. Simply register your pied-à-terre in the name of any foreign government and say it's an "official" guest house.

Here's another thought. During the 1986 corruption brouhaha, it was discovered that Anthony Ameruso, the by then former Koch transportation commissioner who was a partner with the owner of Ponte's restaurant in a secret property deal (chapter ten), had another secret: during his time in the administration, he had been living in the suburbs. Koch, who had ruled that top officials must live in the Big Onion, said he was shocked. As it transpired, at least twenty other administration biggies had been given special permission to leave town. After it was discovered that one of them was based some fifty miles to the north, in a hamlet with the poetic name of Mohegan Lake, a crackdown commenced. Since some of the twenty may be obliged to sell up six-bedroomed $200,000 houses in the suburbs, and face the shock of what $200,000 buys in Koch's New York, you should position yourself at Penn Station and offer a free roof to the first of them whom you spy getting off the train. Just be careful that your initial approach to your target is deferential—"I don't know anybody in the city who is powerful enough to get me the contract to rebuild the Brooklyn Bridge"—because then he'll rationalize the encounter as flattery, not bribery. While the business he slips you won't cost him a penny, you should bear in mind that the cost of the move has forced him to cancel the vacation he planned taking. Suzanne Jaffe, the official who oversaw New York State's $23 billion public employee pension fund, enjoyed a Nile River junket with a group of revelers who included Jerry Zipkin, Ann Getty, Betsy Bloomingdale, Jeane Kirkpatrick, and Alexander Papamarkou, a stockbroker who has done work for the fund. While Papamarkou helped organize the trip, Jaffe said that she had paid her own airfare and her accommodations were picked up by Ann Getty, so these things can be arranged very properly.

The other aspect of the bridge job still to be arranged is a private deal with Local ——'s organizer to supply union cards for all your non-English-speaking employees. They won't know that they're unionized, so you can continue to pay them $3 an hour. You pay their union dues to the organizer, and it's still a saving. Executives at a Brooklyn firm that uses this dodge tell us it can be extraordinarily inexpensive. In return for not blowing the whistle to the wage slaves, the firm's union contact, a minor fish in the mob, collects a case of Corvo white wine once a year plus a check to United Cerebral Palsy, since he has a spastic son.

IF YOU'RE CAUGHT

1. Say you're a priest. During Cardinal Spellman's regnum, according to the biographer John Cooney, men of the Catholic cloth arrested for being drunk and disorderly or caught in a brothel or in any other crime weren't booked but were "routinely handed over to the Powerhouse." The rules have tightened—somewhat. "The cop on the street used to be able to do it, but now the powers that be get together and do a quiet deal," says a source at police headquarters, confiding that archdiocesan officials were livid when a renegade sergeant ignored this procedure and busted a priest for child pornography just six days before Pope John Paul II's pilgrimage to the city. The priest subsequently cut a deal and was relocated to an assignment out of state.

2. Say you're becoming a patron of the peasantry. With only a few hours to go before a new law came into effect banning the demolition of single-room-occupancy hotels, fleabitten buildings which provide one of the city's last refuges for the poor, developer Harry Macklowe had a problem. A man noted for his seminal taste (one reporter caught up with him as he perused the toilet bowls for a new tower) and his patronage of the arts, he wanted to rip down four buildings on West Forty-fourth Street that included an SRO, but he didn't have the required permit. After dark that evening, the bulldozers moved in, bricks flying, pedestrians scattering, water geysering from busted pipes. Macklowe made his deadline. "Most of [the hotel's] business was in foreign tourists," he later said. He silenced the city's squawks by paying $2 million toward housing for the homeless. Of course, if the homeless think they're going to buy into the Toilet Bowl Tower for that, they are in for a shock. Macklowe told *New York* that Sly Stallone was interested in snapping up a floor of it. For about $3.2 million. "A bargain," the developer said.

3. Say you're becoming a stoolie. You may have read about CCS Communication Control in the newspapers. It's the New York firm

that grosses $32 million a year marketing such vital aids to survival in the city as the antibugging equipment we suggested in chapter one, an "Intruder Immobilizer" ("The target experiences involuntary muscle spasms, paralyzing pain and unconsciousness"), and infrared goggles for viewing at night ("Nitefinder could be vital in helping to save lives," so Beirut snipers obviously shouldn't apply). CCS clients include a third of the Fortune 500 companies (like Mobil and General Foods), movie stars, and police departments, the firm told the *Times* in 1984. If the author of that story seemed unaware that three years earlier CCS president Benjamin Jamil had been indicted on charges that he tried to ship wares with potential military uses to Syria, that was exactly how Washington wanted it. The case quickly vanished from public view after Jamil, who claimed he hadn't knowingly broken the law, agreed to turn snitch. The charges against him were dismissed, and customs agents installed hidden cameras and mikes at his Manhattan offices—in an investigation that didn't only go after foreign nationals like the Libyan who was shopping for computer-controlled tank target training systems. The targets also included a security firm that, according to a lawyer for one of its principals, was a CCS competitor. Retorted a CCS executive, "We don't have any competitors. We've always been number one in the field. In fact, we're doubling our office space..."

4. Say you're a woman. Say you're a woman married to an Italian ("You people who are married to Italian men, you know what it's like"). Say you're Italian ("A lot of us who have grown up with vowels at the end of our names faced a lot of discrimination"). You remember Geraldine Ferraro saying all this, don't you, when she was peppered with awkward questions by the media during her 1984 campaign?

5. Say you thought you were working for the CIA. That's how five New York Irishmen got acquitted after admitting that they had been running guns for years to the Irish Republican Army. The CIA came to court to deny it, but the defense successfully reminded the jury that not only are such denials routine, but "the CIA doesn't even know what it is doing."

6. If there's nothing left to say, hire a powerhouse lawyer. When Vitas Gerulaitis got in a bind—a friend of his had boasted to undercover agents posing as narcotics dealers that the tennis star was bankrolling a $20,000 cocaine purchase—he retained Thomas Puccio, the former chief prosecutor in the Abscam investigation of political corruption. Puccio in turn *very quietly* (two

key words at this stage in the game) signed up a heavyweight publicist (the kind who knows people in *government, publishing* ...) and made a preemptive strike. One of the PR man's aides, identifying himself only as a Puccio associate, put in calls to all the metropolitan papers. One by one, reporters were ushered into the attorney's office to interview Gerulaitis, and the next day the feds found themselves staggering under an avalanche of headlines. The *Post,* the *News,* the *Times* ... GERULAITIS SAYS HE IS EXPECTING DRUG INDICTMENT. Of course, the star also asserted his innocence in the stories. After a grand jury declined to indict, Puccio praised it and the government at a news conference for conducting the case in "a highly professional and conscientious manner."

7. If you do go to the slammer, don't forget your old friends. Anthony Scotto, the politically connected former waterfront boss, used elegant blue stationery embossed with his initials to communicate from the pen during his incarceration for extortion. This may have paid off even before his release to the A table (chapter one). Though the mayor has "no recollection" or record of it, the *News* reported that Ed and all five of the Big Onion's borough presidents were among the guests at a "very quiet" dinner at a chic Upper East Side restaurant where a toast was hoisted to the Democratic Party's most loyal racketeer.

In closing, we have one final piece of advice for you.

VERY CONFIDENTIAL! YOU TOO CAN WRITE A BOOK!

If you have been a faithful reader and stuck to white-collar crime, you won't have much to do in jail during your one-year stretch, so, as you lie back in the dentist's chair having your teeth capped, start planning your memoirs. New York State does have a law that is intended to prevent felons from profiting from their misdeeds, but it's highly ambiguous.

As we speak, the Mayflower Madam appears to have successfully challenged it.

When you have finished your manuscript and the first half of your advance is safely salted away in your Burundi bank account, you'll need a picture of the mayor embracing you for the cover. Bludgeon him into posing by threatening to dedicate your epic to him.

That's Edward I. Koch. Or his successor. Gracie Mansion. 212-570-4747.

Whether you're an official overcome by passion for power, a

tourist busted for powerful passion, or just a socially ambitious hostess trying to get Hizzoner to attend the pet puma's declawing party, you never know when that number is going to come in handy. The best thing about living in a friendly town like New York is that someone is always available, twenty-four hours a day, to help you help yourself.

ACKNOWLEDGMENTS

Just as this book has omitted some names, in order to protect enough of the guilty to allow the Big Onion to continue to function, these acknowledgments must omit some of the innocent, so as to protect them. My thanks go to all these "Deep Throats," especially the politicos who explained how everything worked; the expert from Brooklyn District Attorney Elizabeth Holtzman's office who was one of the author's mentors on the Mafia; the holdouts against God's Builders—priests, rabbis, and church officials—who provided insights and files; the Broadway producers who explained the changes in their industry; and the ladies who served up many of the tidbits about the circus.

In addition to the journalists mentioned in the introduction who made up this book's reporting team, I am grateful to many past and present colleagues. At the top of this list is Edward Kosner, the editor and publisher of *New York,* who took a chance and turned over the "Intelligencer" column to me, a job that not only was an investigative reporter's dream, but that ultimately made this book possible. I also am indebted to all those *New York* staffers who shared their knowledge and gave help and encouragement, but particularly to Nicholas Pileggi, Laurie Jones, Florence Fletcher, Melissa Morgan, Paul Abrams, and the three editors who survived the "Intel" endurance test, Dick Babcock, Peter Herbst, and Nancy McKeon. Among the other reporters, writers, and publishing executives who have been incredibly generous with their assistance are Liz Smith, John Cooney, Michael M. Thomas, Steven Gaines, Steven Dunleavy, Guy Hawtin, Cindy Adams, Doug Feiden, Michael Pye, Jonathan Kwitny, Wayne Barrett, Joe Conason, Joe Dolce, Penelope Orth, John Howell, David Harrison, Dotson Rader, Michael Denneny, Rémy Blumenfeld, Josh Friedman, Chuck Ortleb, Eric Nadler, Philip Nobile, V. K. McCarty, Steve Kraus, Philip Seldon, Tony De Stefano, Russell Barber, and Judith Price. Thanks too to Roger Wood, executive editor of the *New York Post,* for allowing the author the run of one of the best editorial libraries in the country.

I also am grateful to dozens of other New Yorkers for their thoughts and expertise. To name just a few of you here: Marianne

Strong, Dallas Boesendahl, Keith Sherman, Steve Rubell, Mark Fleischman, Abe Foxman, Tom Foster, David Powers, Merle Debuskey, Charles Wieland, Frank Hagan, Tim Gilles, Soledad Santiago, Raoul Felder, J. Allen Murphy, Roy Cohn, Tom Marotta, Howard Rubenstein, Dan Klores, David Rothenberg, Edward McDonald, Jerome Piazza, Remo Franceschini, Vic Cipullo, Ed Birns, Jo Coffey, Tony Procino, Jack Clark, Charles Rose, Bruce Baird, Robert Garcia, Deborah Corley, Ned Steele, Bruce Mailman, Ethan Mordden, Joe and Helen Bernstein, Rodger McFarlane, Allen Roskoff, Amanda Jenkins, Ronald Sobel, Richard Chernela, William Daly, Nanette Cavanagh, and Mark Chataway.

Bruce Harris, of Crown Publishers, conceived this project. He and my editors, Betty Prashker and David Groff, my agent, Alice Fried Martell, and lawyer, Slade Metcalf, have been towers of strength and good humor. And, finally, thanks to my family and to Gracie, my dog, who made me realize the significance of Tyler.